335th Assault Helicopter Company
Cowboys Unit History

Dominic Fino

INTRODUCTION

The COWBOYS arrived in Vietnam in April 1965 and officially stood down on 4 October 1971 when they made their last move to Fort Riley Kansas. During their stay in Vietnam, the COWBOYS made several moves, which are captured in the following pages.

Most of the information contained in this book was gathered at the National Archives at 4205 Suitland Road, in Suitland Maryland, which is just outside Washington, DC. Other information was gathered through constant probing of former members of the 335th A.H.C. who managed to retain small portions of Cowboy history over the years. The overview of the COWBOYS / Caspers was assembled by John Hoza and provides an accurate and concise summary of the early years.

The intent of this book is to show those who served in the 335th A.H.C. how certain events occurred and tie them to actual dates, times, and places. If read from beginning to end, the reader will certainly see that the common theme throughout the book is that the COWBOYS were indeed one of the best Aviation Companies to serve in Vietnam, if not the best. Their ability to do a job well under very hazardous conditions is an absolutely outstanding credit to their determination and willingness to make the 335th worthy of such high praise. It also will allow those who never served in the 335th A.H.C. to experience the historical achievements of a great Assault Helicopter Company.

A glossary of abbreviations and definitions is in the back of the book, so the reader can understand the terminology and acronyms used at the time. I have made every effort to include all the abbreviations used in the text. However, one or two may have been missed.

Although the text contained in this book has been retyped from copies of the original documents, some edits were made to correct spelling and grammar. These changes to the original text were necessary to make the book as accurate as possible in grammatical terms only. The pure historical facts contained in this book have not been altered in any way. Sometimes the abbreviations in the original text were changed to the full text descriptions to make the words flow more easily for the reader. Lastly, some portions of the original text were impossible to read due to there poor condition. When a word or words are not decipherable, I used a series of pound signs (###) to denote the unreadable text.

I sincerely hope that you enjoy this historical document and only ask that you take a moment to remember the names of the fine COWBOYS listed on the next two pages that made the ultimate sacrifice.

Dominic P. Fino, Jr.
335TH A.H.C.
Crew Chief, 3rd Platoon Falcons
1969-1971

IN MEMORY OF THE FOLLOWING COWBOYS

COMPANY "A," 82ND AVN. BN. & 335TH A.H.C. KIA LIST

FIRST	MID	LAST	CAUSE	CITY	ST	DOD	WALL_LOC		TOUR	RANK	STATUS
William	R.	Batchelder	KIA	Springvale	ME	06/10/65	02E	006	65-65	PFC	CREW
Raymond	C.	Galbraith	KIA	North Braddock	PA	06/10/65	02E	004	65-65	CWO	PILOT
Walter	R.	Gray	KIA	Big Clifty	KY	06/10/65	02E	003	65-65	PFC	CREW
Zoltan	A.	Kovacs	KIA	Berkley	CA	06/10/65	02E	006	65-65	WO	PILOT
Billy	G.	Hammer	KIA	Enterprise	AL	06/12/65	02E	009	64-65	CWO	PILOT
Kenneth	L.	Reed	KIA	Indianapolis	IN	06/12/65	02E	009	65-65	SSG	CREW
Donald	L.	Baker	KIA	Energy	IL	06/12/65	02E	009	64-65	SP5	CREW
Michael	L.	Wildes	KIA	Callahan	FL	06/12/65	02E	010	65-65	WO	PILOT
William	F.	Covey, Jr.	KIA	Willimantic	CT	06/30/65	02E	025	65-65	PFC	CREW
James	A.	Gruezke	KIA	Newberry	MI	12/23/65	04E	035	65-65	WO	PILOT
Billy	E.	Gipson	KIA	Indianapolis	IN	06/05/66	08E	010	65-66	SGT	CREW
Rutherford	J.	Welsh	KIA	Canada		07/27/66	09E	082	66-66	WO	PILOT
Joseph	C.	Sampson, Jr	KIA	Xenia	OH	07/27/66	09E	082	66-66	WO	PILOT
James	W.	Collins	KIA	Union City	TN	07/27/66	09E	079	66-66	PFC	CREW
Harold	W.	Reinbott, Jr.	KIA	Parma	MO	07/27/66	09E	081	66-66	SP5	CREW
Douglas	L.	Jones	KIA	Erwin	TN	10/12/66	11E	068	66-66	1LT	PILOT
Coley	L.	Andrews	KIA	Mobile	AL	12/19/66	13E	060	65-66	SGT	CREW
Gordon	O.	Walsh	KIA	Johnson City	TN	04/16/67	18E	037	66-67	CPT	PILOT
Pedro		Ortiz	KIA	Selma	CA	05/01/67	19E	007	67-67	SP4	CREW
Robert	F.	Quinn	KIA	Greenville	MS	05/01/67	19E	007	67-67	SP4	CREW
Ewell	E	Acord	KIA	Lester	WV	05/01/67	19E	002	66-67	SSG	CREW
John	M.	Andrews	KIA	Dayton	OH	05/01/67	19E	004	67-67	WO	PILOT
Leyburn	W.	Brockwell, Jr.	KIA	Spartanburg	SC	05/01/67	19E	003	66-67	LTC	PILOT
Lewis	J.	Fogler	KIA	Glen Burnie	MD	05/01/67	19E	005	67-67	PFC	CREW
Charles	C.	Jones	KIA	San Antonio	TX	05/01/67	19E	006	67-67	MAJ	PILOT
John	D.	Legg	KIA	Chickasaw	AL	05/01/67	19E	006	66-67	2LT	PILOT
Carl	F.	Louvring	KIA	Lowell	OR	05/13/67	19E	109	66-67	PFC	CREW
Dewey	A.	Midgett	KIA	Chesapeake	VA	11/25/67	30E	086	67-67	PVT	CREW
Terry	D.	Finch	KIA	Portland	OR	01/26/68	35E	039	67-68	CPL	CREW
Carl	L.	West *	KIA	Nashville	TN	02/02/68	37E	003	67-68	CPT	PILOT
Christopher	M.	Daniels	KIA	Gloucester	NJ	02/03/68	37E	005	67-68	SGT	CREW
Donny	R.	Kidd	KIA	Sioux Falls	SD	03/04/68	42E	067	67-68	CWO	PILOT
Richard	W.	Joles	KIA	New Orleans	LA	04/12/68	49E	033	67-68	SP5	CREW
Jerome	E.	Jacobs	KIA	Bayonne	NJ	05/05/68	55E	018	68-68	PFC	CREW
Richard	G.	Lewis	KIA	Westfield	NJ	05/05/68	55E	021	68-68	WO	PILOT

FIRST	MID	LAST	CAUSE	CITY	ST	DOD	WALL_LOC	TOUR	RANK	STATUS
Glenn	T.	Fey	KIA	Ashley	PA	05/05/68	55E 012	67-68	SP5	CREW
Bobby	R.	Williams	KIA	Spearman	TX	05/05/68	55E 035	67-68	CWO	PILOT
Thomas	F.	Smith	KIA	Roy	NM	12/13/68	36W 017	68-68	SP4	CREW
Robert	A.	Baetzel	KIA	Chicago Heights	IL	03/21/69	29W 095	68-69	WO	PILOT
Albert	O.	Krausser	KIA	Takoma Park	MD	03/21/69	29W 101	67-69	SP4	CREW
Ted	D.	Mills	KIA	Culver City	CA	03/21/69	29W 103	68-69	SGT	CREW
Thomas	M.	Newman	KIA	Saddle River	NJ	03/21/69	29W 104	68-69	1LT	PILOT
Robert	E.	Pierson	KIA	Chatham	NJ	03/21/69	28W 001	69-69	PFC	CREW
Franklin	D.	Ashley, II	KIA	Amma	WV	03/21/69	29W 094	68-69	SP4	CREW
Harry	H.	Gibson	KIA	Lumberton	NC	03/21/69	29W 098	68-69	1LT	PILOT
Thomas	E.	Jones, Jr.	KIA	Beltsville	MD	03/21/69	29W 100	68-69	1LT	PILOT
Thomas	H.	Furnish	KIA	Miami	FL	02/19/70	13W 032	69-70	SP4	CREW
Truman	D.	Norris	KIA	Richmond	VA	03/17/70	12W 014	69-70	CWO	PILOT
Kimball	H.	Sheldon	KIA	Boca Raton	FL	03/31/70	12W 063	70-70	SP4	CREW
Donald	A.	Krumrei	KIA	Enid	OK	07/16/70	08W 022	70-70	WO	PILOT
Robert	L	Shriner	KIA	Hawaiian Gardens	CA	11/20/70	06W 074	70-70	SP5	CREW
Johnie	K.	Woodard	KIA	Pulaski	TN	04/25/71	03W 012	70-71	SP5	CREW
Gerald	F.	Vilas	KIA	Yale	MI	09/19/71	02W 020	71-71	WO	PILOT
Fredrick	A.	Thacker	KIA	Rison	AR	09/19/71	02W 020	71-71	SP5	CREW
Lynn		Jones	KIA	Remerton	GA	09/19/71	02W 020	71-71	SP5	CREW
Donald	J.	Hanning **	KIA	Rockwood	MI	09/03/72	01W 071	72-72	CPT	PILOT

* Capt. Carl Lynn West was in the 235th AWC flying a UH-1H when he crashed with his crew. All were KIA. His tour was 13 Nov 67 – 2 Feb 68. Carl West was a Falcon on an earlier tour.

** Capt. Donald Jerry Hanning was in the 60th AHC flying an AH-1G (cobra) #AH-1G 67-15801 when he crashed in heavy weather. ALSO, KIA was Capt. Frank Oliver. Hanning's second tour lasted 3 Mar 72 – 3 Sep 72. Don Hanning was the Cowboy Ramrod platoon leader most of his first tour from Aug '68-Aug '69.

"THE COWBOYS" 1966-1971

The 335th came into existence in September 1966 with the deactivation of Co. A 82nd Aviation Battalion. Co. A arrived in Vietnam in April 1965 to support the 173rd Airborne Brigade in III Corps. They continued the mission until the 335th Aviation Co. was formed at Bien Hoa. In early 1967 the 335th was renamed the 335th Assault Helicopter Company.

In May 1967 the 335th moved to Pleiku in II Corps with the 173rd Airborne. In August 1967 they relocated to Phu Hiep (also in II Corps). From this base they supported the 173rd Airborne in its desperate fighting against the NVA and VC around Dak To that November. In December 1968 the 335th relocated to III Corps at Bear Cat. In August 1970 they moved to Dong Tam in IV Corps (the Delta). In November 1971 they stood down and returned to the US.

LOCATIONS OF 335TH AHC BASES

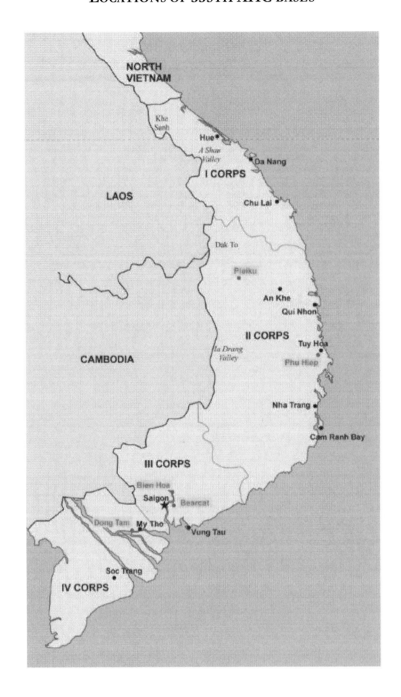

CODE OF THE COW COUNTRY

IT DON'T TAKE SUCH A LOT OF LAWS
TO KEEP THE RANGELAND STRAIGHT,
NOR BOOKS TO WRITE'EM IN, BECAUSE
THERE'S ONLY SIX OR EIGHT.
FIRST ONE IS THE WELCOME SIGN,
TRUE BRAND OF WESTERN HEARTS:
"MY CAMP IS YOURS AND YOURS IS MINE"
IN ALL COW COUNTRY PARTS.

TREAT WITH RESPECT ALL WOMANKIND
SAME AS YOU WOULD YOUR SISTER.
TAKE CARE OF NEIGHBORS' STRAYS YOU FIND,
AND DON'T CALL COWBOYS "MISTER."
SHUT PASTURE GATES WHEN PASSING THRU,
AND TAKIN' ALL IN ALL,
BE JUST AS ROUGH AS PLEASES YOU,
BUT NEVER MEAN OR SMALL.

TALK STRAIGHT, SHOOT STRAIGHT, AND NEVER BREAK
YOUR WORD TO MAN NOR BOSS.
PLUMB ALWAYS KILL A RATTLESNAKE,
DON'T RIDE A SOREBACKED HOSS.
IT DON'T TAKE LAW NOR PEDIGREE
TO LIVE THE BEST YOU CAN,
THESE FEW IS ALL IT TAKES TO BE
A COWBOY----------AND A MAN!

SOMAR BARKER

THE FOLLOWING COWBOY HISTORY WAS PREPARED BY JOHN HOZA

GENERAL BACKGROUND AND PARENT UNIT ASSIGNMENTS OF THE COWBOYS

The 82d Aviation Company was activated at Fort Bragg NC in 1957.

The Company was expanded and redesignated the 82d Aviation Battalion on 1 July 1960 with a total of three (3) Companies and 60 aircraft.

The 82d Aviation Battalion minus Company A deployed to the Dominican Republic in April 1965.

Company A deployed to Vietnam that same month. The Advance Party by plane, from Oakland California, arriving in VN on or about 12 April 1965. The main body of Company A, along with its 3 support units, the 166th Transportation Detachment (Aircraft Maintenance), the 234th Signal Detachment and the 25th Medical Detachment departed San Diego California on 12 April aboard the Helicopter Carrier USS Iwo Jima, bringing with them the first UH–1D model helicopters to enter service in Vietnam. (There was a total of three Avn Companies, with their support units and aircraft and equipment that sailed to Vietnam on the Iwo Jima on 12 April 1965:

- A Company, 82d Aviation Battalion, 82d Airborne Division
- A Company, 1st Aviation Battalion, 1st Infantry Division
- A Company, 101st Aviation Battalion, 101st Airborne Division
- There was a total of 75 new helicopters aboard the ship. Each company was assigned 9 UH–1B and 16 UH–1D helicopters. These were the first "D" model Hueys to enter service in Vietnam.

The Iwo Jima arrived off the coast of Vung Tau Vietnam on 1 May 1965. The ship docked approximately 30 miles off shore and the aircraft were flown from the ship to Vung Tau with limited crews on board. The majority of the company personnel and equipment was taken a shore aboard LSTs.

The company was based at Vung Tau and assigned to the 145th Combat Aviation Battalion. They were given the Call sign "Dallas COWBOYS by Military Assistance Command Vietnam (MACV) SOI. The Company dropped the word: "Dallas" and changed the Call sign to COWBOYS."

The COWBOYS of A/82d were assigned to the 173d Airborne Brigade on 19 October 1965 and co-located with the Brigade at Bien Hoa. As an integral part of the Brigade, Company A provided Direct Support to the 173d Abn Bde from October 1965 until 1 September 1966.

The COWBOYS were redesignated to the 335th Assault Helicopter Company on 1 September 1966 and remained assigned to the 173d Abn Bde where the continued to provide Direct Support to the Brigade. NOTE: The initial designation was: 335th Airmobile Company. It was changed to the 335th Assault Helicopter Company by the 1st Aviation Brigade.

Cowboy Company Commanders

Note 1:	The 82d Aviation Battalion was activated on 1 July 1960 at Fort Bragg NC. Commanders of Company A, at Fort Bragg NC prior to Major Champlin taking command are unknown at this time. Major Donald A. Champlin commanded the unit at Fort Bragg prior to their deployment to Vietnam. (He assumed command of the unit in January 1965).
Note 2:	The Advance Party of A/82d arrived in Vietnam on 12 or 13 April 1965. The main body of the Company arrived in Vietnam on 1 May 1965.
Note 3:	Company A/82d Aviation Battalion was redesignated the 335th Assault Helicopter Company on 1 September 1966.
Note 4:	The 335th Assault Helicopter Company was reassigned to the 1st Aviation Brigade on 1 January 1967.
Note 5:	The 335th stood down and departed Vietnam in November 1971. The 335th was assigned to Fort Riley Kansas with the mission of supporting the 1st Infantry Division and 5th Army.

Company A/82d Aviation Battalion

Major Donald A. Champlin	1 May 1965 – 27 March 1966
Major Larry Baughman	27 March 1966 – 29 June 1966
Major Ernest H. Johnson	29 June 1966 – 1 September 1966

335th Assault Helicopter Company

Major Ernest H. Johnson	1 September 1966 – 20 January 1967
LTC Leyburn W. Brockwell Jr.	20 January 1967 – 1 May 1967 (KIA 1 May 1967)
Major Walter H. Huth	1 May 1967 – 10 June 1967
LTC Charles D. Utzman	10 June 1967 – 1 October 1967
Major Donald R. Drumm	1 October 1967 – 31 December 1967
Major Frank M. Powell	31 December 1967 – 20 June 1968
Major Carl L. Cramer	20 June 1968 – 23 November 1968
Major Paul R. Riley Jr.	23 November 1968 – 25 May 1969
Major Howard J. Stiles	25 May 1969 – 8 November 1969
Major Vance S. Gammons	8 November 1969 – 30 May 1970
Captain Thomas A. Teasdale	30 May 1970 – 19 September 1970
Major Henry J. Raymond	19 September 1970 -?
Major Harold L. Bowen	? - 11 July 1971
Major Marvin W. Schwern	11 July 1971 – 26 November 1971

The 335th Departed Vietnam 5 November 1971

Major Jerry Black	26 Nov 1971 – 11 Apr 1973
Major David A. Measels	11 Apr 1973 – 22 Feb 1974
Major Myron D. Davis	22 Feb 1974 – 07 Jan 1975
Major Stephen D. Ballard	07 Jan 1975 – 00 Jun 1976 ****
Major Barry H. Adams	00 Jun 1976 –?

****These dates may not be correct. History shows dates as 27 May 75 – June 76. If the dates listed in the Unit History were correct it would mean that there was another Unit Commander for 4 months from January 75 to May 75. None is listed in the History.

Unit Awards

Presidential Unit Citation: DAGO 43 dated 9 November 1966
for the period 10 June 1965 to 13 June 1965 for actions during the Battle for Dong Xoai.

Presidential Unit Citation: DAGO 5, 79 Amended DAGO 42, 69
for the period 6 November 1967 to 23 November 1967 for actions during the Battle for Hill 875.

US NAVY Presidential Unit Citation: DAGO 32 dated 24 September 1973
for the period 7 October 1966 to 4 December 1966 awarded to a three (3) aircraft detachment from the COWBOYS, 335th AHC and to the two (2) aircraft detachment from the Caspers, 173d Abd Bde.

Meritorious Unit Citation: DAGO 42, dated 1969
for the period May 1965 to July 1966

Meritorious Unit Citation: DAGO 70, 69 Amended DAGO 48, 68
for the period 1 February 1967 to 31 December 1967

Meritorious Unit Citation: HQ 335th AMB CO, GO 48, dated 1968

Meritorious Unit Citation: HQUSARV GO 904, dated 2 March 1967
for the period 1 August 1966 to 31 January 1967

Meritorious Unit Citation: HQ 173d Abn Bde, GO 17, dated 1968

Valorous Unit Citation: HQ 145th Avn Bn, GO 17, dated 1968

Distinguished Unit Citation:
for the period 10 June 1965 to 13 June 1965 for actions in the Battle for Dong Xoai

Vietnamese Cross of Gallantry w/Palm: GO 162 dated November 1965
for the period 29 December 1964 to 4 November 1965

Vietnamese Cross of Gallantry w/Palm: GO 22 HQ 335th Avn, 1968
for the period May 1965 to July 1966

Vietnamese Cross of Gallantry w/Palm: DAGO 22, dated 1968
for the period 1 March 1966 to 26 March 1967

Vietnamese Cross of Gallantry w/Palm: DAGO 46,69 Amended DAGO 21 Sec III, dtd 8 April 1969
for the period 27 March 1967 to 17 May 1968

Vietnamese Cross of Gallantry w/Palm: DAGO 52, dated 1971
for the period 15 December 1969 to 10 October 1970

Vietnamese Cross of Gallantry w/Palm: DAGO 8, dtd 19 March 1974
Awarded to MAACV units for the period 8 February 1962 to 28 March 1973
Awarded to US ARMY Vietnam Units for the period 20 July 1965 to 28 March 1973

Vietnam Campaigns

Vietnam Defense	8 March 1965 to 24 December 1965
Vietnam Counter Offensive	25 December 1965 to 30 June 1966
Vietnam Counter Offensive Phase II	1 July 1966 to 31 May 1967
Vietnam Counter Offensive Phase III	1 June 1967 to 29 January 1968
TET Counter Offensive	30 January 1968 to 1 April 1968
Vietnam Counter Offensive Phase IV	2 April 1968 to 30 June 1968
Vietnam Counter Offensive Phase V	1 July 1968 to 1 November 1968
Vietnam Counter Offensive Phase VI	2 November 1968 to 22 February 1969
TET 69 Counter Offensive	23 February 1969 to 8 June 1969
Vietnam Summer-Fall 1969	9 June 1969 to 31 October 1969
Vietnam Winter-Spring 1970	1 November 1969 to 30 April 1970
DA Sanctuary Counter Offensive	1 May 1970 to 30 June 1970
Vietnam Counter Offensive Phase VII	1 July 1970 to 30 June 1971
Consolidation I	1 July 1971 to 30 November 1971
Consolidation II	1 December 1971 to 29 March 1972
Vietnam Cease Fire	30 March 1972 to 28 January 1973

Note: The following is written in DA PAM 672-3: "The Arrowhead device is authorized only for members of the 173d Abn Bde who actually participated in a landing in the vicinity of Latum RVN between the hours of 0900 – 0907 inclusive on 27 February 1967."

I assume it is being authorized for those who made the actual parachute jump in Operation Junction City. If so – the date is incorrect. Jump was made on 22 February 1967.

CASPERS', AVIATION PLATOON

173D AIRBORNE BRIGADE (SEPARATE)

The 173d Airborne Brigade (Sep) was formed on the island of Okinawa on 26 March 1963. (Some sources list the activation date as: 25 June 1963).

The 173d Abn Bde deployed to Vietnam, arriving on 5 May 1965, becoming the first U.S. Army ground combat unit to be committed to the Vietnam War.

The 173d Aviation Platoon was a part of the MTOE of Headquarters and Headquarters Company (HHC) of the 173d Abn Bde (Sep) under the operational control (OPCON) of the Brigade S-3, Operations Officer. The aviation platoon deployed to Vietnam along with the rest of the 173d Airborne Brigade (Sep) in May of 1965.

Headquarters and Headquarters Company (HHC) 173D Abn Bde (Sep), along with several other companies, including Company A/82d Aviation Battalion, was assigned to the (Composite) Special Troops Battalion, 173d Abn Bde (Sep), which was created at some later unknown date (Most probably in the mid - late 1966-time frame).

173D AVIATION PLATOON COMPOSITION

The 173d Aviation Platoon consisted of seven (7) Aviators and four (4) Enlisted personnel at the time of its deployment from Okinawa to Vietnam.

The MTOE authorized the platoon eight (8) Utility Helicopters and no other aircraft. The aircraft assigned to the platoon in Okinawa were: Two (2) U-6A fixed wing aircraft, 'Beavers', Four (4) OH-23D Observation Helicopters, 'Ravens', and one (1) UH-1A Utility Helicopter 'Huey'.

Promised they would receive UH-1s when they arrived in Vietnam, they left the helicopters and took the two U-6A fixed wing aircraft with them. According to Don Bliss, the 173d Aviation Platoon Leader at this time, they flew to Vietnam aboard a C-124 and arrived at the Bien Hoa Airbase at almost exactly 12:00 noon on 5 May 1965.

Don said: "We disembarked in full combat gear (steel pots, personal weapons and all), and were greeted by a chorus of teenage Vietnamese girls singing their welcome to us. What a sight."

On or about 7 November 1965, the two (2) U-6A fixed wing aircraft, tail numbers: 757 and 771, and one of the two (2) fixed wing only aviators, Captain Jesse W. (Bob) Watson were transferred to the 74th Aviation Company (SAL), Callsign: "ALOFT", which was part of the 145th Aviation Battalion. The 74th was in Direct Support of the 10th ARVN Infantry Division at Xuan Loc. (The other fixed wing only aviator: Cpt. Rodney S. Beasley returned to CONUS to attend the Advanced Course.)

The 'Casper' platoon was issued two (2) UH-1Bs, tail numbers: 63-13911 and 64-13919. At some point, aircraft #919 was replaced in the Casper Platoon by another B model whose tail number is presently unknown. Aircraft #13919 was transferred to the Falcons armed helicopter platoon and became a 'Heavy' gunship armed with the XM-3 and XM-5 weapons systems. (It is believed, but not yet confirmed, that this aircraft exchange took place in May 1966 to replace the loss of another Falcon 'Heavy' gunship #63-12918, which was shot down and destroyed on 3 May 1966.

At some point during this initial time frame, the Casper Aviation Platoon also received two UH-1D models, tail numbers 64-13611 and 65-10121 (There are indications that acft 64-13610 was initially assigned to the Casper platoon along with 611 and was later replaced by 65-10121. Time frame and reason for this exchange are unknown at this time.)

The platoon also received 6 OH-13s Observation Helicopters, 'Sioux'. (Specific date they were assigned is unknown at this time.). Tail Numbers were: 64-15416, 64-15419, 64-15421, 64-15426, 64-15427, (64-15428 is believed to be the tail number of the 6th acft but this has not been confirmed yet.).

The OH-13s were equipped with wire basket litters (Stokes Litters) giving them the ability to perform Med-Evac missions if necessary. The OH-13s did, on several occasions, perform Med-Evac missions, however, the wounded rode inside the aircraft and, at this time, there are no known Med-Evac missions that were performed utilizing these litters.

ORIGIN OF THE 'CASPER' PLATOON NAME AND CALLSIGN:

According to the 1965 Casper Platoon Commander, Don Bliss, it was during the Aviation Platoons preparation for deployment from Okinawa to Vietnam that the name first arose. On numerous occasions during this critical preparation period, Captain Leonard Small, the Aviation Maintenance Officer from the Brigade Support Battalion was often not readily available to provide the needed assistance to the platoon. Considerable time was frequently spent by platoon members trying to locate him.

On one particular day during preparation, Captain Bob Watson, one of the fixed wing pilots, referred to Captain Small as: 'The Ghost' - someone that you couldn't see but on occasion felt his presence. The name stuck, and it wasn't long before others in the platoon began referring to him as 'The Ghost'.

Don said after they arrived in Vietnam and discovered that everybody had a callsign, the platoon members sat down and discussed various callsigns for the platoon. Bob Watson suggested 'Casper the Ghost' as a platoon name and callsign, adding that even though difficult to see, 'Casper the Ghost' had an impact on various people's lives during this period in time. They decided to shorten the name to 'Casper' and accepted that as the platoon nickname and callsign.

It is believed that Warrant Officer Don McGregor, who joined the platoon after it arrived in Vietnam, was the one most responsible for the original design of the 'Casper' pocket patch. This has yet to be confirmed.

Captain Don Bachali, one of the original Caspers from Okinawa, painted the 'Casper the Ghost' image on the cowlings of the U-6As, doors of the UH-1s they picked up in Vietnam, and on all of the pilot's helmets. The Casper image was also painted on the front of the bubble of the OH-13s. (Who painted it on the OH-13s is unknown.)

In late September 1966, the Casper OH-13s were equipped with the XM-1 Kit, (later designated as the M1), which consisted of two (2) Browning M37C .30 Cal Machine Guns. In keeping with the 'Casper the Ghost' theme, these Armed OH-13s used the callsign: 'HOT STUFF'. During this early time period, the armed OH-13s were flown mainly by 1/LT Gus Bell ('Hot Stuff Lead') and WO Bill Reynolds ('Hot Stuff Chase'). The armed OH-13s continued to retain the Casper image on the bubble. The 'Hot Stuff' image was painted on the pilot's helmets by Captain John Hoza, a former Casper pilot who had transferred to the Falcons armed helicopter platoon.

The remainder of the platoon aircraft continued to use the 'CASPER' callsign with the exception of the brigade commanders' aircraft which used the brigade commanders individual callsign, and the Mortar Aerial Delivery System (MADS) aircraft which used the callsigns: "MAD BOMBER" and "12 O'CLOCK HIGH".

TYPICAL CASPER PLATOON MISSIONS:

- Command and Control
- Psychological Operations: Loudspeaker Missions and Leaflet Drops)
- Mortar Aerial Delivery System: (Bombing Missions)
- Aero Scout Missions: (Reconnaissance, Observation and Surveillance Missions)
- Artillery Fire Adjustment Missions
- Artillery and Bomb Damage Assessment
- Convoy Control Missions
- Resupply Missions
- Med-Evac Missions as necessary
- Troop Lifts/Combat Assaults on a limited basis

Casper Pocket Patches: There are at least 3 different types of Casper Pocket patches that were worn between 1965 and 1971. According to Ned Costa and Bob White, Caspers, 1968-69, there was an additional patch that the 1968-71 Aero Scout crews wore on their survival vests. Bob did not think any of the pilots wore it. A modified version of the patch was also painted on both sides of the LOH 6 main rotor cowling. Bob thinks SP/5 Richard Canning, a Casper Aero Scout, either designed or was involved in the design of the patch.

Early 1965-67 Casper Platoon Commanders:

- Donald Bliss, 1965
- Duane Ingram, 1965-66
- Bruce Cochran, 1966-66
- Thomas J. Terry, 1966-67
- Calvin Gibson, 1967-67

BACKGROUND OF 173D AIRBORNE BRIGADE (SEP)
COWBOY AVIATION SUPPORT:

General background and parent unit assignments of the Cowboys

The 82d Aviation Company was activated at Fort Bragg NC in 1957. The Company was expanded and redesignated the 82d Aviation Battalion on 1 July 1960 with a total of three (3) Companies and 60 aircraft. The 82d Aviation Battalion minus Company A deployed to the Dominican Republic in April 1965. Company A deployed to Vietnam that same month. The Advance Party departed by plane, from Oakland California, and arrived in VN on or about 12 April 1965. The main body of Company A, along with its 3 support units: 166th Transportation Detachment (Aircraft Maintenance) 234th Signal Detachment (Avionics) 25th Medical Detachment departed San Diego California on 12 April aboard the Helicopter Carrier USS Iwo Jima.

There was a total of three Avn Companies, with their support units and aircraft and equipment that sailed to Vietnam on the Iwo Jima on 12 April 1965:

- A Company, 82d Aviation Battalion 82d Airborne Division
- A Company, 1st Aviation Battalion 1st Infantry Division
- A Company, 101st Aviation Battalion 101st Airborne Division

There was a total of 75 new helicopters aboard the ship. Each company was assigned: 9 UH-1B and 16 UH-1D helicopters. These were the first D model Hueys to enter service in Vietnam.

The USS Iwo Jima arrived off the coast of Vung Tau, Vietnam on 1 May 1965. The ship docked approximately 30 miles off shore and the aircraft were flown from the ship to Vung Tau with limited crews on board.

The majority of the company personnel and equipment was taken ashore aboard LSTs. The company was based at Vung Tau and assigned to the 145th Combat Aviation Battalion.

They were given the Callsign: 'Dallas Cowboys' by Military Assistance Command Vietnam (MACV) SOI. The Company dropped the word: 'Dallas' and changed the Callsign to COWBOYS.

The COWBOYS of Company A/82d Aviation Battalion, consisting of two lift platoons and one armed helicopter platoon arrived in Vietnam on 1 May 1965.

- 1st Lift Platoon: 'Ramrods' (Originally named: 'Peacemakers'. Reason for change is unknown.)
- 2d Lift Platoon: 'Mustangs'
- Armed Helicopter Platoon: 'Falcons'

The A/82d COWBOYS were assigned to the 145th Combat Aviation Battalion with the mission of providing General Support to the III Corps Tactical Area.

From May 1965 thru October 1965, the 173d Airborne Brigade received its major aviation support for combat assaults, armed helicopter support and resupply, from the 145th Combat Aviation Battalion. As part of the 145th CAB, the COWBOYS of Company A/82d were actively involved in providing this aviation support to the 173d during this time period. Requested by BG Williamson, 173d Abn Bde Commander, Company A/82d was assigned to the 173d Airborne Brigade (Sep) on 19 October 1965 and their mission changed to Direct Support of the 173d Airborne Brigade (Sep). (Don Bliss, who was instrumental in this action, said he thought the order read: "Attachment For All Purposes.")

The COWBOYS continued to fly operational missions for the 173d while simultaneously preparing for and moving to Bien Hoa. They were released from operational missions on 27 October 1965 to complete the move, which required 53 sorties. The COWBOYS again began flying operational missions for the 173d early the following day.

Company A/82 was redesignated the 335th Assault Helicopter Company (AHC) 173d Airborne Brigade (Sep) on 1 September 1966. Note: The initial designation was: 335th Aviation Company Airmobile Light (AML) The designation was changed to 335th Assault Helicopter Company by the 1st Aviation Brigade that same month.

The company continued to be assigned to the 173d Abn Bde until January 1967 when it was reassigned to the 145th Combat Aviation Battalion, 1st Aviation Brigade.

After this reassignment, its mission was changed to General Support of III Corps, like all of the other 145th CAB aviation units in Military Region Three.

Through the direct intervention of BG John Deane Jr., 173d Airborne Brigade Commander, at that time; the 335th. COWBOYS, were placed under the Operational Control (OPCON) of the 173d Abn Bde and their mission was changed to Direct Support of the 173d. The 335th deployed to the Dak To, Kontum, Pleiku area with the 173d Brigade in May 1967.

On 31 December 1967, the 335th AHC was reassigned to the: 268th Combat Aviation Battalion 17th Combat Aviation Group 1st Aviation Brigade and their base camp moved to Tuy Hoa.

The COWBOYS mission remained Direct Support of the 173d Airborne Brigade.

The COWBOYS were released from the Operational Control (OPCON) of the 173d Airborne Brigade in March 1968, when their mission was changed from providing Direct Support to the 173d Airborne Brigade to providing General Support to the II Corps Tactical Area. The 335th was attached to the: 214th Combat Aviation Battalion 164th Combat Aviation Group 1st Aviation Brigade and moved their base camp to Bear Cat in the Third Corps Tactical Region in December 1968. Their mission was to provide support to the 9th US Infantry Division and the 7th and 9th Vietnamese Divisions.

The 335th was assigned to the 214th CAB in July 1969. The COWBOYS were moved to Dong Tam on 31 August 1970 and provided support to ARVN units operating in the Fourth Corps Tactical Region. The 335th stood down and redeployed to Fort Riley Kansas on: 5 November 1971.

The 335th was assigned to the 1st Aviation Battalion (Provisional) with the mission of providing support to the 1st Infantry Division and 5th US Army. The 335th was deactivated in 1976.

CASPER / COWBOY RELATIONSHIP:

Shortly after the assignment of Company A/82 Avn Bn, to the 173d Abn Bde on 19 October 1965, the decision was made to consolidate all the brigade's aviation assets.

The 173d Aviation Platoon, 'Caspers', and the 161st Reconnaissance Flight (RECCE Flight) of the Royal Australian Army, who used the callsign: 'Possum', were placed under the Operational Control (OPCON) of the Company A/82d Avn Bn Commander, Major Donald A. Champlin.

The 161st RECCE Flight, along with the: 1st Battalion Royal Australian Regiment, the Royal Australian Artillery Battery, the Prince of Whales Light Horse Troop and the 161st Royal New Zealand Artillery, was detached from the 173d Brigade in June of 1966. Note: After their release from attachment from the 173d Abn Bde, the Australians ("Diggers") and the New Zealanders ("Kiwis") formed the: 1st Australian Task Force (Separate).

The Caspers remained OPCON to the Cowboy Company Commanders from October 1965 to March of 1968 when the mission of the COWBOYS changed and the 335th AHC was released from the 173d Airborne Brigade (Sep).

The 173d Aviation Platoon Caspers were the organic brigade aviation support unit and remained in the brigade and reverted to the Operational Control of the Brigade S-3. The platoon increased in size and upgraded their aircraft. The Casper Platoon UH-1 fleet was increased to eight (8), and in March or April 1968, the OH-13s were exchanged for six (6) LOH-6s, which were armed with miniguns and were utilized in the Aero Scout role. The aero scouts used the callsign: 'Inferno'. The remainder of the platoon continued to use the 'Casper' callsign. At some point in mid to late 1970, the LOHs were replaced by OH-58s.

The Casper Platoon remained with and continued to provide aviation support to the 173d Abn Bde (Sep) throughout the remainder of its service. The 173d Airborne Brigade (Separate) departed Vietnam in August of 1971. It was stationed at Fort Campbell, Kentucky until its deactivation on 14 January 1972.

After the 335th, COWBOYS (gunships: Falcons), were released from brigade control, the Combat Assault, and Combat Support missions for the 173d were provided by the 61st and 117th Avn Companies: 1st Aviation Company: Lift Plts: Lucky Stars, Gunships: Star Blazers, 117th Aviation Company: Lift Plts: Warlords, Gunships: Sidewinders.

Additional aviation support was provided by Troop C 7/17th Cavalry (Ruthless Charlie, Yellow Scarf), which had been placed under the Operational Control (OPCON) of the 173d Abn Bde (Sep).

I want to thank the following named individuals for all their efforts and assistance in retrieving this information about the COWBOYS and the Casper Platoon enabling his summary fact sheet to be compiled – *John Hoza*

- Don Bliss: 173d Avn Platoon Ldr, (Casper) / 173d Airborne Brigade, Avn Officer, 1965/66)
- Don Champlin: Company Commander, Company A/82d Avn Bn 'Cowboy 6', 1965/66)
- Chuck Utzman: Company Commander, 335th Assault Helicopter Company, 'Cowboy 6' 173d Abn Bde, Avn Officer, 1967/68)
- Duane Ingram (Casper 6, 1965/66)
- Betty Lou Watson (widow of Jessie Bob Watson, Casper 1965)
- John Tyler (173d Abn Bde S-3, 1965)
- Gus Bell (Casper, Hot Stuff – Lead, 1966/1967)
- Ken Jones (Casper / 166th Maint., 1966/67)
- Bruce Silvey (Casper / 173d Airborne Brigade, Brigade Aviation Officer 1968/69)
- Cliff White (Casper, 1968)
- Steven Spencer (Casper, 1969)
- Sam Keith (Casper, 1971)
- Ned Costa (Casper, 1968/69)
- Bob White (Casper / 'Inferno', 1968/69)
- Don Charlton (Casper, 1968/69)
- Don Bachali, Casper, 1965
- Del McConnel, (1965/66), Commander, 166th Transportation Detachment ('Horsethief')
- Kurt Schultz, Falcon 1965/66

COWBOYS

UNIT HISTORY

5 MAY 1965 -- 31 DECEMBER 1965

History of

173rd Airborne Brigade (Separate)

Prepared by
LT. James B. Channon

Researched by
LT. George A. Russill

BIEN HOA, REPUBLIC OF VIETNAM

The following history was taken from the book *The Fists Three Years*, a pictorial history of the 173D Airborne Brigade (Separate). It was the only history that could be found that describes the activities of **Company "A," 82nd Aviation Battalion**. Although the history below is directed more toward the 173d Airborne Brigade, it does describe some of the COWBOYS activities upon their arrival in Vietnam.

ORGANIZATION:

The 173d Airborne Brigade (Separate) was activated 25 June 1963 and was formed around the nucleus of the 2nd Airborne Battle Group 503d Infantry, a lineal descendent of the World War II 503d Parachute Infantry Regiment of Corregidor fame. It was organized as a balanced airborne combat force consisting of two infantry battalions, an artillery battalion, a support battalion, an engineer company, a cavalry troop, an armor company, and a headquarters company.

Upon activation, it became the first and only separate airborne brigade in the United States Army. This was the beginning of a long series of "Firsts" for the Brigade. It underwent extensive jungle training on Okinawa and made mass parachuted jumps on the Island of Taiwan, in Thailand and on the Island of Mindoro in the Philippines. Through such training, the men of the Brigade were honed to razor sharpness and prepared for deployment to any trouble spot in Southeast Asia.

On 5 May 1965, it became the first U.S. Army ground combat unit committed to the war in South Vietnam, where further organizational changes were to take place. Attached to the Brigade were: 1st Battalion, Royal Australian Regiment and support troops, the Prince of Wales Light Horse Troop, a Royal Australian Artillery Battery, 161st Royal New Zealand Artillery Battery, **Company "A," 82nd Aviation Battalion**, plus special intelligence, transportation, chemical and signal detachments.

The Brigade and attached units distinguished themselves as fierce fighters on the battlefield against the Viet Cong (VC). They have smashed the VC whenever and wherever they found him, and, when not doing battle, they have conducted extensive civic action programs to assist the South Vietnamese people in the attainment of a better life and to bolster their hope for a future of peace and progress.

These programs included medical assistance, support of orphanages, distribution of food and clothing and repair of churches, schools, roads, and construction of wells.

The shoulder insignia (patch) worn by the men of the Brigade came into being with the activation of the Brigade in June 1963. The red bayonet signifies a strike force borne by a white wing denoting that the strike force can be flown by transport aircraft and dropped by parachute onto any assigned objective. The tab reading "AIRBORNE" above the shoulder patch indicates that the men are paratroopers and all equipment of the Brigade is air transportable. The patches' colors, red, white, and blue are our national colors.

"All the Way" is the traditional motto of the paratroopers and was born out of the annals of World War II. It reflects the spirit, drive, and resoluteness of the paratroopers to carry out any assigned task or mission, no matter how difficult, to a successful conclusion.

The paratroopers of the Brigade are called "Sky Soldiers." This nickname was given to the troopers by the people of the Republic of Nationalist China (Taiwan) because of a series of mass parachute jumps conducted on the Island of Taiwan in conjunction with the Chinese airborne forces. The people of Taiwan began calling the paratroopers "Tien Bing" which is Chinese for "Sky Soldier." The name stuck and has since been made the official nickname of the paratroopers of the 173d Airborne Brigade (Sep).

COMBAT SUPPORT:

Within the 173d Support Battalion are three companies without which the Brigade could not function. "B" Company (Medical) provides teams of doctors and aidmen to operate the Brigade Clearing Station. "C" Company (Supply and Transport) hauls and stores the Brigade's supplies and its Aerial Equipment Support Platoon furnishes parachute support. Third echelon maintenance of all equipment is accomplished by "D" Company (Maintenance). Formerly part of support battalion but now separate Company "A" (Administration) handles all the personnel services for the Brigade including Special Services and the post office. The 1st Australian Logistical Support Company provides special support for the Australian troops.

Whether it's a shower point being built or a Viet Cong mine destroyed, the 173d Engineer Company does it. Attached to them is a special detachment of the Third Field Troop of the Royal Australian Engineers. Charged with the responsibility of housing and providing for all the personnel of Brigade headquarters are Headquarters and Headquarters Company.

The two troopship platoons and one gunship platoon of **Company "A," of the 82nd Aviation Battalion** furnished the much-needed independence for the Brigade. With the Hueys of its own helicopter company the Brigade is now certain that its helicopter support will be available as needed. Part of the aviation company are three specialized detachments designed to supplement the company's support platoons. The 166th Transportation Detachment and the 234th Signal Detachment provide the critical third echelon maintenance on the helicopters and signal equipment, while the 25th Medical Detachment provides aidmen and a flight surgeon.

The Brigade's smallest unit is the 51st Chemical Detachment which provides the chemical support needed in clearing tunnel complexes.

THE TROOP LIFT:

To the Brigade's **Company "A," 82nd Aviation Battalion** goes the dangerous job of transporting the "Sky Soldiers" to the objective area. At the staging area, whether Bien Hoa or the field, the units to be lifted are broken down into a series of "lifts." The size of the lift depends upon the number of helicopters available, the size of the objective landing zone (LZ), and the number of troops to be lifted. Generally, about 12 Hueys are used in a lift. For each lift, the troops are separated and prepositioned on the LZ within a few feet of where their helicopter will land.

In just a few well-coordinated seconds, the helicopters will land, the troops pile aboard, and the entire lift will rise from the departure LZ at once and head for the objective area.

As the helicopters approach the LZ, the gunships fan out, circling the LZ waiting to suppress any hostile fire. On board the troopships, the door-gunners are alert for any enemy activity in the surrounding tree line. As the troopships land, the Sky Soldiers spring from the Hueys and quickly take up defensive positions around the LZ or move out immediately into the thick jungles and the troop ships return to the departure LZ for another lift.

A variation of the planned lift employed by the Brigade is an "Eagle Flight" consisting of a reinforced company or less which moves by helicopter to an LZ that generally has not received preparatory fires. Such a flight is made in reaction to a hot intelligence report. During the operations around Pleiku the Brigade employed many eagle flights to deposit quickly platoon-size patrols around the countryside.

HEAVY FIRE TEAM -- LIGHT FIRE TEAM:

The major innovation in this conflict has been the use of the armed Army helicopter. Originally armed for defensive purposes, the four man UH-1B (Hueys) have evolved into a sophisticated aerial fire support system.

A gunship platoon such as the **Falcons of "A," Company 82nd Aviation Battalion**, attached to the Brigade, has eight UH-1Bs heavily armed with 2.75" rockets and 7.62mm machine flexguns with a total of 6,000 rounds. Six of the ships mount four M-6 kits 7.62 machine flexguns, two pods with seven rockets each and two door mounted M-60 machine guns with 1,500 rounds each.

The heavy ships, nicknamed "Frog" and "Hog," provide the saturation fire. The Frog has two 12 shot rocket pods, the door mounted M-60s, and a nose mounted M-5 grenade launcher containing 150 40mm grenades. The beast, the Hog, bears two pods containing 24 rockets each plus the standard door guns. Firing the rockets in pairs, salvo or individually, the heavy ships augment a light gunship fire team, furnishing tremendous suppressive fire against an LZ, a trench system, or an ambush site.

At 80 knots air speed, the Hueys can spot targets of opportunity, provide aerial reconnaissance, and protect a long motor convoy all during its one and a half hour flying time, and its ability to refuel and rearm wherever it lands drastically shortens its down time.

The employment of the gunships and their aerial tactics have been under constant revision as new techniques are devised and tried. Like the fighter pilots of W.W.II, the Falcons represent the daredevils of modern aerial warfare.

COMBAT:

The 173d's first mission was to secure and defend the Bien Hoa Air Base. When asked the morning of his Sky Soldiers' arrival at the base on 5 May 1965, how soon he expected to initiate action against the Viet Cong (VC), General Williamson replied, "Tonight." And that night the Brigade set its first ambush patrols and the security and defense of Bien Hoa Air Base began.

Areas of responsibility were immediately assigned to subordinate units, defensive fires were planned, barriers erected and check points established. But rather than sit and wait for the VC to attack, the Brigade moved out to secure the area by continual, thorough and aggressive patrolling. Twenty-four hours a day, the Bien Hoa area was saturated by the "Sky Soldiers," and in support, the howitzer crewmen of 3/319th Artillery remained on alert. Ranging in size from a rifle squad to a company, patrols combed the area, examining trails for recent use, investigating likely assembly and ambush sites and recording every new trail and clearing. Usually each patrol had a mortar or artillery forward observer with it, and when needed, specially trained demolition's men were included. In addition, Vietnamese policemen accompanied the patrols as interpreters and to interrogate suspected VC.

While securing the immediate area, the troopers simultaneously moved into adjacent areas, patrolling and clearing a series of zones extending in radials out to 15 kilometers from the air base. Once cleared, a "measle" approach was used extensively in conjunction with other tactical concepts to maintain the security of the Tactical Area of Responsibility (TAOR).

This approach entailed the selection of numerous helicopter landing zones and patrol base positions throughout the TAOR out to 105mm artillery range. These areas were coded and plotted on the Brigade's immediate defense map, which became commonly known as the "Measle Sheet." Eagle flights and motor and foot moves were employed in positioning elements up to company size in these preselected areas. The exact areas to be occupied were arbitrarily selected, but when possible, the selection was based on available intelligence. Several areas were selected for occupation at a time and the units occupying them would remain there from one to three days. In this way the VC was kept guessing. He never knew where the "Sky Soldiers" would show next and was caught by surprise time and time again by the fast-moving resolute troopers.

While the infantry battalions were employing eagle flights and foot patrols, E/17th Cavalry and D/16th Armor were making a show of force, scouting the road networks, selecting fording sites and checking the banks of the Dong Nai Rivers, or conducting a reconnaissance in force in the TAOR. By varying the time, type and manner of patrols, the Brigade was able to secure the roads. Once secure, the roads sprang alive with bicycles, ox carts, Lambretta scooters, buses and trucks as the grateful Vietnamese people journeyed to visit long abandoned markets, friends and families.

In conjunction with the securing of Bien Hoa Air Base, the Brigade perfected techniques in airmobile operations such as the movement of artillery by helicopter and establishment of a fire support base prior to the introduction of the infantry into objective areas by helicopters. Outmoded procedures were revamped and the Brigade began preparation for battalion and larger size operations.

In less than two weeks after its arrival in Vietnam, the first battalion size operation was conducted. The 2/503d Infantry was heli-lifted into an LZ in the extreme eastern sector of the Brigade TAOR, and conducted an overnight sweep through the thick jungles, emerging the next day in the adjoining rice paddies. The 3/319th Artillery with E/17th Cavalry and D/16th Armor attached moved out by convoy to a location from which it could support the operation and was in position well before the first heliborne troops of the 2/503d Infantry was landed in the selected LZ. Very light enemy resistance was encountered.

One week later, the 1/503d Infantry with C/3/319th Artillery struck out from Vung Tau against the VC. The battalion task force swept through an area near the resort, meeting only sporadic sniper fire from the VC.

At the end of May 1965, the Brigade committed almost all its combat assets in an airmobile operation for the first time as the 1/503d Infantry and 2/503d Infantry swept through an area just south of the junction of the Song Be and Dong Nai Rivers. The four-day operation included airmobile assaults on three different objectives and security of a fourth. It was the largest and most unusual airmobile operation ever conducted in Vietnam.

Brigade elements were organized into three task forces (TF): Task Force SURUT, composed of 3/319th Artillery (less two batteries), reinforced by E/17th Cavalry, one platoon of Brigade engineers and one composite platoon made up of volunteers of the administrative, supply and maintenance personnel of the Support Battalion; Task Force DEXTER, consisting of 2/503d infantry, plus attached Brigade engineers.

All individuals in TF SURUT, even the artillery gun crews, made an Infantry type airmobile assault to secure LZ BLUE. The TF landing area was pounded by U.S. Air Force and U.S. Army Aviation 25 minutes prior to the first touchdown of troops. As soon as the area was secured, H-37 helicopters brought in six 105mm howitzers with their ammunition. The howitzers were promptly laid and fires for the landing of TF DEXTER on LZ RED were initiated.

Three hours after the landing of TF SURUT, TF DEXTER began landing on LZ RED. Its landings were protected by a twenty-minute artillery preparation, a fifteen-minute air strike and five minutes of reconnaissance and suppressive fires from the armed helicopters. The initial assault was supported by fire from armed helicopters and all door gunners of the personnel carrying UH-1B and D's (Hueys).

While landings were going on in objective BLUE and RED, TF BOLAND was being flown by C-130 and C-123 aircraft from Vung Tau to Bien Hoa Air Base. Bien Hoa served as the staging field for all helicopter lifts.

The next day at first light, fire support from objectives BLUE and RED were used to support landings of TF BOLAND on objective WHITE. After support from ground weapons, the U.S. Air Force again assisted in paving the way with a high volume of bombs, rockets and machine-gun fire. Again, under the protective fires of helicopters, the TF landing was accomplished against light opposition.

A total of 7 VC were killed as the swift moving "Sky Soldiers" encountered light resistance. They uncovered and destroyed many VC camps and bunkers but found the VC unwilling to stand and fight.

Thus, the mold was cast. Many of the techniques and procedures employed in this operation would be used again in later operations. The "Sky Soldiers" were now ready to press the "offensive defense" of the Bien Hoa area, and began planning for thrusts into infamous War Zone "D" which lay just across the Dong Nai River to the north of the Brigade TAOR.

On 31 May 1965, the 1st Battalion, Royal Australian Regiment, arrived in country and was attached to the Brigade. Many of the men of this experienced and highly trained battalion were veterans of the Malayan counter guerrilla campaign and were eager to show their mettle in battle against the VC.

Early in the morning of 13 June 1965, the Brigade was alerted for possible movement to assist ARVN forces heavily engaged in a fierce battle with the VC near the town of Dong Xoai north of War Zone "D." The decision was made to send a battalion task force. Within hours the 1/503d Infantry and A/3/319th Artillery were lifted from Vung Tau and Bien Hoa to the vicinity of Phuoc Vinh on the northern edge of War Zone "D." By dusk, the battalion task force had set up blocking positions and secured the town and vital airstrip there.

In spite of aggressive patrolling, TF 1/503d had no VC contact as the enemy chose again to avoid the "Sky Soldiers." After four days, ARVN forces had secured the Dong Xoai area and TF 1/503d returned. The Brigade had successfully demonstrated its ability to respond to combat operational requirements on a moment's notice and had proved to all its eagerness to carry the battle to the VC.

On 19 June, the 1/503d and attachments were moved permanently from Vung Tau to rejoin the Brigade at Bien Hoa.

In late June, the Brigade penetrated War Zone "D" for the first time. Long a VC stronghold and formerly used as a redoubt by the Vietminh and Vietnamese bandits, War Zone "D" reportedly was an impregnable VC fortress. Here the VC trained, treated their sick, stored supplies and relaxed.

Preceded by artillery, air and armed helicopter strikes, the 2/503d assaulted War Zone "D" by helicopters on the morning of 23 June. Their mission was to search and destroy, and the fast-moving troopers fanned out quickly from their LZ. With the artillery support based just south of the Dong Nai River, the men of the 2/503d Infantry were assured of continuous fire support. Again, the VC chose not to fight as the troopers swept through the area. Hot chow and glowing fires were abandoned by the VC. Bunkers, camps and supplies were destroyed by the "Sky Soldiers" and tons of rice rendered useless. A few VC suspects were detained but no significant contact was made with the enemy. But the "Sky Soldiers" proved that War Zone "D" was not an impregnable VC position.

As American troop strength in Vietnam increased, the Brigade was assigned the responsibility for clearing and securing the base areas for incoming units. The first mission was to secure the base area for the 2nd Brigade, 1st

Infantry Division. On 25-26 June, the newly arrived 1/RAR, on its first major operation, cleared an area southeast of Highway 1A. The Aussies found only a few VC camps and made no contact with the VC. Within days' elements of the 2nd Brigade moved into the area without a shot being fired at them.

On 27 June, the Brigade participated in the largest troop lift and its first joint American-Vietnamese combat operation of the war. In all, nine battalions were involved: five infantry, one artillery, one support and a composite battalion of cavalry, armor and engineers. The targets were objectives deep inside War Zone "D." With the 3/319th fire support base established north of TAN UYEN in War Zone "D" and secured by the 1/RAR, D/16 Armor, with E/17th screening, the 1/503d Infantry and 2/503d Infantry were heli-lifted to the west of TAN UYEN deep into the VC redoubt--farther than any sizable friendly force had ventured in over one year. The two infantry battalions swept south while two battalions of ARVN airborne troops, who landed south of the "Sky Soldiers," swept north in an adjacent zone of operation. The operation lasted for four days and was the first time the newly arrived 1/RAR had taken their place with the Brigade as part of its combat formation. Killing 25 VC and destroying or capturing over 200 tons of rice and food stuff plus three trucks, the "Sky Soldiers" mapped enemy installations for future actions and proved again that the enemy redoubt was not impenetrable.

From 6 to 9 July, the Brigade again attacked into "D" Zone. With the fire support base (3/319th, D/16th, and 173d Eng. Co.) south of the Dong Nai River, the 1/503d, 2/503d with E/17th attached and 1/RAR, conducted successive heliborne assaults north of the Dong Nai River just south of the combined operation of 27-30 June. They swept south to trap the enemy against the river. On the west flank, the ARVN 48th Regiment blocked enemy escape routes and coordinated their movements with the Brigade. The ARVN 3d Battalion, 43d Regiment was attached to the Brigade on the second day of the operation and blocked VC escape routes to the east along the Dong Nai River. This was the first time that an ARVN combat unit had been attached and under the direct command of the U.S. commander. This thrust into War Zone "D" was the most complex yet most successful operation to date and resulted in over 400 VC casualties (later intelligence indicated, in fact, over 600 casualties), 28 VC captives, the destruction of over 300 VC buildings, 100 tons of rice and many domestic animals, and the recovery of a ton of documents, thirty weapons and four radios.

In the first major engagement with the VC, the men of the Brigade had the satisfaction that they emerged eminently victorious. The hard-core VC battalion they encountered had been decimated. The enemy had proved no match for the tough, hard driving "Sky Soldiers" in spite of their well-prepared entrenchment's and booby-trapped facilities.

During the period 10 to 27 July, the Brigade conducted patrols up to two companies in size in its TAOR at Bien Hoa as shows of force and in conjunction with the Measle Sheet. The 161st Field Battery of the Royal New Zealand Army (RNZA) arrived in country on 17 July and was attached to the Brigade.

The Brigade's next major operation from 28 July to 2 August was in Phuoc Tuy Province where a VC supply route was believed located. Task Force 6A (3/319th, E/17th, D/16th, and elements of the Engineers and Support Battalion moved by convoy down Highway 15 to Position NICKEL in Phuoc Tuy Province on 28 July (D-1) and in the process cleared the highway for the first time in months which allowed the ARVN to resupply their Binh Gia garrison near Vung Tau. The 1/503d moved by C-130 aircraft to Vung Tau early in the morning of 29 July.

The airmobile assault on 29 July was preceded by a massive B-52 strike. Following this, the normal Air Force and artillery fires prepared the LZ for the landing of the first troop lift of the 2/503d from Bien Hoa. The seventy-five Hueys used to lift the battalion then moved on to Vung Tau and in two lifts placed the 1/503d on the LZ. Then the helicopters returned to Bien Hoa and picked up the rest of the 2/503d. In this manner, the 145th Aviation Battalion was able to complete the entire troop lift with only two refueling stops.

On 30 July the 2/18th Infantry, 1st Division relieved E/17th and D/16th from their security mission of Position NICKEL and allowed the cavalry and armor units to establish blocking positions for the infantry's push through the valley. D/16th mounted patrols with composite platoons of the Support Battalion and Engineers to check out reported VC locations and caches.

The Brigade logistics operation center operated out of Vung Tau throughout the operation. For the first time in Vietnam, the Brigade used parachutes for the delivery of supplies. Low Level Extraction (Lolex) was used partially to supply TF 6A at Position NICKEL.

This complicated operation was conducted smoothly and effectively. The Brigade showed its flexibility and proved that it was not tied to the Bien Hoa area, and the "Sky Soldiers" dispelled the myth that this Phuoc Tuy area was a heavily fortified VC fortress and encouraged the ARVN military forces to conduct bolder and more ambitious operations in the area.

During the period 7 to 11 August, the Brigade again invaded "D" zone as the 1/RAR supported by B/3/319th moved through on another search and destroy operation. Only light contact was made with the VC, but the Aussies killed 4 snipers and destroyed numerous VC camps and installations.

On the morning of 10 August, the Brigade received a warning order to move to the Pleiku area for possible airmobile operations. Minutes later came the movement order and within hours the first elements of the Brigade were landing by C-130 and C-123 aircraft in the Montagnard country in central Vietnam.

Under siege was the Special Forces CIDG camp at Du Co, only 5 kilometers from the Cambodian border. With the VC strength estimated at more than regimental size, immediate reinforcements in the Pleiku area were necessary to allow the ARVN II Corps Commander to commit his reserves to relieve the VC pressure at Duc Co. The 173d provided the reserve and secured the strategic Thanh Binh pass, allowing ARVN relief forces to pass through to Duc Co. While securing the pass, the Brigade conducted numerous eagle flights and patrols throughout the area seeking out the VC.

A total of 43 company, 116 platoon and 22 squad size operations were conducted in the area, thoroughly saturating every hill and valley with "Sky Soldiers," but the enemy again chose to run rather than fight. After the VC siege of Duc Co had been broken, the ARVN relief column was ordered to return to the Pleiku area. The Brigade was given the mission to secure the passage of the relief force back to Pleiku. This force returned through the Brigade secured area without a shot being fired at them. Brigade planning and coordination for the security of the ARVN forces served as an outstanding example as to how this type mission should be carried out. The ARVN Task Force Commander was so impressed that he told his staff to learn the technique employed by the Brigade. Having mastered the technique, the favor was later returned in kind when the same ARVN task force secured the return of Brigade elements from Kontum.

The Brigade returned to Plieku and was immediately alerted for commitment to the Kontum area. A VC buildup there was in progress and an attack at any time was feared. The Brigade dispatched 1/503d, C/3/319th and E/17 to Kontum, opening the Pleiku-Kontum road for the first time in five weeks. At Kontum, the VC again chose not to fight the "Sky Soldiers."

During the Brigade's presence in the highlands, VC activity decreased to its lowest rate in 18 months. Consequently, most of the Brigade's efforts there were directed towards civic action. Over 50 villages were visited by medics who treated over 5,000 patients. A leprosarium was refurbished, and many schools were repaired, painted and cleaned. After 28 days, the "Sky Soldiers" moved back to Bien Hoa from the highlands.

One week later, 14 September 1965, War Zone "D" was penetrated again as the Brigade moved into the Ben Cat sector north of the Iron Triangle and conducted search and destroy operations until 28 September. Saturation patrolling was employed utilizing squad and platoon size units from battalion patrol bases.

An impressive list of accomplishments marked this operation. In order to extend the fire support base, A/3/319th and the 161st RNZA Battery were moved into the center of the TAOR with the indispensable help of the APC's of the Prince of Wales Light Horse Troop. Acting on intelligence garnered from a VC, the 1/503d was heli-lifted into the northern operational area. In four days the swift moving "Sky Soldiers" destroyed two hospitals, a signal school, several large training camps and numerous VC buildings. C/1/503d captured 62 Russian sniper rifles with telescopic sights and 36 military radios plus 4,500 Chinese hand grenades and 91 bangalore torpedoes. One of the sniper rifles was to later be permanently displayed in the Presidential Library in Washington, DC.

In all, the VC lost 46 killed and 80 captured. Over 9,000 documents and 500 pounds of medical supplies were captured and twenty-three VC camps were located for future air strikes or destroyed as found.

Concurrent with combat operations, an extensive civic action program was conducted. Seventeen village chiefs who had not ventured out of Ben Cat in over a year returned to their villages, elections were held, and Mass was said for the first time in a year. The roads sprung alive as long abandoned markets were supplied with fresh produce. Tons of foodstuffs were distributed along with 900 magazines for the news starved villagers.

During September 1965, the 1/RAR was reinforced by the 105 Field Battery, Royal Australian Artillery (RAA), the 3d Field Engineer Troop, the 161st Reconnaissance Flight and the 1st Australian Logistical Support Company (ALSC).

From 4 to 6 October, the 1/503d supported by 3/319th conducted another search and destroy operation into "D" Zone. On this rapidly moving three-day operation, the battalion killed 15 VC, destroyed numerous VC camps and bunkers and captured many documents.

Two days later, the Brigade returned to the Ben Cat area but met only light and scattered VC resistance northwest of Ben Cat. The Brigade then turned south to challenge the "Iron Triangle"--a VC physical, psychological and military bastion. Many stories had been told about the Triangle and it was believed by the Vietnamese that the area was impenetrable.

Employing all three infantry battalions and the first B-52 strike of the war in direct support of ground troops, the "Sky Soldiers" and Aussies moved into the Iron Triangle and cracked it wide open. The fast-moving Brigade elements killed 106 VC, destroyed numerous camps, a VC hospital and sank 7 sampans. The fifty square kilometers of the unknown no longer existed. The few VC installations that could not be destroyed were pinpointed for destruction at will by air attacks. As Brigadier General Williamson stated succinctly to his troops after the operation, "The Iron Triangle is no more." Another myth of VC invincibility was laid to rest.

On 19 October, the Brigade received its own aviation company, **Company "A," 82nd Aviation Battalion**. This was to be a most valuable addition to the Brigade for it provided much needed mobility and greatly enhanced the operational capability of the Brigade.

From 21 to 27 October, the 2/503d and B/3/319th cleared the Phu Loi-Di An area, a future location for elements of the U.S. 1st Infantry Division. The seven-day operation resulted in slight contact and only two VC were killed. At the same time the 1/RAR supported by the RAA and RNZA batteries combed War Zone "D" again, encountering only occasional sniper fire from the VC. Three VC were killed.

From 5 to 9 November, the Brigade again invaded "D" Zone in Operation HUMP, which resulted in the biggest single U.S. ground engagement of the war to date. The 1/RAR entered south of the Dong Nai River while the 1/503d was heli-lifted in northwest of the river. The first three days of the operation were quiet with most of the action occurring in the Australian sector where two enemy were killed and one captured.

On the fourth day, the 1/503d, acting on an intelligence report, moved westerly and immediately encountered a large enemy force. The lead elements of C/1/503d made contact first and soon Charlie Company was enveloped by the larger force. B/1/503d moved up to secure Charlie Company's flank and quickly had to fight to secure its own flanks. With this, A/1/503d was committed, attacking the enemy's left flank. The 1/503d was now engaged with a regiment of hard core VC and the battle raged for four hours.

Shortly past noon Bravo and Charlie Companies were able to consolidate and readjust their lines to allow heavy artillery and air strikes to pound the entrenched enemy. As the "Sky Soldiers" moved back in to attack, the enemy, leaving their trenches and blowing bugles, counterattacked. Combat raged at close quarters throughout the afternoon and when the VC withdrew at dusk they left behind 403 dead, most of whom were killed by small arms fire. Hundreds of VC were killed and carried away and many wounded escaped on their own. Later reports indicated that the three companies of "Sky Soldiers" had decimated a front-line regiment, armed with the latest Communist bloc automatic weapons and clothed in standard uniforms with steel helmets. The "Sky Soldiers," though seriously outnumbered and in the enemy's home ground, had routed and destroyed a major VC force.

Operation NEW LIFE in the La Nga River valley north of Vo Dat commenced on the morning of 21 November. Moving by helicopter, C-130, CV-2 and C-123 aircraft, within a few hours three infantry battalions, four artillery batteries, the cavalry troop and command sections had landed on the Vo Dat airstrip.

The mission of the Brigade was to prevent the rice harvest in the rich Rice Bowl from falling into the enemy's hands and to return the valley to government control.

Moving south on the road to Gia Ray the 2/503d cleared the area, eventually joining up with the overland elements consisting of two infantry battalions and two artillery batteries of the 1st Infantry Division, and brigade armor, logistical and engineer elements. With the road cleared, 600 troop-filled vehicles of the ARVN 10th Division passed through the Brigade to the eastern part of the Rice Bowl and began operations.

The 1/503d with C/3/319th was heli-lifted across the unfordable La Nga River into the northwest corner of the Rice Bowl. Through close cooperation with the village chief of Phuong Lam and acting on intelligence received, a series of highly successful night attacks were employed, proving to the startled villagers that the night did not belong to the VC.

All units carried out saturation patrolling, and the constant activity with supporting artillery and air strikes coupled with the active civil affairs program resulted in 207 VC ralliers to the government side and 63 weapons turned in.

Used extensively for the first time were the Long Range Patrols (LRP) of the Cavalry Troop who conducted a river patrol on the La Nga River. Twice the LRP swam rivers to get into their patrol areas and some patrols ranged out as far as 12 miles in their intelligence efforts.

The intensive civic action program resulted in the relocation of the people of entire villages to safer areas and cultivated a friendly attitude among the people throughout the area. Soon the villagers assisted Brigade elements in locating VC caches of rice, weapons, and ammunition and were volunteering to tape broadcasts for psychological warfare missions.

From Operation NEW LIFE, the Brigade moved on the morning of 17 December directly to Operation SMASH in the Courtenay Rubber Plantation area 35 miles southeast of Bien Hoa. Intelligence sources indicated a sizable VC buildup there.

The 1/503d, 2/503d and 1/RAR were moved into three LZ's and immediately began saturation patrolling to find the enemy. On the next day the 2/503d ran into a strongly defended VC trench system manned with heavy machine guns. First encountered by the reconnaissance platoon and then C/2/503d, the battalion size VC force stubbornly held on. As B/2/503d came forward to reinforce the reconnaissance platoon, it smashed and overran an enemy position.

In the late afternoon, both Bravo and Charlie Companies 2/503d assaulted the trench system and the enemy chose to pull out rather than fight. The heavy firepower brought to bear on the enemy cost him 62 dead.

On 22 December, the Brigade returned to the Bien Hoa area to celebrate Christmas, host the Army Chief of Staff and watch the Bob Hope Show.

The Brigade launched the New Year with a swift move into the Mekong Delta and the notorious "Plain of Reeds." Operation MARAUDER I marked the first time American ground combat troops had fought in the Delta. The Brigade's mission was to cut the VC Oriental River supply route and seek out and find a hard-core VC battalion long known to operate in the area.

With the fire support base and logistical and command elements set up at Bao Trai air strip 30 miles west of Saigon, the 1/503d and 1/RAR were heli-lifted into two LZ's west and east of the Oriental River. With the employment of these two battalions the Oriental River was effectively cut.

The next morning the 2/503d landed east of the Oriental River and immediately the "Sky Soldiers" met strong resistance between the LZ and the river. The battalion fought through a series of fortified positions and employed tear gas, and air and artillery strikes to dislodge the enemy. Late in the afternoon, a strong coordinated assault by the battalion routed the VC and they fled under the cover of darkness leaving behind 93 of their dead and machine-gun tripods and mortar base plates.

Meanwhile the 1/503d continued the mop-up on the west side of the river with numerous platoon size patrols. The 1st Battalion "Sky Soldiers" found extensive fortifications brought back 326 VC suspects and destroyed quantities of VC equipment and supplies. On the east side of the river the 1/RAR also found numerous enemy positions and heavy entrenchment's while encountering only light resistance.

E/17th and D/16th conducted search operations around the support base area. They made a systematic search of a 4,000-meter radius of Boa Trai accompanied by Vietnamese National Policemen. In one operation, E/17th conducted a search of a 22,000-meter area on the eastern edge of the Brigade TAOR. Attached to E/17th was D/16th, two companies of the 38th ARVN Ranger Battalion, a light fire team, and one HO-13 helicopter for command and control. This was the Brigade's first experience with controlling all ground elements entirely from the OH-13. This technique proved very successful and was used on subsequent operations. Twenty-one VC were captured and two VC killed.

In another instance D/16th, with two companies of ARVN Rangers attached rapidly surrounded a village into which personnel were observed fleeing. A number of military age suspects were captured and one, who had a powder burn on his cheek, proved to be a sniper who admitted that he had been firing on aircraft in the Bao Trai area.

The effectiveness of E/17th and D/16th efforts was such that the province Chief informed the Brigade commander that the VC had issued orders to cease firing upon aircraft in the area because it had become too costly in personnel and equipment.

During this operation, a further exploitation of the helicopter's mobility produced a variation of eagle flight tactics termed "Hopscotch." As an eagle flight of company size or smaller touched down on an LZ another eagle flight was airborne, ready to react to reinforce the first flight if needed. If not, it landed on a second LZ while a third eagle flight was airborne serving as its reaction force. In this manner, a large area could be rapidly saturated with troops and quickly covered and all of the troops could be within fire support range. In one day, the Hopscotch tactics enabled the Brigade to cover an area that would normally take two or three days to cover with the same size force.

When Operation MARAUDER terminated early in the morning of 8 January the Brigade had killed over 111 VC and literally torn up the VC 267th Battalion and headquarters of the VC 506th Battalion. Many important documents were taken, including the roster of the 506th personnel who lived by day in the villages and on the farms and fought at night as guerrillas. With proper follow-up, this spelled the end of the 506th.

The 173d, the first allied unit to operate in the Mekong Delta, proved again that the Brigade could go anywhere, anytime, and decisively defeat the enemy whenever contact was made.

At 0630 hours, 8 January, the Brigade swung immediately into Operation CRIMP, the largest U.S. operation conducted in the war to date.

The mission was to drive through the Ho Bo Woods region in Binh Duong Province and to destroy the political-military headquarters of the VC Military Region 4 that controlled enemy activities in the greater Saigon area.

The 1/RAR moved in first, initially encountering light resistance, but a few hours later a VC company engaged them in a vicious fight that continued into the night with the Australians overrunning successive bunker and trench systems. As the operation progressed, the Aussies and "Sky Soldiers" uncovered a multilevel labyrinth of underground tunnels. The Aussies captured dozens of weapons, including four new 12.7mm anti-aircraft machine-guns and more than 100,000 pages of important documents.

In all, 128 VC were confirmed killed, 91 captured and 509 suspects detained. The enemy lost 90 weapons, 22,000 rounds of small arms ammunition, grenades, 9 sampans, 57 tons of rice and various items as diverse as tape recorders, a duplication machine, and four typewriters.

The headquarters of the VC Military Region 4 was found, fixed and destroyed by the Brigade, thus causing the enemy untold damage by destroying one of his most secure base areas in Vietnam and taking from him many of his weapons and capturing thousands of documents and records which revealed his organization, plans, and much of his past activity.

To make sure use was not made of the tunnel complexes again, crystallized CS tear gas was placed on detonation cord and exploded throughout the system.

From 4 to 7 February the 1/RAR and E/17th supported by B/3/319th, the RAA and RNZA, conducted Operation ROUNDHOUSE in the vicinity of Phuoc Loc. It was a costly one for the VC as three VC were killed with a possible 17 more, and captured were 235 tons of rice, 5,250 pounds of salt, 700 lbs of peanuts, seven 5 ton and one 1/4-ton trucks, 9 bicycles, 2 typewriters and a quantity of weapons, ammunition and documents.

Throughout the Brigade's ten months in Vietnam, it and its attached units have proved themselves time and time again in battle. They beat the VC at his own game in his own back yard, and through their courage and drive, the VC have suffered heavy losses of personnel and equipment. To date, Brigade has killed enough guerrillas and hard-core enemy to form a regiment, and over two battalions of VC surrendered rather than face the Brigade in battle.

COWBOYS

UNIT HISTORY

1 JANUARY 1966 -- 31 DECEMBER 1966

History of

335th Assault Helicopter Company
145th Combat Aviation Battalion
APO San Francisco, Calif., 96227

Prepared by
Cpt. John L. Wood
&
Cpt. Troy Reeves Jr.

Approved by
Leyburn W. Brockwell Jr.
LTC Infantry
Commanding

Headquarters
335 Assault Helicopter Company
145th Combat Aviation Battalion
APO San Francisco, Calif. 96227

From 1 January until 31 August 1966 the COWBOYS of the 335th were members of Company "A," 82nd Aviation Battalion. As of 1 September 1966, the COWBOYS were redesignated. The 335th Aviation Company (Airmobile Light) came into being. Subsequently, this designation was changed to the 335th Assault Helicopter Company (AML).

Throughout the year the mission of the unit, regardless of designation, was the same--to provide the 173rd Airborne Brigade (Separate) with the best, most professional airmobile support available anywhere in the world.

To provide this close support, the 335th was attached to the 173rd Airborne Brigade.

The organization of the company with its attached units remained the same. That is, internally the 335th consisted of two airlift platoons, known as the Ramrods and the Mustangs, an armed helicopter platoon, known as the Falcons, and the service platoon that owned the well-known recovery ship, Horsethief. Attached to the 335th were the 25th Medical Detachment, the 166th Transportation Detachment and the 234th Signal Detachment. Additionally, the 173rd Aviation Platoon, the organic aviation element of the 173rd Airborne Brigade, was under the operational control of the company, and Casper was their name.

The area of operation for the company, in support of the Brigade, was the entire III Corps tactical area of the Republic of Vietnam. Within this III Corps there were some sectors that caused anxiety in the hearts of the aviators such as War Zone "D," the area around Song Be, and around Xuan Loc. But wherever the Brigade went, the COWBOYS of the 335th were always present.

To speak of the deeds of the COWBOYS in an adequate manner, a short summary of the various operations and occurrences must be made.

1966 began in the appropriate manner -- a combat lift on New Year's Day to open Operation "Marauder" in the Bao Trai area. Then becoming Operation "Crimp," the COWBOYS entered the Hobo Woods, just South of War Zone "C." The greater part of January was spent in crushing the Viet Cong in the Hobo Woods. Miss Jo Collins, of Playmate fame, visited the COWBOYS. Subsequent mention of this was made in Playboy magazine.

The majority of February involved supporting the Brigade in its TAOR (Tactical Area of Responsibility) at Bien Hoa. Code named "Uniontown," this TAOR work was continued by elements of the Brigade during the remainder of the year. Additional support was provided the 1st Infantry Division at Di An.

Possibly one of the finest hours, to date, of the COWBOYS occurred during Operation "Silver City," in March, in War Zone "D." Specifically, on the evening of 15 March a force of two thousand VC encircled the 2/503rd Infantry, a Battalion of the 173rd Airborne Brigade. Throughout the night the VC remained silent, but as the first resupply helicopter arrived just after sunrise, the attack began. The resupply helicopter was shot down, ammunition was critical. The COWBOYS, responding to the emergency, sling-loaded ammunition into the LZ under withering hostile fire. At the time the first sling load of ammunition arrived, the Battalion was using the last that it had on-hand. When the VC broke contact after a day-long battle, they left behind four hundred of their dead. To say that the COWBOYS saved the day would be an understatement.

On 27 March Major Larry J. Baughman took command of the company from Major Donald A. Champlin who returned to CONUS.

April was the start of Operation "Denver" in the Song Be area. For this, the company moved in its entirety to the Special Forces camp at Song Be. Numerous Combat Assaults were performed throughout the heavily jungled area. Very few hits were taken on this operation.

Operation "Dexter," during May, took place in an area East of Bien Hoa, yet West of Xuan Loc. A search and clear operation, it was of short duration. Following this was Operation "Hardihood," by Xa Binh Gia, just North of Vung Tau. The purpose was to secure a base camp position for the newly arrived Royal Australian Regiment. Many long range patrol missions were accomplished, to include the first recorded emergency night extraction of the LRRP under fire.

On 9 June Operation "Hardihood" became "Hollandia," a search and destroy mission in the mountains on the seacoast just North of Vung Tau. Another first for the COWBOYS -- the first night Combat Assault in the III Corps area of RVN ever -- was the assault to begin the operation. 29 June saw Major Ernest H. Johnson take command of the company from Major Larry J. Baughman. After "Hollandia," Operation "Yorktown" commenced. Again, it was a search and destroy mission. It was during this operation that six hundred and forty U.S. troopers were heli-lifted from the area of operation, just South of Xuan Loc, to a shower point located near the Xuan Loc airfield. This proved the COWBOYS flexibility.

In the second week of July, "Yorktown" was completed and Operation "Aurora I" began. Both a road clearing and search and destroy operation, its interest was highway 20, from Xuan Loc North to Da Hoa just inside the II Corps Area. The highway was being used rather heavily by the VC. In addition, the rich rice country around Vo Dat was feeding the VC. As the Brigade cleared the highway and moved into the Vo Dat area, the operation became "Aurora II." The COWBOYS then garrisoned themselves at the Vo Dat airfield. The event most probably remembered is the flood that swept everything into the nearby wooded area. But a very tragic occurrence was the crash of a troop-carrying COWBOY and the attendant ten (10) fatalities.

Xuan Loc was the base of operations for the COWBOYS in the month of August during Operation "Toledo." The Brigade, with ARVN units attached, combed the area East of Xuan Loc. Extensive use was made of the long range patrols. Most notable was the rescue, in the fog and rain, of the lone-surviving crewman of a downed medevac aircraft.

The Brigade returned in Operation "Sioux City" to its stamping ground, War Zone "D," during September and early October. The Casper platoon employed its armed OH-13 aircraft for the first time. The VC seemed to stay out of sight during this operation, probably remembering vividly their defeat in March during "Silver City."

Operation "Robin" began on 10 October. Elements of the 4th Infantry Division were arriving at Vung Tau from CONUS and were to garrison at Bear Cat, about ten miles Southeast of Bien Hoa. The operation was then a road security mission, keeping open highway 15 between Vung Tau and Bear Cat. Concurrently, the COWBOYS provided three (3) UH-1Ds and two (2) 37's from the Caspers for Operation "Winchester" at Da Nang Airbase in the I Corps area. It was also during October that the VC sabotaged the Falcon helicopter parking area at Bien Hoa. Before the helicopters could be evacuated, one (1) gunship was destroyed and another severely damaged.

With ARVN units attached, the Brigade began Operation "Meridian" in November. The area was War Zone "C" above Tay Ninh. Making numerous Combat Assaults and Eagle Flights, it was soon discovered that the VC were in the area in force. Thus Operation "Attleboro," a multi-divisional operation was born. Despite the terrible terrain, over one thousand VC were killed. There were almost constant Combat Assaults by the COWBOYS throughout the period.

Upon the completion of "Attleboro" on 20 November the COWBOYS reverted to their continual mission of supporting Brigade elements in the TAOR at Bien Hoa. An eventual operation, "Waco," developed from the TAOR mission in late November. A search and destroy mission, it covered the area between Bien Hoa and Xuan Loc.

The COWBOY element that was supporting the 4/503rd Infantry at Da Nang returned in early December to Bien Hoa. Operation "Canary/Duck," again a mission of securing highway 15 between Vung Tau and Bear Cat, began on 7 December. This time the road was secured for elements of the 199th Light Infantry Brigade and the 9th Infantry Division that were arriving from CONUS. Activities during the operation were normal until 23 December when the 4/503rd Infantry was to be withdrawn from PZ "Stump" because of the forthcoming Christmas truce. The Battalion had minor contact with unknown enemy forces, and no particular problems were expected during the extraction. However, a surprise was in store. During the extraction a large enemy force made its presence felt by ruthlessly attacking both the troops on the PZ and the COWBOYS who were making the extraction lifts. After thirteen lifts by the COWBOYS under extremely heavy fire the extraction was complete. The COWBOY aircraft were riddled with holes and two (2) crewmen were injured. This sort of action by the COWBOYS was indicative of their skill and their valor.

After the Christmas truce, Operation "Canary/Duck" continued. And the COWBOYS were there. The year closed on that note.

An example of the tremendous efforts expended by the 335th Assault Helicopter Company in the accomplishment of its mission is evidenced by the following statistical data accumulated during the period 1 January--31 December 1966.

Company size Combat Assaults	1,560
Flying Hours	25,671
Sorties	66,329
Cargo (Tons)	3,486
Passengers	95,577
Aircraft Hit by Hostile Fire	184
Aircraft Destroyed	7
Major Aircraft Accidents	9
Personnel Killed in Action	6
Personnel Wounded In Action	29

The following awards were presented to members of the company during the period, 1 January--31 December 1966.

Legion of Merit	2
Distinguished Flying Cross	52
Bronze Star for Valor	4
Bronze Star	60
Air Medal for Valor	180
Air Medal	4,865
Army Commendation Medal	74
Purple Heart	32

Company "A," 82nd Aviation Battalion was awarded the Meritorious Unit Commendation for Achievement in the performance of outstanding service in the Republic of Vietnam for the period May 1965--July 1966.

History of

COMPANY "A," 82ND AVIATION BATTALION

173rd Airborne Brigade (Separate)

APO 96250 San Francisco, California

1 January 1966 through 28 February 1966

Prepared by

1/Lt. GEORGE W. MURRAY

Approved by

ERNEST H. JOHNSON

Major Infantry

Commanding

For

DONALD A. CHAMPLIN

Major Armor

Commanding

Headquarters

335 AVIATION COMPANY (AML)

173rd Airborne Brigade (Separate)

APO 96250 San Francisco, California

COMPANY "A," 82ND AVIATION BATTALION

173rd Airborne Brigade (Separate)

APO San Francisco 96250

AVBE-AM   4 November 1966

Subject: Monthly History for Company "A," 82nd Aviation Battalion

To: Commanding Officer
     335th Aviation Company (AML)
     173rd Airborne Brigade (Separate)
     APO San Francisco 96250

1 January 1966 through 31 January 1966

I. OPERATIONS:

a. The year 1966, began with the lifting of 700 troops on New Year's Day, into Bao Trai, an airstrip Northwest of Saigon. The Company set up operations with the Brigade at Bao Trai and supported the Brigade on Operation Marauder.

b. 2 January 1966-normal support missions for the Brigade were flown. Captain Alfred L. Dovre was hit by enemy ground fire. The wound in the foot, kept him out of action for several days.

c. Normal support of the Brigade continued through 6 January, with a 324-troop lift on the 6th.

d. Operation Marauder ended on 7 January 1966.

e. The 173rd Airborne Brigade moved into Hobo Woods on 8 January to begin Operation Crimp. The COWBOYS led by Major Champlin lifted 420 troops to secure the Brigade CP. Two (2) aircraft were damaged by ground fire.

f. An assault in the Hobo Woods on 9 January cost the COWBOYS three (3) aircraft damaged by ground fire.

g. On 11 January 1966, normal support of the Brigade's Operation Crimp continued. One (1) UH-1D was assigned the pleasant mission of transporting Miss Jo Collins, the Playmate of the Year, who was in Vietnam visiting the 173rd Airborne Brigade.

WO James Hunter and WO Ronald Basney were WIA. WO Hunter was evacuated to the States with a .30 Caliber round through his shin. WO Basney was flying again after medical treatment for shrapnel wounds.

h. 12, 13, and 14 January, were the final days of Operation Crimp. The COWBOYS lifted 748 troops of the 173rd Airborne and 1st Infantry Division during these three days. The COWBOYS moved back into Bien Hoa as Operation Crimp terminated on 14 January 1966.

i. The COWBOYS flew normal support of the Brigade from the "Corral" at Bien Hoa from January 15th through the 18th.

j. 356 troops of the Brigade's 2nd Battalion, 503rd Infantry were lifted on 19 January by the COWBOYS with Falcon cover.

k. The COWBOYS lifted 100 troops of 2/503 from Phu Loi to Bien Hoa, and the Falcons flew overhead cover for the Battalion's road convoy that traveled from Phu Loi to Bien Hoa on 20 January.

l. January 21, 22, and 23, were normal support of the Brigade.

m. On January 24th Major Gibbons led a lift moving 99 1st Division troops. Major Champlin led a 10-ship lift to move 140 troops of the 173rd Airborne.

n. 25, 26, and 27 January, were in normal support of the 173rd Airborne.

o. 28 through 31 January, saw the COWBOYS lift 1606 troops with one ship being damaged by enemy fire.

II. MONTHLY STATISTICS:

	OH-13	UH-1B	UH-1B(A)	UH-1D	TOTAL
Sorties	1	250	445	3556	4252
Hours	1	86	493	1120	1700
Pax					8228
Cargo (tons)					257
Aircraft Hits					17

1 February 1966 through 28 February 1966

I. OPERATIONS:

a. The COWBOYS and Falcons began February with normal Brigade support missions.

b. The 3rd of the month found the COWBOYS and Falcons attached to the 1st Aviation Battalion for a Combat Assault. Major Champlin led the 226-troop lift mission.

c. The 145th Aviation Battalion at Bien Hoa requested help from the COWBOYS on the 4th day of February. The COWBOYS used ten (10) UH-1Ds to lift 215 troops, while the Falcons supplied two (2) Light Fire Teams as escorts for the "Slicks."

d. The 4th through the 8th of February found the COWBOYS in normal support of the 173rd Airborne.

e. Again, on February 9th, the COWBOYS with Falcon cover aided the 145th Aviation Battalion.

f. Nine (9) COWBOYS on 10 February 1966 participated in a flyby for the 173rd.

g. Training was the order of the day for 11 February. "Peeping Tom" techniques were practiced by a UH-1D and a Falcon Light Fire team. Decca navigation training was conducted by two (2) UH-1Ds.

h. February 12th - 15th brought only normal Brigade Support missions.

i. 16 February brought several lifts for the COWBOYS. Three ships put a 20-man patrol of the 2/503 into an LZ. Three ten (10) ship lifts moved A/2/503. Five (5) ships extracted the 4.2 mortar platoon of the 1/503. Ten (10) "Slicks" in eight (8) lifts moved the 1/503.

j. 17, 18 February -- normal Airborne Brigade missions.

k. On 19 February five (5) UH-1Ds lifted 70 troops from Di An to Lai Khe. Eight (8) COWBOYS lifted a 96-man reaction force of 1/RAR (1st Battalion/Royal Australian Regiment) into Phuoc Vinh, a town North of Bien Hoa in the notorious "War Zone Delta."

l. On 20 February a Light Fire Team from the Falcons provided air cover for E Troop, 17th Cavalry as they convoyed from Bien Hoa to Phu Loi.

m. The COWBOYS, demonstrating their ability to support any combat unit, lifted 113 troops for the "Big Red One" and delivered 23.5 tons of cargo for the Division. A COWBOY aircraft, 610 on an R&R flight from Dalat to Bien Hoa stooped at Phan Thiet to refuel. Receiving an emergency call for a medevac, the crew voluntarily evacuated 16 wounded ARVN's from a raging ambush site. Aircraft Commander 1/Lt. Fred G. Zabarsky and Flight Surgeon Captain Lonnie Hammargren received the Air Medal with the "V" device for valor as a result of this action.

n. On 22 February 300 troops were lifted in conjunction with the 145th Aviation Battalion.

o. February 23rd and 24th are spent in normal support of the 173rd Airborne.

p. 306 troops of the 1st Infantry Division were lifted by 10 COWBOYS and 5 Falcons.

q. 518 troops of the 173rd were lifted by the COWBOYS on 26 February.

r. The month of February closed with the COWBOYS and Falcons supporting the paratroopers of the 173rd and the aviation units of the 145th Aviation Battalion.

II. MONTHLY STATISTICS:

	OH-13	UH-1B	UH-1B(A)	UH-1D	TOTAL
Sorties	734	147	442	2936	4259
Hours	315	85	357	926	1683
Pax					5705
Cargo					247
Aircraft Hits					23

History of

COMPANY "A," 82ND AVIATION BATTALION

1 MARCH -- 31 MARCH 1966

Prepared by

Capt. Francis C. Bennett

Unit Historian

Approved by

Larry J. Baughman

Major, Infantry

Commanding

Headquarters

173rd Airborne Brigade (Separate)

San Francisco, California 96250

COMPANY "A" 82D AVIATION BATTALION
APO 96250
San Francisco, California

1 April 1966

Subject: Monthly History for Company "A," 82d Aviation Battalion
              1 March through 31 March 1966

To: Commanding Officer
      Company "A," 82d Aviation Battalion
      173rd Airborne Brigade (Separate)
      APO San Francisco 96250

I. Mission:

The mission of Company "A," 82d Aviation Battalion for the entire month of March 1966 was to augment the aviation capabilities of the 173rd Airborne Brigade (Separate) by providing support in combat operations and providing tactical and administrative air mobility.

II. Operations:

a. Company "A" is capable of providing continuous (day and night) operations during visual weather conditions and limited operations under minimum visual weather conditions. It can provide airlift support for one infantry or dismounted mechanized infantry company. The unit during the month of March, was involved in supporting only the 173rd Airborne Brigade. Company A's UH-1Ds performed air landed assaults (ALA) air landed resupply (ALR) and command and liaison (CL) missions, while the UH-1Bs-Falcons, performed visual recon (VR), and escort helicopter (EH) missions.

b. 1 March 1966 Company "A" extracted 2/503rd Infantry (156 troops) from field locations and transported them to the Brigade Base Camp Area at Bien Hoa. Major Addiss flew lead for this extraction. All other missions for this day were normal administrative types.

c. 2 March 1966 All missions were normal administrative support for the 173rd Airborne Brigade.

d. 3 March 1966 Company "A" participated in a troop lift for 300 ARVN troops. Major Champlin flew lead.

e. 4 March 1966 All missions were normal administrative support for the 173rd Airborne Brigade.

f. 5 March 1966 Company "A" participated in a troop lift for the 1st Bd., 1st Inf. Div. Ten (10) UH-1Ds transported 140 troops from a location South of Tay Ninh to a field location. Major Champlin flew lead. During this lift one of the Falcon gunships was shot down with no casualties.

g. 6 March 1966 Company "A" was attached to the 145th Aviation Battalion to lift elements of the 15th ARVN Division. 10 UH-1Ds and 5 UH-1Bs flew in this operation and 2 separate lifts were made. A total of 264 ARVN Troops were transported. Major Champlin flew lead.

h. 7 & 8 March 1966 All missions were normal administrative support of the 173rd Airborne Brigade.

i. 9 March 1966 Company "A" was attached to the 145th Aviation Battalion for a lift involving 400 troops. Ten (10) UH-1Ds and five (5) UH-1Bs flew on this lift. Major Champlin flew lead. This lift was the start of operation "Silver City" in War Zone "D" involving the entire 173rd Airborne Brigade. The troops were located at LZ #12, 083426, which became the base for support of the extensive operation. The first lift of the day was at 0730 hours and the move was completed at 1130 hours. The remainder of the day involved logistical resupply for the elements of the 173rd Airborne Brigade.

j. 10 March 1966 Company "A" supported the 173rd Airborne Brigade with six (6) UH-1Ds flying logistical resupply during all daylight hours to various tactical locations in War Zone "D."

k. 11 March 1966 In addition to supporting the 173rd Airborne Brigade on operation Silver City, Company "A" was attached to the 145th Avn. Bn. for a Combat Assault that required ten (10) UH-1Ds and five (5) UH-1Bs. The lift involved 140 ARVN troops. Major Champlin flew lead. Logistical resupply to the 173rd Airborne Brigade maintained from sunup to sundown.

l. 12 March 1966 Continued logistical support for the 173rd Airborne Brigade in War Zone "D" requiring six (6) UH-1Ds during daylight hours.

m. 13 March 1966 Operation "Silver City" continued requiring six (6) UH-1Ds from "A" Company for resupply to all elements of the 173rd Airborne Brigade.

n. 14 March 1966 Company "A" continued to support the 173rd Airborne Brigade in War Zone "D" with six (6) UH-1Ds performing logistical resupply from Phuoc Vinh. One (1) UH-1B suffered a hard landing while on a training flight.

o. 15 March 1966 Company "A" provided six (6) UH-1Ds for logistical support during daylight hours in War Zone "D" in tall, dense jungle terrain requiring maximum performance of the aircraft.

p. 16 March 1966 This day was the most significant of all during operation "Silver City." During the night 2000 Viet Cong troops encircled the 2/503rd Infantry in a tight area 50 meters in diameter the center of which was the resupply LZ. Their plan of attack was to wait until the first resupply helicopter of the day arrived and then to attack from all directions. The first UH-1D was to be flown by Lt. Roush and Cpt. Bennett, but generator trouble delayed the takeoff. UH-1D 737, flown by CWO Geishauser and WO McHenry made the first approach to the LZ with A/rations for the 2/503rd. Upon approach to the LZ the helicopter tail rotor gear box was shot off and the main transmission was hit by an estimated four 50 caliber bullets. The helicopter crashed in the trees on the Northeast side of the LZ. The gunner suffered an injured back, while the remainder of the crew suffered only minor cuts and bruises. The VC attack lasted for four hours, with the crew of UH-1D 737 trapped in the middle of the fire fight. As the fight between the VC and the 2/503rd progressed an urgent request for resupply of ammunition went out to Company "A" and only through the determined efforts of four crews dropping sling loads of small arms ammunition into this small LZ was the 2/503 able to beat back the VC attack with light casualties, while the VC suffered 400 killed 1000 wounded.

At the end of this day 7 UH-1Ds had suffered combat damage from this resupply effort. Another gunner was wounded by ground fire, and UH-1D 737 was completely destroyed. Several aviators from Company "A" were recommended for combat decorations following this action.

q. 17 March 1966 Following the battle of the previous day Company "A" had an increased resupply and extraction requirement from 2/503 Infantry in order to remove large numbers of captured weapons and fly in personnel replacements, as well as to maintain the normal logistical resupply of rations and ammunition. The Viet Cong broke contact for the remainder of the operation.

r. 18 March 1966 Company "A" continued to provide logistical support to operation "Silver City."

s. 19 March 1966 Elements of the 173rd Airborne Brigade moved to various tactical locations in War Zone "D," and established many new resupply LZ's requiring maximum performance from aircraft.

t. 20 March 1966 Company "A" provided the logistical needs of the 173rd Airborne Brigade, still operating in War Zone "D."

u. 21 March 1966 In addition to providing continued logistical support for the 173rd Airborne Brigade on operation "Silver City," Company "A" lifted 100 ARVN troops with ten (10) UH-1Ds in a Combat Assault. Following this lift of ARVN troops, the first extraction of troops from War Zone "D" was made by Company "A." Eight UH-1Ds lifted 261 troops of the 173rd Airborne Brigade.

v. 22 March 1966 Extraction of troops from War Zone "D" continued with Company "A" lifting 260 troops of the Royal Australian Regiment from LZ 12 back to Bien Hoa. This extraction concluded operation "Silver City."

w. 23 March 1966 All missions were normal administrative support of the 173rd Airborne Brigade. Repair of combat damaged aircraft continued.

x. 24, 25, 26, March 1966 All missions were normal administrative support of the 173rd Airborne Brigade.

y. 27 and 28 March 1966 All missions were normal administrative support of the 173rd Airborne Brigade. Ten (10) UH-1Ds and five (5) UH-1Bs were placed on 30 minute's standby for operation Mohawk.

III. MONTHLY STATISTICS:

	OH-13	UH-1B	UH-1B(A)	UH-1D	TOTAL
Sorties	627	237	330	3561	4755
Hours	302	84	463	1098	1947
Pax					5826
Cargo (tons)					508
Aircraft Hits					28

HISTORY OF

COMPANY "A," 82ND AVIATION BATTALION

173RD AIRBORNE BRIGADE (SEPARATE)

APO SAN FRANCISCO, CALIFORNIA 96250

1 APRIL -- 30 APRIL 1966

Prepared by

CPT. TROY REEVES JR.

Approved by

LEYBURN W. BROCKWELL, JR.

LTC Infantry

Commanding

For

LARRY J. BAUGHMAN

Major Infantry

Commanding

HEADQUARTERS

335TH ASSAULT HELICOPTER COMPANY (AML)

145TH COMBAT AVIATION BATTALION

APO SAN FRANCISCO, CALIFORNIA 96227

COMPANY "A" 82D AVIATION BATTALION
173RD AIRBORNE BRIGADE (SEPARATE)
APO SAN FRANCISCO, CALIFORNIA 96250

AVBE-AM   12 March 1967

Subject: Monthly History for Company "A," 82d Aviation Battalion
             1 April 1966 through 30 April 1966

To: Commanding Officer
      335th Aviation Company (AML LT)
      173rd Airborne Brigade (Separate)
      APO San Francisco, Calif. 96250

I. OPERATIONS:

a. The month of April opened with the COWBOYS lifting 180 troops from the Brigade into the local TAOR. All other missions were in normal support of the 173rd Abn. Bde.

b. On the 2nd of April the 335th began the day by airlifting two (2) ARVN companies, 220 ARVN troops, into a landing zone near Saigon. After these two (2) lifts the company returned to the TAOR and extracted 180 U.S. troops into the Brigade base at Bien Hoa in three (3) lifts. All other missions were in normal support of the 173rd Abn. Bde.

c. All mission flown 3 April were in normal administrative support of the 173rd Abn. Bde.

d. Two (2) UH-1Ds escorted by one (1) Light Fire Team began 4 April at 0530 hours by infiltrating a DELTA team into the Mangrove Swamp South of Saigon. This team was extracted that afternoon, under enemy automatic weapons fire, by the same COWBOY crews. In the afternoon 190 troops of the 1/503 were lifted from the Brigade Pad to the TAOR. All other missions were in normal administrative support of the 173rd Abn. Bde.

e. On 5 April the COWBOYS lifted 520 173rd Abn. Bde. troops in nine (9) ten (10) ship lifts within the 173rd Abn. Bde. TAOR. All other missions were in support of these troops.

f. The 173rd Abn. Bde. was still moving troops within the TAOR as the COWBOYS repositioned 310 U.S. troops in five (5) ten ship (10) lifts. All other missions were in support of these troops within the TAOR.

g. On 7 April from 0100 to 0300 hours' one (1) UH-1D with the MAD system and one (1) Light Fire Team flew a reconnaissance for Field Artillery Control in the Northern part of War Zone "D." One (1) Light Fire Team was supporting the 25th Infantry Division on a sweep operation when Falcon 601 was shot down and destroyed. All personnel were rescued with only minor injuries. Falcon 928 received several hits but was flown safely to Cu Chi with no injuries received. One platoon of the 2/503, 35 U.S. troops, was repositioned within the 173rd Abn. Bde. within the TAOR.

h. All missions flown on 8 April were in support of the 173rd Abn. Bde. in preparation for Operation Austin. In the late afternoon, the 173rd Abn. Bde. received word that they had no commitment for Operation Austin but to initiate tentative plans for air loading all equipment for an airlift. Company "A," 82nd Aviation Battalion began to make preparations for an airlift.

i. All missions flown on 9 April were in support of the 173rd Abn. Bde. in preparation for Operation Denver to be conducted in the Song Be area. The company continued planning and loading preparation for movement to Song Be for troop insertion.

j. On 10 April ten (10) UH-1Ds and one (1) Light Fire Team were attached to the 11th Aviation Battalion to move 140 U.S. troops of the 173rd Abn. Bde. from the Snake Pit to the Song Be airstrip to secure the airfield. All other missions were in normal support of the 173rd Abn. Bde. Preparation and loading continued for movement in support of Operation Denver.

k. On 11 April the COWBOYS began movement by UH-1Ds to Song Be in support of the 173rd Abn. Bde. during Operation Denver. After closing at Song Be nine (9) UH-1Ds and one (1) Light Fire Team returned to Bien Hoa and lifted 54 173rd Abn. Bde. troops to Song Be. Two (2) missions were flown for B/34th Special Forces. All other Missions were in normal support of the 173rd Abn. Bde's. Operation Denver.

l. On 12 April eight (8) UH-1Ds and one (1) Light Fire Team extracted six (6) patrols and 300 U.S. troops, for the 173rd Abn. Bde. in six (6) separate lifts. All other missions were in support of the 173rd Abn. Bde. Operation Denver and B/34th Special Forces compound at Song Be.

m. Four (4) Combat Assaults were flown by the COWBOYS on 13 April for the 173rd Abn. Bde. lifting 360 troops in support of Operation Denver. Five (5) UH-1Ds carried three (3) tons of rice from the city strip in Song Be to Be Dung for B/34th Special Forces at Song Be. All other missions were in support of the 173rd Airborne Brigade.

n. Three (3) Combat Assaults and eight (8) extractions were flown by ten (10) COWBOYS for the 173rd Abn. Bde. on 14 April lifting 840 U.S. troops in support of Operation Denver. All other missions were in support of the same Operation.

o. One (1) dummy extraction and seven (7) Combat Assault, lifting 480 troops for the 173rd Abn. Bde. were flown on 15 April in support of Operation Denver. All other missions were normal support for the Brigade.

p. At dawn on 16 April, 162 Royal Australian Regiment troops were lifted in two (2) Combat Assaults in support of the 173rd Abn. Bde. Operation Denver. Nine (9) "Slicks" and two (2) Light Fire Teams repositioned 162 U.S. troops for the 173rd Abn. Bde. Aircraft 556 crashed on takeoff from Song Be city strip due to power failure. All other missions were in normal support of the 173rd Abn. Bde. Operation Denver.

q. On 17 April, eight (8) "Slicks" and two (2) Light Fire Teams repositioned 259 RAR troops in support of Operation Denver. Six (6) COWBOYS and two (2) Light Fire Teams lifted 72 U.S. troops of the 1/503 in Operation Denver. All other missions were normal support of the 173rd Abn. Bde. Operation Denver.

r. Ten (10) UH-1Ds and two (2) Light Fire Teams lifted 120 troops from E/17th Cav. Eleven (11) Combat Assaults with these fourteen (14) aircraft was performed moving 710 U.S. troops into a new location in the Denver Operational area. All other missions were normal support of the 173rd Abn. Bde. operation.

s. On 19 April nine (9) "Slicks" and two (2) Light Fire Teams repositioned 107 E/17th Cav. troops. One gunner was wounded during the repositioning. All other missions were in normal support of the 173rd Abn. Bde.

t. On 20 April all missions were in support of the 173rd Abn. Bde's. Operation Denver. Nine (9) UH-1Ds and four (4) gunships stood-by for the Chief of Staff (Army) at Song Be.

u. On 21 April all missions were in normal support of Operation Denver.

v. Ten (10) extractions were made by ten (10) "Slicks" and two (2) Light Fire Teams on 22 April. 620 U.S. troops of the 173rd Abn. Bde. were moved to Song Be airfield for shipment back to Bien Hoa. All other missions were in direct support of Operation Denver.

w. At 1005 hours on 23 April the COWBOYS closed at Bien Hoa from Operation Denver near Song Be. All missions flown were in support of the 173rd Abn. Bde's. move from Operation Denver to Bien Hoa.

x. All missions flown on 24 April were of the administrative type in support of the 173rd Abn. Bde.

y. On 25 April two (2) UH-1Ds took part in a demonstration of the MAD system and Chemical spray system for representatives of the Commercial Research and Development Board. All other missions were in normal support of the 173rd Abn. Bde.

z. On 26 April all missions were in normal support of the 173rd Abn. Bde.

aa. The COWBOYS were attached to the 11th Aviation Battalion for a lift on 27 April. Nine (9) "Slicks" and two (2) Light Fire Teams lifted 252 U.S. troops in support of the 11th Aviation Battalion.

bb. All missions flown on 28 April were administrative flights in support of the 173rd Abn. Bde. except four (4) Combat Assaults flown in support of the 145th Combat Aviation Battalion lifting 360 ARVN troops with ten (10) "Slicks" and two (2) Light Fire Teams.

cc. On 29 April nine (9) "Slicks" and two (2) Light Fire Teams lifted 382 U.S. troops in three (3) Combat Assaults in support of the 11th Aviation Battalion in the Tay Ninh area. Three (3) aircraft were hit by enemy ground fire but all aircraft were recovered with no injuries received.

dd. All missions on 30 April were in support of the 173rd Abn. Bde.

II. MONTHLY STATISTICS:

	OH-13	UH-1B	UH-1B(A)	UH-1D	TOTAL
Sorties	407	162	976	3957	5502
Hours	319	78	498	1274	2169
Pax					9158
Cargo (tons)					210
Aircraft Hits					27

III. TRAINING:

a. On 1 April a two-hour helicopter troop loading class was conducted for Brigade elements. On 5 April the MAD system, developed and proved effective by this unit, was sent to the 145th Combat Aviation Battalion for support and training. The emphasis this month was placed on inclement weather and operational hazards during the coming wet weather season.

IV. COMPANY AREA:

Improvements during the month of April were made in the Company area in the form of new buildings.

V. CIVIL AFFAIRS:

a. The school in Nqu Phouc is ready for the roof to be placed over parts of the building.

b. The 25th Med-Cap team treated over 1200 Vietnamese.

HISTORY OF

COMPANY "A," 82ND AVIATION BATTALION

1 MAY THROUGH 31 MAY 1966

173RD AIRBORNE BRIGADE (SEPARATE)

APO 96250 SAN FRANCISCO, CALIF.

Prepared by

Captain Donald L. Peters

Approved by

LARRY J. BAUGHMAN

Major Infantry

HEADQUARTERS

173rd Airborne Brigade (Separate)

APO San Francisco, Calif. 96250

COMPANY "A," 82ND AVIATION BATTALION
173RD AIRBORNE BRIGADE (SEPARATE)
APO SAN FRANCISCO, CALIFORNIA 96250

AVAB-AM   1 June 1966

Subject: Monthly History for Company "A," 82d Aviation Battalion
               1 May through 31 May 1966

To: Commanding Officer
       Company "A," 82nd Aviation Battalion
       173rd Airborne Brigade (Separate)
       APO San Francisco 96250

I. OPERATIONS:

a. Company "A," 82nd Aviation Battalion started the month of May by supporting the 1st Infantry Division at Tay Ninh on operation "Birmingham." Eight (8) UH-1Ds and one (1) Light Fire Team, after performing six (6) extraction's while attached to the 11th Aviation Battalion at Tay Ninh, remained over night at a forward area, South of Tay Ninh, to prepare for one of the largest heliborne assaults in Vietnam up to that date.

b. On 3 May 1966, Company "A" was planning for Operation "Dexter," a search and clear operation Northeast of Bien Hoa. The next day Company "A," attached to the 145th Aviation Battalion, air lifted 457 troops from the Snake Pit to the operational area. On this day aircraft number 614 received two (2) hits on an approach into LZ "Diamond" in the heart of the operational area -- there were no injuries. Also, on this day A/C #918, Falcon 87, was hit while making a firing pass on a target that had been firing at aircraft all that day. The aircraft caught fire on the way down but was landed successfully in a rice paddy despite the intense flames. The aircraft burned and became a total loss -- there were no injuries. At 1600 hours on 5 May 1966, an alert was called. The COWBOY'S plus attachments were combat ready by 1615 hours. A briefing for all detachments and platoon leaders was given on the physical security plan for the Company. On 6 May 1966, Operation "Dexter" ended with the COWBOYS attached to the 145th Aviation Battalion. Seven (7) lifts were made out of LZ "Diamond." Six COWBOY Aircraft were hit by enemy ground fire during the extraction's. One man was wounded by shrapnel.

c. From the period 6 May 66 to 9 May 66, the COWBOYS were attached to the 11th Aviation Battalion on Operation "Birmingham" at Tay Ninh. On 9 May, the COWBOYS completed their part in Operation "Birmingham" by resupplying elements of the 1st Infantry Division. At 1500 the COWBOYS started their logistical task. The last ship came back to the corral at 2030 hours. The COWBOYS carried 65 passengers, 32 tons of cargo, and flew 268 sorties in that short span of time.

d. The next day the COWBOYS were alerted to be ready to bring a security force from the 173rd Airborne Brigade (Separate) to a point Northwest of Vung Tau where a CH-47 helicopter had crashed. The security Force never had to go because the Chinook was destroyed by fire. At 2200 hours that evening the CO was notified to be ready to move to the Song Be area in support of the 2/503. Intelligence reports stated that elements of the 101st had pushed a badly beaten force of VC to a point between Song Be and an area about 25K's to the North. The 2/503 was called upon to prevent the VC from moving any farther South and to squeeze them in between the 101st and themselves. After preparation was made, the COWBOYS moved out early the next morning. A part of the COWBOYS was left behind to participate in Operation "Hardihood," a 173rd Airborne Brigade effort to the Northeast of Vung Tau. On the first Combat Assault at Song Be the COWBOYS received automatic weapons fire from a tree line while on short final to an LZ in a mountain village. A crew chief, Sp/4 Woodrum, was hit in the chest from enemy ground fire. He was quickly evacuated to the rear area at Bien Hoa. The bullet punctured a small portion (5%) of his lung and went completely through his spleen. He is now recuperating and is expected to be back within a few months. On 12 May 1966, three (3) UH-1Ds and one (1) Light Fire Team deployed a long range patrol into a dense jungle area to the Northwest of Song Be, near the Cambodian border. Three separate locations were chosen and at sunset the three (3) UH-1Ds completed their mission. The next day the COWBOYS returned from Song Be and prepared for Operation "Hardihood."

e. On 15 May 1966, Falcon 81 and 82 fire teams were scrambled to a location North of Tan Uyen. VC were reported in a rubber plantation. The Falcons struck the area and three (3) confirmed VC were found dead.

f. 17 May 1966 saw the start of Operation "Hardihood" for the COWBOYS. On the initial Combat Assault one Falcon ship was hit twice in the main rotor blades. On a resupply mission on the 19th of May 1966, Aircraft number 609 was hit four (4) times forcing it down into an LZ. It had been hit in the transmission twice and was barely flyable. WO Harrell elected to fly the aircraft to Vung Tau because the unit in the LZ had to move on thereby leaving an aircraft in an unsecured area. He made the flight without incident. The gunner on the aircraft received minor wounds from shrapnel. On the 19th of May A/C #945 took 5 hits while escorting a "Dust Off" medevac ship into a forward area. There were no injuries.

g. On 25 May 1966 two (2) UH-1Ds conducted Long Range Patrol (LRP) Recovery Techniques in conjunction with E Troop 17th Cav. Some of the techniques used were: rappelling from a 50-foot rope, using a rope ladder to climb out of an inaccessible area and using two 125 feet ropes to lift 2 personnel at one time out of a simulated unimproved area where a helicopter could not land and speed would be essential in recovering the personnel to keep them from falling into enemy hands.

h. On 30 May 1966, A/C #421, an OH-13, crashed in the forward Brigade CP area. Investigation is still underway at the time of this writing.

i. On 31 May 1966, an orientation class was given to newly arrived personnel into the 173rd Airborne Brigade (Separate). Approximately 200 people participated in the Airmobile Class. After the class, a demonstration ride was given to familiarize the new troops with loading and unloading during a Combat Assault.

II. MONTHLY STATISTICS:

	OH-13	UH-1(A)	UH-1B	UH-1D	TOTAL
Sorties	827	1539	184	4306	6856
Hours	354	417	125	1404	2300
Pax					9257
Cargo (tons)					363
Aircraft Hits					28

III. TRAINING:

a. The emphasis this month was placed on Command Information Classes. Classes were given on security, Code of Conduct, survival, Escape and evasion, and CBR. A class on the .45 cal. pistol was given to all officers before they went out on the range for their annual familiarization firing. The Company and its attachments then fired their TO&E weapon for familiarization.

b. The Inspector General's team had their annual inspection during the latter part of May. The inspection ended in favorable results for Company "A."

IV. AWARDS AND DECORATIONS:

CWO Lerner	Air Medal W/ "V" device
Maj. Addis	Basic Air Medal
Maj. Gibbons	Basic Air Medal
Capt. West	Basic Air Medal
CWO Waters	Basic Air Medal
Sgt. Casey	Basic Air Medal
Sgt. Witcher	Basic Air Medal
Sp/5 Nahon	Basic Air Medal
Sp/5 Rushin	Basic Air Medal
Sp/4 Davis	Basic Air Medal
Sp/4 Partch	Basic Air Medal
Sp/4 Fettig	Purple Heart
WO Rasney	Purple Heart

V. COMPANY AREA:

a. Improvements during the month of May were as follows: a new permanent latrine with porcelain urinals, completion of a new arms room adjoining a new supply room, a movie screen placed where it was best suited for the Company. Other small improvements were made to individual billets. A beautification project was started when Doctor (Capt.) Hammargren planted the first tree outside his new office.

VI. CIVIL AFFAIRS:

a. The school house in Nqu Phouc is now 85% completed with the roof being put in place over the 1st classroom.

b. The 25th Med-Cap team again treated over 1200 Vietnamese. They performed first aid and administered shots to the people.

HISTORY OF

COMPANY "A," 82ND AVIATION BATTALION

1 June -- 30 June MAY 1966

Prepared by

Capt. Donald L. Peters

Unit Historian

Approved by

Ernest H. Johnson

Major Infantry

Commanding

HEADQUARTERS

173rd Airborne Brigade (Separate)

APO San Francisco 96250

I. OPERATIONS:

a. Co. "A," 82nd Aviation Battalion began the month of June by continuing to support the 173rd Abn. Bde. (Separate) in operation "Hardihood." During this period E/17th Cav. with its attached Long Range Patrol, performed many reconnaissance type missions. The Long Range Patrol Teams are usually sent out in six (6) man elements. They are infiltrated at dusk by helicopter so that they may not be seen by the enemy. Two (2) teams have been put in previously during this operation and were extracted on the second of June. At 1430 hours on the 2nd of June 66, one patrol was extracted from a PZ under fire. The LRP left three (3) dead VC in the PZ. That evening aircraft number 736 with Capt. Peters as aircraft commander and 1st Lt. Roush as pilot made an emergency extraction of an LRP at night under fire from a hole in the woods, about seventeen (17) Kilometers North of the Fire Support Base. This marked the first successful completion of an LRP extraction at night.

b. On 9 June 66 at 0400 hours' eight (8) UH-1D and two (2) Light Fire Teams left the corral at Bien Hoa enroute to a forward area about eight (8) kilometers Northeast of Vung Tau. The COWBOYS lifted one hundred ninety-eight (198) troops in three (3) LZ's. Two of the LZ's were unsecured. Under moonlight the COWBOYS skillfully placed the troops into these LZ's making another "first" for "A" Co., 82nd Avn. Bn. This was the first night Combat Assault in the III Corps area in the history of Vietnam. This also initiated operation "Hollandia," a search and destroy mission, in the mountain range East of Vung Tau.

c. On 15 June 66 a scramble was called about 1545 hours to have the COWBOYS report to the forward area. Ten (10) UH-1Ds and two (2) Light Fire Teams quickly reacted to the situation. The COWBOYS heli-lifted two hundred twenty-two (222) troops into an LZ to the South of a Fire Support Base. This only proved the readiness of the COWBOYS to react to any situation at any time. Operation "Hollandia" ended on the 18th of June 1966.

d. For the next four days the COWBOYS supported the 173rd Abn. Bde. (Separate) on operation "Uniontown." This operation took place in Bde. TAOR.

e. On the 20th of June 1966 the COWBOYS supported the 13th Avn. Bn. at Soc Trang. The United States Navy had run aground a VC vessel full of weapons and ammunition. The COWBOYS heli-lifted 390 ARVN troops to that location so that they could secure the area and keep the VC from obtaining the ammo and weapons. It was a very successful day for the United States Army in that they confiscated many tons of ammo and numerous Chinese and Russian weapons.

f. 21 June 1966 saw the start of operation "Yorktown," a search and destroy mission approximately seven (7) kilometers South of Xuan Loc. The remaining days of the month were spent in numerous Combat Assaults in the Yorktown TAOR.

II. MONTHLY STATISTICS:

	OH-13	UH-1B(A)	UH-1B	UH-1D	TOTAL
Sorties	502	622	298	3721	5143
Hours	297	391	215	1352	2238
Pax					8985
Cargo (tons)					316
Aircraft Hits					20

III. TRAINING:

a. During the month of June Company "A" was engaged in numerous training activities. The 2nd Platoon "Mustangs" flew a night training mission landing to various fields and lighting systems.

b. The "Falcons," 3rd Platoon, conducted a night firing exercise along with the "MAD" (Mortar Aerial Delivery) ship.

c. The Casper Platoon participated in a night exercise using five (5) UH-1Ds.

d. Elements of Company "A" dropped troops of E/17th Cav. (Approx. 40) in a simulated parachute assault in the Brigade TAOR.

IV. AWARDS AND DECORATIONS:

NAME	RANK	AWARD
Richardson	CWO	Air Medal with "V" Device
Waters	CWO	Air Medal with "V" Device
Patterson	WO	Air Medal with "V" Device
Dorf	CWO	Basic Air Medal
Lind	WO	Basic Air Medal
Jones	WO	Basic Air Medal
McHenry	WO	Basic Air Medal
		Purple Heart
Tilley	SSG	Basic Air Medal
Usher	SP/5	Basic Air Medal
Priest	SP/4	Basic Air Medal
Bowen	SP/4	Basic Air Medal
Shultz	SP/4	Basic Air Medal
Mangram	MAJ.	Purple Heart
Dumas	WO	Purple Heart
Geishauser	WO	Purple Heart
Boliver	SGT.	Purple Heart
Spires	SP/4	Purple Heart
Eaton	PFC	Purple Heart

V. COMPANY AREA:

a. During the month of June a few invocations were made in the company area. Porcelain sinks were installed in the shower-wash room complex thereby alleviating the problem of leaking faucets and wasted water.

b. June also saw the start of new officer's semi-permanent type quarters to accommodate the newly arrived officers. Cement pads were laid by the officers of the Company.

c. A pad was laid for the new "All American Club." This complex will house an EM and NCO club, Bar, Tailor Shop, Barber Shop, and Laundry Shop.

d. On 30 June Maj. Baughman was replaced by Maj. Johnson as the new Commanding Officer of Company "A."

VI. CIVIL AFFAIRS:

a. The Company Project, a three-room school in Ngu Phuc, is nearly completed. It is expected to be finished within two weeks.

b. The 25th Med. Detachment's Med-Cap team treated over 1000 people in the Duc Tu Province this month. They performed first aid treatments in addition to giving medical advice to the people.

HISTORY OF

COMPANY "A," 82ND AVIATION BATTALION

173RD AIRBORNE BRIGADE (SEPARATE)

APO SAN FRANCISCO, CALIFORNIA 96250

1 July -- 31 July 1966

Prepared by

CPT. TROY REEVES, JR.

Approved by

LEYBURN W. BROCKWELL JR.

LTC Infantry

Commanding

FOR

ERNEST H. JOHNSON

Major Infantry

Commanding

HEADQUARTERS

335TH ASSAULT HELICOPTER COMPANY (AML)

APO SAN FRANCISCO, CALIFORNIA 96227

**335TH ASSAULT HELICOPTER COMPANY
173RD AIRBORNE BRIGADE (SEPARATE)
APO SAN FRANCISCO, CALIFORNIA 96250**

AVBE-AM   12 March 1967

Subject: Monthly History for Company "A," 82d Aviation Battalion
                 1 July through 31 July 1966

To: Commanding Officer
       335th Assault Helicopter Company
       173rd Airborne Brigade (Separate)
       APO San Francisco, Calif. 96250

I. OPERATIONS:

a.   This month began with the COWBOYS in normal support of the 173rd Airborne Brigade's Operation "Yorktown."

b.   On 2 July, all missions were in normal support of the 173rd Abn. Bde. in Operation "Yorktown." One Falcon ship received a hole in the main rotor blade when a rocket prematurely exploded after it was fired. There were no crew injuries.

c.   Early on the 3rd of July all aircraft were dispatched to the Yorktown area for a possible lift of a reaction force. Ten (10) UH-1Ds and two (2) Light Fire Teams lifted 360 U.S. troops in six (6) Combat Assaults in support of Operation Yorktown. Aircraft 935 received one round of small fire through the pilot's compartment. All other missions were in support of the 173rd Abn. Bde. operation Yorktown.

d.   On the 4th of July all missions flown were in support of the 173rd Abn. Bde. Operation Yorktown.

e.   Ten (10) UH-1Ds and two (2) Light Fire Teams airlifted 180 U.S. troops, on the 5th of July, for the 173rd Abn. Bde. in three (3) Combat Assaults. All other missions were in support of Operation Yorktown.

f.   On 6 July, ten (10) "Slicks" and two (2) Light Fire Teams lifted 180 troops as the COWBOYS repositioned units of the 173rd Abn. Bde. Six (6) UH-1Ds carried 640 173rd troops from field positions in the Yorktown operational area to a Xuan Loc shower point and return them to their field positions. All other missions flown were in support of 173rd Abn. Bde. Operation Yorktown.

g.   All missions were in support of the 173rd Abn. Bde. Operation Yorktown.

h.   On the 8th of July six (6) UH-1Ds lifted 120 ARVN troops in support of a 173rd Abn. Bde. Med-Cap Operation South of Xuan Loc. All other missions were in support of the 173rd Abn. Bde.

i.   Ten (10) UH-1Ds and two (2) Light Fire Teams supported the 173rd Abn. Bde. in six (6) Combat Assaults for the beginning of Operation Aurora, on the 9th of July. All other missions flown were in support of Operation Aurora.

j.   On July 10, ten (10) "Slicks" and two (2) Light Fire Teams lifted 180 U.S. troops in three (3) Combat Assaults in support of Operation Aurora. Six (6) UH-1Ds and one (1) Light Fire Team extracted 190 U.S. troops of the 4/503 from their company training area in the TAOR into the Brigade forward area. All other missions were in support of the 173rd Abn. Bde. Operation Aurora.

k.   All missions flown on the 11th of July were in normal support of the 173rd Abn. Bde. Operation Aurora.

l.   On the 12th of July five (5) UH-1Ds and two (2) Light Fire Teams lifted 210 U.S. troops in six (6) Combat Assaults in support of Operation Aurora. All other missions were in support of the same Operation.

m. Ten (10) UH-1Ds and two (2) Light Fire Teams lifted 640 173rd Abn. Bde. troops in several Combat Assaults in support of Operation Aurora on 13 July. One gunship received a hit that wounded the gunner in the leg, knocked out the hydraulics and punctured a fuel line. The aircraft was landed at the Brigade Command Post without further damage. All other missions were in support of the 173rd Abn. Bde.

n. On 14 July ten (10) UH-1Ds and two (2) Light Fire Teams lifted 690 U.S. troops in support of the 173rd Abn. Bde. Operation Aurora. All other missions were in support of the same operation.

o. Ten (10) UH-1Ds and two (2) Light Fire Teams flew (9) Combat Assaults repositioning 476 troops for the 173rd Abn. Bde. in support of Operation Aurora, on the 15th of July. All other missions were in support of Operation Aurora.

p. On 16 July all missions were in support of the 173rd Abn. Bde. in support of Operation Aurora.

q. Aurora II began on 17 July with the COWBOYS attached to the 145th Aviation Battalion for movement of the 173rd Abn. Bde. into the Vo Dat area. Ten (10) UH-1Ds and two (2) Light Fire Teams made six (6) Combat Assaults in the area of operation carrying 360 U.S. troops. All other missions were in support of the 173rd Abn. Bde. Operation.

r. Early on the 18th of July an advance party from the company moved to the Aurora II area of operation. After five (5) Combat Assaults with the "Slicks" (ten) and two (2) Light Fire Teams, moving 300 173rd Abn. Bde. troops, all elements of the company were moved to Vo Dat. All other missions were in support of the 173rd Abn. Bde.

s. Ten (10) UH-1Ds and two (2) Light Fire Teams made one (1) Combat Assault in support of operation Aurora II, on 19 July. The COWBOYS moved 60 173rd Abn. Bde. troops in the Combat Assault and supported the Brigade by flying normal missions after the Combat Assault.

t. Nine (9) "Slicks" and two (2) Light Fire Teams made three (3) lifts in support of the 173rd Abn. Bde. on 20 July, moving 162 U.S. troops. All other missions were in support of Operation Aurora II.

u. On the 21st of July, the COWBOYS using nine (9) "Slicks" and two (2) Light Fire Teams repositioned 360 173rd Abn. Bde. troops in four (4) lifts in support of Operation Aurora II. All other missions were in normal support of the operation.

v. Eight (8) "Slicks" and two (2) Light Fire Teams conducted fourteen (14) Combat Assaults, carrying 642 173rd Abn. Bde. Troops, on the 22nd of July. Aircraft 735 crashed in one of the LZ's. The aircraft was a total loss; the crew was evacuated with only minor injuries. All other missions were in support of Operation Aurora II.

w. All missions flown on the 23rd of July were in support of the 173rd Abn. Bde. Operation Aurora II. The Falcon Fire Team sank thirteen (13) sampans and were credited with two (2) KIA's. A slick on a medical evacuation mission received one hit while aiding "Dust Off" aircraft in the evacuation of 173rd Abn. Bde. Troops.

x. On 24 July all missions flown were in support of Operation Aurora II. COWBOY 884 received one round while delivering supplies to the forward 173rd Abn. Bde. element. The pilot was slightly wounded and the aircraft was evacuated to Bien Hoa for repairs. The Falcons sank sixteen sampans and received credit for one (1) KIA.

y. Nine (9) "Slicks" and two (2) Light Fire Teams made three (3) lifts while repositioning 162 173rd Abn. Bde. troops in support of Operation Aurora II on July 25. All other missions were in support of this operation.

z. On the 26th of July ten (10) "Slicks" and two (2) Light Fire Teams made four (4) Combat Assaults carrying 240 U.S. troops in support of the 173rd Abn. Bde. Operation Aurora II. All other missions were in support of this operation.

aa. Ten (10) UH-1Ds and two (2) Light Fire Teams repositioned the 4/503 in four (4) Combat Assaults in support of Operation Aurora II, on 27 July. On the first lift aircraft 571 crashed with a load of six (6) 173rd Abn. Bde. Troops. There were ten (10) fatalities in the accident. A security platoon was lifted to the crash site. All other missions were in support of the 173rd Abn. Bde. Operation.

bb. On 28 July all missions flown were in support of the 173rd Abn. Bde. in Operation Aurora II.

cc. All Missions flown on the 29th of July were in support of the 173rd Abn. Bde. Operation Aurora II. Five (5) UH-1Ds and one (1) Light Fire Team lifted a large security force into the crash site of 571 to secure the area so that a CH-47 could recover parts of the wreckage. Aircraft 557 received one round during this lift.

dd. Nine (9) UH-1Ds and one (1) Light Fire Team made one Combat Assault on 30 July repositioning 94 173rd Abn. Bde. troops in Operation Aurora II. Ten (10) "Slicks" and two (2) Light Fire Teams lifted 240 troops of the 1/503 to the Brigade area in four (4) lifts. All other missions were in normal support of the 173rd Abn. Bde.

ee. The COWBOYS were attached to the 145th Combat Aviation Battalion on 31 July for movement of the 173rd Abn. Bde. back to Bien Hoa. Six (6) extractions were flown moving 360 troops back to their base camp.

II. TRAINING:

a.   Due to the operational commitment of this month very little training was accomplished other than training new pilots and crew members reporting into the unit.

III. COMPANY AREA:

Construction began on the officers' lounge during this month and work continued on individual living quarters.

IV. CIVIL AFFAIRS:

The 25th Med. Detachment's continued Med-Cap operations in the Duc Tu District.

HISTORY OF

COMPANY "A," 82ND AVIATION BATTALION

1 August -- 31 August 1966

Prepared by

Cpt. Donald L. Peters

Unit Historian

Approved by

ERNEST H. JOHNSON

Major Infantry

Commanding

HEADQUARTERS

173rd AIRBORNE BRIGADE (SEPARATE)

APO SAN FRANCISCO 96250

Dominic Fino

335TH AVIATION COMPANY (AIRMOBILE LIGHT)
173RD AIRBORNE BRIGADE (SEPARATE)
APO 96250 SAN FRANCISCO, CALIFORNIA

ARAV-AM   1 September 1966

Subject: Monthly History for Company "A," 82d Aviation Battalion
                 1 August 1966 through 31 August 1966

To: Commanding Officer
       335th Aviation Company (Airmobile Light)
       173rd Airborne Brigade (Separate)
       APO San Francisco, Calif. 96250

I. OPERATIONS:

a. 1 August 1966 found Co. "A," 82nd Aviation Battalion in Bien Hoa after terminating support of the 173rd Airborne Brigade's Operation Aurora II on 31 July. Extensive post-operation aircraft maintenance was in process and recovered parts of the company's crashed COWBOY 571 were flown to Cam Ranh Bay for inspection to determine the cause of the fatal accident of 27 July 1966.

b. On 2 August 1966, Company "A" held an Awards and Decorations Ceremony in the company area. The Company Commander, Major Johnson, pinned awards on 26 members of the company. In the afternoon the COWBOYS, with Falcon cover, lifted troops of 4th Battalion, 503rd Infantry, 173rd Airborne Brigade into the local TAOR in support of Operation Uniontown. Later in the afternoon pilots flew to Vung Tau to ferry UH-1Ds 902 and 910 to Bien Hoa as replacements for UH-1Ds 735 and 571 destroyed on Operation Aurora II.

c. From 3 August 1966 until 9 August 1966, Company "A" continued to support the Brigade in Operation Uniontown and Provided aircraft for Long Range Reconnaissance Patrol Training. Training of the LRRP's consisted of practice in methods of infiltrating and exfiltrating patrols in enemy territory. The new "Palmer Snatch," rappelling and rope ladder methods were practiced. On the afternoon of 5 August, the Falcons with a 173rd Aviation Platoon put on a fire power demonstration in War Zone "D" for the new unit commanders within the Brigade.

d. On 10 August, the 173rd Airborne Brigade opened a search and destroy operation East of Xuan Loc. Labeling the operation, Toledo, the Brigade Headquarters moved into position Castle at the base of Gia Ray Mountain, with the COWBOYS supporting from Xuan Loc airfield.

e. The COWBOYS on 13 August with elements of the 145th Aviation Battalion lifted 1/503 and 4/503 into LZ Grenada in support of Operation Toledo. At approximately 2000 hours, COWBOY operations at Xuan Loc received a call that a "Dust Off" helicopter was missing near LZ Grenada. Captain Wayne Davis and Lt. Fred Zabarsky took COWBOY 674 on a rescue mission through darkness and marginal weather. The crew chief of the "Dust Off" was found and rescued and elements of 2/503 were directed to the crash site.

f. On 14 August, the COWBOY'S lifted an ARVN unit from An Loc to a position East of Castle in support of Operation Toledo.

g. On 16 August Falcon 86, Major William MacPhail, flying a UH-1B armed with a new chemical dispersing unit made a CS run on a location suspected to be harboring large VC units. The CS was effective as Falcon 86 took four (4) hits. Immediately after spraying, the Falcons struck the area with their machine guns, rockets and grenades.

h. In the late afternoon of 17 August, an OH-13s, Casper 419, lost power and settled into the trees in a small LZ near position Granada. There were no injuries and the aircraft was repaired and flown to Bien Hoa on 18 August.

60

i. On 20 August 1966, Falcon 86 was slightly wounded on another successful CS mission. COWBOY 567 was forced down by an engine compartment fire at position Castle. Several crew chiefs in the LZ quickly extinguished the fire saving the aircraft and preventing injury to the crew.

j. On 21 August, Major Clark and Captain Reeves made an emergency extraction of an LRRP being chased by the Viet Cong. There was not a suitable LZ available. The "Palmer Snatch" was employed for the first time by the COWBOYS under combat conditions.

k. On 22 August, the COWBOYS with Falcon cover lifted 360 U.S. and 180 ARVN troops in support of Operation Toledo. The MAD System (Mortar Aerial Delivery) deployed from a UH-1B of the 173rd Aviation Platoon attacked positions in "War Zone D" where Viet Cong elements had been sighted.

l. During the morning of 23 August, the Company working with the 145th Aviation Battalion, lifted elements of the 173rd Airborne Brigade as Operation Toledo turns to the Southeast in pursuit of the Viet Cong. Just past noon the COWBOYS were beginning resupply of elements of the Brigade. COWBOY 674 had an engine failure and was autorotated by Captain Troy Reeves into an open field two miles South of Xuan Loc. There were no injuries and the aircraft was lifted to Bien Hoa by CH-47.

m. On 24 August 1966, 356 troop of the 173rd Abn. Bde. were lifted in support of Toledo. The COWBOYS are alerted for overnight standby to lift a reaction force for the Brigade.

n. On 29 August, a UH-1B received one hit in support of Operation Toledo. There were no injuries and only incidental damage to the aircraft.

o. The month of August closed with the COWBOYS continuing to support Operation Toledo in the dense jungle South of Xuan Loc.

II. MONTHLY STATISTICS:

	OH-13	UH-1B(A)	UH-1B	UH-1D	TOTAL
Sorties	396	431	309	3021	4157
Hours	292	398	187	1228	2105
Pax					4355
Cargo (tons)					242
Aircraft Hits					7

III. TRAINING:

The training time this month was devoted to familiarizing the pilots and crews of the UH-1Ds with the Long Range Reconnaissance Patrol infiltration and exfiltration tactics. Often these patrols are place in or removed from locations requiring rappelling, use of rope ladders or use of the "Palmer Snatch." The "Palmer Snatch" is an emergency exfiltration method operated from a helicopter hovering over the jungle. A length of rope is lowered from the helicopter to the troops on the jungle floor. The troops are hooked onto the rope by a Swiss Seat and a Chest Harness. The helicopter hovers straight up until the troops are clear of the trees, and flies to the nearest secure landing area. All the methods were practiced and studied.

IV. AWARDS AND DECORATIONS: (PREPARED BY Sp/4 Michael A. De Marco)

RANK	NAME	AWARD
Major	Gibbons, Bruce H.	D. F. C.
Captain	Overholser, William H.	B.S. ACM "V"
Captain	Pitchard, Donald G.	B.S. BAM
SSGT	Tilley, Rosco C.	B.S.
Sp/4	Koziol, Theophil J.	AM "V"
Sp/4	Platt, Richard W.	AM "V" BAM
Major	Cochran, Bruce S.	BAM
Major	Victor, Henry J.	BAM
Captain	Reeves, Troy Jr.	BAM
Captain	Albrecht, Richard D.	BAM
1/Lt.	Beasley, Lonnie S.	BAM
1/Lt.	Murray, George W. Jr.	BAM
CWO	Dorf, Harold A.	BAM
CWO	Richardson, Harold F.	BAM
WO	Jones, Kenneth R.	BAM
WO	McCormac II, Gordon	BAM
WO	Norton, Daniel S.	BAM
WO	Stoudt, Charles F.	BAM ACM "V"
WO	Lind, Clarence R.	BAM
WO	Sanders, Gary G.	BAM
WO	Basney, Ronald A.	BAM
SSG	Renmey, James	BAM
Sp/5	Pete, Davis S.	BAM
Sp/5	Lucas, Delbert G.	BAM
Sp/5	Emerick, Thomas J.	BAM
Sp/5	Cooper, Homer A.	BAM
Sp/5	Ferrall, Frank V.	BAM
Sp/5	Roberts, Curtis	BAM

RANK	NAME	AWARD
Sp/5	Payne, Melvin L.	BAM
Sp/5	Lampman, Richard R.	BAM
Sp/5	Larson, Larry	BAM
Sp/4	Nelson, Gary M.	BAM
Sp/4	Brecht, William C.	BAM
Sp/4	Bell, Philip G.	BAM
Sp/4	Tippett, Jerry W.	BAM
Sp/4	Patterson, Richard G.	BAM
Sp/4	Ingles, Michael J.	BAM
Sp/4	Luneckas, Peter T.	BAM
Sp/4	Norris, Mickel J.	BAM
Pfc.	Keil, David A.	BAM
Pfc.	Price, Larry D.	BAM
Pfc.	Epstein, Lewis D.	BAM
Pfc.	Anthony, Everett	BAM
Pfc.	Kinkella, Alan J.	BAM
Pfc.	Pike, John V.	BAM
Pfc.	Jackson, Walter C.	BAM
Pfc.	Eby, Benny E.	BAM
Pfc.	Hanshaw, David L.	BAM ACM
Pfc.	French, Ray	BAM
Sp/5	Schultz, Kurt E.	ACM
Sp/5	Shatzer, John R.	ACM
WO	Dumas, Robert E.	P.H.
WO	Geishauser, Anthony J.	P.H.

V. COMPANY AREA:

Construction and beautification projects continued in the Company area. The Officers, under the close supervision of Major Victor, put the finishing touches on a COWBOY-Falcon-Casper Lounge joining the patios of the BOQ. The lounge will have a bar, TV, a hand painted helicopter aerial combat mural designed by 1/Lt. John Hoza and a Company Officers DEROS snapshot sequence.

The All-American club had its grand opening and is serving the Enlisted Men with a bar, Lounge and day room. The club building also houses a barber shop and a laundry that serves the entire Company.

VI. CIVIL AFFAIRS:

a. On 19 August 1966 Company "A," 82nd Aviation Battalion, working hand in hand with the 38th Artillery Battalion, ARVN, completed construction of a three-classroom school in Duc Tu District of Ngu Phuc area, Republic of Vietnam. The school, now being used by the Vietnamese people, was completed under direction of First Lieutenants Guillot and Zabarsky with many hours of hard, voluntary work by the men of the Company.

The Vietnamese orphanage directly across the street from the school project in Duc Tu was treated to a party by the COWBOYS. Food and drinks were provided for the children and staff of the orphanage. Major Johnson, Commander of the COWBOYS, with Major Victor and 1/Lt. Zabarsky attended the big party to represent the Company and reported that the party was a tremendous success.

The 25th Medical Detachment of Company "A" continued MED-CAP operations in Duc Tu District. In conjunction with the medical work, articles of food, milk and clothing were distributed to needy Vietnamese people.

HISTORY OF

335TH AVIATION COMPANY (AIRMOBILE LIGHT)

173RD AIRBORNE BRIGADE (SEPARATE)

APO 96250 SAN FRANCISCO, CALIFORNIA

1 September -- 30 September 1966

Prepared by

1/Lt. GEORGE W. MURRAY

Approved by

ERNEST H. JOHNSON

Major Infantry

Commanding

HEADQUARTERS

173rd Airborne Brigade (Separate)

APO 96250 SAN FRANCISCO, CALIFORNIA

335TH AVIATION COMPANY (AML-LT)
173RD AIRBORNE BRIGADE (SEPARATE)
APO 96250 SAN FRANCISCO, CALIFORNIA

AVBE-AM   1 October 1966

Subject: Monthly History for Company "A," 82d Aviation Battalion
           1 September through 30 September 1966

To: Commanding Officer
      335th Aviation Company (Aml-Lt)
      173rd Airborne Brigade (Separate)
      APO 96250 San Francisco, California

I. OPERATIONS:

a. The 335th Aviation Company (Aml-Lt) continued to support into September the 173rd Airborne Brigade (Separate) on a search and destroy operation labeled Toledo being conducted near Xuan Loc, Republic of Vietnam. Eight (8) COWBOYS with Falcon support flew four (4) Combat Assaults as the Paratroops searched-out the Viet Cong.

b. The second of September found the COWBOYS and Falcons with elements of the 145th Aviation Battalion lifting 354 troops of the Brigade in a massive heliborne assault. COWBOY 902 loaded with troops lost power on departure from LZ Washington and was autorotated. Damage was suffered to the tail boom and tail rotor. 902 was evacuated to Bien Hoa by CH-47.

c. The COWBOYS, Falcons, and Caspers from 3 through 6 September supported the 173rd Airborne with resupply, courier service, reconnaissance, command and liaison and aerial fire support.

d. The 7th of September marked the termination of Operation Toledo as the 335th led three airmobile companies in lifting the paratroopers from the operations area into the "Snake Pit" at Bien Hoa.

e. Early morning the 8th of September found the COWBOYS and Flacons winging Westward to support the 1st Infantry Division in the Phu Loi -- Lai Khe area. 216 members of the "Big Red One" were Eagle Flighted into a rough, brush landing zone. The proud COWBOYS shamed 1st Infantry Airmobile Companies with their tight, exact formation flying and the deadly Falcons put on an impressive demonstration of aerial fire support.

f. Operation Uniontown underway in the 173rd local TAOR was supported on 9 September by the 335th. Vietnamese National Elections are approaching and alertness is the word, for all allied intelligence sources expect maximum Viet Cong interference with the elections.

g. The period of 10 September through 14 September was quiet for the 335th. The Battalions operating in the local TAOR were provided hot "A" rations and other supplies each morning and evening by the UH-1Ds.

h. On 15 September 4th Battalion moved Northwest to secure an airstrip at Dau Tieng for an operation by the 1st Infantry Division. The security operation was labeled Operation Atlantic City. A "Slick" pulled an injured man from the jungles on the end of a rope, took three (3) bullet hits, and flew a scary night emergency resupply of damaged radio parts to the 4th Battalion.

i. September 16th at 1015 hours CWO Dorf and WO Gregg working out of Dau Tieng in support of the 4/503 received three (3) rounds of light automatic weapons fire as they were on short final to medevac wounded Americans. The hits ruptured the fuel cells, and by the time CWO Dorf nursed the crippled 701 into Dau Tieng, JP-4 was flowing ankle deep through the cargo compartment. A survival kit under the crew chief's seat caught one enemy round headed for Sp/5 Meredith. 701 was finally repaired by the maintenance crew on "Horsethief" and was flown to Bien Hoa.

At noon the COWBOYS and Falcons lifted elements of the Brigade into a loading zone in the TAOR. COWBOY 738 in formation at tree top altitude experienced an engine failure. WO Ron Jones, aircraft commander, and Captain John Wood, who was on his first heliborne assault in Vietnam, made a perfect zero airspeed autorotation into dense jungle. There were no injuries, but the jungle was so dense that a landing to rescue the crew was impossible. An emergency message was relayed to the Brigade Long Range Reconnaissance Patrol to prepare their rescue rope ladders for use. The LRRP responded instantly with the entire unit trying to climb on helicopters to rescue the COWBOYS from the hands of the Viet Cong. However, the LRRP was finally convinced that only a rope ladder was needed to rescue the crew. A few nervous moments after plunging into the jungle, the crew scrambled up the rope ladders into the hovering rescue helicopter. Later in the afternoon 738 was evacuated to Bien Hoa by CH-47.

j. At 0800 on 17 September 1966 an Awards and Decorations Ceremony was held. Major Johnson, Commander of the COWBOYS, decorated ten (10) officers and enlisted men for acts of valor and periods of meritorious service. The Company received notice that the COWBOYS, as of 1 September 1966, are redesignated the 335th Aviation Company (Airmobile-Light). Company "A" will be returned to its parent 82nd Aviation Battalion at Fort Bragg, North Carolina. This return to the United States involves only our name, a disappointment to every COWBOY.

k. The period of 15 September to 23 September was a period of training and experimentation with a new item of equipment. Col. Parmeter introduced us to a system deployed on the roof of the jungle by a UH-1D. This system was labeled the jungle canopy and CWO N. Dorf and WO R. Jones worked with Col. Parmeter in preparation for a demonstration to show how troops and equipment could be placed on this canopy by helicopter, then lowered to the otherwise inaccessible jungle floor.

l. At last light on the afternoon of 20 September five (5) LRRP teams were infiltrated by UH-1Ds into the hostile area North of Bien Hoa known notoriously as War Zone "D." Two (2) Light Fire Teams from the Falcons provided cover for the operation; there was negative enemy contact.

m. The COWBOYS and Falcons spent the day of 21 September on extraction stand-by for the LRRP teams working in "D" Zone. Three of the teams made contact with the Viet Cong and three times the COWBOYS scrambled to snatch the patrols from the hands of the Viet Cong.

n. On 22 September, Light Fire Teams from the Falcons were called upon to provide aerial fire support for LRRP's in contact with the Viet Cong. At 1030 COWBOYS reacted to an urgent request for a patrol extraction, pulling the patrol in without incident. Again, at last light two (2) LRRP's were scheduled for infiltration into "D" Zone. The first COWBOY approaching his LZ spotted VC on the edge of the woods. A quick drawing COWBOY crew chief beat a VC with an automatic weapon to the draw. Partners of the dead VC opened fire and the LRRP mission was aborted. The second COWBOY began his approach and received fire, a hot gun battle ensued as the COWBOYS pulled out of the approach and the Falcons rolled in with their guns blazing. Both LRRP's missions were aborted and returned to Bien Hoa because of the VC presence in primary and alternate LZ's.

The Casper's OH-13s armed with machine-guns went out for a test fire of their new systems. The OH-13s are to be utilized as scout units to detect Viet Cong concentrations for destruction by quick reaction COWBOY - Falcon Eagle Flights.

o. At 0800 on the 23rd of September, CWO Harold Dorf and WO Ronald Jones flew the jungle canopy demonstration for the Brigade staff. Col. Parmeter gave the staff members an initial briefing on the uses and operation of the canopy. The net became fouled in the jungle and the demonstration was terminated with observers skeptical of the feasibility of the jungle canopy system.

At 1300 two (2) UH-1Ds conducted training with pathfinders from E/17 Cav.

The last light of day saw three (3) COWBOYS spiral down into the jungles of War Zone "D" with LRRP's to search for Viet Cong. WO Charles F. Stoudt and WO William M. Manker placed their patrol in a small rough jungle clearing. Immediately after the helicopter departed the LRRP engaged a platoon size VC force; an immediate extraction was requested. WO Stoudt and WO Manker went back into the LZ and picked up the patrol under fire. A rotor blade was damaged, but the aircraft returned safely to Bien Hoa.

p. LRRP's called for help at 1300 hours on 25 September. The COWBOYS and Falcons snatched the patrols from the jungle and assaulted a reaction force into the area where the LRRP's had discovered the Viet Cong.

The 173rd Airborne Brigade began Operation Sioux City, aiming at the Viet Cong elements the LRRP had made contact with in "D" Zone.

q.   0800 hours, 26 September 1966 the COWBOYS delivered 120 paratroopers into "D" Zone LZ's. The Falcons shot white phosphorous into a position that was directing ground fire at the COWBOYS. Two (2) VC with their clothes in flames sprinted into the open and were cut down by the "Saber" gunships.

r.   Three (3) assaults put 170 paratroopers into LZ's in support of Sioux City on the morning of 27 September.

s.   On 28 September Eagle Flights were conducted in War Zone "D" as the 173rd Airborne continued to search for the elusive Viet Cong. OH-13s armed with their side arms conducted Aero-Scout Training with E/17 Cavalry. Three (3) LRRP's were placed in the Brigade operational area in "D" Zone. Thirty minutes after infiltration one team was calling for help. Captain Troy Reeves and Captain Don Moss made a daring extraction of the team under intense automatic weapons fire. The Falcon fire team led by Captain Vance Gammons provided ravaging fire support for the extraction. The LRRP's reported that Falcon fire was providing close-in support against VC only 20 meters from their position.

t.   The COWBOYS, Falcons, and Casper's continued on September 29 and 30 to provide the Brigade with aviation support for Operation Sioux City. Eagle Flights and assaults were made, supplies were delivered, LRRP's were supported and CS gas was showered on suspected Viet Cong targets. The month of September closed with the following monthly statistics:

	OH-13	UH-1B(A)	UH-1B	UH-1D	TOTAL
Sorties	225	642	325	2552	3744
Hours	127	450	162	964	1703
Pax					4381
Cargo (tons)					206
Aircraft Hits					3

II. TRAINING:

Training during the month of September was devoted to new pilots and crew members. Pilots were given the usual unit aircraft checkout and the area orientation. New gunners and crew chiefs were given the weapon checkout and briefed on crew procedures and responsibilities.

III. AWARDS AND DECORATIONS: Prepared by Sp/4 Michael De Marco.

MacPhail, William Jr.	Major	DFC, Bronze Star,
		AM w/ "V," Purple Heart
Addiss, Daniel A.	Major	Bronze Star
Bell, Glenn B.	1/Lt.	AM w/ "V"
Kuhblank, Richard C.	1/Lt.	AM w/ "V"
Sanders, Gary G.	WO	AM w/ "V"
Peters, Donald L.	Captain	AM
Ferrall, Frank V. Jr.	Sp/5	AM
Klinefelter, John W.	Sp/4	AM
Houchin, Zelner M. Jr.	Pfc.	AM
McHugh, Leo P.	Pfc.	AM

IV. COMPANY AREA:

Construction work in individual rooms continues at an enthusiastic pace. CWO Bill Easton persists in his running water project. A large water tower has been constructed and piping to deliver running water to the company area is being laid.

V. CIVIL AFFAIRS:

MED-CAP and food distribution projects in the Bien Hoa area were carried out to aid the sick and needy Vietnamese people.

HISTORY OF

335TH AVIATION COMPANY (AIRMOBILE LIGHT)

173RD AIRBORNE BRIGADE (SEPARATE)

APO 96250 SAN FRANCISCO, CALIFORNIA

1 October -- 30 October 1966

Prepared by
1/Lt. GEORGE W. MURRAY

Approved by
Leyburn W. Brockwell, Jr.
LTC Infantry
Commanding

For
Ernest H. Johnson
Major Infantry
Commanding

HEADQUARTERS

173rd Airborne Brigade (Separate)

APO 96250 SAN FRANCISCO, CALIFORNIA

335TH ASSAULT HELICOPTER COMPANY
173RD AIRBORNE BRIGADE (SEPARATE)
APO SAN FRANCISCO 96250

AVBE-AM   12 March 1967

Subject: Monthly History for 335th Aviation Company
           1 October 1966 through 30 October 1966

I. OPERATIONS:

a. The month of October began with the COWBOYS, Falcons and Caspers continuing to provide the 173rd Airborne Brigade (Separate) with dependable aviation support as the "Sky Soldiers" carried on Operations Sioux City and Uniontown. A Casper OH-13s darting across the operations area near position Fox picked up two rounds of small arms fire. The pilot was able to reach a secure area, where he found minor damage to his ship. The company made two (2) small lifts to reposition the paratroopers as their unrelenting pursuit of the crafty Viet Cong in "War Zone D" continued.

b. On the 2nd of October two (2) OH-13s armed with machine guns provided overhead cover for E/17 Cav. The Viet Cong chose not to interfere with the Cavalry and thus avoided incurring the wrath of the Aero Scouts.

c. One hundred and sixty U.S. troops were lifted by seven (7) COWBOYS with cover from a Falcon Light Fire Team on 4 October. Light contact was made but "Charlie" avoided major contact with the paratroopers of the 173rd.

d. The COWBOYS moved two hundred troops of the Brigade as Operation Sioux City continued on 6 October.

e. On 7 October, ten (10) COWBOYS with cover from two (2) Falcon Light Fire Teams repositioned 120 U.S. troops in War Zone "D."

f. On 8 October 1966, paratroopers of the 173rd began to withdraw from the area of Operation Sioux City. 360 troops were extracted by the COWBOYS. As the COWBOYS approached the Song Deng Nai River, the Southern boundary of "War Zone D," the Viet Cong opened fire on the formation. Four ships were damaged. The COWBOYS, in formation, returned the fire and the hungry Falcons rolled in to remind "Charlie" that the luxury of firing at the COWBOYS can cost dearly. Later in the day, 5 COWBOYS moved 60 cavalry men into position to secure the route of travel for the Brigade convoy moving out of "D" Zone.

g. On 9 October, the COWBOYS cleaned up the Sioux City area with an extraction of 92 U.S. troops in 4 lifts. Aerial reconnaissance for Operation Robin began as 5 aircraft checked Route #15 from Bien Hoa to Vung Tau to prepare for road clearing operations.

h. 10 October 1966 was the opening day of Operation Robin as the "Sky Soldiers" provided security for elements of the 4th Infantry Division moving from Vung Tau to Bear Cat.

i. The morning of 11 October the COWBOYS lifted troops of the 173rd into an LZ in the vicinity of the Brigade CP on Highway #15 South of Bien Hoa, Operation Robin continued as the 335th provided a Light Fire Team, a courier ship and resupply ships used to supplement the road supply convoy.

j. On 12 October four (4) UH-1Ds and a Light Fire Team infiltrated two (2) LRRP's into suspected Viet Cong areas South of the Brigade CP. At approximately 1805 Casper #416, an OH-13s piloted by 1/Lt. Douglas L. Jones, departed the Brigade CP enroute to Bien Hoa. At approximately 1815, #416 fell 50 feet to the ground and burst into flames. 1/Lt. Jones and his passenger S/Sgt. E-6 Freeman were killed instantly. The accident investigation board was appointed and began its investigation at first light on the 13th of October.

At 1830 hours on the 12th five (5) UH-1Ds with a Light Fire Team conducted night training. They landed in formation at Bear Cat, Vung Tau and the Snake Pit in Bien Hoa.

k. Early on the morning of 13 October 1966 two (2) OH-13s were carried by Air Force C-130 to Da Nang. Two (2) UH-1Ds flew to Da Nang via the coastal route. These four helicopters were placed in support of the 173rd Airborne Brigade's 4/503 Infantry on Operation Winchester supporting allied operations in I Corps near the

Demilitarized Zone. At 1700 hours' three (3) UH-1Ds extracted a LRRP that had made contact with a Viet Cong force. The extraction was made without any enemy interference.

l. Again, on 14 October a LRRP called for extraction at 1700 hours. The extraction was made with no enemy fire received. At 1800 hours a flight of six (6) UH-1Ds (the Mustangs) with a Light Fire Team made a night formation training flight to Vung Tau, the Snake Pit, and then back into the CORRAL.

m. At 0900 hours on 15 October, UH-1Ds covered by a Light Fire Team extracted 42 U.S. paratroopers from a pick-up zone in A/O Robin. A second Light Fire Team came on station at 0900 hours to provide convoy cover for Brigade vehicles traveling Highway 15 in the Robin area.

n. 16 October 1966 dawned with a Falcon fire team making a reconnaissance, which was repeated at last light of day. This was a daily chore to observe any Viet Cong activity near the Crucial highway.

o. Termination of the 173rd Airborne Brigade's road runner operation on Highway #15 began at 0730 hours on 17 October as seven (7) COWBOYS and two (2) "Falcon" Light Fire Teams extracted 126 U.S. paratroopers from the Robin area. A convoy began moving toward Bien Hoa with a "Falcon" team providing overhead cover. By the afternoon Operation Robin was terminated. The 335th Aviation counts Operation Robin a loss because of the tragic accidental death of 1/Lt. Douglas L. Jones.

p. At 0730 hours on 18 October two (2) UH-1Ds began airborne refresher training with elements of E Troop, 17th Cav. At 0900 hours' one (1) UH-1D departed the CORRAL for Da Nang to provide additional support for 4/503 in Operation Winchester. At 2245 hours a Viet Cong unit attacked the armed helicopter parking area at the South boundary of the Brigade perimeter. A Claymore mine or fragmentation grenade was detonated under UH-1B #932. The resulting fire, and fuel-ammunition explosion completely destroyed #932 and severely damaged #930. Captain Vance Gammons and Sp/4 Lyle Travis saved #930 from destruction by flying it off the pad. Both were later presented the Bronze Star with "V" Device for heroism by Major General Paul Smith, Commanding General of the 173rd Airborne Brigade (Separate). Falcon aircraft #919 parked next to #932 also was in danger and was evacuated by 1/Lt. Willoughby Goin; Lt. Goin received the Air Medal with a "V" Device for heroism.

q. At 0700 hours on 19 October 1966, seven (7) COWBOYS and two (2) Light Fire Teams departed Bien Hoa to support the 25th Infantry Division in the Cu Chi-Duc Hoa area. Combat Assaults moved 150 ARVN and U.S. troops during the day. On the last extraction of the day the COWBOYS," on short final to an open rice field pick-up zone, were ambushed by heavy small arms and automatic weapons fire. COWBOY door gunners whipped out white smoke to mark for the Falcons and opened fire with their own M-60s. The Falcons rolled in and the supposedly "Secure LZ" was engulfed in a wild fire fight. Airborne again, the COWBOYS found five of seven ships carrying combat damage--no crew members wounded. Two of the ARVN's extracted were seriously wounded by enemy fire and were flown to 7th Surgical Hospital at Cu Chi.

One (1) Light Fire Team at Bien Hoa conducted reconnaissance of the Brigade TAOR (Tactical Area of Operational Responsibility) at 0730 and 1830. These recons provide more security for the Brigade perimeter, which is obviously not as secure as everyone had previously hoped.

r. Before daylight on the morning of 20 October, seven (7) "COWBOY" and two (2) "Falcon" fire teams pulled pitch and headed into the Delta South of Saigon. Arriving at Ben Tri, the company joined the "Outlaws" and "Knights" of the Delta Aviation Battalion (13th Aviation Battalion) and lifted 280 ARVN in four (4) assaults. On an extraction toward the end of the afternoon, the "Falcons" detected Viet Cong on a landing zone about to be assaulted. Rolling in, the guns put CS gas, machine-gun fire, and rockets on the enemy elements and successfully upset any plans the enemy had of firing on the incoming "Slicks."

The company returned to the CORRAL happy, as the units visited in the Delta expressed amazement at the excellent formation flying by the COWBOYS and the spirited aggressiveness of the bloodthirsty "Falcons."

s. October 21 and 22 were spent in normal support of the 173rd Airborne in Bien Hoa and Da Nang. A number of recons were conducted in the TAOR and one recon covered Highway #15 from Bien Hoa to Vung Tau.

t. On 23 October 1966 Light Fire Teams conducted recons in the TAOR. At 1300 a fire team from the Falcons went out to cover CH-47s (Chinooks) flying out of Xom Cat Special Forces Camp on the North bank of the Song Deng Nai River Northeast of Bien Hoa.

At 1800, three (3) UH-1Ds covered by a fire team positioned two (2) LRRP teams in the Brigade TAOR.

u. At 1120 hours on 24 October three (3) UH-1Ds and a "Falcon" fire team scrambled to extract a LRRP team that had been compromised. The extraction was successful with no combat damage received.

At 1800 hours another LRRP was positioned by the COWBOYS."

v. Just after day break on 25 October 1966, the COWBOYS and "Falcons" received request for an emergency extraction of a LRRP team. The LRRP had made contact with a small Viet Cong element and had captured two of the enemy. The extraction was successful, and the two VC were delivered to Brigade Headquarters for interrogation. On departure from the pick up, the "Falcons" spotted sampans in the area and rolled in on firing passes. When the smoke cleared there were two (2) positively destroyed enemy boats.

In the afternoon one (1) UH-1D flew a reconnaissance in the vicinity of Tanh Linh for possible operations on the 26th of October.

w. 26 October was spent in normal support of the 173rd Airborne in Bien Hoa and the Brigade's 4/503 at Da Nang.

x. On 27 October 1966 at 1045 hours' seven (7) UH-1Ds escorted by two (2) Light Fire Teams lifted 180 paratroopers of the 1/503. At 1500 hours' four (4) UH-1Ds (Mustangs) and a team of "Falcons" repositioned 72 troops of the 1/503 in the TAOR. Two (2) UH-1Ds received hits and one gunner suffered minor neck wounds. Operation Trojan Horse (Joplin) began today for the 1/503.

y. At 0700 hours on 28 October, seven (7) COWBOYS supplemented by three (3) UH-1Ds from the 145th Aviation Battalion and two (2) "Falcon" fire teams lifted 600 ARVN troops into the Tanh Linh area to aid the 1/503 in Operation Joplin. One (1) "Falcon" received a small arm hit in the main rotor blade and one (1) of the "Falcon" door gunners was hit in the leg by ground fire. The gunner was taken to the 93rd Medical Evacuation Hospital at Bien Hoa for treatment. A week later he returned to duty.

z. 29 October 1966, the COWBOYS with four (4) 145th Aviation UH-1D and a "Falcon" fire team in four (4) lifts moved 219 troops in the Operation Joplin area. At 1400 hours, UH-1D #614 commanded by WO Ronald G. Jones showed fluctuations of transmission gages and was landed safely near Dong Xoai Special Forces with a failing transmission. The ship was returned to Bien Hoa by Chinook.

aa. On 30 October 1966, 1/503 terminated Operation Joplin as Chinooks lifted the troops from Tanh Linh to Bien Hoa.

bb. The month of October ended with three (3) UH-1Ds and two (2) OH-13s supporting 4/503 on Operation Winchester in I Corps Area. The remainder of the COWBOYS - Falcons - Caspers" continued to provide the main force of the 173rd Airborne Brigade (Separate) in Bien Hoa with the FINEST COMBAT AIRMOBILE SUPPORT IN THE WORLD!

II. MONTHLY STATISTICS:

	OH-13	UH-1B(A)	UH-1B	UH-1D	TOTAL
Sorties	543	571	571	3238	4923
Hours	204	250	307	1387	2148
Pax					7045
Cargo (tons)					206
Aircraft Hits					12

III. TRAINING:

Training time during October, in addition to the normal transition and initial new pilot briefings, included a night formation flight by each lift platoon escorted by the "Falcons." A new program of Officers Call was set up on a bi-monthly basis. This conference session is designed to emphasized to pilot's information pertinent to maintenance, operations, aviation safety, intelligence, company administration and any information that the Commander chooses to emphasize.

IV. AWARDS AND DECORATIONS:

An awards ceremony was not held during the month of October because of the heavy operational commitment of the COWBOYS." However, this month has produced many Air Medals as the Company participated in several Combat Assaults. Also, General Smith, Commanding General of the 173rd Airborne Brigade (Separate) decorated Captain Gammons and Sp/4 Lyle Travis with Bronze Stars with "V" Devices for the evacuation of the "Falcon" gunship from its parking area during a Viet Cong attack.

V. COMPANY AREA:

The living area of the company improves each day as the Officers and men develop "Green Thumbs." Grass is growing and trees have been set out. Soon the area will look so much like home, that except for the VC, the men of the COWBOYS will think they are back in the United States.

VI. CIVIL AFFAIRS:

Following the theory that the war will be won by diligent civil affairs work as well as by hot pursuit of the Viet Cong guerrilla, the 335th Aviation Company continued an active program of MED-CAP through the 25th Medical Detachment.

HISTORY OF

335TH AVIATION COMPANY (AIRMOBILE LIGHT)

173RD AIRBORNE BRIGADE (SEPARATE)

APO 96250 SAN FRANCISCO, CALIFORNIA

1 November -- 30 November 1966

Prepared by
1/Lt. GEORGE W. MURRAY

Approved by
HENRY J. VICTOR
Major Artillery
Commanding

PROVIDING THE 173RD AIRBORNE BRIGADE (SEPARATE)
WITH THE MOST PROFESSIONAL AIRMOBILE SUPPORT
AVAILABLE ANYWHERE IN THE WORLD

HEADQUARTERS
335TH Aviation Company (Airmobile Light)
173rd Airborne Brigade (Separate)
APO 96250 SAN FRANCISCO, CALIFORNIA

335TH AVIATION COMPANY (AIRMOBILE LIGHT)
173RD AIRBORNE BRIGADE (SEPARATE)
APO 96250 SAN FRANCISCO, CALIFORNIA

1 December 1966

Subject: Monthly History for 335th Aviation Company (Airmobile Light)
1 November 1966 through 30 November 1966

To: Commanding Officer
335th Aviation Company (Airmobile Light)
173rd Airborne Brigade (Separate)
APO 96250 San Francisco, California

I. ORGANIZATION AND DESIGNATION:

(A) Airlift Platoons: COWBOYS -- 20 UH-1D "Slicks"

1st Airlift Platoon -- Ramrods
2nd Airlift Platoon -- Mustangs

(B) Armed Helicopter Platoon: Falcons -- 8 UH-1B "Armed" Helicopters)

(C) 173rd Aviation Platoon: Caspers
2 UH-1D Command & Control
1 UH-1B Command & Control
1 UH-1B "12 O'clock High" MAD System
6 OH-13s "Hot Stuff" Aero Scouts

(D) Maintenance:
1 UH-1B Horsethief

II. OPERATIONS:

a. The month of November began as the longed for dry season seems never to be coming. Rain, thunder storms and poor visibility continued to be a nuisance, but the 335th continues to support the "SKY SOLDIERS" on Operation Uniontown. Three (3) UH-1Ds and two (2) OH-13s continue support at Da Nang.

At 1030 hours a Light Fire Team was scrambled to provide the 120th Aviation Company with fire support in the Saigon area.

Five (5) UH-1Ds and a Light Fire Team move 145 U.S. troops in three (3) Combat Assaults.

b.   At 0945 on the 2nd of November seven (7) UH-1Ds with a Light Fire Team conduct seven (7) Combat Assaults in the Bear Cat area. In support of the 4/25 Infantry, 306 American troops are lifted into the landing zones in the Bear Cat area of operation.

c. From 0730 to 1800 on the 3rd of November seven (7) UH-1Ds, a Light Fire Team and a UH-1B Command and Control ship from the CASPERS conducted seventeen (17) Combat Assaults for 453 troops of the 4/25 Infantry. The troops are resupplied by 8.9 tons of cargo by the COWBOYS.

d. At 0800 hours on the 4th of November four (4) UH-1Ds conduct Combat Assault training with the ARVN. Training was extended to 480 Vietnamese during sixteen (16) practice assaults.

At 0800 hours, Maj. Johnson decorated ten (10) members of his command in ceremony. Other individuals were due awards but were flying -- they will be decorated at a later date.

At 1030 hours' one (1) COWBOY conducted a Psy War leaflet drop in support of Brigade S-5.

At 1630 hours' five (5) UH-1Ds covered by a Light Fire Team in three (3) CA's placed 90 paratroopers into ambush sites.

e. 300 troops of the 3rd Brigade, 4th Infantry Division were deployed by the COWBOYS in ten (10) CA's on 5 November 1966. At 1600 hours, the 90 troops of ambush patrol were extracted from local TAOR after twenty-four hours of negative contact. Also, at 1600 hours' four (4) UH-1Ds in three (3) lifts placed 54 paratroopers of the 1/503 in the TAOR. At dusk four (4) UH-1Ds and a Light Fire Team infiltrated two (2) Long Range Reconnaissance Patrols into the local TAOR.

f. At 1700 hours on the 6th of November one of the LRRP working just East of the TAOR placed a call for an emergency extraction to escape a Viet Cong trap that had surrounded them. Three (3) UH-1Ds and a Light Fire Team scrambled to aid the LRRP and found the patrol in an area that did not offer a suitable LZ. The three (3) UH-1Ds employed the emergency rope rescue system, lowering ropes 120 feet to the jungle floor and lifting the patrol members clear of the jungle. There were no injuries and no aircraft damaged as the six (6) man patrol was evacuated to the safety of the Bien Hoa Compound.

g. 0700 hours, 7 November 1966: Five (5) UH-1Ds and a Light Fire Team supported the 3/4th Division at Bear Cat lifting 260 American troops. At 1000, two (2) UH-1Ds and a Light Fire Team extracted 57 ambush patrol members from sites in the TAOR.

h. At 0730 on 8 November six (6) COWBOYS and a Falcon Light Fire Team arrived at Bear Cat to support 3/4 Infantry Division. Twelve (12) assaults were conducted as 455 troops were moved; resupply was conducted at conclusion of the lift. In the TAOR, three (3) LRRP teams were extracted at the conclusion of their mission. Operation Meridian was initiated by 2/503 today.

i. 9 November was devoted to Eagle Flights as eight (8) UH-1Ds and a Light Fire Team supported the 1/503 Infantry.

j. 10 November 1966: Operation Meridian in the Tay Ninh - Dau Tieng - Minh Thanh area North of Saigon near the Cambodian border has the COWBOYS, Falcons, and CASPERS working hard. Supplemented by two (2) UH-1Ds from the 145th Aviation Battalion from Bien Hoa, 700 ARVN and 180 U.S. troops are lifted in the area of Operation Meridian.

k. On 11 November, all company aircraft are working at the Minh Thanh Special Forces Compound in support of Operation Meridian. With the two (2) UH-1Ds from the 145th, the COWBOYS conducted six (6) assaults to deploy 460 American troops.

l. On 12 November, four (4) UH-1Ds in the Minh Thanh area reposition 50 U.S. troops. The company is now regulated to stand-by status at Minh Thanh through the 13th. Everyone is squirming for action as American units to the West of Minh Thanh are killing VC at a phenomenal rate. All 335th Action is limited to the Falcons making reconnaissance flights into the area of Operation.

m. 14 November 1966 finds Operation Meridian renamed Operation Attleboro; as it becomes clear that this Operation is rapidly becoming the biggest operation to date in the Vietnam War. On this day the COWBOYS and Falcons transported 486 American and Vietnamese troops to search for the enemy.

n. Early in the morning on the 15th of November, a fake assault of two (2) lifts follow the TAC Air into an LZ North of Minh Thanh. The plan is a block to contain the VC in an area where he can be destroyed. No fire received, but chalk 4 tries to chop down a tree with his main rotor -- slight blade damage, and the tree is still standing. Later in the morning two (2) assaults received fire going into an LZ -- negative hits.

o. 16, 17, & 18 November 1966 again find the company on standby at Minh Thanh. Over the three-day period only 239 U.S. and ARVN troops are lifted.

p. On the 19th of November, the COWBOYS in seven (7) assaults moved 384 U.S. and ARVN troops in support of Operation Attleboro. At 0830 hours the CASPERS employed Psy Warfare against Viet Cong in the Minh Thanh area. A UH-1 with the MAD system aboard delivered a cargo of death dealing 81mm mortar rounds on an area suspected to harbor enemy elements.

q. The 20th of November 1966 concluded the 173rd Airborne Brigades participation in Operation Attleboro. The Brigade moved from Minh Thanh to Bien Hoa by road. The Falcons flew overhead cover, and the COWBOYS and CASPERS provided ready reaction and C&C.

r. At 1400 on the 21st of November three (3) assaults lifted 144 paratroopers of the 1/503 into an LZ at TAOR. At 1700 hours the Brigade Aviation Officer alerted the company the 3rd Brigade of the 4th Infantry Division was heavily engaged with enemy elements in the Rung Sat Special Zone Southeast of Saigon. Five (5) UH-1Ds scrambled to the aid of the unit working from Nha Bhe Naval Base on the Song Dong Nai River. The COWBOYS breaking a cardinal rule by working without the Falcons, all UH-1Bs were down for maintenance, moved 78 troops into reinforced positions in three (3) assaults. A gun team from the 145th Aviation Battalion covered the COWBOYS. Major Johnson flying lead drew fire and his ship, 884, took a hit in the left underside. The round stopped against the armor plate on which SP/5 Davis Trice was sitting. Major Johnson flew 884 safely back to Bien Hoa, but Rice was visibly shaken as he had only a few days to completion of his Vietnam tour. The COWBOYS flight returned to corral at 2200 hours.

s. On 22 November 1966, three (3) UH-1Ds and a Light Fire Team support 3/4th Infantry Divisions as 126 U.S. troops and a large quantity of supplies were moved.

t. 23 November 1966 was spent on LRRP stand-by, with several recons for Operation Waco being conducted. The COWBOYS - CASPERS elements supporting the 4/503 at Da Nang was alerted for return to Bien Hoa.

u. 24 November 1966: The Falcons conducted morning and evening recons in the Brigade TAOR. One LRRP team in the TAOR was extracted without incident.

v. At 0800 hours on the 25th of November eight (8) UH-1Ds and a Light Fire Team made five (5) assaults into the LZ's in the Operation Waco area, North of Highway #1 between Bien Hoa and Xuan Loc. At 1800 hours' two (2) LRRP teams were emplaced South of Bear Cat. Enemy fire was received, but there were no casualties or aircraft damage. Two (2) OH-13s returned by Air Force C-130 from Da Nang.

w. 26 November was devoted in support of the 1/503 in Operation Waco and 4/503 at Da Nang.

x. On 27 November normal support of Waco and LRRP was performed. Training was conducted by all flyable ships not committed to operational missions. (NOTE: See item IV Training)

y. At 0800 hours on the 28th of November the company lifted 282 ARVN and U.S. troops in support of Operation Waco. The landing zone being utilized was a roughly cultivated field with stumps and rocks. As the lift approached, rotor wash stirred up dense clouds of dust and COWBOY 614, caught in the turbulence, ran out of power causing loss of directional control. The ship turned to the right approximately 270 degrees, struck a stump shearing part of one tail rotor blade. The pilot cut the power and 614 remained upright. The tail rotor was repaired on the spot by Horsethief and flown back to Bien Hoa. Major frame damage from the accident sent the ship to Depot Maintenance for overhaul.

At 1100 hours' two (2) LRRP teams were extracted from the Waco area without incident.

z. The closing days of November were spent in support of Operation Uniontown in the Brigade TAOR, Operation Waco East of Bien Hoa and the 4/503 at Da Nang.

III. MONTHLY STATISTICS:

	OH-13	UH-1B(A)	UH-1B	UH-1D	TOTAL
Sorties	631	1086	540	5219	7476
Hours	206	475	171	1297	2149
Pax					11464
Cargo (tons)					243
Aircraft Hits					2

IV. TRAINING:

The training highlights for November was the on-the-job type of training conducted as the COWBOYS and Falcons supported the 3rd Brigade of the 4th Infantry Division. The Unit, just arrived in country, was conducting operations to the Southwest of Bear Cat as they prepared themselves for the demanding environment of the war in Vietnam. The 335th, provided academic introduction to helicopter operations and utilization and then provided the 3rd Brigade with the capability of conducting airmobile operations, resupplying by aircraft and using armed helicopters in support of ground operations.

Training with the LRRP's was conducted providing refresher training for aircraft crews and for patrol members. Finally, normal training of new pilots and standardization training for veteran pilots continued as a large number of hours were logged in extensive cross-country training. The cowboys ranged to Phan Thiet, Can Tho, and Vung Tau logging training time.

V. AWARDS AND DECORATIONS:

A ceremony was held at 0800 hours on 4 November 1966 in the company area as Maj. Johnson decorated ten (10) members of the unit.

NAME	RANK	AWARD
Kuhblank, Richard C.	Captain	Distinguished Flying Cross
Zabarsky, Frederick G.	Captain	Distinguished Flying Cross
		Air Medal W/ "V"
		Bronze Star
Sanders, Gary G.	WO1	Distinguished Flying Cross
Hammargren, Lonnie L.	Captain	Air Medal W/ "V"
		Bronze Star
Vance, John D.	1/Lt.	Army Commendation W/ "V"
Lovgren, Paul W.	Captain	Basic Air Medal
Payne, Melvin L.	SGT.	Basic Air Medal
Hancock, William A.	PFC	Basic Air Medal
Lucas, Delbert G.	SP/5	Purple Heart

HISTORY OF

335TH AVIATION COMPANY (AIRMOBILE LIGHT)

173RD AIRBORNE BRIGADE (SEPARATE)

Bien Hoa, Republic of Vietnam

APO SAN FRANCISCO 96250, CALIFORNIA

1 December -- 31 December 1966

ERNEST H. JOHNSON
Major Infantry
Commanding

PROVIDING THE 173RD AIRBORNE BRIGADE (SEPARATE)
WITH THE MOST PROFESSIONAL AIRMOBILE SUPPORT
AVAILABLE ANYWHERE IN THE WORLD

Prepared by
GEORGE W. MURRAY
1/Lt. Armor
Unit Historian

HEADQUARTERS
335TH Aviation Company (Airmobile Light)
173rd Airborne Brigade (Separate)
APO SAN FRANCISCO 96250

335TH AVIATION COMPANY (AIRMOBILE LIGHT)
APO 96250 SAN FRANCISCO, CALIFORNIA

1 January 1967

Subject: Monthly History for 335th Aviation Company (Airmobile Light)
1 December 1966 through 31 December 1966

To: Commanding Officer
335th Aviation Company (Airmobile Light)
173rd Airborne Brigade (Separate)
APO San Francisco 96250

I. ORGANIZATION AND DESIGNATION:

(A) Airlift Platoons: COWBOYS

> 20 UH-1D "Slicks"
> 1st Airlift Platoon -- Ramrods
> 2nd Airlift Platoon -- Mustangs

(B) Armed Helicopter Platoon: Falcons

> 8 UH-1B "Armed" Helicopters)

(C) 173rd Aviation Platoon: Caspers
2 UH-1D Command & Control, 1 UH-1B Command & Control
1 UH-1B "12 O'clock High" MAD System
6 OH-13s "Hot Stuff" Aero Scouts

(D) Maintenance 166th Transportation Detachment
1 UH-1B Horsethief

(E) 25th Medical Detachment

(F) 234th Signal Detachment

II. OPERATIONS:

a. December began with the COWBOYS, Falcons and Caspers providing the 173rd Airborne Brigade (Separate) with Army Aviation support on Operation Uniontown and Waco II. Three (3) UH-1Ds continued to support the Brigade's 4th Battalion 503rd Infantry operation out of Da Nang in the I Corps area.

Everyone feels that the month of December will be a slow flying month with very little enemy action. However, these optimistic predictions will by New Year's have proved very inaccurate.

b. At 0700 hours on 2 December, a message from the element at Da Nang reported that COWBOY 902, a UH-1D, supporting the 4/503rd sustained extensive combat damage when a booby trap was detonated against it. WO Ted H. Bingham and WO Basil D. Freeman were resupplying an element in a secure landing zone. As the ship came to a hover on a rough PSP helipad, a scrap of paper on the pad was swirled up through the air by the rotor turbulence. This paper was attached to a wire that pulled the pin on a fragmentation grenade. The resulting explosion damaged the skids, fuselage and rotor blades. The pilots, although badly shaken, got the ship on the ground safely. One passenger had shrapnel in his leg, and the gunner, Sp/4 Mark Seabury, had minor wounds in one leg. Investigation revealed that one of the Vietnamese boys playing near the landing zone had been trained and paid by the Viet Cong to set the booby trap.

This incident was a costly reminder that the Viet Cong are determined to destroy aircraft and are extremely crafty and skillful in their methods. The landing area had been checked by the infantry for mines and traps, but the metal in the PSP disguised the grenade from mine detectors and the human eye was deceived by the ingenious camouflage and innocent firing method.

At 0800, ten (10) UH-1Ds and a Light Fire Team lifted 260 ARVN and U.S. troops to Bien Hoa in termination of Operation Waco II. Additional support for the move was provided by ten (10) UH-1Ds and fire teams from the Warriors, an airmobile company based at Soc Trang as a member of the 13th "Delta" Aviation Battalion.

c. At 0800 on 3 December, an awards ceremony was held in the Company area. Major Johnson decorated 19 officers and 23 enlisted men (NOTE: Item V). Six (6) UH-1Ds and a Light Fire Team worked out of Saigon transporting a 59-man security force ready to react to any trouble connected with a speech being made in Saigon by South Vietnamese Premier Nguyen Cao Ky. No trouble was encountered.

Two (2) UH-1Ds returned to Bien Hoa after supporting the 4/503rd at Da Nang.

d. December 4th and 5th were spent in support of the 173rd Airborne Brigade on Operation Uniontown. On 5 December, five (5) UH-1Ds supported FF VII in the III Corps area.

e. At 1400 hours on 6 December, a Falcon Light Fire Team flew convoy cover as the 4/503rd moved from Bien Hoa to Position Lark (YS 173868) on Highway 15 South of Bien Hoa. This move opened the Brigade's Operation Canary/Duck, a road runner operation designed to secure the highway from Vung Tau to Bien Hoa for new combat units arriving in Vietnam.

f. At 0800 on 7 December, ten (10) UH-1Ds and a Light Fire Team moved 162 paratroopers into positions around Lark. At 1600 hours, three (3) UH-1Ds and a Light Fire Team infiltrated two (2) LRRP teams into landing zones in the Canary/Duck area. All other missions on 7 and 8 December were in support of Brigade Operations Uniontown and Canary/Duck.

g. On 9 December normal support was flown with 62 troops repositioned in the Canary/Duck area. One (1) UH-1D supported Field Forces VII.

h. On 10 December, 140 paratroopers were lifted in three (3) assaults in the Canary/Duck area. At 0800, Major Johnson decorated fourteen (14) members of the Company. 98 troops were repositioned in three (3) CA's on 11 December.

i. Ten (10) UH-1Ds and a fire team conducted four (4) assaults from Bear Cat to Position Lark, moving 269 paratroopers. On one landing at Lark COWBOY 674 lost power on approach, turned 90 degrees to the right, slammed into the road and struck his fast-moving main rotor blades into the spinning tail rotor of COWBOY 557. Damage was sustained by both ships, but a little green tape in the right places and a change of tail rotors made them safe for maintenance flights to Bien Hoa. At approximately 1500 hours, a Falcon Light Fire Team testing weapon systems over War Zone "D" received a call from an Air Force FAC who had spotted men in black pajamas fleeing into a wood line. The fire team scrambled to the spot and put rockets and machine-gun fire on the target with unknown results.

j. At 0930 on 13 December, UH-1D 738 was hit in the tail boom by small arms fire while involved in a repositioning of troops in the Canary/Duck area.

k. December 14th and 15th were normal support days. However, on the night of the 15th, two (2) UH-1Ds and a Light Fire Team conducted a night observation mission over the Rung Sat Special Zone to the Southwest of the Canary/Duck area. Sampans had been operating on the waterways at night, and with the aid of artillery and PUFF THE MAGIC DRAGON thorough surveillance of the area was conducted. The results were not spectacular, the VC would not venture from hiding with the blood thirsty Falcons prowling overhead.

l. At 1300 hours on 16 December, the Falcon 87 fire team was scrambled to support a platoon of E Troop, 17th Cavalry in contact with the Viet Cong at Coordinates YS 305863. The fire team put in rocket and machine-gun strikes. The Air Force fighters hit the area, then 12 O'clock High brought smoke on the VC. "Dust Off" 104 came in to medevac the wounded. Falcon 87 covered as 104 did an outstanding job with a hoist and jungle penetrater. Contact apparently broken, Falcon 87 went to Lark to refuel as "Dust Off" headed to the 93rd Evac hospital at Long Binh. TONTO II, an Air Force FAC, called that the Cavalry was in contact again and had more wounded. The Cavalry was now reinforced as six (6) UH-1Ds rushed 36 Horse Soldiers into an LZ 200 meters South of the embattled force. "Dust Off" 104 came back on station and pulled three more wounded to safety. 104 put on an outstanding exhibition of flying skill as he hovered at the top of the jungle hoisting the wounded to safety. His skill was a tribute to Army Aviation and an example of the immeasurable aid these pilots provide to the American fighting man. The 335th

Aviation Company (Airmobile Light) tips its hat to "Dust Off" 104 of the 254th Medical Detachment, (Helicopter Ambulance) Long Binh, Republic of Vietnam.

The harassed platoon of E/17th Cavalry finally was extracted from the battle as the COWBOYS pulled them from a rough jungle landing zone.

m. All missions on 17 and 18 December were in normal support of the Brigade on Operations Canary/Duck and Uniontown. Ten (10) UH-1Ds lifted 420 troops in seven (7) assaults.

n. Early on the morning of 19 December 1966, five (5) UH-1Ds from the Ramrods with a Falcon Light Fire Team began an Aero Rifle problem with E/17 Cavalry. The Ramrods worked in the open, wet marsh land East of Bear Cat along the Dong Nai River. Placing troops into positions and reinforcing when contact was made, several Viet Cong were killed or captured. COWBOY 849 landed to pick up a prisoner and an automatic weapon opened up from a concealed position. Sgt. Coley L. Andrews, 849's door gunner, mortally wounded by the fire was rushed to the 93rd Medical Evacuation Hospital where he died several hours later. The aircraft had extensive damage to the fuel system.

Casper 611, a UH-1D C&C ship, later in the day landed near the spot 849 had been hit. Surprise!! the Viet Cong shot him too, slight damage and no injuries.

333 troops of the 4/503rd were extracted in the afternoon by ten (10) COWBOYS with Falcon cover. Viet Cong were in the area, but there was negative fire. As the final extraction was made the infantry fired Claymore mines on four sides of the PZ toward the wood line.

o. On 20 December at 0800 hours, seven (7) UH-1Ds repositioned 143 paratroopers in support of Operation Uniontown.

p. At 0800 on 21 December 1966, the 335th Aviation Company (Airmobile Light) opened the Battle of Stump, a campaign that was to entail two (2) assaults and two (2) extractions from the same Landing Zone. The landing zone was an opening in dense jungle South of Bear Cat at YS 308857. The area was approximately the size of a football field with 200-foot trees surrounding it; inside this hole, trees of various heights were scattered about, and a thick carpet of underground covered fallen trees, stumps, ditches and pits. Running from North to South in the LZ was a belt of trees and brush 10 meters wide that cut the LZ in half. This LZ had been used by three COWBOYS in an emergency extraction of two (2) elements of E/17th Cavalry on 16 December 1966.

The COWBOYS using ten (10) ships in two (2) flights of five (5) ships each, stormed into "Stump" at 0800 hours with paratroopers of 4th Battalion, 503rd Infantry. Alpha flight cleared the LZ under the leadership of COWBOY 6, Major Ernest H. Johnson. Bravo Flight, led by COWBOY 5, Major Henry J. Victor, hit the LZ and the troops were leaping off from five to ten feet hovers. As Bravo flight lifted off, the radio cracked "Lead this is trail, we just lost our tail rotor and gear box." Horsethief roared in from his eagle eye position above the flight, and the battle was under way. The COWBOYS poured troops onto the LZ to secure the aircraft under repair, and the Viet Cong, coming alive around the LZ sprayed automatic weapon and small arms fire up through the jungle at the COWBOYS and Falcons. The gunships rolled in on firing passes as the "Slicks" marked with smoke and suppressed. The Air Force sent in fighters to strike the enemy positions, and artillery hammered the approach and departure paths from the landing zone. However, the VC proved to be extremely tenacious as each lift received fire. UH-1D 910, commanded by WO Rodney G. Heckerman, took seven (7) hits. One round exploded a smoke grenade in the gunner's compartment, burning Pfc. Thomas A. Sanchez's eyes and burning Mr. Heckerman on the arm.

At the first fueling stop, Major Victor with several hits and suffering violent in-flight vibrations shut down 701, jumped into 674 and continued to lead his flight. Finally, after eleven lifts there were 563 paratroopers in Stump looking for Charlie, and 799 had been repaired to the point of being safe to fly to Bien Hoa.

q. An OH-13s, Casper 419, flown by WO Bill Reynolds received two (2) hits in the vicinity of LZ Stump while marking enemy structures for ground troops. Mr. Reynolds made a precautionary landing at position Lark. A Chinook was called in, and 419 was sling loaded to Bien Hoa for repairs.

r. On 23 December 1966, the COWBOYS began the day with ten (10) UH-1Ds and two (2) Light Fire Teams lifting 772 troops of the 1/503 Infantry and the 199th Infantry Brigade into LZ's South of Bien Hoa. At noon the COWBOYS returned to the "Corral" for a briefing and change of some aircraft commanders.

At approximately 1300, ten (10) UH-1D and four (4) UH-1Bs departed Bien Hoa for Pick up zone Stump (YS 308857). The 4th Battalion, 503rd Infantry was operating in the area of Stump and was to be extracted to Bien Hoa prior to night fall in order to be out of enemy contact prior to the beginning of the Christmas Truce at 0700 24 December. The pick up zone was entered five (5) ships at a time, and because of the extremely high barriers on all four sides the PZ, limited fuel loads and five (5) troops per aircraft were scheduled. Two (2) extractions by each flight were accomplished before any fire was received. On the third approach Alpha Flight began receiving intense automatic weapons fire. Flight routes, approaches and departures, were altered every possible way to avoid the intense ground fire, by Major Johnson in COWBOY lead. Shutting down for fuel after eight (8) lifts from Stump, Captain Tucker and WO Danitz found a 50-caliber hole in one blade of the main rotor. Captain Wood and 1/Lt. Steed found fuel draining from a wound in the belly of their aircraft and a bullet hole in the fuselage behind Lt. Steed's head. Both crews made quick repairs and were ready for the next lift. On takeoff Major Cochran and WO Legg lost power and put their ship back on the refueling field. Sp/4 Paul White, their Crew chief, made a rapid survey and found the engine intake clogged with grass and dirt. After a rapid cleaning job, the ship was back in the flight.

The afternoon wore rapidly on as lift after lift brought the paratroopers out of the PZ. As the troops in the 4th Battalion area dwindled, the Viet Cong, in spite of TAC Air, Artillery and the armed helicopters, were closing into the very edges of all four sides of the PZ. Each lift into the PZ found the Falcons pouring tremendous suppressive fire under the COWBOYS, suppressing several .50 caliber positions. The Falcon pilots flew suicide runs on the positions to draw fire away from the vulnerable "slick" aircraft. Many of these passes were made with little or no ammunition, one pilot flying and one pilot firing pistols out the cockpit windows.

On the last refueling stop, Pfc. Newsome, accidentally was thrown from the Crew chief seat of his aircraft at 5 feet. He was evacuated to the 93rd Evac Hospital at Long Binh with a back injury. Lt. Stribling, now had only one door gunner and was told to fly his ship to Bien Hoa for repair -- it was not capable of further flight. Lt. Stribling, however, knowing that if he left the area the troop helicopters would be hurting for cover, explained the situation to his crew and then led his fire team back on station.

Rain was now falling in the area of the operation, and as the time passed it became obvious that the Viet Cong were doing their utmost to delay the extraction so that a small group of Americans would be trapped in the PZ overnight. The ground fire grew intense with each lift, the rain made visibility poor and the approaches and departures to the obstacle-studded pickup zone became a horrible nightmare. But the COWBOYS and Falcons, following Major Johnson to the last man, were not to be denied the accomplishment of their mission. With sixty (60) paratroopers remaining on "Stump," Major Johnson asked the COWBOYS if there was a ship that could not lift six (6) troops on the last lift. There was no reply to his question, the tense silence indicating that maximum effort was going to be expended on this last load, even though some of the weaker ships with only five (5) troops had been barely staggering over the 200-foot trees around the PZ on previous lifts. As the two flights came in very close together, the Viet Cong fire was returned with marked violence. The troops on the ground, now forming a tight perimeter around the small rise the COWBOYS were using as a pickup point and placing M-79 fire behind them, attested to the deadly dream that was being played out in the jungle PZ. The last COWBOY cleared the trees safely, and the two flights joined for the trip to Bien Hoa. Heavy rain showers blocked the path home, Major Johnson, talking to the COWBOYS all the way, led the flight through a light spot in the storm. Just out of the storm, Lt. Beasley and WO Heckerman reported an electrical fire aboard their ship. Making a precautionary landing in a Cavalry position South of Bien Hoa, the crew extinguished the fire and determined that the ship was safe to fly to Bien Hoa.

At final assessment, the COWBOYS had transported a total of 772 troops during the relatively quiet morning lifts and extracted approximately 700 troops from PZ Stump. The Falcons and COWBOYS with the Air Force's nine F-100's and two (2) F-5's and the artillery's 105mm and 8-inch weapons expended: twenty (20) 500 lb. bombs, twelve (12) 750 lb. bombs (napalm), six (6) CBU's, 100 Rockets, 4,400 rounds of 40mm ammunition, 420 2.75 rockets, 457 rounds of 105mm ammunition, and 8 rounds of 8-inch ammunition.

s. At 0700 hours on 24 December 1966, the 48-hour Christmas truce went into effect. Liaison, logistical and reconnaissance missions were flown on the 24th with no enemy initiated incidents reported.

Christmas Day was a quiet day as the truce continued with only light missions.

t. The Christmas Truce ended at 0600 on 26 December 1966. Six (6) UH-1Ds repositioned 131 paratroopers in support of Operation Canary/Duck. Three (3) UH-1Ds covered by a Light Fire Team lifted 30 troops in support of the 1/503rd conducting operations in the Brigade TAOR.

u. Normal support of the Brigade was flown during the day of 27 December.

v. At 1430 hours the Mustang element was supporting E/17th Cavalry in the open rice paddies West of Bear Cat. UH-1D 567 received sniper fire while unloading troops in a LZ, one round struck the engine combustion section. WO John Legg lifted off to approximately 10 feet but put his ship on the ground as the engine failed. Horsethief came in to begin recovery work and a sniper hit one of the maintenance personnel in the hand. A Chinook was called to the rescue, and the ship was lofted to Bien Hoa.

At 1815 hours a LRRP extraction was called for in an area to the Southwest of Bear Cat. Three (3) UH-1Ds covered by a Light Fire Team moved in to make a routine pick up. As a COWBOY set down to make the extraction, Viet Cong opened fire from positions around the pick up zone. The Falcon 81 fire team rolled in to suppress the enemy fire. As Falcon 82, flown by CWO Dan Norton and WO Gary Peyton, broke from his firing pass a heavy automatic weapon shot the engine away and destroyed the cyclic controls. CWO Dan Norton entered autorotation at treetop level and plunged into a small, rough clearing, whipping off a pair of rockets as he crashed through the trees. WO Peyton, on the flex-machine-guns, fired the weapons until the ship finally came to rest. All crew members were alive, but the crew chief, Sp/4 Luther, was severely burned and had to be helped away from the wreckage. SSGT Kilgore, the S-2 aerial observer aboard the ship, made two (2) trips into the burning wreckage to obtain weapons for defense. Viet Cong in the area were firing at the downed crew, but a UH-1D flown by WO Ralph Hicks and WO William Hanker, swooped down and snatched the downed crew from the hands of the Viet Cong.

The aircraft was destroyed and totally consumed by fire. The crew was flown to the 93rd Evac Hospital, all returned to duty except the crew chief who was sent to the United States.

w. On 29 December 1966, 300 troops of the 1/503 were lifted in five (5) CA's in support of Operation Uniontown. Ten (10) UH-1Ds and two (2) Light Fire Teams lifted 545 troops of the 2/503 in support of Canary/Duck and the Battle of LZ "Stump." The 2/503 was sweeping the area around LZ Stump.

x. On 30 December at 1630 hours an assault was made on a tax collection point South of Bear Cat. No resistance was encountered. After this lift an LRRP was extracted, and elements of E/17th were extracted from positions West of Bear Cat. Small units were left in place as ambush patrols.

y. The year of 1966 ended quietly as the 173rd Airborne Brigade (Separate) continued to operate South of Bear Cat. The COWBOYS, Falcons and Caspers continued to provide the 173rd with the finest Army Aviation support available in the world. Paratroopers of the Brigade continued to search the area around the notorious position Stump. Very little enemy contact was made; however, the Viet Cong continue to snipe, booby trap and ambush. Promise of the COWBOYS returning to LZ Stump was strong and every man expects to encounter heavy resistance.

III. MONTHLY STATISTICS:

	OH-13	UH-1B(A)	UH-1B	UH-1D	TOTAL
Sorties	577	1206	591	5956	8330
Hours	259	554	219	1650	2682
Pax					12031
Cargo (tons)					177
Aircraft Hits					16

IV. TRAINING:

Training during December was restricted by the extreme operational commitments. The month recorded an exceptional number of flying hours plus many hours not logged while LRRP, Eagle Flight and Fire Teams stood by for any missions the Brigade might have. Normal standardization and orientation was conducted for new pilots arriving in the unit.

V. AWARDS AND DECORATIONS:

a. At 0800 on 3 December 1966, Major Johnson decorated CWO Daniel S. Norton with a Distinguished Flying Cross for actions in March of 1966. Captain Paul W. Lovgren was presented a Bronze Star for meritorious service as Aircraft Commander of the Brigade Commanding General's UH-1D. Eighty-two (82) other officers and enlisted men were presented Basic Air Medals in the Company.

b. At 0800 on 10 December 1966, Major Johnson decorated fourteen (14) members of the Company. Included was an Air Medal with "V" device for heroism presented to 1/Lt. Willoughby S. Goin III for his bravery in flying a fully armed UH-1B out of a parking area, at night, when the Viet Cong had sabotaged another armed helicopter.

c. Colonel Robert C. Shaw, acting Brigade Commander, decorated sixty-four COWBOYS and Falcons for their action on 23 December 1966 at the Battle of "Stump." Crew chiefs and gunners were decorated with Army Commendation Medals with "V" devices. Major Johnson and Captain Wood are being recommended for the DFC as flight leaders on the mission. 1/Lt. Stribling is pending a Silver Star for exceptional gallantry demonstrated while flying a battle-damaged gunship through heavy enemy fire.

PROVIDING THE 173RD AIRBORNE BRIGADE (SEPARATE)
WITH THE MOST PROFESSIONAL AIRMOBILE SUPPORT
AVAILABLE ANYWHERE IN THE WORLD

173rd Pilot Awarded DFC For Heroic Flying

BIEN HOA, (173rd-IO) -- Warrant Officer Richard F. Landrum, A Co, 82nd Aviation Bn, shook hands with Brig. Gen. Ellis W. Williamson as the commander of the 173rd Airborne Brigade presented him with the Distinguished Flying Cross.

Landrum won his cross for his heroic flying during a 173rd operation in the "Iron Triangle." As commander of a rocket and machine gun armed helicopter, Landrum flew reconnaissance for the paratroopers.

Flying at treetop level, he exposed his helicopter to enemy groundfire. When fired at, he dived into action, attacking the position, scattering and killing many of the enemy.

As the paratroopers penetrated further into the jungle, enemy resistance grew and Landrum stayed on station, above the ground troops for more than eight hours, landing only to rearm and refuel. A medical evacuation helicopter, attempting to land and aid the wounded, drew so much enemy groundfire that a landing was impossible.

The pilot of the medevac chopper called for support, and Landrum raced to the scene. Circling the area, the 20-year-old Texan located the VC positions and charged in, pouring out a hail of bullets. As the VC abandoned the area, the ambulance chopper landed, carrying the wounded away without further harassment.

Holder of the Vietnamese Cross of Gallantry, more than 30 air medals, and a Presidential Unit Citation, Landrum has finished his one-year tour in Vietnam. First assigned to flying troop carrying helicopters when he arrived last year, Landrum soon transferred to jockeying the gunships on a voluntary basis. "You get to do a lot more flying in the gunships," he said, "and see a good deal more action."

The following article was originally printed in *The Army Reporter* newspaper on July 16, 1966. It was contributed to the Cowboy History by Billy R. Childs.

No Mission Too Tough
For 82nd 'Cowboys'

BIEN HOA, (173d ABN-IO) --Shortly after arrival in Vietnam in April 1965, A Company of the 82nd Aviation Battalion took their name from an equally tough group of football heroes from Dallas, Texas, and became the COWBOYS."

Formerly a subordinate unit of the "All American" 82nd company attached to the 173rd Airborne Division the COWBOYS are an airmobile light helicopter company attached to the 173rd Airborne Brigade. Their job is to carry troops into combat, bring them back and to provide all the supplies and combat aviation support while the troopers are engaged with the enemy.

The COWBOYS are a hard-flying, hard-fighting team, interdependent on themselves, with their goal being the successful accomplishment of each mission. Each Cowboy is essential to the team's success.

The quarterback for this team is the company commander, Maj. Larry J. Baughman. He calls the plays based on established procedures, the enemy situation, and his wealth of personal experience. The fullback is the armed helicopter platoon leader Maj. Abb W. Mangram. It's his job to smash through the enemy and clear the way for the ball carrying halfbacks. The halfbacks are the platoon leaders of the troop-carrying helicopters. These platoons are the work horses of the company and take the ball over the goal line after the other COWBOYS have done their jobs. The COWBOYS' center is the operation officer, Maj. Bruce Gibbons. He receives word of pending mission and passes it to the commander. The "play" is started and the operation is complete after the goal has been reached and the mission is accomplished.

The COWBOYS line consists of all the officers and warrant officers who fly the helicopters and the crew-chiefs and gunners that complete each crew. These are the men who bring the food, water, and ammunition to the ground soldiers, fly him to medical aid in minutes after he is wounded, act as his eyes above the ground, and get him out of tight spots when nothing but the helicopter can do the job.

The COWBOYS have a combat record and professional team would be proud to display. After one year and some 400 airmobile combat operations in Vietnam, A Company of the 82nd Aviation Battalion has transported 85,000 combat troops, carried 2500 tons of supplies, and has flown 22,500 hours on over 85,000 combat sorties.

This rough and ready "All American" unit stand always ready to do whatever task is asked of them. Dallas, as well as the 82nd Airborne Division, is justly proud of their representation in Vietnam, the "All American" COWBOYS.

COWBOYS

UNIT HISTORY

1 JANUARY 1967 -- 31 DECEMBER 1967

Dominic Fino

DEPARTMENT OF THE ARMY
HEADQUARTERS, 335TH ASSAULT HELICOPTER COMPANY
268th Combat Aviation Battalion
APO San Francisco 96316

FORWARD

The 335th Assault Helicopter Company (COWBOYS) began the new year, 1967, with a new parent organization. Released from the 173rd Airborne Brigade (Separate) and reassigned to the 145th Combat Aviation Battalion, 1st Aviation Brigade, the COWBOYS continued their familiar role of direct support for the 173rd Airborne Brigade (Separate), better known as the "Sky Soldiers."

Regardless of their parent organization, the 335th Assault Helicopter Company has become closely identified with the 173rd Airborne Brigade, and the "Sky Soldier's" many successful operations and major battles. This identification has been made by the "Sky Soldiers" as well as the COWBOYS themselves; the history of the COWBOYS closely parallels that of the 173rd Airborne Brigade (Separate).

During the year 1967, the highest decoration to be awarded to a COWBOY, was the award of the Silver Star to First Lieutenant Arville W. Stead, 054-18-581, Infantry, United States Army, for his heroic extraction of a Long Range Reconnaissance Patrol on the 3rd of March 1967.

On the 22nd of June 1967, fifty-seven COWBOYS were cited and decorated for heroic actions in support of A 2/503rd Infantry, 173rd Airborne Brigade near Dak To, Republic of Vietnam. Twelve of the fifty-seven were awarded Distinguished Flying Crosses.

In November 1967, COWBOYS were again in the thick of things, supporting the 173rd Airborne Brigade during Operation McArthur, which included the famous Battle of Dak To and the Assault of Hill 875. Thirty-two COWBOYS were recommended for Air Medals for heroism during this action and one COWBOY was recommended for the Distinguished Service Cross. The 335th Assault Helicopter Company was commended by General Westmoreland in a letter to the unit, and unofficial word was received that the COWBOYS were recommended for a Valorous Unit Award.

The following statistics concerning decorations awarded individuals indicates total numbers of the decorations received. A breakdown by name is included in each monthly history.

SILVER STAR	1	AIR MEDAL W/V	89
DISTINGUISHED FLYING CROSS	25	AIR MEDAL*	12
BRONZE STAR W/V	2	ARMY COMMENDATION W/V	17
BRONZE STAR	21	ARMY COMMENDATION	29
PURPLE HEART	13		

* Basic Air Medals only. Clusters were not counted.

January 1967 found the COWBOYS in their base camp located at Bien Hoa, Republic of Vietnam. In May, the Company was moved to Plieku to support the 173rd Brigade in combat operations there. Flight Operations shifted to Dak To early in June and the COWBOYS found themselves operating in three areas; a situation that would continue for the remainder of the calendar year and longer. A critical shortage of senior non-commissioned officers hampered many phases of the Company's operation, and incredibly adverse weather, working and living conditions became the lot of the COWBOYS. Despite these obstacles, aircraft availability and unit sprit remained outstanding.

90

In August, Flight Operations of the Company shifted from Dak To to Phu Hiep, near Tuy Hoa, on the South China Seacoast, and COWBOYS were billeted in buildings for the first time since the company's departure from Bien Hoa.

In September, the COWBOY element located at Plieku convoyed to Phu Hiep, and the company seethed with rumors of an impending return to Bien Hoa.

A lightning move in November, shifted the COWBOY Flight Operations to Kontum and COWBOYS commenced their heroic participation in Operation McArthur, which included the Battle of Dak To and the Assault on Hill 875.

Returning to Phu Hiep on the 5th of December, COWBOYS were confronted with the fact that the base camp they had built at Bien Hoa was to be cleared and turned over to the 101st Airborne Division.

The company became a hotbed of rumor once more. Rumor and counter rumor flew as from day to day evidence of a reassignment to another Battalion was refuted by the 145th Combat Aviation Battalion.

On the 31st of December 1967, Official word was received of the reassignment of the 335th Assault Helicopter Company to the 17th Combat Aviation Group and the 268th Combat Aviation Battalion located at Phu Hiep, Republic of Vietnam. Year's end found the COWBOYS at home.

During the year 1967 the following statistical evidence of operational ability and accomplishment accumulated:

TOTAL SORTIES		66,959
	UH-1B	8,468
	UH-1D	58,491
TOTAL COMBAT SORTIES		55,149
	UH-1B	7,302
	UH-1D	47,847
TOTAL FLYING HOURS		22,075
	UH-1B	4,456
	UH-1D	17,619
TOTAL PASSENGERS		86,045
TOTAL CARGO (TONS)		5,772

**HISTORY OF THE
335TH ASSAULT HELICOPTER COMPANY
145th Combat Aviation Battalion
APO San Francisco 96227**

1 January 1967 through 31 January 1967

Prepared by

CPT. GEORGE W. MURRAY

Approved by

**LEYBURN W. BROCKWELL JR.
LTC Infantry
Commanding**

335TH ASSAULT HELICOPTER COMPANY
145th Combat Aviation Battalion
APO San Francisco 96227

1 February 1967

Subject: Monthly History of the 335th Assault Helicopter Company for the period
1 January through 31 January 1967

To: Commanding Officer
335th Assault Helicopter Company
145th Combat Aviation Battalion
APO San Francisco 96227

NOTE: The 335th Aviation Company (Airmobile Light), 173rd Airborne Brigade (Separate) became the 335th Assault Helicopter Company, 145th Combat Aviation Battalion in compliance with USARV Order #102 on 15 January 1967.

I. ORGANIZATION AND DESIGNATION:

A.   Flight Platoons (2) -- COWBOYS

    (1)   First Airlift Platoon -- Ramrods
    Platoon Commander: Major Wayne Davis
    Aircraft: 10 UH-1D "Slicks" -- Troop Carriers.

    (2)   Second Airlift Platoon -- Mustangs
    Platoon Commander: Captain John L. Wood
    Aircraft: 10 UH-1D "Slicks" -- Troop Carriers.

    (3)   Armed Helicopter Platoon -- Falcons
    Platoon Commander: Major Vance Gammons
    Aircraft: 8 UH-1B "Guns" -- Armed Escort.

B.   173rd Airborne Brigade (Separate) Aviation Platoon - Caspers
Platoon Commander: Captain Thomas J. Terry
Aircraft: 3 UH-1   Command & Control
        1 UH-1B Mortar Aerial Delivery System -- 12 O'clock high
        6 OH-13s (A) Aero Scouts - Hot Stuff.

C.   166th Transportation Detachment.
(1) Commander: Captain Paul Lovgren.
(2) 1 UH-1B recovery helicopter -- Horsethief.

D.   25th Medical Detachment.

E.   234th Signal Detachment.

II. OPERATIONS:

a. The New year came in with a bang as the COWBOYS, on normal support missions for the 173rd Airborne Brigade (Separate), had two (2) ships in position Stump when the Viet Cong decided to lob a few mortar rounds into the area. Both ships scrambled out of the LZ in a hurry, and only one gunner received a slight leg wound.

b. 2 January found continued support being provided to the paratroopers engaged in Operation Uniontown in the Brigade TAOR and Operation Canary/Duck along Highway 15 from Bien Hoa to Vung Tau.

c. On 3 January 1967, the battle crazy COWBOYS crashed back into PZ Stump to extract the 2/503rd Infantry who had probably decided we were crazy, for they could find very little sign of the Viet Cong who had shot at us a few days before. Surprise!! The Viet Cong opened up on the COWBOYS with automatic weapons. Two (2) flights of six (6) UH-1Ds each extracted 542 troops under constant fire. The six (6) UH-1B gunships from the Falcons got a wild work-out as they attempted to suppress the Viet Cong. Only one COWBOY, 561, took hits and that caused only minuet damage.

d. On 4 January 1967, the 1st Battalion, 503rd Infantry, 173rd Airborne Brigade (Separate) kicked-off Niagara Falls in the Phu Loi area. This area is highly classified and promises plenty of action.

e. The morning of 5 January found four (4) CA's assaulting the 35th Ranger Battalion (ARVN) into landing zones South of Ben Cat, RVN. Speculation has a big push aimed at the notorious Iron Triangle.

f. Operation Niagara Falls became Operation Cedar Falls on 6 January as the American and ARVN units aimed a killing blow at the Viet Cong bastion used to terrorize III Corps and the Saigon area. The mighty Iron Triangle was the target of the 173rd Airborne Brigade (Separate), 1st Infantry Division, 25th Infantry Division, 199th Light Infantry Brigade, 11th Armored Cavalry Regiment and the 35th ARVN Ranger Battalion.

Two (2) OH-13s helicopters from Casper on a Scout Mission on the Southeast side of the Triangle engaged several Viet Cong in open rice fields. Aircraft #426 took a hit in the fuel tank and the aerial observer aboard from E/17th Cavalry had four machine-gun rounds laced up the side of his right ankle.

g. On 7 January 1967 normal mission support was provided to the paratroopers. At 1530 Hot Stuff lead called two-minute final for the corral. Trail was limping home with a hot engine. The smell of smoke got things up tight over the old French mine fields one minute out of the corral. Daring not abandon ship in a mine field, WO Bill Reynolds screamed into the Unit maintenance pad, unsaddled and shut down his potential fire bomb. There was a lot of scrambling before the situation was under control, and the broken fan belt was discovered.

h. 8 January began early as the COWBOYS and Falcons joined six (6) other airmobile companies on the airfield at Dau Tieng for an assault. Lifting a Battalion of the "Big Red One," the seventy (70) ship troop armada was so frightening that Charlie fired not a shot as allied elements continued to drive forward into the Iron Triangle.

At 1230 the Company moved over to support the paratroopers of the 173rd Airborne Brigade (separate) in seven (7) lifts in the Cedar Falls Operation Area.

i. At dawn on the morning of 9 January, ten (10) UH-1Ds and a Light Fire Team arrived at Lai Kai to participate in a large airmobile operation. Elements of the 1st Division and the 173rd Airborne were moved into blocking positions North of the Iron Triangle. Armor and engineer units were moving in areas around the Triangle preparing to wreck Viet Cong installations. The allied plan appears to be centered around crushing all cover and concealment, storage areas and tunnel systems available in the Triangle.

j. Missions in normal support of the 173rd included resupply, C&C and courier service on 10 January 1967.

k. On 11 January from 0900 to 1100 eight (8) UH-1Ds and a Light Fire Team supported the 35th ARVN Ranger Battalion, moving 362 troops into the operation area. No enemy contact was involved.

l. The bright, sunny morning of 12 January found the COWBOYS, Falcons and Caspers working with E/17th Cavalry in Eagle Flights in the rice paddy area on the Southwest edge of the Iron Triangle. The Hot Stuff team, two (2) OH-13s were down on the tree tops hunting Viet Cong. Using their skid mounted 7.62 machine-guns and hand-held M-79 grenade launchers the team destroyed fifteen (15) structures, damaged four (4) structures, sunk two (2) sampans, zapped two (2) VC and wounded three (3) bad guys. Finding things hot, as aircraft #427 took a light hit in the stabilizer bar, the Hot Stuff team shared their targets with the Falcons who came screaming on target like their blood thirsty namesakes. Spraying machine-gun and rocket fire over the area the armed Hueys ripped apart four (4) enemy structures. Close on the heels of the hunters, the UH-1D "Slicks" assaulted crack Horse Soldiers of E/17 Cavalry into the target areas to police up stray personnel and burn Viet Cong structures and supplies.

m. 13 January 1967 brought more Eagle Flights into the Viet Cong infested rice paddies. As two (2) UH-1Ds screamed into an open rice paddy to pick up fourteen (14) troops, COWBOY 570 decided to find out what effect a fast spinning tail rotor had on standing water. Surprise! The tail rotor slowed down, the aircraft did a 180 degree right turn and smacked into the mud. The main rotor clipped the tail rotor drive shaft in half, came on around and wiped out the top of the right cockpit and slapped WO R. Sims on top of his head. The crew came out safe with WO Sims a bit dazed. The second COWBOY told the Cavalry platoon leader to secure the wreckage and rushed the crew to medical attention. The wreck was extracted by a CH-47 later in the day.

Casper 911 on approach to a secure area received a minuet hit. Nothing is "secure" when the Viet Cong are alive. No injuries, thus the old lesson is emphasized free of charge.

n. 14 January 1967 came and went with normal support being provided to the 173rd Airborne Brigade as the paratroopers aggressively rip into the Viet Cong stronghold in the Iron Triangle. Missions for the day consist of 2 C&C, 9 C 7 L, 1 FAD, 1 Light Fire Team, 4 resupply and 1 Hot Stuff mission. Two VC die, 2 enemy sampans are demolished and 13 structures are flattened as the COWBOYS, Falcons and Caspers support the infantry in their favorite way -- Killing VC.

o. Eagle Flights are the program for 15 January. The Company is enjoying this work as we can see the results of our support as the Viet Cong are driven from hiding and captured or killed. Two (2) huts and a bridge were destroyed and the always blood thirsty Falcons become much more accurate as they are presented moving targets in the form of running guerrillas.

By General Order No. 102, Headquarters USARV, the 335th Aviation Company is assigned to the 145th Combat Aviation Battalion as of 15 January 1967. We did not hear about this until several days later.

p. On 16 January 1967, the deadly Eagle Flights hit the open, wet rice fields at the Southwest corner of the Triangle again. Two (2) VC are killed by an observer aboard one of the OH-13 Hot Stuff ships. Five (5) structures are destroyed with one secondary explosion.

q. Operation Cedar Falls in the Iron Triangle continues. Normal resupply and C&C missions together with the Eagle Flights continue to keep the COWBOYS busy.

r. Normal support continues in the Iron Triangle on the 18th. COWBOY 736 on a routine mission to Vung Tau experienced a partial engine failure on takeoff to the South. Captains' Lonnie Beasley and Bill Jones whipped their crippled ship back toward dry land and set it down just off the main runway. There were no injuries and a CH-47 brought the ship to the Corral for an engine change.

s. Normal support of Cedar Falls continued. Today, 19 January, the orders assigning us to the 145th Finally arrive. It is with mixed emotions that the Company reads these orders. We have been highly independent as we supported the gung-ho paratroopers of the 173rd Airborne Brigade (Separate). We have learned to work with these people, giving them the maximum support we were capable of giving. We had come to recognize their problems, and there isn't a COWBOY who wouldn't fly through a Viet Cong Division to help a paratrooper. However, the 145th Combat Aviation Battalion is a crack aviation unit, and we are honored to be considered qualified for membership in so excellent an outfit. Without a doubt, our toughest problem will be the loss of our independence that we prize so highly.

t. On 20 January 1967, our new Commander, Lieutenant Colonel Leyburn W. Brockwell, Jr., takes actual control of the Company. The Company staff sections receive their initial briefing from the 145th staff in the morning and by afternoon we are convinced that the 145th shuffles paper rather than flies.

u. On 21 January 1967, five (5) UH-1Ds with a Light Fire Team made twelve (12) eagle flight CA's moving 148 troops of E/17 Cavalry in the Southwest of the Iron Triangle. Sixty-six (66) of these troops were removed later in the day and the remainder conducted a night ambush.

At 1130 hours, COWBOY 610, flown by Captain William O. Jones and 1/Lt. A. W. Steed, approached the Bien Hoa base camp of the 173rd Airborne Brigade (Separate) to make a passenger drop. At short final to a small helipad at the 2nd Battalion perimeter, a command detonated Claymore exploded within ten yards of the ships left side. Thirty to forty deadly scraps of steel ripped into the aircraft, wounding both pilots, one crew member, and one passenger. The pilots, realizing that the passenger was bleeding profusely from a head wound, flew the badly damaged helicopter to the pad at 3rd Surgical Hospital. All wounded recovered in time to wear their Purple Hearts.

v. 22 January was spent in normal resupply support of the paratroopers. A small eagle flight conducted moving 24 Cavalrymen.

At 1430 hours a brief ceremony was held in the Company area officially marking the 335th membership in the 145th Combat Aviation Battalion.

w. Resupply and administrative air support was provided to the 173rd Airborne on 23 January.

x. Nine (9) "Slicks" a Light Fire Team and a C&C supported a Battalion of the 199th Light Infantry Brigade in operations in the Nha Be area on 24 January, 425 troops were moved in 140 sorties. The Falcons were turned loose to support a unit in contact. They shot up everything in sight, giving the infantry unit superb support.

At approximately 1430, COWBOY 674 in trail formation (Chalk #7) on approach to a road with a load of troops got stacked in the formation by a steep approach. Losing RPM on termination, control of the aircraft was lost. The ship bounced off the road and rolled on its side. No injuries; the ship was evacuated to Saigon.

y. 25 January was spent in III Corps General Support. Six (6) UH-1Ds flew resupply for the 1st Infantry Division. Five (5) UH-1Ds flew General Support for the 173rd Airborne Brigade. Two (2) Light Fire Teams supported the 173rd Airborne Brigade.

z. General support of the 9th Division was flown on 26 January.

aa. On 27 January, the 25th Infantry Division received General Support from the COWBOYS.

bb. 28 January 1967: Resupply and General Support was provided to the 25th Infantry Division.

cc. Ten (10) UH-1Ds and a Light Fire Team worked for the 25th Division and the 196th Light Infantry Brigade on 29 January.

dd. On 30 January, WO Roger Aveni and 1/Lt. Tom Anderson, supporting the 173rd Airborne Recon Patrols, experienced an engine failure at 100 feet in UH-1D 609. An outstanding autorotation was performed with little aircraft damage.

LRRP teams were introduced and extracted. One American was wounded and three (3) VC Killed.

ee. The month of January closed as the COWBOYS supported the 173rd Airborne Brigade and the 9th Infantry Division with resupply and long range patrol aircraft.

III. MONTHLY STATISTICS:

	UH-1B	UH-1D	TOTAL
TOTAL SORTIES	1983	8926	11410
COMBAT SORTIES	1778	8339	10578
HOURS	628	1722	2350
PAX			17299
CARGO (TONS)			596

IV. TRAINING:

Normal standardization and new pilot training was conducted while the Company was heavily committed to support missions.

V. AWARDS RECEIVED DURING THE MONTH OF JANUARY 1967

CPT. REEVES	DFC
WO1 PEYTON	AM "V"
CPT. ALBRECHT	AM "V"
WO1 AVEN	AM "V"
WO1 DRAKE	AM "V"
WO1 HECKERMAN	AM "V"
WO1 TEMEYER	AM "V"
CPT. GAMMONS	AM "V"
CPT. KUHBLANK	AM "V"
CPT. TUCKER	AM "V"
WO1 VILLAREAL	AM "V"
MAJ. DAVIS	AM "V"
WO1 GREGG	AM "V"
WO1 LEGG	AM "V"
CPT. FINEGAN	AM "V"
WO1 HAMVAI	AM "V"
1 Lt. GOIN	AM "V"
CPT. VANCE	AM "V"
CWO NORTON	AM "V"
CPT. JONES	AM "V"
1 Lt. STEED	AM "V"
WO1 DANITZ	AM "V"
WO1 FREEMAN	AM "V"
CPT. HOZA	AM "V"
WO1 SANDERS	AM "V"
CPT. ALBRECHT	AM "V"
CPT. MOSS	AM "V"
SP5 SHOOK	AM "V"
SP4 CURTIS	AM "V"
CPT. ZABARSKY	AM "V"

CWO NORTON	BS
SSG SELLERS	BS
SP5 ZACK	BAM
SP5 COOPER	BAM
SP5 PENNINGTON	BAM
SP4 EASTMAN	BAM
PFC MCDONALD	BAM
CWO NORTON	PH
WO1 PEYTON	PH
WO1 CROTEAU	PH
SP4 SNYDER	PH
SP5 WATERS	GCM

HISTORY OF THE
335TH ASSAULT HELICOPTER COMPANY
145th Combat Aviation Battalion
APO San Francisco 96227

1 February 1967 through 28 February 1967

Prepared by

CPT. BILLY D. TUCKER

Approved by

LEYBURN W. BROCKWELL JR.
LTC Infantry
Commanding

Dominic Fino

335TH ASSAULT HELICOPTER COMPANY
145th Combat Aviation Battalion
APO San Francisco 96227

1 March 1967

Subject: Monthly History of the 335th Assault Helicopter Company for the period
1 February through 28 February 1967

To: Commanding Officer
335th Assault Helicopter Company
145th Combat Aviation Battalion
APO San Francisco 96227

I. ORGANIZATION AND DESIGNATION:

A. Flight Platoons (2) -- COWBOYS

   (1) First Airlift Platoon -- Ramrods
        Platoon Commander: Major Wayne Davis
        Aircraft: 10 UH-1D "Slicks" -- Troop Carriers.

   (2) Second Airlift Platoon -- Mustangs
        Platoon Commander: Major Daniel Stefanowich
        Aircraft: 10 UH-1D "Slicks" -- Troop Carriers.

   (3) Armed Helicopter Platoon -- Falcons
        Platoon Commander: Major Vance Gammons
        Aircraft: 8 UH-1B "Guns" -- Armed Escort.

B. 173rd Airborne Brigade (Separate) Aviation Platoon - Caspers
    Platoon Commander: Captain Thomas J. Terry
        Aircraft: 3 UH-1   Command & Control
                   1 UH-1B Mortar Aerial Delivery System -- 12 O'clock high
                   6 OH-13s (A) Aero Scouts - Hot Stuff.

C. 166th Transportation Detachment.
    (1) Commander: Major Robert A. Lawson
    (2) 1 UH-1B recovery helicopter -- Horsethief.

D. 25th Medical Detachment.

E. 234th Signal Detachment.

II. OPERATIONS:

a. February's dawn again found the COWBOYS supporting the "Sky Soldiers" of the 173rd Airborne Brigade (Separate), starting a new operation "Big Spring" in War Zone "D," North of Bien Hoa. "D" Zone is expected to be hot and this operation was to show all expectations lived up to. COWBOYS on the move lifted 753 airborne troops and legs of the 9th Infantry Division to battle from the Snake Pit, Bear Cat and Xom Cat. Ten (10) LZ's were used with fire received in many of them. Resupply missions began when Combat Assaults were completed. One (1) UH-1D aircraft was hit six (6) times making a Med Evac. No injuries were received and the mission was completed with a shook pilot.

b. 2 February 1967 found continued support being provided to the Paratroopers in "D" Zone. A total of 239 sorties of "Beans and Bullets" missions moved 39 tons of cargo and 296 troops to forward areas from the Corral and BSOC. It was a relatively quiet day as far as fire being received. However, the COWBOYS saw the birth of a new problem, finding flight routes to forward areas through the vast maze of artillery.

c. On 3 February the COWBOYS introduced LRRP's of E/17 Cav. and again found it necessary to extract them under fire. Captain Conger and Captain Moss, both exposing their aircraft to enemy fire, did excellent jobs of saving the Brown Beret boys. Both were suggested for awards. No hits received but anxious moments were passed. Also, UH-1Ds flew 116 resupply sorties carrying 86 troops and 31 tons of cargo. Fire again was received sporadically during the day.

d. Direct support of the 173rd Airborne was again on 4 February the mission of the day for COWBOYS. Ten (10) "Slicks" and two (2) Light Fire Teams were committed to lift 169 troops and six tons of cargo in a Combat Assault. Other missions were normal if anything can be considered normal in Vietnam. COWBOYS received fire again and returned it again as usual -- no hits.

e. On 5 February the days' activities were started with a Combat Assault from position "Chevy" occupied by the 173rd Airborne Brigade, to forward areas in "D" Zone. Eight (8) "Slicks" were involved moving 165 troops and eight (8) tons of cargo. The remainder of the day was devoted to moving chow to the troopers, approximately 31 tons of it this day. The COWBOYS were called out again after dark to resupply the 9th Division. We also were called on for medical evacuation and cover of medical evacuation, indicating the upswing in shooting on this operation.

f. 6 February Long Range Reconnaissance Patrols were again installed in the "D" Zone jungle by COWBOYS. They didn't stay long before they fell into bad problems. They got out again with both sides shooting.

g. On 7 February COWBOYS conducted five (5) ship lift with a Light Fire Team, but most of the flying of the day could be considered Command and Logistical missions. Captain Beasley went to the free fire area to test the guns on 868 and got shot at for his troubles. He received one hit, but the Falcons took care of him--very little damage and no injuries. The Company promoted thirteen brand new SP/4's.

h. Platoon missions were normal for the day. Six (6) "Slicks" carried 44 tons of cargo and 283 passengers. The Long Range Reconnaissance Patrols of the 173rd Airborne also had normal missions. Two (2) teams were introduced in "D" Zone. Both lasted less than a day before the going became too hot. The Falcons got the target of every gunship pilot's desires, trucks in the open. COWBOY 879 reported receiving fire from them and called the Falcons who came in a hurry and wiped them out. COWBOY 879 got a hit.

i. 10 February: Long Range Reconnaissance Patrols and resupply again today. General support for the 173rd. No action.

j. 11 February: The COWBOYS get a long-needed rest both to the pilots and to the equipment. Only two (2) UH-1Ds were committed and they were loaned to the 68th Aviation Company. Only maintenance flights were flown by the unit.

k. 11 February: Apparently, we are growing up in the world. We got a new name today -- 335th Assault Helicopter Company of the 145th Combat Aviation Battalion. The mission remained the same and was demonstrated. Long Range Reconnaissance Patrols, Combat Assault, and resupply missions all in one day. Aircraft 738, on loan to the 71st Assault Helicopter Company was laced down by Charlie. It was hit nine (9) times and down it went. A crew chief was wounded, and the aircraft went to Saigon via good nature.

l. The days' activities on 13 February 1967 were considered normal most of the day with direct support missions for the 173rd Airborne Brigade. Resupply aircraft carried 41 tons of food and ammunition to troopers in the field. As luck would have it LRRP's again changed the day from normal to one of those better forgotten. It all started when Captain Wecas had an engine failure on short final to a confined area that he was attempting to land in to introduce the LRRP team. He got the aircraft down in a very fine manner hitting only a few stumps. The trouble came when a security force had to be lifted into the area. Probably no country has ever seen such a dark night as that. The COWBOYS proved that they can respond in a fine manner to any situation though. They completed the job with very little damage to the other aircraft. They were very happy to return to the Corral, nevertheless. We have a new platoon leader today, Major Stefanowich took the reins of the Mustangs.

m. The COWBOYS worked hard again today for the "Sky Soldiers" of the 173rd Airborne Brigade. Most of the support was in the form of small Combat Assaults and resupply. A force of approximately 20 VC was spotted just outside the Brigade Perimeter and the Falcons were called on to search for them. When they got back from the fruitless chase they blamed the whole incident on a nervous guard.

n. On 15 February 1967 the COWBOYS lifted the 4th Bn 39th Infantry 9th Division from their field position above Xom Cat to the Snake Pit in six (6) lifts. Almost 350 troops were moved. Operation Big Springs was actually a training exercise for elements of the 9th Inf. Div. Rumor has it that they will be going to the Delta to make a few changes there. The day was quite with no reports of fire.

o. 16 February 1967: More troops of the 9th Infantry were extracted today. A total of 728 troops were moved with only light fire being received. The Falcons ran into some real fun at Duc Hoa. A Light Fire Team flying support for the 199th Infantry Brigade opened up on a VC in the open. They got credit for eight (8) enemy KIA's. At times they reported that they were flying cover for TAC Jets as they made their runs. At 1945 the COWBOYS received alert for a possible lift after dark, and at 2000 received confirmation. At 2035 ten (10) "Slicks," one (1) Light Fire Team, and one (1) C&C ship were off to support ARVN units in the Delta. A Battalion of 338 troops were lifted from Boa Tri to Duc Hoa. Fire was received at both places and returned. There were some bad feelings when the COWBOYS accidentally shot up Duc Hoa, even if they were shooting at us. We had three (3) ships hit.

p. On 17 February 1967 the COWBOYS realized that the tide was slowly turning from the direct support role to General Support role toward the 173rd Airborne. COWBOYS flew all day but this time in support of the 199th Light Infantry Brigade.

q. Slicks moved 486 ARVN's and members of the 25th Inf. Div. on 18 February 1967. The day was patie time for tired COWBOYS. Another welcome rest in the form of a maintenance stand down grounded the Company.

r. On 19, 20 and 21 February 1967 the 335th provided helicopter support again for the Inf. Division at Cu Chi. Only a little fire was received.

s. On 22 February 1967 one of the biggest if not the biggest operations of the Vietnam conflict started. Operation Junction City began with a flair. COWBOYS flew over eleven hours without let up lifting the 173rd Airborne to attack from Quan Loi to the Cambodian border Northeast of Tay Ninh. Strangely enough the day was quite as fire goes. Only after the day's exercise was over and the flight was enroute home did we get any fire. The 173rd Airborne Brigade also made the first combat jump of the war. The Falcons attacked with unknown results, but it became very quiet down there. Sp/5 Meehan was wounded in the leg when his M-60 exploded and was submitted for a Purple Heart. Major Van Wert flew his new "Horsethief" today for the first time. Old Horsethief ran into dust and beat herself to death, Rest in Peace. Captain Conger also bounced one in at Quan Loi due to dust problems.

t. On 23 February 1967, the 335th flew General Support again with the 173rd Airborne. The shooting started early on this day. Aircraft 567 received one hit, but the COWBOYS completed all missions including resupply missions that moved 110 troops and 10 tons of cargo. The Falcons fired over 7000 rounds of 7.62 ammo.

u. Normal activities were conducted on 24 and 25 February 1967. Again, the COWBOYS supported the 173rd Airborne Brigade with resupply and small troop lifts.

v. On 26 February 1967 the 335th Assault Helicopter Company worked with the "Big Red One." Two (2) Combat Assaults moved 112 soldiers of the 1st Infantry Division to a blocking position Northwest of Phu Chong to stop the VC movement across the Saigon River from the Iron Triangle. Another LRRP team was introduced near the Cambodian Border. Falcon 978 received a single hit when light small arms fire was received. Most of the COWBOYS spent the better part of the day in support of the 173rd Airborne.

w. Operation Junction City continues on 27 February 1967. The COWBOYS flew resupply and troop lifts for the 1st Infantry Division and the 173rd Airborne Brigade. Falcons continue to standby for quick reaction taking on the enemy whenever and wherever the opportunity arises.

x. Some days are good days, a few are bad. On 28 February 1967 the COWBOYS ended a long hard month with a very bad day. COWBOYS in support of the 1st Infantry Division were called on to make an emergency assault into an LZ Northeast of Soui Da late in the afternoon. The first lift in was met with a hail of enemy fire that cost the COWBOYS several hits in six (6) different aircraft. Warrant Officer Jackson, the pilot of 736, received a bullet hit in the leg that ended the war for him. He was evacuated to Tay Ninh and will eventually go home. If it was bad for the COWBOYS, it was worse for the "Big Red One." Of the 172 troop's air lifted into the heat of battle 24 were killed and 22 wounded. They cleaned the VC's clock though, killing 142 by body count in just a few hours. Most of the pilots say that the count would have been higher if only the Falcons had been there.

III. MONTHLY STATISTICS:

a. Total sorties by type aircraft for combat missions:

	ARMED HELO	COMBAT ASSAULT	RE-SUPPLY	CMD & CNT	RECON	MED EVAC	MIS	TOTAL
UH-1B	859				12		33	904
UH-1D		2714	4020	305	16	13	993	8065
TOTAL	859	2714	4020	305	28	13	1026	8969

b. Monthly Summary of Performance:

	UH-1B	UH-1D	TOTAL
TOTAL SORTIES	1005	8639	9644
COMBAT SORTIES	904	8061	8965
HOURS	503	1845	2348
PASSENGERS			10341
CARGO (TONS)			753

c.	Troop Lifts:		
	Combat Assault	92	
	Extraction's	9	
	Repositioning	59	
d.	Armed Helicopter Missions	141	
e.	Average Aircraft Hours	87.0	
	UH-1B	71.9	
	UH-1D	92.3	
f.	Average Aviator Hours	89.6	
	High Aviator	WO John D. Legg	155.9
	Low Aviator	Cpt Willoughby S. Goin	5.9
g.	Ammunition Expenditures	7.62	340,000
		2.75in	857
		40mm	4,890
h.	Med Evacs Carried	6	
i.	VC KBA	3	
j.	Total Aircraft Hit	UH-1D	10
		UH-1B	4
k.	U.S. Wounded	3	
l.	Total Accidents	1	
m.	Forced to Land, but Recovered	1	

IV. AWARDS RECEIVED DURING THE MONTH OF FEBRUARY 1967

SSG BERGMAN	BAM
PFC CARTER	BAM
PFC CORMIER	BAM
WO1 JACKSON	BAM
SP4 KOOP	BAM
SP4 BLODGETT	BAM
WO1 HOLLINGSWORTH	BAM
SP5 MENCER	BAM
SP5 WARREN	BAM
WO1 MAGONIGAL	ACM
SP5 PETE	ACM
SP4 EPSTEIN	PH
PFC TRAVIS	PH
PFC LAWLER	PH

HISTORY OF THE
335TH ASSAULT HELICOPTER COMPANY
145th Combat Aviation Battalion
APO San Francisco 96227

1 March 1967 through 31 March 1967

Prepared by

1 Lt. PAUL C. HOWELL

Approved by

LEYBURN W. BROCKWELL JR.
LTC Infantry
Commanding

335TH ASSAULT HELICOPTER COMPANY
145th Combat Aviation Battalion
APO San Francisco 96227

1 April 1967

Subject: Monthly History of the 335th Assault Helicopter Company for the period
1 March through 31 March 1967

To: Commanding Officer
335th Assault Helicopter Company
145th Combat Aviation Battalion
APO San Francisco 96227

I. ORGANIZATION AND DESIGNATION:

A. Flight Platoons (2) -- COWBOYS

(1) First Airlift Platoon -- Ramrods
Platoon Commander: Captain Ronald Wecas
Aircraft: 10 UH-1D "Slicks" -- Troop Carriers.

(2) Second Airlift Platoon -- Mustangs
Platoon Commander: Major Daniel Stefanowich
Aircraft: 10 UH-1D "Slicks" -- Troop Carriers.

(3) Armed Helicopter Platoon -- Falcons
Platoon Commander: Major Vance Gammons
Aircraft: 8 UH-1B "Guns" -- Armed Escort.

B. 173rd Airborne Brigade (Separate) Aviation Platoon - Caspers
Platoon Commander: Captain Thomas J. Terry
Aircraft: 3 UH-1   Command & Control
1 UH-1B Mortar Aerial Delivery System -- 12 O'clock high
6 OH-13s (A) Aero Scouts - Hot Stuff.

C. 166th Transportation Detachment.
(1) Commander: Major Robert A. Lawson
(2) 1 UH-1B recovery helicopter -- Horsethief.

D. 25th Medical Detachment.

E. 234th Signal Detachment.

II. OPERATIONS:

a. March began with a little excitement for some of the COWBOYS, shortly after takeoff WO's Legg and Andrews experienced hydraulics failure and made a successful landing at the corral. The COWBOYS again found themselves supporting the "Sky Soldiers" of the 173rd Airborne Brigade (Separate) and also the 1st Infantry Division. They flew a total of 215 sorties, carrying 42 tons of cargo, 235 troops, and extracting 7 tons of captured rice.

b. 2 March 1967 found continued support being provided to the paratroopers in "C" Zone. Two (2) CA's were conducted carrying 97 troops into an LZ with no enemy resistance. A total of 254 sorties, 35 tons of cargo and 325 passengers were carried for resupply of the 173rd and 1st Division. The LRRP's of E/17 Cav. again made the day a little interesting for the COWBOYS. They had to be extracted under small arms fire. Eight (8) VC were killed and one was wounded and captured.

c. 3 March was a rather quiet day for the COWBOYS. Two (2) LRRP teams were introduced and later extracted. UH-1Ds flew 105 sorties carrying 15 tons of cargo and 192 passengers.

d. 4 March found the COWBOYS supporting the 173rd Airborne Brigade (Separate) in seven (7) CA's. They lifted 120 troops in an LZ and extracting 76 troops from another LZ. 111 Sorties were conducted carrying 18 tons of cargo and 191 passengers. Fire was received during the day with one hit being taken, no injuries and only slight damage.

e. 5 March the COWBOYS flew resupply and General Support for the 173rd and 1st Div. 206 Sorties were flown carrying 345 passengers and 29 tons of cargo. Fire again was received -- no hits.

f. 6 March 1967 began by the COWBOYS supporting the 173rd in eleven (11) CA's carrying 579 troops. Moderate automatic weapons and small arms fire was received. Three (3) gunships took hits and PFC Dubin, gunner on a slick, received a bullet wound in the leg and was evacuated to Tay Ninh. The rest of the day was rather calm flying 109 Sorties and carrying 114 troops and 18 tons of cargo.

g. Three (3) CA's were flown in support of the 1st Div. from Phu Loi, on 7 March. 57 troops were carried. 315 troops and 37 tons of cargo were carried for the 173rd Airborne Brigade and the 1st Div. in 218 Sorties. One (1) UH-1D received one hit of automatic weapons fire while on a resupply mission. No injuries received and only slight damage to the aircraft.

h. 8 March found the COWBOYS in resupply and General Support missions for the 173rd and 1st Div.

i. 9 March began seeing the COWBOYS doing what they like to do most. Four (4) CA's were flown in support of the 1st Div. five (5) CA's were for repositioning were flown for the 173rd. Resupply and General Support mission completed the rest of the days' activities in support of the 1st Div. No fire was reported. Several new aviators were given stan rides and check rides were also flown by other aviators.

j. On 10 March the 335th provided support for the "Sky Soldiers" and the "Big Red One."

k. 11 March began as a rather quiet peaceful day. At 1100 hours the stillness of the day was broken. A/C 569 flown by Lt. Anderson and WO Hollingsworth were carrying a sling load into an LZ, which they had been in several times earlier in the day. This time they were greeted with Heavy Automatic Weapons fire and upon dropping their load made a hasty retreat. The aircraft took six (6) hits and WO Hollingsworth took one in the leg. The A/C was flown back to Soui Da and WO Hollingsworth was evacuated to Tay Ninh.

l. 12 March was found to be a good day. Resupply and General Support missions were flown for the 173rd and 1st Div. Light automatic weapons fire was received with no hits reported.

m. On 13, 14, 15, and 16 March the 335th was mostly engaged in General Support missions of III Corps, II FFV, 145th. No fire was reported during these days.

n. St. Patrick's Day found the COWBOYS flying for the paratroopers of the 173rd and also adding some support to the 25th Infantry. An Emergency Standby Light Fire Team was scrambled to the aid of a Cozy Cabin Unit near Bear Cat. Another Light Fire Team flying the Dong Nai Recon received fire with one (1) gunship taking one (1) hit. Slight damage and no injuries. All of the COWBOYS showed their interest in St. Patrick's Day. They all wore green to help commemorate the day.

o. The 18th of March found the COWBOYS doing what they like to do most. They flew six (6) CA's in support of the 25th and 4th Inf. Divisions. Resupply and LRRP training completed the day's operation. No fire was received and none was reported.

p. 19 March began the move of the COWBOYS from Bien Hoa to their new home for a 2-week RON at Tay Ninh, RVN. An operation was established by the time the COWBOYS arrived in force at 1800 hours.

q. The first full operational day at Tay Ninh started in a big way. The COWBOYS flew four (4) CA's in support of the 173rd and 25th Inf. The remainder of the day was spent in resupply and General Support of the 25th Inf. Div. Fire was received and returned as per usual. No hits.

r. 21 March found the COWBOYS flying five (5) CA's for the 173rd, 196th and 1st Div. The LRRP created two (2) extractions for the COWBOYS no fire was received during these, however some fire was received during the day and the Falcons found their mark and estimated ten (10) VC KBA. No hits taken.

s. The 22nd found the COWBOYS flying resupply and General Support. The Falcons reported receiving fire several times and returned same.

t. 23 March found the COWBOYS supporting the 173rd in nine (9) CA's lifting 486 troops and 2 tons of cargo. Fire was received and returned today per COWBOY tradition.

u. 24 March again saw the 335th in active support of the 173rd participating in six (6) CA's. A Falcon Light Fire Team was called to support a unit that was under attack N.E. of Tay Ninh. They responded with unknown results.

v. 25 March found the COWBOYS receiving fire frequently during the day and always returning some. On one occasion the gunner of 884 had his M-60 jam and in his excitement to continue engaging the enemy he grabbed his M-16 and fired three (3) holes in the floor of the aircraft.

w. 26 March proved to be what has lately seemed like a common day for the aircraft Commanders. Fire again was received and returned. At approximately 1300 hour's tragedy struck the COWBOYS. Aircraft 609 had a forced landing on T/O from Tay Ninh and crashed, killing the pilot, Captain Kirby of the 71st Avn. Co.

x. 27 and 28 March the COWBOYS flew resupply and General Support for the troops participating in Junction City. Fire was received and returned with negative results.

y. 29 March started out in a bad way with 2 shook up pilots. They saw 50 Cal tracer fire going by the aircraft lighting up the morning sky. They took one hit in the sync elevator but didn't return it due to the close proximity of the fire to friendly positions. A Light Fire Team on counter mortar standby were called on. They tallied fifteen (15) VC confirmed and one (1) structure destroyed.

z. 30 March the COWBOYS participated in two (2) CA's and one (1) repositioning for the 1st Div. A little fire was received but none returned.

aa. March ended in what could be considered on normal COWBOY missions. Two (2) CA's were flown for the 1st Division and the remainder of the day was spent on resupply and General Support. Again, fire was received. No hits. The 31st of March ended in what could be considered the biggest and best month in the COWBOY'S history.

III. MONTHLY STATISTICS:

a. Total sorties by type aircraft for combat missions:

	ARMED HELO	COMBAT ASSAULT	RE-SUPPLY	CMD & CNT	RECON	MED EVAC	MIS	TOTAL
UH-1B	706				31			737
UH-1D		1280	4680	325	113	9	1152	7561
TOTAL	706	1280	4680	325	144	9	1152	8298

b. Monthly Summary of Performance:

	UH-1B	UH-1D	TOTAL
TOTAL SORTIES	901	8080	8981
COMBAT SORTIES	737	7561	8298
HOURS	354	2516	2870
PASSENGERS		11867	11867
CARGO (TONS)		988	988

c. Troop Lifts:
    Combat Assault   50
    Extraction's   8
    Repositioning   18

d. Armed Helicopter Missions   100

e. Average Aircraft Hours   102.5
    UH-1B   44.3
    UH-1D   125.8

f. Average Aviator Hours   92.1
    High Aviator   WO William O. Idell   206.6
    Low Aviator   WO Ted H. Bingham   5.0

g. Ammunition Expenditures   7.62   137,000
    2.75in   458
    40mm   1,045

h. Med Evacs Carried   11

i. VC KBA   33

j. Total Aircraft Hit   UH-1D   6
    UH-1B   4

k. U.S. Wounded   2

l. U.S. Killed   1

m. Total Accidents   1

n. Forced to Land, but Recovered   0

IV. AWARDS RECEIVED DURING THE MONTH OF MARCH 1967

MAJ. VICTOR	BS
CWO EASTON	BS
SP4 DEMARCO	BS
MAJ. JONES	BAM
CPT. OWENS	BAM
WO1 ANDREWS	BAM
WO1 BROAD	BAM
WO1 HOOKS	BAM

HISTORY OF THE
335TH ASSAULT HELICOPTER COMPANY
145th Combat Aviation Battalion
APO San Francisco 96227

1 April 1967 through 30 April 1967

Prepared by

1 Lt. PAUL C. HOWELL

Approved by

LEYBURN W. BROCKWELL JR.
LTC Infantry
Commanding

335TH ASSAULT HELICOPTER COMPANY
145th Combat Aviation Battalion
APO San Francisco 96227

1 May 1967

Subject: Monthly History of the 335th Assault Helicopter Company for the period
1 April through 30 April 1967

To: Commanding Officer
335th Assault Helicopter Company
145th Combat Aviation Battalion
APO San Francisco 96227

I. ORGANIZATION AND DESIGNATION:

A. Flight Platoons (2) -- COWBOYS

    (1) First Airlift Platoon -- Ramrods
Platoon Commander: Major Charles Jones
Aircraft: 10 UH-1D "Slicks" -- Troop Carriers.

    (2) Second Airlift Platoon -- Mustangs
Platoon Commander: Major Daniel Stefanowich
Aircraft: 10 UH-1D "Slicks" -- Troop Carriers.

    (3) Armed Helicopter Platoon -- Falcons
Platoon Commander: Captain Claude Stults
Aircraft: 8 UH-1B "Guns" -- Armed Escort.

B. 166th Transportation Detachment.
(1) Commander: Major Robert A. Lawson
(2) 1 UH-1B recovery helicopter -- Horsethief.

C. 25th Medical Detachment.

D. 234th Signal Detachment.

II. OPERATIONS:

a. The dawn of April found the COWBOYS of the 335th Assault Helicopter Company supporting the 1st Infantry Division and the "Sky Soldiers" of the 173rd Airborne Brigade (Separate), in resupply and General Support missions. They lifted 314 troops in 363 sorties and also performed two (2) Med. Evacs missions.

b. 2 April the 1st Infantry Division and the 173rd Airborne Brigade again found the COWBOYS waiting to support them. Five (5) "Slicks" flew CA's for the 1st Infantry Division, carrying 588 troops in 254 sorties. Lt. Tarr and WO Quiberg were flying a resupply mission for the 173rd Airborne Brigade when their aircraft received a heavy volume of fire, taking five (5) hits. WO Quiberg was wounded in the leg and Lt. Tarr skillfully took over the controls and guided the ship into the LZ.

c. 3 April turned out to be a bad day for the Falcons. Two (2) Falcon aircraft took a total of fourteen (14) hits, while covering resupply ships, for the 173rd Airborne Brigade, but no injuries were incurred. The remainder of the day was spent flying administrative missions.

d. 4 April found the COWBOYS flying a five (5) ship lift for the soldiers of the 1st Infantry Division. After the lift, the COWBOYS flew resupply for the 1st Infantry Division and the "Sky Soldiers" of the 173rd Airborne Brigade, lifting a total of 394 troops and performing 252 sorties.

e. 5 April was a rather slow day for the COWBOYS. The day was spent flying resupply for the 9th Infantry Division and General Support for the Navy out of Nha Be.

113

f. Aircraft 567 crashed due to an engine failure on 6 April. The aircraft commander, Major Jones, received a minor back injury, but the pilot, WO Hooks was not as fortunate receiving a compression fracture of the lower vertebra. The gunner received facial cuts as a result of the crash. Later in the day Aircraft 557 went down in the Quan Loi area; no injuries incurred by the crew. The COWBOYS flew a total of 257 sorties and carried 380 passengers.

g. A Combat Assault began the day of 7 April for the COWBOYS, followed by an extraction of the "Sky Soldiers." The COWBOYS rounded out the day, by flying resupply missions for the 173rd Airborne Brigade and the Falcons flew General Support -- type missions for the 173rd. No fire was reported or received during the day.

h. The COWBOYS flew six (6) Combat Assault Missions on the 8th in support of the 25th Inf. Div. 350 troops were lifted in 120 sorties. Following the lift, the remainder of the day was spent flying resupply and General support missions for the 25th Inf. Div., and the "Sky Soldiers." It was a relatively quiet day, until aircraft 868 received fire and took one (1) hit, no injuries were received.

i. On 9 April, the COWBOYS found themselves doing what they enjoyed doing most; flying Combat Assaults for the 173rd Airborne Brigade. Major Huth, Executive Officer of the 335th, received a minor wound while flying as pilot of the lead ship. The day became hectic before it was over; Artillery and Air Strikes delayed, and mingled with the lifts on numerous occasions. A total of 270 troops were lifted and 198 were extracted.

j. Early in the morning of the 10th the Falcons had to scramble a Light Fire Team to support the Rung Sat river backup. Later that afternoon, eight (8) "Slicks" and a Light Fire Team were scrambled to Tan An, for a lift in support of the 9th Infantry Division. Fire was reported being received, but no aircraft were reported hit.

k. April 11th again found the COWBOYS lifting troops of the 9th Inf. Div. Aircraft 868 went down due to engine failure. No damage was done to the aircraft and no injuries were incurred by any members of the crew or the passengers. Aircraft 561 took one (1) round while placing troops into the area to secure 868. An ammunition box flew up and out of Aircraft 610, and struck the main rotor blade, with the lid of the box flying into the exhaust stack of 569. The Falcons had a busy and productive day destroying fourteen (14) huts!

l. On 12 April, twelve (12) extraction's and five (5) repositionings were flown for the "Sky Soldiers" of the 173rd Airborne Brigade. Aircraft 610 crashed on takeoff during the Combat Assault and had to be destroyed in the field. WO Broad received numerous cuts and a sprained wrist, and the gunner, Specialist Retterer, had one of his toes crushed. During the day, fire was received and returned in typical COWBOY fashion. No hits were reported by any ship.

m. The 13th of April was a relatively quiet day for the COWBOYS. Six (6) UH-1Ds flew General Support Missions. Aircraft 569 was being flown on a test flight when it developed hydraulic failure. A successful landing was performed on the Bien Hoa airstrip by WO Villerreal with no further damage incurred by the aircraft. April 13th terminated Operation Junction City II. The COWBOYS extracted the last troops of the 173rd out of their operational area on the 12th.

n. Eleven (11) UH-1Ds and a Heavy Fire Team flew three (3) Combat Assault Missions, and two (2) repositionings on the 14th for the 9th Inf. Div. Automatic and semi-automatic weapons fire was received during the day and was returned, per COWBOY and Falcon fashion, destroying five (5) houses and killing four (4) VC (Confirmed). A total of 224 sorties were flown carrying 554 troops.

o. The COWBOYS had a rather uneventful day on the 15th of April. The morning was spent flying four (4) lifts for the "Sky Soldiers" of the 173rd, Carrying 236 troops.

p. The morning of the 16th found the COWBOYS flying seven (7) CA's for the 9th Inf. Div. at Tan An, in the afternoon four (4) extractions were flown for the 1st Australian Task Force at Nu Dat. The COWBOYS said that the 1st Australian Task Force is, by far, the best organized and most cooperative unit for Airmobile operations that they have ever worked for. Fire was reported during the day, but no hits were taken.

q. A relatively quiet day was spent by the COWBOYS on the 17th, flying General Support and resupply missions for USAID, II FFV and the 1st ATF. The Falcons were credited with one (1) sampan destroyed during the day.

r. The 18th and 19th again found the COWBOYS flying Combat Assaults. A total of 684 troops were air lifted and 16 tons of cargo was carried. One (1) VC was confirmed killed. The 18th began operation Newark for the 173rd Airborne Brigade in "D" Zone North of Bien Hoa.

s. On 20 April the COWBOYS flew one (1) Combat Assault and ten (10) repositionings lifts for the "Sky Soldiers." The remainder of the day was spent flying resupply and General Support missions for the 173rd and USAID. No fire was reported or received during the day.

t. On the 21st a LRRP team was inserted, and discovered, and later extracted. The rest of the day was devoted to flying resupply and General Support Missions for the 173rd and USAID. 179 troops and 35 tons of cargo were carried.

u. The 22nd saw a very welcome and well-deserved rest for the COWBOYS. In the morning one (1) ship was called upon to make an R&R run leaving the rest of the ships on standby. They were never called. The Falcons were kept busy on the Dong Nai Recon and escorting Med-Evacs ships.

v. After a day of rest 486 passengers, 12 tons of cargo and 215 sorties were flown in support of the 25th Inf. Div. and the III Corps. No enemy activity was noted and no fire was received.

w. On April 24th the COWBOYS resumed their support of the 173rd LRRP's with four (4) UH-1Ds and a Light Fire Team. Three (3) UH-1Ds flew resupply for the "Sky Soldiers." 177 sorties were flown carrying 202 troops and 25 tons of cargo. COWBOY 916 received fire, taking two (2) hits in the tail boom. No injuries were sustained and the aircraft proceeded back to the corral, for repair, without further damage. The Falcons got in a few licks themselves when they received light automatic weapons fire and returned same, results unknown. No Falcons were hit.

x. On the 25th the COWBOYS supported the 173rd with six (6) ships, three (3) for the LRRP's and three (3) for resupply of the troops in the field. Three (3) other UH-1Ds were placed in support of the II FFV for their General Support.

y. The morning of the 26th found the COWBOYS in familiar sky's. They carried 178 troops of the 173rd into Combat during the morning hours. The afternoon found the COWBOYS standing by on one-hour alert. They were not called and they rested up for tomorrow's missions.

z. The 27th and 28th of April found the COWBOYS supporting the 173rd in LRRP missions, Eagle Flights, and resupply. II FFV and III Corps were both supported by General Support missions. No enemy resistance was met.

aa. On April 29th the Falcons on emergency standby were called out to investigate some possible enemy activity. When they arrived over the area in question they began receiving small arms fire from two (2) hooches. No Falcons were hit, but both hooches were destroyed.

bb. On 30 April, eleven (11) COWBOYS and a Falcon Light Fire Team were involved in an extraction of the "Sky Soldiers." In the afternoon the COWBOYS, with the aid of a Heavy Fire Team, could be found in the sky supporting the 36th ARVN Ranger Battalion in a Combat Assault. Another successful month in the history of the COWBOYS came to a close while supporting the 173rd Airborne Brigade and the 25th Infantry Division with resupply missions. Operation Newark was brought to an end by the extraction of the 173rd Airborne Brigade.

III. AWARDS RECEIVED DURING THE MONTH OF APRIL 1967

WO1 JONES	BS
1SG KEMP	BS
SP4 LOCKWOOD	BAM
PFC SAMMONS	BAM
SP4 VICK	BAM
WO1 BASS	BAM
SP5 BRIGGANS	BAM
WO1 NIELSEN	BAM
WO1 OSTERMAN	BAM
WO1 QUIBERG	BAM
SP4 SCOTT	BAM
PFC TOLLIVER	BAM
PFC MILLARD	BAM
SP4 ORTIZ	BAM
PFC TAYLOR	BAM
WO1 JEFFREY	BAM

HISTORY OF THE
335TH ASSAULT HELICOPTER COMPANY
145th Combat Aviation Battalion
APO San Francisco 96227

1 May 1967 through 31 May 1967

Prepared by

1 Lt. PAUL C. HOWELL

Approved by

WALTER H. HUTH
MAJ. Artillery
Commanding

335TH ASSAULT HELICOPTER COMPANY
145th Combat Aviation Battalion
APO San Francisco 96227

1 June 1967

Subject: Monthly History of the 335th Assault Helicopter Company for the period
1 May through 31 May 1967

To: Commanding Officer
335th Assault Helicopter Company
145th Combat Aviation Battalion
APO San Francisco 96227

I. ORGANIZATION AND DESIGNATION:

    A.   Flight Platoons (2) -- COWBOYS

        (1)   First Airlift Platoon -- Ramrods
              Platoon Commander: Captain Ronald Wecas
              Aircraft: 10 UH-1D "Slicks" -- Troop Carriers.

        (2)   Second Airlift Platoon -- Mustangs
              Platoon Commander: Major Jon Dickerson
              Aircraft: 10 UH-1D "Slicks" -- Troop Carriers.

        (3)   Armed Helicopter Platoon -- Falcons
              Platoon Commander: Captain Claude Stults
              Aircraft: 8 UH-1B "Guns" -- Armed Escort.

    B.   166th Transportation Detachment.
        (1) Commander: Major Robert A. Lawson
        (2) 1 UH-1B recovery helicopter -- Horsethief.

    C.   25th Medical Detachment.

    D.   234th Signal Detachment.

II. OPERATIONS:

a. 1 May 1967 began as a normal and productive day in the life of the COWBOY'S, 335th Assault Helicopter Company, by lifting the "Sky Soldiers" of the 173rd Airborne Brigade (Separate), during the morning. In route to Bear Cat to begin a Combat Assault early in the afternoon for the 9th Inf. Div., tragedy struck in one quick and forceful blow. Chalks one (1) and two (2) exploded in air, tumbling to and burning on the ground, fatally wounding all personnel on board. In one short minute the company lost eight (8) of its best and most respected personnel. The Company Commander, Lieutenant Colonel Leyburn W. Brockwell; 1st Platoon Leader, Major Charles C. Jones; 1st Platoon Sergeant, SSG Ewell E. Acord; CW2 John D. Legg, WO John M. Andrews; Crew Chief, SP4 Pedro Ortiz, and PFC Lewis J. Fogler; and Gunner SP4 Robert F. Quinn.

b. With the tragedy of the first still turning in their hearts the COWBOY'S were awakened early in the morning of the second to support the 9th Infantry Div. on a tactical emergency in the Delta near Tan An. The emergency was covered in COWBOY fashion and then the days normal missions were undertaken.

c. On 3 and 4 May Eagle Flights were flown in support of the 173rd Airborne Brigade General Support missions for II FF Artillery and USAID rounded out the remainder of the days' agendas. No significant enemy activity was noted.

d. The 5th of May found the COWBOY'S supporting the "Sky Soldiers" in a Combat Assault carrying 466 troops in eleven (11) lifts. Two (2) aircraft were damaged when they had hard landings at the pickup zone at Black Horse Strip, RVN. No injuries resulted in either mishap.

e. The COWBOY'S were again supporting the 173rd Abn. Bde. on 6 May, with all available aircraft. Fire was received twice during the day and returned both times, no hits were taken. 125 - 40mm and 42 - 2.75mm rocket rounds were expended during the day.

f. Resupply of the forward troops of the 173rd Abn. Bde. took up most of the 7th and 8th of May for the COWBOYS. The 8th also found five (5) COWBOY ships supporting the II Field Forces Artillery and Engineers and USAID in the General Support role. Small arms fire was received on the 8th and returned in the COWBOY tradition.

g. The 9th found the COWBOYS supporting LRRP's of the 173rd Abn. Bde. in its normal fashion. One of the teams called for an emergency extraction and they were extracted without injuries involved, under fire, causing a few anxious moments for some of the pilots. II Corps Field Forces Artillery is now finding out without question what a superior job of support the COWBOY'S will do for you.

h. Five (5) ships were committed today on the 10th to support the 173rd Abn. Bde. for resupply and LRRP standby. They performed one (1) LRRP extraction and carried 96 troops and 26 tons of cargo for resupply. Another five (5) ships supported the II Field Forces and MACV in General Support. No significant enemy activity was noted.

i. The 11th began with the COWBOY'S supporting the 173rd Abn. Bde. in ten (10) lifts of a Combat Assault; eleven (11) "Slicks" and four (4) Falcons were utilized for the assaults. 500 "Sky Soldiers" participated in the assault. Fire was received and returned during the day. No aircraft were hit and negative results were available on the outcome of fire returned.

j. 12 May, five (5) ships were used in resupply of the forward elements of the 173rd Abn. Bde. with 110 troops and 29 tons of cargo being the totals for the day. Four (4) ships were utilized by the 173rd and II FFV in the General Support role. One (1) ship was also used by the 335th for training to help keep standardization up to date.

k. 13 May found the COWBOY'S supporting the 173rd Abn. Bde. in various types of missions. Fire was received during a Combat Assault with no hits reported. During a resupply mission, in the afternoon, Warrant Officer Osterman took a load to a kickout resupply point. After about half of the load was dropped, the aircraft began to lose power and settled into the trees. The crew came out unscathed but not as much can be said for the aircraft.

l. The morning of the 14th found the COWBOY'S of the 335th Assault Helicopter Company in relatively unfamiliar sky supporting the 9th Inf. Div. in a Tactical Emergency with ten (10) "Slicks" and a Heavy Fire Team. The only major problem arose after the COWBOYS arrived on the scene. The 9th Inf. Div. decided that there no longer was an emergency and had no further use that day for the COWBOYS. All ships were then diverted to there originally scheduled missions of resupply and General Support of the 173rd Airborne Brigade.

m. On May 15th the COWBOYS supported the 173rd using four (4) "Slicks" and a Light Fire Team for an extraction of two (2) LRRP teams. Eight (8) "Slicks" carried 300 troops and 25 tons of cargo to help resupply the forward units of the 173rd. One (1) Light Fire Team was used on the III Corps emergency standby light arms fire was received during the day, no hits were taken.

n. The 16th was used entirely to support the 173rd and its forward elements. With resupply and General Support 282 troops and 41 tons of cargo were carried making the day a very quiet one.

o. On the 17th of May the 173rd Airborne Brigade terminated Operation Dayton in the area Southeast of Black Horse and commenced Operation Cincinnati as a training operation for the Brigade and as a security force for the Bien Hoa areas. On final approach into a pickup zone, light automatic weapons fire was received with aircraft 849 taking two (2) hits. The Falcons assaulted the area of reported fire with results unknown. With four (4) Chinooks for support, a total of 1700 troops were lifted from the area. Mortar fire was received in the pickup zone with no hits being taken.

p. On the 18th of May again found the COWBOYS on a Combat Assault for the 173rd Abn. Bde. (Separate) as they were lifted in "D" Zone and the surrounding area due to bad weather the days' operations were delayed 3 hours and 30 minutes. 700 "Sky Soldiers" of the Brigade were lifted into the area. Light to moderate Automatic weapons fire was received with aircraft 456 and 201 each taking one (1) hit in the tail boom. After the lift was completed the COWBOYS had the remainder of the afternoon to rest up.

q. On 19 and 20 May five (5) "Slicks" and two (2) gunships for Eagle Flights, the troops were lifted into an area of suspected enemy locations, sweeping through the area and then being extracted upon completion of their sweep. One (1) LRRP team was also inserted during the 19th. Resupply for the 173rd and General Support missions for II FFV, III Corps and MACV constituted the remainder of the days' activities. No fire was received on either day.

r. On 21 May a LRRP team was extracted without incident. Resupply missions were flown for both the 199th Light Infantry Brigade and the 173rd Airborne Brigade (Separate), carrying 152 troops and 30 tons of cargo in 35 sorties. General Support missions were flown for the II FFV and 79th Engineers. The Falcons were on emergency standby. Fire was received on numerous occasions and was returned. Approximately 10,000 rounds of 7.62 and 48 rockets were expended. Falcon ship 934 flew its last mission today, covering a Medical Evacuation ship. On its orbit to cover the "Dust Off" low level the ship lost power and settled into the trees, completely destroying itself. Neither WO Gregg, WO Quiberg, the pilots, nor the crew were injured.

s. 22 May found seven (7) COWBOYS supporting the 173rd by moving 126 "Sky Soldiers." The remainder of the day found the COWBOYS supporting the 199th Light Infantry Brigade with eight (8) "Slicks" for resupply. 200 troops and 27 tons of cargo were carried in support of the 199th. One (1) slick for General Support for II FFV. One (1) ship was used, each for badly needed training and maintenance flights. Fire was again received and returned COWBOY fashion.

t. 23 May five (5) "Slicks" and two (2) gunships supported the 173rd Abn. Bde. in extracting the remainder of their personnel from war Zone "D" terminating Operation Cincinnati. The remainder of the day found the COWBOYS supporting the 199th Light Infantry Brigade with resupply in 140 sorties and the II FFV Artillery in the General Support role with 41 sorties. No fire was reported or received during the day.

u. 24 May started with the COWBOYS supporting the 9th Inf. Div. in the Delta, near Ra Khiem, RVN. 300 troops were lifted in 128 sorties. At approximately 1100 hours the COWBOYS received a call from higher headquarters and told to return to home station when the mornings' activities were over. At 1630 hours we were notified that we were to be a member of Operation Winchester (Code name for deployment to vicinity of Pleiku). We were also informed that we were to be under Operational Control of the 173rd Airborne Brigade (Separate) in their operation in the Pleiku area. Commenced immediately by Operation Francis Marion.

v. Minor maintenance and administrative flights were all that were flown on the 25th, 26th, and 27th in preparation for the move. The movement of equipment from the company area began by Air Force C-130 at approximately 0400 hours on the morning of the 26th.

w. 28 May 1967. Briefing was held at 0700 hours. Twenty-one (21) UH-1D, six (6) UH-1B gunships, and one (1) CH-47, chase ship, departed Bien Hoa in route to Pleiku at 0800 hours. The light of twenty-seven (27) UH-1 type aircraft and one (1) CH-47 arrived at Hensel AAF, Camp Enari home of the 4th Inf. Div., at approximately 1630 hours on the day of the 28th. Two (2) minor maintenance errors were encountered in route, but all ships were able to close on Hensel at the same time.

x. No missions were flown on the 29th of May. On 30 May a minimum of missions were flown. A LRRP team was inserted and later extracted and one (1) recon mission was flown in support of the 173rd Airborne Brigade.

y. No missions were flown on the 31st. All members of the 335th continued to work on getting their tents erected and make living quarters for everyone. All personnel waited in eager anticipation for a new month and a new chapter to unfold in the history of the COWBOYS.

III. AWARDS RECEIVED DURING THE MONTH OF MAY 1967

LTC BROCKWELL	DFC
CWO LEGG	DFC
CPT. HOZA	BS
CPT. KUHBLANK	BS
CPT. JONES	ACM "V"
1Lt. STEED	ACM "V"
PFC ERICKSON	BAM
SP4 HATTON	BAM
PFC MILLS	BAM
SP4 TRACE	BAM
SP4 MOSLEY	BAM
SP4 AUMACK	BAM
WO1 GRAHAM	BAM
PFC GRANT	BAM
SP4 KNOX	BAM
PFC WILLIAMS	BAM

HISTORY OF THE
335TH ASSAULT HELICOPTER COMPANY
145th Combat Aviation Battalion
APO San Francisco 96227

1 June 1967 through 30 June 1967

Prepared by

1 Lt. PAUL C. HOWELL

Approved by

CHARLES D. UTZMAN
LTC Infantry
Commanding

335TH ASSAULT HELICOPTER COMPANY
145th Combat Aviation Battalion
APO San Francisco 96227

10 January 1968

Subject: Monthly History of the 335th Assault Helicopter Company for the period
1 June through 30 June 1967

To: Commanding Officer
335th Assault Helicopter Company
145th Combat Aviation Battalion
APO San Francisco 96227

I. ORGANIZATION AND DESIGNATION:

A. Flight Platoons (2) -- COWBOYS

    (1) First Airlift Platoon -- Ramrods
        Platoon Commander: Captain Ronald N. Wecas
        Aircraft: 10 UH-1D "Slicks" -- Troop Carriers.

    (2) Second Airlift Platoon -- Mustangs
        Platoon Commander: Major Jon R. Dickerson
        Aircraft: 10 UH-1D "Slicks" -- Troop Carriers.

    (3) Armed Helicopter Platoon -- Falcons
        Platoon Commander: Captain Donald N. Moss
        Aircraft: 8 UH-1B "Guns" -- Armed Escort.

B. 166th Transportation Detachment.
    (1) Commander: Major Robert A. Lawson
    (2) 1 UH-1B recovery helicopter -- Horsethief.

C. 25th Medical Detachment.

D. 234th Signal Detachment.

123

II. OPERATIONS:

a. June began by the COWBOYS beginning their work in the new operational area of Pleiku. Four (4) slick ships were committed to LRRP missions. One (1) team was placed in and later extracted without incident. Two (2) ships were used on resupply carrying 14 troops and 12 tons of cargo. Everything went fairly smooth; however, the COWBOYS were beginning to find out what was meant by the Pleiku Monsoon season. Everyone is looking forward to a good and productive month at their new location.

b. 2nd and 3rd of June were both relatively quiet days for the COWBOYS of the 335th Assault Helicopter Company and the "Sky Soldiers" of the 173rd Airborne Brigade (Separate) two (2) LRRP Combat Assaults, and one (1) extraction took place. Three (3) ships were committed to resupply on both days flying a total of 44 hours and carrying 114 passengers and 37 tons of cargo. On 3 June an Eagle Flight was performed. No enemy contact was noted during the days' activities.

c. On 4 June 1967 the COWBOYS and the 173rd Airborne Brigade had their first Combat Assault in the new area. 125 troops were lifted into an area with no enemy contact received on the initial lifts. One (1) LRRP team was extracted. The remainder of the day was spent on resupply and General Support missions for the Brigade.

d. On 5 and 6 June one (1) insertion was made and no extractions were needed. Resupply missions were beginning to pickup intensity as 66 hours were flown carrying 223 passengers and 68 tons of cargo. Fire was received on 5 June and returned. Warrant Officer Allen R. Johnson had approximately 10 hours in country when he was wounded in the legs when the aircraft he was flying resupply in received fire.

e. On 7 June the COWBOYS participated in a repositioning for the Mortar Platoon of the 2/503 Inf. 173rd Abn. Bde. carrying 50 passengers and 13 tons of Cargo. Five (5) "Slicks" supported the Brigade the remainder of the day carrying 103 troops and 19 tons of cargo. Fire was received during the day but was not returned. No hits were taken.

f. 8 June began with the COWBOYS flying an extraction for the 173rd. The extraction was delayed 3 hours due to weather. 240 troops were extracted in the 3-hour operation. Two (2) LRRP teams were inserted with negative resistance. Six (6) ships flew resupply for forward elements of the Brigade carrying 45 passengers and 27 tons of cargo during the remainder of the afternoon.

g. On 9 and 10 June the COWBOYS supported E/17th Cav. of the 173rd in LRRP missions placing two (2) teams and extracting one (1) team. A total of ten (10) ships supported the Brigade for the two days in resupply missions. Almost 40 tons of cargo was carried during the two days. No fire was reported, during the days' activities. The morning of the 10th, missions were delayed for approximately 2 1/2 hours because of the change of Command ceremonies. Major Walter H. Huth turned the Company over to Major Charles D. Utzman. Major Huth was also presented with his BAM and 5 clusters to the Air Medal, a Purple Heart for wounds received in action on 9 April 1967 and a Bronze Star Medal for Service.

h. Fire was received and returned today, 11 June, while extracting an LRRP team. It looks as if the LRRP's are getting back into the action again, putting the COWBOYS also in the center of it. Another LRRP team was placed in later in the afternoon without incident. Six (6) COWBOYS flying resupply filled the remainder of the days' activities. Fire was also received and returned during these flights.

i. Weather is becoming more and more a determining factor in the missions. This morning 12 June 1967 the mission a repositioning of E Troop 17th Cavalry from the home base of the 173rd at Caticka to the Special Forces Camp at Plei Me. During the three (3) lifts the best weather at Plei Me was approximately 200 feet with light rain and haze. LRRP teams again kept four (4) ships busy for the remainder of the day. Placing one (1) team in, extracting them and staying in the air for radio relay. Six (6) ships also aided the Brigade by flying 132 sorties of resupply to its forward elements. Fire was received by the resupply ships and reported to control as Heavy Automatic Weapons.

j. The LRRP's placed a patrol in on the morning of the 13th and extracted them later in the evening. Five (5) ships flew resupply and one (1) ship flew in the General Support role. Negative enemy contact was made.

k. 14 June saw ten (10) "Slicks" and two (2) Falcons supporting the 173rd on the extraction of the 2 Battalions of the 503rd Infantry in seven (7) lifts. Approximately 260 troops were extracted from two (2) separate locations. No fire was received, and the extractions were made with no enemy incidents. Some troops of the 4th Infantry Division

"Ivy Division" were placed in one of the pickup zones by accident. They were also picked up by the ships that placed them in the area when they noticed their error. Resupply and General Support missions rounded out the remainder of the day.

l. 15 June began with COWBOY ships supporting the LRRP's with a CA and an extraction. No enemy resistance was met in either instance. All COWBOY aircraft were then called upon to extract 230 "Sky Soldiers" from a forward location. Resupply and General Support were again placed on today's agenda.

m. On 16 June the COWBOYS again made an extraction for the 173rd. 182 troops in 98 sorties were lifted. Four (4) ships were again used for LRRP extracting two (2) teams without incident. Resupply and General Support missions rounded out the day of flying. Word was received today that one (1) platoon of Slick ships and a Light Fire Team will be going up to Dak To to support a Battalion size operation in that vicinity for a period of approximately 30 days. The 2nd Platoon was selected.

n. 17 June found the COWBOYS supporting the 173rd again in extraction of their troops for preparation of the movement to Dak To. 11 tons of cargo and 65 passengers were carried during resupply. An advanced party of one was sent up to Dak To to lay claim to an area for the COWBOYS to bed down and build hitching racks. The advanced party came back the same day and made final coordination for the move. The second platoon spent the afternoon preparing for the move.

Major Utzman took his advanced party back up to Dak To to check out the area and then went back to Hensel. It was learned that overnight Dak To had received a total of over 250 rockets and mortars. One tent was set up and one very deep foxhole was dug. No incidents were received during the night.

On 18 June Major Utzman and Captain Wecas flew up in advance of the Second Platoon to further check out the area and discuss further movement plans with the Battalion. They were informed upon arrival that a lift was to take place and notified the Company at Hensel to send up a total of ten (10) "Slicks" and a Light Fire Team. The COWBOYS arrived in force early in the afternoon and placed 160 "Sky Soldier" on a pinnacle for their first Combat Assault at Dak To in Operation Greeley. The COWBOYS found out the first day that flying at Dak To in its mountainous terrain was going to be a big change from the flying they had been used to. The COWBOYS went back to Hensel to bed down for the night.

o. On 19 June the COWBOYS arrived at Dak To as early as the weather would permit. When they arrived, they were informed that they would again have to perform for the Brigade by making another Combat Assault. 270 troops were lifted in eight (8) lifts. Fire was received and returned, no ships were hit and no results were obtained for the returned fire. The Second Platoon and one (1) Light Fire Team were notified that they would begin to RON at this time. Minimum resupply was carried to the troops in the field.

p. The Brigade has continued to move troops out into the underbrush. Today they again called on the COWBOYS to haul "Sky Soldiers" out in another Combat Assault. 230 troops were lifted. The Brigade is continually moving more of their elements up to Dak To. Rumors are going around that the operation will last more than 30 days and also that the entire Company will have to move up. Only time will tell. After the Assault most of the personnel were used within the Company area to build bunkers and make their home more habitable. All reports tend to point to another mortar attack soon.

q. A Combat Assault for E Troop 17 Cav. and an extraction for the 1st Battalion 503rd Infantry took up most of the days' time for the COWBOYS on the 21st of June. No fire was received during the day. The Falcons put in a good pre-strike for the Combat Assault. The 52nd Combat Aviation Battalion has given us the PSP necessary to build all of our revetments. The 173rd Airborne Brigades Engineers are making good time at getting them up for us. Almost every day now the weather is holding us up for a couple of hours at least on the days Operations.

r. "A" Company 2nd Battalion 503rd Infantry was walking down a mountainside early the morning of the 22nd when they met a Battalion size unit of an NVA Regiment. They immediately became engaged in a running battle. The Falcons were called upon immediately to give vitally needed air support to the Company. Even though bad weather prevailed at the dawn of the day the Falcons flew continuous cover for the Company, hampered frequently by A1E "Sky Soldiers," airstrikes, artillery and the ever-present threat of rain and low cloud cover. The COWBOYS were called upon to give the Company support in other ways also. Resupply of Ammo was badly needed and eventually a Combat Assault was placed in within 200 meters of the heaviest fighting to attempt to reinforce the surrounded Company. The Falcons and COWBOYS braved the enemy's fire and successfully accomplished their mission in protecting and preventing the possible annihilation of the company. The Falcons in covering the company expended over 230 rockets and 36,000 rounds of 7.62 ammunition. As the COWBOYS returned at the end of the day everyone turned and looked solemnly to the scared face of the mountain less than three miles South where fierce and ferocious hand to hand Combat had been fought earlier that day.

s. On 23 June the COWBOYS supported the 4th Battalion in a Combat Assault lifting 168 troops onto a field location. Suppression was placed in on the initial lift, no enemy resistance was met. Three (3) slick ships were utilized to support the forward elements of the Brigade in resupply carrying 18 troops and 2 tons of cargo. An additional ship was used for a recon mission.

t. Three (3) ships were utilized to support the forward elements of the Brigade in Recon for the LRRP missions. No teams were placed in or extracted. Four (4) "Slicks" were utilized for resupply carrying 23 troops and 16 ton of cargo. No enemy resistance was met during the day by the COWBOYS. Two (2) Gunships were used on training missions to further their ability and precision.

u. The COWBOYS kept themselves busy on the 25th by flying formation most of the day. A repositioning began the day for the COWBOYS by moving 46 troops of the 4th Battalion 503rd Infantry. Early in the afternoon elements of the 1st Cav. Division got to see first-hand some of the flying capabilities of the COWBOYS when their troopers were moved during Combat Assault. In the late afternoon the COWBOYS performed an extraction for the 1st Battalion 503rd Infantry 173rd Airborne Brigade when 80 "Sky Soldiers" were lifted from a forward area back to their base camp. Seven (7) "Slicks" supported the Brigade for the remainder of the day with resupply. 16 tons of cargo were lifted, although numerous flights were made throughout the days' activities and no fire was received.

v. The COWBOYS began the 26th of June with resupply and General Support of the 173rd Airborne Brigade. 66 "Sky Soldiers" and 9 tons of cargo were carried. The afternoon became a busy day for the COWBOYS as 190 troopers were extracted for the 1st Battalion, back to the vicinity of Dak To for a day or so of rest.

w. The 27th and the 28th were relatively quiet days for the Brigade and ultimately for the COWBOYS. General Support and resupply absorbed most of the day's activities. 42 hours were flown for resupply, carrying 170 "Sky Soldiers" and 26 tons of cargo.

x. Five (5) UH-1D "Slick" helicopters and a Heavy Fire Team extracted 330 "Sky Soldiers" for the 173rd. No enemy resistance was met on the extraction. One (1) LRRP team was infiltrated into a suspected enemy infested area. Three (3) "Slick" ships performed resupply while the additional six (6) ships completed the days' activities with General Support and administration missions for the 173rd and the 335th.

y. 151 troops were lifted on a Combat Assault into a forward area of the Brigade. An extraction was made of 24 troopers from a forward element to the vicinity of Dak To. Eight (8) Ships rounded out the day and the month with resupply for the 173rd Airborne Brigade (Separate).

III. MONTHLY STATISTICS:

	UH-1B	UH-1D	TOTAL
TOTAL SORTIES	706	5096	5802
COMBAT SORTIES	612	4480	5092
HOURS	273	1515	1788
PAX		5966	5966
CARGO (TONS)		645	645
AMMO - 2.75	269		269
7.62	60,300		60,300
40MM	253		253

	UH-1B	UH-1D	TOTAL
MEDIVACS-VC/KBA	55		55
AIRCRAFT HITS	1		1
U.S./WIA/KIA	1 WIA		1 WIA
UH-1B MISSIONS	115		115
AVG. ACFT HOURS	17	88	105
CA'S	25		25
EXTRACTION'S		18	18
REPOSITIONING		4	4
HIGH AVIATOR			175.3
LOW AVIATOR			4.1
AVG. AVIATOR HRS			81.3

IV. AWARDS RECEIVED DURING THE MONTH OF JUNE 1967

1Lt. STRIBLING	SILVER STAR
MAJ. JOHNSON	DISTINGUISHED FLYING CROSS
CPT. SPANJERS	DISTINGUISHED FLYING CROSS
CPT. WOOD	DISTINGUISHED FLYING CROSS
CPT. STULTS	BRONZE STAR
CPT. WOOD	BRONZE STAR
SP4 BONACORDA	AIR MEDAL W/ "V"
PFC WALLER	AIR MEDAL W/ "V"
PFC GRANT	BASIC AIR MEDAL
WO1 BRYAN	BASIC AIR MEDAL
SP4 CLARK	BASIC AIR MEDAL
PFC CODY	BASIC AIR MEDAL
SP4 GRODES	BASIC AIR MEDAL
SP4 MIDGET	BASIC AIR MEDAL
PFC ALLEN	BASIC AIR MEDAL
SP4 OLSON	BASIC AIR MEDAL
SSG ROSES	BASIC AIR MEDAL
CPT. TARR	ARMY COMMENDATION W/ "V"
MAJ. DAVIS	ARMY COMMENDATION
WO1 MANKER	ARMY COMMENDATION
SSG WOOD	ARMY COMMENDATION
SP5 GAMBOA	ARMY COMMENDATION
SP4 GALUEN	ARMY COMMENDATION
SP4 EATON	ARMY COMMENDATION
SP4 SAMUELSON	ARMY COMMENDATION

BATTLE OF THE SLOPES

Hill 1338

173D AIRBORNE BRIGADE (SEPARATE)
APO San Francisco 96250

Subject:

Combat Operations After Action Report - Battle of The Slopes, Hill 1338

Task Organization:

Companies A and C, 2nd Battalion; Company B, (Reserve) 2nd Battalion, 503rd Infantry, 173rd Airborne Brigade

Date of Operations:

18 - 22 June 1967.

Location:

YB 988153, ZB 001171, Map Series L7015, Sheet 6538 III.

Sources, Excerpts:

SKY SOLDIERS, BATTLES OF DAK-TO
Copyright 1988 By Lawrence D. Okendo.
ISBN: 0-9620333-0-8
DAK TO, America's Sky Soldiers in South Vietnam's Central Highlands
Copyright 1993 By Edward F. Murphy
ISBN: 0-671-52268-X

Background Information:
Arriving early June in Dak-To proper, the Sky Soldiers of the 2/503rd Airborne Infantry were briefed. Intelligence reported an unknown enemy force had attacked U.S. and CIDG installations in the Dak-To area with mortar and rocket fire during the period of June 17-21, 1967. The enemy was estimated to be within the 2/503rd AO.

Mission: Search and Destroy:
The 2/503rd Infantry was to conduct search and destroy operations against possible enemy forces and installations south of the Dak-To Special Forces Camp. The concept was to deploy the A/2/503rd and C/2/503rd Infantry by helicopter and assault the area on 18th and 20th of June, respectively. B/2/503rd Infantry was to remain as the reaction force and rotate with the line units when instructed.

From 18th, through 21st, June, both Companies had negative contact, and on 211700H (June 21st, at 5 p.m.), A Company received orders to return overland to Dak-To proper (Base Camp). The Commander of A Company chose a route that would allow him to close not later than 221500H.

Many are the facts of war that darkens the path of history. The Battle of the Slopes (dubbed by the Sky Soldiers) in Dak-To, Kontum Province on June 22, 1967, is no exception. John L. Leppelman of C/2/503rd made this report, "We moved through the hills of Dak-To, not keeping track of time. It was an endless search for Charlie and occasionally taking sniper fire with no head on contact" These hills were actually mountains, steep, muddy and leech infested. We were usually under triple canopy jungles which made it appear dark and dreary."

Intelligence information indicated that the enemy situation prior to the operation were elements of the 24th NVA Regiment, 304th VC Battalion, 200th VC artillery Battalion and H-15 LF Battalion. The enemy had the capability to attack in up to regimental strength, to defend and reinforce with above mentioned elements, and to withdraw at the time and place of his choosing.

The Sky Soldiers arrived in the Dak-To area with little or no knowledge of the North Vietnamese Regular Army or their capabilities. In early June, there was a solid indication that the B-3 front was moving the bulk of its regiments from Laos and Cambodia into the Central Highlands under the control of the 1st NVA Division. These were well-trained and seasoned soldiers.

On June 21, A and C Company made their laager site in one common perimeter on a ridge extending perpendicular to Dak-To proper about 2,000 meters away. As they were setting up their positions, both Companies sent out their clearing and reconnaissance patrols in front and around their respective areas. The patrols were an insurance that the area was clear of enemy activity prior to the Sky Soldiers digging in for the night. Shortly after the patrols returned, SP4 Cook of C/2/503rd accidentally strayed outside the safety of the perimeter and was cut down by friendly fire.

Some of the tragedies of war are at times unexplainable and much less justifiable. Some of the tragedies are leadership foul-ups, troops being jumpy from prior actions, or troops being tired and weary. There are many other factors that can be a major cause for such accidents. The well-trained Sky Soldiers kept accidents to the minimum.

The morning of June 22, the Commanders got together for their briefing of respective AO's and final instructions for the mission ahead. C Company was to continue their search and destroy mission and A Company was to return to base camp by overland. Captain Milton commanding A Company had selected his route so that his Company could close at Dak-To base camp NLT 1500 hours. The night before, the men were told they would be returning to Dak To via the same trail they had been monitoring for the past few days. It was gospel among the grunts to avoid repeat use of trails. The crafty enemy frequently booby-trapped them or set up ambushes along their length. Captain Milton had little choice in his Company's route of march. The ridge finger they were on had such steep sides, covered with the typical dense jungle growth, that any other route would have taken several days to traverse. He gave his Officers and NCO's their final instructions prior to moving out.

Milton assigned Lieutenant Judd's 2d Platoon to the point position. Next came 3d Platoon led by Lieutenant Hood. Milton's CP group would follow, and behind them would come Weapons Platoon. Lieutenant Sexton's 1st Platoon was given the task of spreading the CS crystals over the LZ and laager site before falling in at the column's rear.

At 0625, Lieutenant Judd started off. As the tail end of his platoon disappeared downhill into the jungle, Hood started his platoon forward. The Weapons Platoon members, all eighteen of them, squatted along the trail waiting their turn to move. Lieutenant Sexton's platoon had donned their gas masks and were spreading the tear gas around the LZ.

As the Companies moved out from their night laager site, SP4 John L. Leppelman became the point man for C/2/503rd. As his Squad moved out, he reported, "As we moved and wound our way through A Company's positions we greeted our buddies with idle guff and chatter, many of whom we went to jump school with or came to Nam (Vietnam) with.

We continued our search and destroy mission from ridge to ridge, while A Company moved down the slope towards base camp at Dak-To, some 2,000 meters away. A few hours into our mission, the point element started taking sniper fire and within a 20-minute period, we had 3 WIA's. One was serious; he was hit through the neck.

The area was triple canopy jungles and the lower ground area was heavy brush and foliage, just too thick to cut out an LZ so we had to transport him (the WIA) on a make shift stretcher. We made the stretcher by cutting two poles long enough to carry a person then rolling both poles around the edge of a poncho till it was wide enough for a person. We continued to move on our AO, then suddenly we got a radio call from A Company that they were in heavy contact with an entrenched NVA force. Shortly after we got another call from Colonel James Steverson, Commander of the 2nd Battalion, 503rd Infantry, to move out to assist A Company."

A Company's Point Squad moved down near a well-used trail, shortly after they walked into five or six NVA soldiers crossing the trail, the startled NVA's opened fire. Contact was established with an estimated 5-6 NVA's at 0658 hours.

The area was steep with single to triple canopy jungles, thick bamboo, and heavy low foliage. The sun was just breaking through the tops of the jungles sending flowing eloquent rays of light down to the jungle floor. The peacefulness of the jungle turned into a chorus of automatic weapons firing, the sound sending vibrations throughout the Dak-To mountains.

Captain Milton radioed Judd. The young lieutenant reported that his point squad had walked smack into ten to fifteen NVA coming toward them on the same trail. The NVA had opened up first, hitting some of Judd's men. He didn't know how many, or how badly. Judd had put his remaining men into a defensive perimeter.

After getting off the radio with Judd, Milton radioed the battalion TOC. He reported the contact to Capt. Ken Smith.

Colonel Partain and his executive officer, Maj. H. Glenn Watson, were also present in the TOC. While Partain and Smith plotted the coordinates in order to bring in supporting artillery fire, Watson stayed on the radio with Milton.

Major Watson was not overly concerned. Alpha seemed to have the situation under control. He advised Captain Milton to "develop the fight and keep us informed."

A Company's Point Squad was in the middle of a firefight, and the startled NVA's fire was ineffective at the moment, Capt. Milton ordered the 2nd Platoon to assist. As the remainder of the 2nd Platoon moved down to assist, they in turn came under heavy fire from the front and both flanks.

After a brief period, and sizing up the situation, Capt. Milton ordered the 2nd Platoon to withdraw, requesting heavy artillery fire to cover their movement back up the ridge. The artillery fire initiated, gave only minimum results, since the enemy was at close proximity with the Sky Soldiers. The 3rd Platoon was ordered to link up with the 2nd Platoon and assist them to move up the ridge to a more defendable area.

Then both elements began moving back up hill approximately seventy-five (75) meters and forming a common perimeter along the ridgeline, with 2nd Platoon on the west and 3rd Platoon on the east.

At 0810 hours, the elements of the 2nd and 3rd Platoon came under attack from the north by an estimated reinforced NVA Platoon. The attack was repulsed but renewed with increased intensity. As the attack continued for the next half hour. Captain Milton reported to Battalion that his two lead elements were in heavy contact.

Based on the information he had, Partain called in an air strike. In order to bring in the jets, or fast movers, the artillery had to be shifted while the planes were in the area. Not everyone thought air strikes should be used. Because air strikes were less accurate than artillery, the NVA knew that the closer they moved to an allied unit, the safer they were.

Major Watson knew this, too. When the order for use of the fast movers came to him, he thought it was a mistake. "Negative," he responded to the order to shift the artillery.

General Deane, who had arrived in the area, came up on the Battalion net. "Shift the artillery," Deane ordered, overriding Watson.

From 0820 to 0825, the jets dropped their bombs along the east side of the ridge. At 0835, Huey gunships arrived on the scene. To help mark their Platoons' perimeter for the close-in support from the gunships' weapons systems, Lieutenants Judd and Hood had their men toss out smoke grenades, or "pop smoke" in the grunts' jargon.

Another reality about fighting in the highlands became apparent. The thick jungle dispersed the smoke so widely that the gunships couldn't get an accurate fix on the Paratroopers' location.

On the ground, the effects were disastrous. The rising columns of smoke told the NVA right where the Americans were. Specialist Patterson noticed the increase in small-arms fire immediately. Seconds later NVA mortar rounds began crashing into the perimeter, tearing American flesh. Amid the renewed cries of "Medic!" Paratroopers were yelling, "No more smoke. No more smoke." But it was too late. The NVA now had an accurate fix on their positions.

Even while the gunships were firing blindly into the jungle around them, the NVA were massing for another ground attack. At 0850 Lieutenant Judd radioed back to Milton, "Six, we're bracing for an all-out attack. We're laid out well. About a hundred gooks are getting ready to hit us."

Before Milton could respond the roar of M16, fire filled the handset. He was starting to wonder if the two platoons would make it. They had been in contact for almost two hours.

The attack was repulsed with heavy casualties to the Sky Soldiers, despite the fact that the Sky Soldiers inflicted heavy casualties on the NVA's. The NVA's kept moving through their own dead and wounded in a frenzied attack.

Air, artillery and gun-ships strikes continued throughout the firefight, to include napalm to the north side of the perimeter. At 0900 hours, Captain Milton committed his 1st Platoon to relieve the pressure on the besieged 2nd and 3rd Platoons, at the same time Capt. Milton had his Weapons Platoon assist in evacuating the wounded back up the hill to his CP (command post).

The 1st Platoon had to assault through the NVA's lines to get to the embattled 2nd and 3rd Platoons perimeter. The Weapons Platoon carrying party was unable to reach the battle area. By this time the NVA had the area surrounded and continued their attack on the perimeter despite heavy losses to themselves.

As the battle progressed with A Company's Rifle Platoons being surrounded with no resupply of ammunition or ground support, Capt. Milton reported that his units were in a desperate situation requiring immediate assistance.

General Deane had arrived at the Brigade TOC by this time. Based on reports from Milton and from Partain's aerial observation, General Deane surmised that Alpha Company had not fallen into a prepared ambush but had stumbled into a moving NVA column of indeterminate size. Deane figured the main body of the NVA unit would continue its movement while holding Alpha at bay. He looked over his maps, identifying likely routes of movement, and then barked off the coordinates to the artillery liaison officer. The latter relayed those figures to 3/319th's fire direction center. The 105's poured howitzer shells into those areas, hoping to catch the fleeing NVA.

Colonel Partain reported his findings to General Deane. When Deane learned that Partain had had two choppers shot out from underneath him, he gave Partain his own chopper and crew and sent him back into the air. Before Partain departed, he ordered his remaining company, Bravo, to vacate its base security positions and chopper into an LZ north of where Alpha's three Platoons were fighting for their lives.

The Commander of C Company was reporting heavy movements to their front and flanks, and were carrying dead and wounded with them, were thought to be moving too slow. Battalion ordered C Company to ignore the movements to his front and flanks and to proceed rapidly to the assistance of A Company.

Col. Steverson had alerted Bravo Company 2/503rd who was the Battalion reserve unit, back at Dak-To proper. They were making preparations and planning for their movement, since the contact area was not approachable by helicopter, nor were there any good landing zones close up to the embattled area.

At approximately 1000 hours, the forward elements of Alpha in contact with the NVA, reported they were in heavy contact and their elements were down to fifteen effective. All Platoon Leaders were killed; all Platoon Sergeants were wounded, some several times.

The 2nd Platoon Sergeant and ranking survivor directed that the wounded and the effective be moved back to the ridge, towards the Company's CP. Before action could be initiated on the request, radio contact was broken, and at 1034 hours, Captain Milton reported that he had lost radio contact with his forward elements. At the same time, he requested that Battalion terminate the airstrikes that were pounding the western approaches to the forward positions with napalm and rockets and to use artillery instead. At this time, Captain Milton's CP was not under fire but all available personnel were helping to evacuate the wounded.

Company B 2/503rd Airborne Infantry was inserted into a one ship LZ. The process of this insertion was complicated by a fire in the high kunai grass (caused by smoke grenade). The lead elements (2nd Platoon B/2/503rd) moved out of the LZ towards the battle area about 300 meters south. They received small arms fire with no casualties. Other elements of Bravo Company landed, they moved to join their 2nd Platoon, which was now directing artillery fire against the NVA's.

Members of A Company reported to the CO that heavy movements were noted on the northwest portion of the perimeter. At 1030 and 1100 hours, Capt. Milton made this report to Battalion and requested supporting fire in that area. He then dispatched a guide element back up the ridge to the old laager site to assist C Company 2/503rd back into A Company's perimeter. There was intermittent radio contact with the forward element of A Company and shortly after 1100 hours, radio contact was permanently lost. While trying to make radio contact with his forward element, a group of survivors, led by the 2nd Platoon Sergeant reached the Company's CP.

The disposition of A Company 2/503rd was now about thirty-five wounded and thirty effective, a hasty perimeter was made around the wounded. Then at 1140 hours, Capt. Milton decided to move the Company further up the ridge to a better defendable position. With heavy artillery cover fire, he moved all his wounded and personnel back to a more secure position.

The new position was assaulted from the northwest at 1220 hour and again on 1245 hours, then continued with sporadic small arms fire. As some defended others were feverishly cutting out an LZ as the situation permitted, Captain Milton was wounded during this action. A medical and ammunition re-supply was made into the partially completed LZ.

As Captain Willoughby's Bravo Company 2/503rd completed their insertion into their LZ the Company was ready to move out at 1205 hours and at 1240 hours, they made contact with an estimated NVA Platoon, small-arms fire erupted around them before they had covered much ground. Calling artillery support on the enemy, Willoughby also detected the NVA moving around his left, or east, flank and formed a defensive perimeter.

Airstrikes were called in, at 1335 to 1440 hours the A-1E Skyraiders pounded the suspected enemy area with 500-pound bombs, CBU (Cluster bomb units), napalm and strafing runs were directed against the NVA.

At about the same time the air strikes began for Bravo, Charlie Company reached Alpha's earlier LZ. The CS crystals sown by Sexton's platoon had a disastrous effect on Leonard's Paratroopers. They donned their gas masks, but most found the mask's filters had become wet in all the downpours and were no good. Soon, half the Company were on their knees, retching and with snot running from their noses and tears pouring from their eyes.

Company C finally made it to the old laager site where the B Company party met them, then led them back to the besieged perimeter of A Company 2/503rd. Company C 2/503rd was burdened with 2 KIA's from the night before and this made their progress to assist A Company more difficult. The link up with A and C Companies were effected at 1420 hours, and immediate attention was directed towards the completion of the LZ.

A team from Company C was sent out to the battle area to locate WIA's and to gain information on the enemy's situation. Their retrieval attempt was met with heavy sniper fire from the trees and surrounding area. C Company secured the area and got all WIA's and the remainder of A Company 2/503rd extracted to the Brigade main base camp, and the extraction was completed at 1850 hours.

Company C 2/503rd laagered on the ridge in A Company's perimeter with one Platoon placed on ambush. And B Company laagered in their area with one Platoon in ambush. Throughout the night, artillery was directed against potential NVA routes of withdrawal.

On June 23, 1967, both B and C companies 2/503rd linked up to clear the battlefield, police the area for all members of their units, WIA's, KIA's, and MIA's. They discovered a horrendous situation committed by the NVA's, over half the KIA's (43 personnel) had suffered head wounds inflicted at close range, indicating that the NVA had executed the wounded during the night. One MIA who was recovered alive had survived the ordeal. The coup de grace had merely stunned him, however his head was split open exposing the skull. The Sky Soldiers that were never in a firefight were sick and horrified.

Search and destroy missions conducted on June 24th through 28th, by B and C Company, the Recon Platoon 2/503rd and augmented by E/17th Calvary, produced substantial evidence of the NVA losses. Much NVA equipment was captured and U.S. equipment recovered. Intelligence findings produced documents and three NVA POW's captured by E/17th Calvary. The enemy unit was identified as the K-6 Battalion, subordinate to B-3 Front (this unit was formerly the 6th NVA Battalion, 24th NVA Regiment and detached to the B-3 Front in August 1966).

HISTORY OF THE
335TH ASSAULT HELICOPTER COMPANY
145th Combat Aviation Battalion
APO San Francisco 96227

1 July 1967 through 31 July 1967

Prepared by

1 Lt. PAUL C. HOWELL

Approved by

CHARLES D. UTZMAN
LTC Infantry
Commanding

335TH ASSAULT HELICOPTER COMPANY
145th Combat Aviation Battalion
APO San Francisco 96227

18 January 1968

Subject: Monthly History of the 335th Assault Helicopter Company for the period
1 July through 31 July 1967

To: Commanding Officer
335th Assault Helicopter Company
145th Combat Aviation Battalion
APO San Francisco 96227

I. ORGANIZATION AND DESIGNATION:

A.   Flight Platoons (2) -- COWBOYS

(1)   First Airlift Platoon -- Ramrods
Platoon Commander: Captain Ronald N. Wecas
Aircraft: 10 UH-1D "Slicks" -- Troop Carriers.

(2)   Second Airlift Platoon -- Mustangs
Platoon Commander: Major Jon R. Dickerson
Aircraft: 10 UH-1D "Slicks" -- Troop Carriers.

(3)   Armed Helicopter Platoon -- Falcons
Platoon Commander: Captain Donald N. Moss
Aircraft: 8 UH-1B "Guns" -- Armed Escort.

B.   166th Transportation Detachment.
(1) Commander: Major Robert A. Lawson
(2) 1 UH-1B recovery helicopter -- Horsethief.

C.   25th Medical Detachment.

D.   234th Signal Detachment.

II. OPERATIONS:

a. July 1st opened another calendar month in the history of the COWBOYS, supporting the 173rd Airborne Brigade (Separate) at Dak To. Seven (7) ships were utilized during the day's activities. Four (4) ships were flown on a lift in the morning, lifting 108 "Sky Soldiers" of the Brigade, and were then released to fly Brigade missions, and were then released to fly resupply missions for the completion of the day, 13 tons of cargo was carried. The three (3) remaining ships were used on LRRP standby, being called on later in the day to extract a team. The morning of the 1st was a quiet day and all personnel had high hopes that this was an indication for the tone of the entire months' activities. At 1615 all hopes were shattered as news arrived to operations that aircraft 900 had crashed on a resupply mission. Warrant Officer Bobby Manning was flying at the time, luckily no one was injured. Material failure was the cause of the accident.

b. On 2 July the COWBOYS started the day with a Combat Assault of "Sky Soldiers" of the Brigade. An LRRP extraction and resupply took up most of the remainder of the days' activities. The troops that were lifted in the morning were all extracted in the late afternoon upon completion of their search and destroy mission.

c. On 3 July the COWBOYS supported the 173rd Airborne Brigade with five (5) ships for resupply. Because of a delay of weather in the morning 26 hours was all that they were able to fly. The Long Range Reconnaissance Patrol also called on three (3) COWBOY aircraft and a Falcon Light Fire Team. A team was placed in and later extracted under fire, this gave the Falcons a good chance to practice with their weapons. A recon was made for a Combat Assault and an extraction that is scheduled to take place tomorrow, weather permitting.

d. July 4th. The Combat Assault that was planned yesterday went off as scheduled. No real problems with the weather however fire was received and returned per COWBOY fashion. An extraction was also made, removing 192 "Sky Soldiers" from the field to the rear location for a needed rest from the rigors of the forward Combat elements. One LRRP team was extracted with negative contact. Six (6) ships completed the days' activities with resupply missions. 23 tons of cargo and 60 passengers were carried. The 173rd Airborne Brigade (Separate) helped the COWBOYS celebrate the 4th of July Holiday at the Special Forces Camp of Dak To in Kontum Providence. The Brigade Artillery Battalion put out for all to see, a fireworks, Artillery display.

e. 5, 6, and 7 July were fairly routine operations in support of the paratroopers of the 173rd Airborne Brigade. Resupply missions took up most of the days' activities, over 70 tons of cargo and 100 passengers. Two (2) Combat Assaults, Reconnaissance and General Support missions comprised the remainder of the activities. Sporadic enemy fire was received during the completion of the missions. No hits were sustained by any of our aircraft.

f. The morning of 8 July began with a five (5) ship Combat Assault. The remainder of the day was spent in resupplying the forward elements of the Brigade. Fire was received and returned and negative results available, no ships were hit.

g. 9 July began with ten (10) UH-1Ds, a Light Fire Team and the C&C ship, supporting the Brigade in a Combat Assault. Five (5) lifts were made into an area in the vicinity of Dak Seang. No enemy contact was made during the lifts. Resupply took up most of the days' activities with the exception of the infiltration of one LRRP team.

h. LRRP missions took up the major portions of the days' activities. One (1) team was lifted in and another was extracted. Two (2) ships were called up to haul resupply and a Light Fire Team was used to cover a "Dust Off" on its mission to extract wounded personnel.

i. 11 through 14 July all missions were flown in support of the 173rd Abn. Bde. Operation Greeley. 12 July aircraft 201 on a kick-out resupply mission lost power and settled into the trees. No injuries resulted.

j. 15 July. 90 "Sky Soldiers" of E/17 Cav., 173rd Airborne Brigade (Separate) were lifted into an LZ for the purpose of sweeping a suspected area of enemy concentration and were extracted in the late afternoon. Light small arms fire was received, on the initial assault into the area and the Falcons suppressed, driving the enemy from the area.

k. On 16 July 1967 we supplied four (4) ships for resupply of the 173rd. They carried 20 tons of cargo and 122 passengers. One (1) slick and three (3) Falcons were able to accomplish some training and standardization rides which they were in need of.

l. 17 and 18 July found the company supporting the 173rd Abn. Bde. with aircraft to reposition and extract some of their paratroopers. Resupply, training and General Support took up most of the days' activities. The Falcons got to test out their weapons systems when they received permission for suppression on the last lifts out of the areas.

m. Five (5) UH-1D troop carriers from the company performed an extraction of 86 troopers from a forward location to the airfield at Dak To. Ten (10) UH-1D "Slicks" and two (2) Falcons supported the Brigade for the remainder of the day in resupply and General Support missions. No fire was reported or received during the day. Warrant Officer Manker and Warrant Officer Burton were flying a resupply mission. Upon taking off from the feed bag, POL point, they lost RPM rapidly, and aircraft 884 crashed from 4 feet and rolled on its left calf. Specialist Four Daniel Trace sustained a bruised left knee and was taken to the 173rd Airborne Brigade, "B" medical facilities for treatment, he was returned to the company later in the day.

n. The COWBOYS with the aid of five (5) UH-1Hs from the 189th AHC, at Holloway, and a Casper UH-1D from the 173rd Abn. Bde. flight platoon as a smoke ship rappelled cavalry and engineer troops of the Brigade into a crater formed during a B-52 strike. With the smoke used as screening during the rappelling operations, no enemy contact was made. It took the engineers over seven hours to improve a suitable site to accept a UH-1 helicopter for a single ship assault.

o. E Troop 17th Cav., 173rd Abn. Bde. was lifted into Combat Assault by the COWBOYS with the aid of three (3) UH-1H (Ghost Riders) and CH-47s. The entire lift was hampered frequently by low clouds, short turn around and artillery blocking fire. A total of five (5) lifts on behalf of the COWBOYS was required. Pathfinders were used at the pickup zone and the landing zone to help expedite the flow of traffic.

p. The LRRP teams have again begun to get back into the action. On the 22nd Recon's were made for the possible infiltration of troops. For the three-day period 22 July through 24 July LRRP teams were infiltrated and later extracted under fire. No ships were hit. General support and resupply took up the remainder of the days' activities in support of the Brigade. 49 tons of cargo and 360 passengers were transported.

q. At approximately 2000 hours in the evening of 25 July word was received that the Special Forces Camp at Dak Seang was under an intense attack by mortar and recoilless rifle. Less than 20 minutes later a Falcon Light Fire Team led by Lieutenant Thomas L. Anderson and wing ship piloted by Lieutenant Charles F. Jackson had fought their way through the intense low cloud cover and ground fog. They received a situation briefing and began suppressing identified targets by their muzzle flashes. After completely expending their ammo they returned to Dak To, rearmed, refueled and returned to the area of Dak Seang, although they had to fly through steady deteriorating weather. The Falcons showed to all their extremely superior courage and bravery tonight by flying to the aid of the Dak Seang Special Forces camp and lifting the siege when other Light Fire Teams were forced to turn back due to the extremely poor weather conditions.

r. The low cloud cover that affected the Falcons flying the evening of the 25th hung in around Dak To late into the mornings through the 28th causing as much as five hours delay in order for the ships to begin their daily missions. LRRP teams were placed in with negative contact, resupply was the major mission for this period. Over 52 tons of cargo and 230 passengers were carried during the weather shortened and interrupted working days.

s. The Falcons got a lot of practice on the 29th of July as they were called upon to put suppressive fire into a landing zone awaiting the COWBOYS and also to attack several other likely targets of enemy resistance or strength. Over 128 rockets and 11,000 rounds of 7.62 ammo were expended.

t. Two (2) LRRP teams and an ARVN Mike, ten-man, force team were extracted on the 30th without enemy resistance on contact. Two (2) COWBOYS were used for resupply and another slick with gunships escort was used for General Support.

u. The COWBOYS completed another month with the aid of CH-47s in the extraction of a forward fire support base. The CH-47s lifted out all the large equipment and many of the personnel, leaving for the COWBOYS the 64-man security force remaining in the area. The pathfinders were utilized in both the pickup zone and landing zone. Neither weather nor the enemy effected the extraction of the personnel or equipment. The month of July ended with another well-run operation.

III. MONTHLY STATISTICS:

	UH-1B	UH-1D	TOTAL
TOTAL SORTIES	829	4967	5796
COMBAT SORTIES	717	4503	5210
HOURS	721	1291	2012
PAX		6571	6571
CARGO (TONS)		591	591
AMMO - 2.75	890		890
7.62	183,200		183,200
40MM	42		42
MEDIVACS-VC/KBA	33		33
AIRCRAFT HITS			
U.S./WIA/KIA			
UH-1B MISSIONS	205		205
AVG. ACFT HOURS	20	12	32
CA'S	19		19
EXTRACTION'S		21	21
REPOSITIONING		11	11
HIGH AVIATOR			141.6
LOW AVIATOR			4.2

IV. AWARDS RECEIVED DURING THE MONTH OF JULY 1967

PFC DELMONACO	BASIC AIR MEDAL
SP4 ASHE BACK	BASIC AIR MEDAL
SP4 CARITHERS	BASIC AIR MEDAL
SP4 BROWN	BASIC AIR MEDAL
SP4 BYNUM	BASIC AIR MEDAL
SP4 CLEGG	BASIC AIR MEDAL
SP4 FOSSETT	BASIC AIR MEDAL
PFC GIBSON	BASIC AIR MEDAL
PVT GRODE	BASIC AIR MEDAL
SP4 KING	BASIC AIR MEDAL
WO1 KORTH	BASIC AIR MEDAL
SSG MORI	BASIC AIR MEDAL
PFC PRATER	BASIC AIR MEDAL
SP5 ROOK	BASIC AIR MEDAL
SP4 STORSTEEN	BASIC AIR MEDAL
SP4 TUPPER	BASIC AIR MEDAL
SP4 MULLEN	BASIC AIR MEDAL
SP5 FRELAK	BASIC AIR MEDAL
SSG EPSTEIN	ARMY COMMENDATION
SSG WITCHER	ARMY COMMENDATION
SP5 FRELAK	PURPLE HEART
SSG MEEHAN	PURPLE HEART

HISTORY OF THE
335TH ASSAULT HELICOPTER COMPANY
145th Combat Aviation Battalion
APO San Francisco 96227

1 August 1967 through 31 August 1967

Prepared by

1 Lt. PAUL C. HOWELL

Approved by

CHARLES D. UTZMAN
LTC Infantry
Commanding

335TH ASSAULT HELICOPTER COMPANY
145th Combat Aviation Battalion
APO San Francisco 96227

20 January 1968

Subject: Monthly History of the 335th Assault Helicopter Company for the period
1 August through 31 August 1967

To: Commanding Officer
335th Assault Helicopter Company
145th Combat Aviation Battalion
APO San Francisco 96227

I. ORGANIZATION AND DESIGNATION:

A.   Flight Platoons (2) -- COWBOYS

    (1)   First Airlift Platoon -- Ramrods
        Platoon Commander: Captain Ronald N. Wecas
        Aircraft: 10 UH-1D "Slicks" -- Troop Carriers.

    (2)   Second Airlift Platoon -- Mustangs
        Platoon Commander: Captain William O. Jones
        Aircraft: 10 UH-1D "Slicks" -- Troop Carriers.

    (3)   Armed Helicopter Platoon -- Falcons
        Platoon Commander: Captain Phillip P. Osterli
        Aircraft: 8 UH-1B "Guns" -- Armed Escort.

B.   166th Transportation Detachment.
    (1) Commander: Major Robert A. Lawson
    (2) 1 UH-1B recovery helicopter -- Horsethief.

C.   25th Medical Detachment.

D.   234th Signal Detachment.

II. OPERATIONS:

a. Another month, that of August, is beginning to unfold for the COWBOYS at the 335th Assault Helicopter Company. The month began with a Combat Assault in support of the 4th Battalion 503rd Infantry, 173rd Airborne Brigade (Separate). The operation was initially delayed for four hours due to the bad weather. Once the operation commenced it moved rapidly as two (2) troop carriers and a Light Fire Team assaulted a pinnacle at 1245 with full suppression by all concerned. 125 passengers in all were lifted onto the pinnacle.

b. Perhaps 3 August will be best remembered as the day the COWBOYS supported everyone with every type of conceivable mission. General Support and resupply missions began the days' operations. At 1320 hours the 1/42 Inf. (ARVN) were air lifted into a Combat Assault. 180 ARVN soldiers were lifted. Artillery preparation by the ARVN units was excellent. At 1530 hours the company swiftly extracted "A" Co. 1/503rd Abn. Bde. from a one (1) ship pinnacle pickup zone. At 1604 hours 60 ARVN's of the 8/11 Abn Inf. were repositioned on a very short notice, at 1837 hours' two (2) lifts were completed for "C" Co. 4/503rd Inf. to complete their extraction. Fire was received and returned on several occasions today. One (1) gunship received three (3) hits but continued to fly. The Falcons received credit for ten (10) confirmed NVA KIA by body count.

c. On 4 August the COWBOYS conducted a repositioning of troops and cargo from Dak To to two (2) landing zones adjacent to the Special Forces camp at Dak Pek. Due to weather the first lift was forced to return to Dak To after being enroute. The Falcons were not utilized for the lift. 238 troops were lifted in six (6) separate assaults. The Falcons and their marksmanship were called upon to place suppression around the ARVN troops that were placed in the day before West of Dak Seang. They were given credit for five (5) confirmed KIA's and several more possible. The ARVN's are in tough contact and putting up a good fight for it.

d. The ARVN troops remained in contact with the NVA West of Dak Seang. The Ramrods, led by Lieutenant Arville Steed, furnished the ARVN's by means of sling loads the necessary ammunition, food and medical supplies to sustain them. Fire was received by all ships going into the area. Late in the evening of the 6th Warrant Officer Garry Bass took a sling load in and dropped it on target even though his ship 701, commonly called "Magnet Ass," received several rounds and was forced to land at Dak Seang to be evacuated. Because of the darkness and poor weather conditions no more supplies or assistance could be offered to them until the morning of the 7th.

On the 7th as soon as the weather broke the COWBOYS once again were out supporting the ARVN's that were in contact. The Ramrods under the supervision of Lt. Steed and the cover of the Falcons immediately began resupply. Warrant Officer Garry Wong was in charge of the Falcon Fire Team, on one of his breaks after his firing pass he received fire and sustained a bullet wound in the calf of his right leg. Warrant Officer Tillman Jefferey flying with, Warrant Officer Wong, he flew the ship back to Dak To and landed without the assistance of hydraulics. It was a good landing and Warrant Officer Wong was taken to "B" Med for treatment.

Lieutenant Steed was later awarded the Vietnamese Cross of Gallantry with Bronze Star, for heroism in this action. Lieutenant Steed accepted his in person while Warrant Officer Jefferey accepted Warrant Officer Wong's for him since he was in the hospital at that time.

e. August 8th, the missions today were all delayed due to weather. The weather broke only long enough for the company to perform three (3) lifts in a Combat Assault and one (1) lift in an extraction in support of the 173rd Airborne Brigade during Operation Greeley.

f. The COWBOYS began 9 August by repositioning 181 troops for the Brigade. They were placed into two (2) separate locations to hopefully capture someone while closing on each other. Heavy automatic weapons fire was received during the day and was returned in routine Falcon suppression. No results were available for the Falcon strikes. One (1) LRRP team was extracted, this was done without enemy contact.

g. The 10th found the COWBOYS supporting the LRRP's with Combat Assaults (infiltration's) of two (2) teams. No enemy resistance was met making it a relatively quiet peaceful day. Four (4) "Slicks" supported the Brigade the rest of the day with resupply hauling 5 tons of cargo and 31 "Sky Soldiers."

Word came up today from Bien Hoa that we were going to be getting in "H" model Hueys to replace the old "D" models we are using. No one up North at either Pleiku or Dak To believed it. Perhaps they should have as it turns out the ships or at least a couple of them awaiting us at Saigon and Vung Tau already.

h.   11 August began with eight (8) "Slicks" of the 335th Assault Helicopter Company, COWBOYS, repositioning 219 "Sky Soldiers" of the 173rd Airborne Brigade to a fire support base from the forward area. Resupply was then carried on by four (4) of the ships while the additional four (4) were placed on LRRP standby for possible extraction. At approximately 1630 hours' one (1) team requested extraction. The extraction was performed in the usual superior manner of the COWBOYS. Light small arms fire was received and returned in what is now considered COWBOY fashion and excellence by the forward troops in the field that they support.

i.   At 0849 on the 12th the COWBOYS began a repositioning of the 1st Abn Task Force (ARVN) from the Special Forces airstrip at Dak Seang to the airstrip at Dak To I. It was a routine move and all went smoothly. The COWBOYS lifted 285 troops with CH-47s lifting the remaining troopers. Upon completion of the move the COWBOYS gave a well done to the ARVN soldiers for the job that they performed in the hills West of Dak Seang. In the late afternoon the COWBOYS were requested for an emergency extraction of an LRRP team in the field that was under heavy contact. Immediately responding to the call, they removed the team under an intensive volume of enemy automatic weapons fire. No ships were hit, and the Falcons got in a few punches of their own for attempting to interfere with the mission of the LRRP and the COWBOYS.

j.   On 13 August at 1440 hours the COWBOYS began the cleaning operation on a pickup zone that the CH-47s had started. They lifted out 106 passengers and then proceeded back to their normal missions of resupply and General Support. At 1630 hours while flying resupply Lieutenant Hallinam's ship (736) lost power and crashed. The crew was evacuated, and the ship was surrounded with security until the next morning when recovery operations were completed.

k.   Weather caused a 2 1/2-hour delay in the scheduled lift consisting of both a Combat Assault and an extraction. Artillery and gunships plus radar bombing were the pre-strike on the landing zone. A total of 308 "Sky Soldiers" were moved during the lifts. Light automatic weapons fire was received during the lift and consequently assaulted by the gunships. No results were available on the Falcon suppression. Today the first of the company's new "H" models was flown in from Bien Hoa. We are supposed to receive a total of 23 within the near future and turn in all of our "D" models.

l.   The 16th to 18th found most of the ships in support of the 2/503rd Inf., 173rd Airborne Brigade. Several extractions were performed in the days' activities 270 "Sky Soldiers" were extracted and one (1) Combat Assault also for the 2nd Battalion was performed in which 130 troopers were assaulted.

On the 18th during a resupply mission heavy automatic weapons fire was received and returned. One round was taken, but the ship was able to continue to fly and complete its mission. No injuries resulted from the incident. The second flight of "H" models flew in today. We're getting the numbers built up fast. They reported having several more waiting for us at Bien Hoa on the pads in the COWBOY corral.

m.   19 August began was a normal support day for the 335th Aslt Hel Co., while supporting the 173rd Airborne Brigade in operation Greeley.

n.   20 August began with a Combat Assault of 200 paratroopers of the 2nd Battalion at 0935. Low level flight was required on the assault into the landing zone due to the low ceilings and poor visibility enroute. The Falcons placed a pre-strike into the area.

At 1100 hours an extraction for the 4th Battalion was commenced. 180 paratroopers were extracted from Dak Pek back to Dak To. Five (5) Ghost Riders were utilized to help expedite the move. Fire was received by one of the COWBOYS new "H" models that was being used on its first Combat Assault, fortunately no hits were taken.

At 1600 hours the paratroopers of the 2nd Battalion that were assaulted during the morning were extracted. The unit had completed its sweep of the area and had negative enemy contact.

o.   At 0836, nine (9) COWBOYS, five (5) Alligators and a CH-47 left Dak To for Dak Pek to begin an extraction of the 1st Battalion 173rd Airborne Brigade, as scheduled. One turn around was accomplished when weather moved in and delayed the operation. After a six hour delay it was again commenced and then proceeded without further delay. No enemy resistance was met and the operation was terminated at 1910 hours upon touchdown at Dak To with the last troopers. 270 "Sky Soldiers" were extracted on the COWBOY ships.

p.   Eight (8) COWBOYS began a Combat Assault at 0900 hours for the 4th Battalion. 130 troopers were carried on the assault into the tall grassy landing zone.

At 1130 hours' eight (8) COWBOYS and five (5) Ghost Riders extracted a mike force from a 4500-foot pinnacle. The pickup zone was only large enough to accommodate one aircraft at a time. Weather was marginal with rain showers causing low visibility during the extraction.

q. 23 through 26 August were routine days for the COWBOYS in support of the 173rd Airborne Brigade participation in operation Greeley. Missions in support of the LRRP -- none emergency, and resupply with several small, short Combat Assaults and extractions took up most of the time on hand for the COWBOYS. Weather frequently interfered with the rapid accomplishment of the missions and frequently delayed them.

r. 27 August was a busy day for the COWBOYS in support of the 173rd LRRP teams. Two (2) teams were placed into separate locations. Almost immediately after the second team was placed in they made heavy contact with the enemy and requested immediate emergency extraction. The COWBOYS and Falcons responded and removed the team under a heavy volume of small arms and automatic weapons fire. The Falcons showed their excellence by placing in closely concentrated fire around the area to protect the team and the ship. All had a busy day all together, being called on several times for their support. 82 rockets, 200-40mm rounds, and 20,000-7.62 rounds were expended during the day.

s. On 28 August the COWBOYS repositioned 200 "Sky Soldiers" for the Brigade. They also carried 28 tons of cargo and 121 passengers, while on the missions of resupply.

Major Lawson went to Quin Nhon to pickup the last three (3) "H" models for the company. As it turned out when he arrived he found out that the 335th Transportation Company had received the word of the aircraft for them and came down from Chu Lai the day before and picked them up. The discrepancy was settled, and Major Lawson made arrangements to go to Chu Lai and pick them up on the 30th.

t. Normal support of the Brigade took place, on the 29th and 30th, in the 335th participation of operation Greeley.

The weather at Pleiku caused the cancellation of the trip to Chu Lai to pick up the aircraft for at least another day.

u. On 31 August the COWBOYS participated in a Combat Assault, an extraction, a repositioning and resupply missions. All in support of the 173rd Airborne Brigade. 450 troopers and 28 tons of cargo were carried. No enemy contact was noted by the COWBOYS.

Major Lawson and crews were able to get to Chu Lai and pick up the remaining three (3) "H" models. The COWBOYS now have a total of 23 new "H's," with high expectations of what is too, and can be done. The Falcons have now got that gleam in their eye that perhaps the new Huey Cobra will not be far from the grasps of the COWBOYS. Only time will tell for sure. Maybe next month!

III. MONTHLY STATISTICS:

	UH-1B	UH-1D	TOTAL
TOTAL SORTIES	813	5873	6686
COMBAT SORTIES	729	5345	6074
HOURS	341	1211	1552
PAX	5939		5939
CARGO (TONS)	257		257

IV. AWARDS RECEIVED DURING THE MONTH OF AUGUST 1967

1Lt. LUNGARELLA	DISTINGUISHED FLYING CROSS
WO1 MAGONIGAL	DISTINGUISHED FLYING CROSS
CPT. STULTS	DISTINGUISHED FLYING CROSS
WO1 TEMEYER	DISTINGUISHED FLYING CROSS
MAJ. DAVIS	DISTINGUISHED FLYING CROSS
LTC UTZMAN	BRONZE STAR
CPT. GOIN	BRONZE STAR
SFC WARREN	BRONZE STAR
PVT MIDGETT	AIR MEDAL W/ "V"
MAJ. GAMMONS	AIR MEDAL W/ "V"
WO1 HAMNAI	AIR MEDAL W/ "V"
2Lt. MUSCI	AIR MEDAL W/ "V"
CPT. STULTS	AIR MEDAL W/ "V"
SP4 LOCKWOOD	AIR MEDAL W/ "V"
SP5 BOUTIA	AIR MEDAL W/ "V"
CPT. WECAS	AIR MEDAL W/ "V"
WO1 GREGG	AIR MEDAL W/ "V"
WO1 AVONI	AIR MEDAL W/ "V"
SP4 SADDLER	AIR MEDAL W/ "V"
SP4 CHANDLER	AIR MEDAL W/ "V"
SP5 MERIDETH	AIR MEDAL W/ "V"
SP4 HICKEY	AIR MEDAL W/ "V"
SP4 NELSON	AIR MEDAL W/ "V"
WO1 FREEMAN	AIR MEDAL
MAJ. DICKERSON	ARMY COMMENDATION
CPT. CONGER	ARMY COMMENDATION
SP4 HICKEY	ARMY COMMENDATION
PVT MIDGETT	PURPLE HEART
WO1 QUIBERG	PURPLE HEART
SSG NOVALLIS	GOOD CONDUCT

HISTORY OF THE
335TH ASSAULT HELICOPTER COMPANY
145th Combat Aviation Battalion
APO San Francisco 96227

1 September 1967 through 30 September 1967

Prepared by

1 Lt. PAUL C. HOWELL

Approved by

CHARLES D. UTZMAN
LTC Infantry
Commanding

335TH ASSAULT HELICOPTER COMPANY
145th Combat Aviation Battalion
APO San Francisco 96227

22 January 1968

Subject: Monthly History of the 335th Assault Helicopter Company for the period
1 September through 30 September 1967

To: Commanding Officer
335th Assault Helicopter Company
145th Combat Aviation Battalion
APO San Francisco 96227

I. ORGANIZATION AND DESIGNATION:

A.   Flight Platoons (2) -- COWBOYS

(1)   First Airlift Platoon -- Ramrods
Platoon Commander: Captain Ronald N. Wecas
Aircraft: 11 UH-1H "Slicks" -- Troop Carriers.

(2)   Second Airlift Platoon -- Mustangs
Platoon Commander: Captain William O. Jones
Aircraft: 11 UH-1H "Slicks" -- Troop Carriers.

(3)   Armed Helicopter Platoon -- Falcons
Platoon Commander: Captain Phillip P. Osterli
Aircraft: 8 UH-1B "Guns" -- Armed Escort.

B.   166th Transportation Detachment.
(1) Commander: Major Robert A. Lawson
(2) 1 UH-1H recovery helicopter -- Horsethief.

C.   25th Medical Detachment.

D.   234th Signal Detachment.

II. OPERATIONS:

a. September 1st began as a new day in a new month in the history of the COWBOYS. The COWBOYS arose to the realization that they were still supporting the 173rd Airborne Brigade out of Dak To in Operation Greeley.

Ten (10) "Slicks" and a Heavy Fire Team were called on at 0800 hours to move a company of the 1st Battalion. No enemy contact was made and the operation went off smoothly. Five (5) ships hauled LOC (resupply) and four (4) ships plus a Light Fire Team remained on LRRP standby the remainder of the day.

Word has come down that the COWBOYS will be moving sometime soon. All hopes are focused on the possibility that the move may be back to Bien Hoa. Time will tell that these hopes were later destroyed.

b. 2, 3, and 4 September found the COWBOYS supporting the 173rd Airborne Brigade with General Support, LRRP standby, and an occasional movement of personnel. No enemy contact was met while moving 80 tons of cargo, 750 "Sky Soldiers" of the Brigade.

c. On 5 September 260 paratroopers were extracted from a forward position and placed back at a fire support base.

In the late afternoon the LRRP called on the COWBOYS for an emergency extraction of one team that was in contact and unable to lose the enemy force in the jungle. The team was extracted safely while the Falcons placed rockets and suppressive fires into the positions. No hits were received by any of the ships.

d. The morning of the 6th began with the COWBOYS repositioning 315 paratroopers of the Brigade from two forward elements back to a fire support base. The repositioning was done smoothly and without incident. The remainder of the day consisted of resupply missions carrying 18 tons of cargo and 77 passengers.

e. On 7 September 1967 LRRP standby and resupply were the missions for the day. Midafternoon a call was received for emergency extraction of a team. The extraction was accomplished in a rather exemplary manner with light small arms fire received and returned.

f. 8 September found the COWBOYS performing numerous Combat Assaults. An LRRP team was placed in without incident. 386 "Sky Soldiers" were lifted in by five (5) COWBOY aircraft on a Combat Assault with a small turn around time. Late in the afternoon 76 troopers of the 42 ARVN were heli-lifted on a Combat Assault. The COWBOYS kept themselves busy today but did not notice any enemy movement.

g. Today the COWBOYS seem to have located the enemy. While flying resupply fire was received on several occasions. One (1) Ship was hit and the gunner, PFC Waller, was wounded in the leg and taken to "B" Med, 173rd Abn. Bde. for treatment.

h. Again, on the tenth the COWBOYS seem to have stirred up a hornet nest frequently throughout the day fire was received. On one occasion the pilots reported that they had received rocket fire that was directed at their ship. Fire was returned, but with negative results available.

i. Rumors are beginning to spread around a lot faster now about the COWBOYS moving. The COWBOYS as versatile as they are, are about ready for a change now and are really beginning to expect one. On the 11th the COWBOYS supported the 173rd Abn. Bde. with LRRP, resupply and General Support. No fire was received and no enemy movement was noted.

j. On 12 September 220 "Sky Soldiers" were placed into a landing zone on a Combat Assault. 116 troopers of E/17 Cav. were extracted back to the rear area of Dak To. 24 tons of cargo were also extracted. No enemy contact was met.

k. On 13 September the COWBOYS with the aid of four (4) CH-47s extracted the 3rd ARVN Abn Bn from Dak Seang back to their home base at Dak To I. Lack of coordination slowed the extraction at first, but it then proceeded as scheduled without any further complications.

l. On 14 and 15 September the COWBOYS performed extractions for the 1st and 4th Battalions, 503rd Infantry, 173rd Airborne Brigade (separate). The troopers were all lifted without incident. The COWBOYS have received word to move on the 17th to a place called Phu Hiep on the coast, just South of Tuy Hoa. An advanced party of Major Spanjers and Lt. Anderson have been sent ahead to reconnoiter the area and plan for the company's arrival.

m. On the 16th the COWBOYS supported the Brigade with two (2) "Slicks" and a Light Fire Team. Most of the day was used for packing and preparing for the move to Phu Hiep. Everyone kept themselves busy preparing the area for the move.

n. At 1300 hours on the afternoon of the 17th the COWBOYS departed Dak To enroute to Phu Hiep. They closed at Phu Hiep at approximately 1600 hours with the delightful surprise of discovering that they would not have to stay in tents but would be moving into already constructed buildings. The detachment at Pleiku will remain at that location until arrangements can be made to transport them to Phu Hiep.

o. The 18th was a free day for the COWBOYS to set up in the new area, awaiting the arrival of the 173rd Abn. Bde. to close tomorrow and commence Operation Bolling.

p. On 19 September the COWBOYS organized lead Combat Assaults for the 173rd Airborne Brigade with the units of the 268th Combat Aviation Battalion forming a lift of 60 ships in support of the Brigade. Minor difficulties occurred in the lifts, but all problems were worked out without much of a delay. No enemy resistance was met in today's operation the first in the Tuy Hoa area for the Brigade and the COWBOYS of the 173rd. Operation Bolling has begun.

q. The 20th through the 22nd of September found the COWBOYS in direct support of the Brigade. Numerous small lifts were intermingled with LRRP and resupply in support of the Brigade. No significant enemy contact was made, no fire was received by any of the COWBOY ships.

r. On 23 September the COWBOYS supported the 4th Battalion and E/17 Cav. on two separate Combat Assaults. 512 "Sky Soldiers" were lifted in the first assault in support of the 4th Battalion. 60 troops of the Cav. were lifted. Poor planning on the part of the supported units caused a slower operation and made the requirement necessary for an additional refueling stop. No enemy resistance was met.

s. On 24 September three (3) separate lifts were performed to reposition units of the 1st and 4th Battalions. No difficulties resulted with the units moving as scheduled. 290 "Sky Soldiers" were carried in all. The remainder of the day was spent in General Support and resupply of the Brigade. 133 passengers were carried along with 28 tons of cargo.

t. The 25th and 26th of September found the COWBOYS in normal support of the 173rd Abn. Bde. (Separate). One (1) small Combat Assault took place on the 25th. Resupply and General Support took up most of the days' operations carrying 360 passengers and 32 tons of cargo.

u. On 27 September 1967, ten (10) UH-1Hs and two (2) Light Fire Team's lifted 420 "Sky Soldiers" of the 4th Battalion into a total of six (6) separate landing zones. All landing zones were five (5) ship rice paddy areas. 116 troops and 24 tons of cargo were lifted in support of the forward elements of the 173rd Abn. Bde. No fire or enemy contact was noted during the day.

v. Today's missions of the COWBOYS were in normal support of the 173rd Abn. Bde. (Separate) and its units in the field on Operation Bolling.

w. 29 September found the COWBOYS and four (4) Falcons gunships in support of the Brigade by lifting 489 "Sky Soldiers" in a Combat Assault. An LRRP team was extracted under fire when they came under heavy contact and were unable to break contact. All members of the team were extracted and none of the aircraft received any hits. 63 passengers and 15 tons of cargo were carried during resupply and 177 passengers were carried on General Support of the Brigade. The Falcons had a good day while logging 21 hours and expending 107 -- 2.75 rockets and 10,000 -- rounds of 7.62 ammunition.

x. September came to an end with the COWBOYS supporting the 173rd Abn. Bde. out of Phu Hiep. Resupply, LRRP, General Support and a short lift concluded the months' activities. The company is still divided among three locations, one at Bien Hoa for coordination with the 145th Combat Aviation Battalion and its logistical support. The remainder, majority -- all flight elements, are located at Phu Hiep in support of the 173rd Abn. Bde. Perhaps October will find the COWBOYS all back together again at one location.

III. MONTHLY STATISTICS:

	UH-1B	UH-1D	UH-1H	TOTAL
TOTAL SORTIES	300	105	2,000	2405
COMBAT SORTIES	300	64	910	1274
HOURS	231	128	950	1309
PAX		148	4300	4448
CARGO (TONS)		28	230	258

IV. AWARDS RECEIVED DURING THE MONTH OF SEPTEMBER 1967

1Lt. STEED	SILVER STAR
WO1 PEYTON	DISTINGUISHED FLYING CROSS
MAJ. WOOD	DISTINGUISHED FLYING CROSS
WO1 QUIBERG	DISTINGUISHED FLYING CROSS
1Lt. ANDERSON	DISTINGUISHED FLYING CROSS
WO1 WONG	DISTINGUISHED FLYING CROSS
CPT. WECAS	DISTINGUISHED FLYING CROSS
WO1 ANDERSON	DISTINGUISHED FLYING CROSS
1Lt. JACKSON	DISTINGUISHED FLYING CROSS
CPT. MOSS	DISTINGUISHED FLYING CROSS
WO1 JEFFEREY	DISTINGUISHED FLYING CROSS
LTC UTZMAN	DISTINGUISHED FLYING CROSS
MAJ. DICKERSON	BRONZE STAR
CPT. CONGER	BRONZE STAR
WO1 SIMS	AIR MEDAL W/ "V"
WO1 BRYAN	AIR MEDAL W/ "V"
SP4 MERITT	AIR MEDAL W/ "V"
SP4 SEABURY	AIR MEDAL W/ "V"
SP4 FOSSETT	AIR MEDAL W/ "V"
1Lt. HALLINAN	AIR MEDAL W/ "V"
SP4 BROWN	AIR MEDAL W/ "V"
WO1 FREEMAN	AIR MEDAL W/ "V"
PFC ALLEN	AIR MEDAL W/ "V"
SP4 BYNUM	AIR MEDAL W/ "V"
SP5 FRELAND	AIR MEDAL W/ "V"
SP4 GOSSETT	AIR MEDAL W/ "V"
WO1 BARLY	AIR MEDAL W/ "V"
WO1 BURKS	AIR MEDAL W/ "V"
WO1 BURTON	AIR MEDAL W/ "V"
SP4 KNOX	AIR MEDAL W/ "V"
WO1 GRAHAM	AIR MEDAL W/ "V"
SP4 CODY	AIR MEDAL W/ "V"
SP4 EASTMAN	AIR MEDAL W/ "V"
WO1 BRUAD	AIR MEDAL W/ "V"
WO1 CAMPBELL	AIR MEDAL W/ "V"
WO1 NIELSON	AIR MEDAL W/ "V"
PFC BENNETT	AIR MEDAL W/ "V"
MAJ. DICKERSON	AIR MEDAL W/ "V"
SP4 HAVENS	AIR MEDAL W/ "V"
WO1 OSTERMAN	AIR MEDAL W/ "V"
PFC SIMMONS	AIR MEDAL W/ "V"
WO1 BASS	AIR MEDAL W/ "V"
WO1 FOGLE	AIR MEDAL W/ "V"
PFC SWAUZE	AIR MEDAL W/ "V"

SP4 TRACE	AIR MEDAL W/ "V"
SP4 WILLIAMS	AIR MEDAL W/ "V"
WO1 IDELL	AIR MEDAL W/ "V"
SP4 HATTON	AIR MEDAL W/ "V"
SP4 MARCHBANKS	AIR MEDAL W/ "V"
SP5 MERIDETH	AIR MEDAL W/ "V"
SP4 FULLER	AIR MEDAL W/ "V"
SSG LYON	BASIC AIR MEDAL

AWARDS RECEIVED DURING THE MONTH OF SEPTEMBER 1967

WO1 SAXTON	BASIC AIR MEDAL
WO1 SHELSTAD	BASIC AIR MEDAL
PFC SMITH	BASIC AIR MEDAL
SP4 STACEY	BASIC AIR MEDAL
CPT. STEWART	BASIC AIR MEDAL
SP4 TORRES	BASIC AIR MEDAL
SP4 WATSON	BASIC AIR MEDAL
SP4 CARROL	BASIC AIR MEDAL
SP4 CHAMBERS	BASIC AIR MEDAL
SP5 CORBETT	BASIC AIR MEDAL
PFC CORLISS	BASIC AIR MEDAL
WO1 DIBBLE	BASIC AIR MEDAL
SP5 DRIVER	BASIC AIR MEDAL
SP4 KIRKMAN	BASIC AIR MEDAL
WO1 MACHIN	BASIC AIR MEDAL
WO1 MCLAUGHLIN	BASIC AIR MEDAL
SP4 MICHEL	BASIC AIR MEDAL
WO1 MILLS	BASIC AIR MEDAL
WO1 MORRIS	BASIC AIR MEDAL
SP4 O'DELL	BASIC AIR MEDAL
WO1 OLLIFF	BASIC AIR MEDAL
WO1 REZNAK	BASIC AIR MEDAL
WO1 ENRIGHT	BASIC AIR MEDAL
1Lt. FLETT	BASIC AIR MEDAL
PFC LOESCH	BASIC AIR MEDAL
SP4 GOSSETT	BASIC AIR MEDAL
PFC BENNETT	BASIC AIR MEDAL
WO1 HOWARD	BASIC AIR MEDAL
PFC WISE	BASIC AIR MEDAL
SP4 BROWN	ARMY COMMENDATION W/ "V"
PFC ALLEN	ARMY COMMENDATION W/ "V"
SP4 BYNUM	ARMY COMMENDATION W/ "V"
SP5 FRELAK	ARMY COMMENDATION W/ "V"
SP4 GOSSETT	ARMY COMMENDATION W/ "V"
SP5 OLSON	ARMY COMMENDATION W/ "V"
SP4 CARITHERS	ARMY COMMENDATION W/ "V"

SP4 CHANDLER	ARMY COMMENDATION W/ "V"
PFC ERICKSON	ARMY COMMENDATION W/ "V"
SP4 MULLEN	ARMY COMMENDATION W/ "V"
CPT. JONES	ARMY COMMENDATION W/ "V"
1Lt. STEED	ARMY COMMENDATION W/ "V"
CPT. CONGER	ARMY COMMENDATION
SP5 BAKER	GOOD CONDUCT

**HISTORY OF THE
335TH ASSAULT HELICOPTER COMPANY
145th Combat Aviation Battalion
APO San Francisco 96227**

1 October 1967 through 31 October 1967

Prepared by

1 Lt. PAUL C. HOWELL

Approved by

**DONALD R. DRUMM
Major, Artillery
Commanding**

335TH ASSAULT HELICOPTER COMPANY
145th Combat Aviation Battalion
APO San Francisco 96227

22 January 1968

Subject: Monthly History of the 335th Assault Helicopter Company for the period
1 October through 31 October 1967

To: Commanding Officer
335th Assault Helicopter Company
145th Combat Aviation Battalion
APO San Francisco 96227

I. ORGANIZATION AND DESIGNATION:

A. Flight Platoons (2) -- COWBOYS

    (1) First Airlift Platoon -- Ramrods
        Platoon Commander: 1Lt. Thomas L. Anderson
        Aircraft: 11 UH-1H "Slicks" -- Troop Carriers.

    (2) Second Airlift Platoon -- Mustangs
        Platoon Commander: Captain Albert R. Stewart
        Aircraft: 11 UH-1H "Slicks" -- Troop Carriers.

    (3) Armed Helicopter Platoon -- Falcons
        Platoon Commander: Captain Phillip P. Osterli
        Aircraft: 8 UH-1B "Guns" -- Armed Escort.

B. 166th Transportation Detachment.
    (1) Commander: Major Robert A. Lawson
    (2) 1 UH-1H recovery helicopter -- Horsethief.

C. 25th Medical Detachment.

D. 234th Signal Detachment.

II. OPERATIONS:

a. October began with the COWBOYS at Phu Hiep supporting the 173rd Abn. Bde. A change of faces took place in the COWBOYS this morning, Lt. Col. Charles D. Utzman turned over command of the company to Major Donald R. Drumm. Col. Utzman is assuming the duties as the 145th Combat Aviation Battalion Executive Officer. The first activity of the new month for the COWBOYS and its new commander was a Combat Assault of the 4th Battalion. 275 "Sky Soldiers" were transported on the assault. ARA -- aerial rocket artillery, and Falcon gunships placed in the pre-strike on the landing area just prior to the COWBOYS arrival.

b. On 2 October the COWBOYS conducted a Combat Assault with the Recon Platoon of the 1st Battalion, 503rd Infantry to secure a fire support base site. ARA and gunships assisted in the assault. For the remainder of the day 164 troopers and 22 tons of cargo were hauled to the forward area on resupply.

c. On 3 October the COWBOYS were called off their normal missions at 1030 hours to make an assault with a company of the 1st Battalion into an area where an LRRP team was in contact earlier in the day. No enemy contact was made as the Falcons placed in the accurate preparatory suppressive fires.

d. Three (3) lifts in support of E Troop 17 Cav. commenced the operation for 4 October. A 90-minute delay was incurred to delay the operation at first, due to weather. Once the operation started it was completed without delay. 192 passengers and 8 tons of cargo were carried on resupply and General Support.

e. 5 October was spent in normal support of the 173rd Airborne Brigade in Operation Bolling.

f. On 6 October the COWBOYS assaulted "A" 1/503rd Infantry into LZ Basin. The remainder of the Battalion was repositioned into LZ Care that had been secured by a CIDG force. ARA played a slightly different role today as it was used in place of the Falcons. The Falcons had been sent to Dalat yesterday on a reaction mission and were weathered in and unable to return in time for the lift.

g. On 7 October the COWBOYS, supporting the 4th Battalion conducted six (6) lifts into LZ Saddle. Artillery and gunships supported the assault. The COWBOYS were then called upon to clean up Fire Support Base Goose, lifting nine (9) sorties to LZ Basin and three (3) to LZ Saddle.

h. Combat Assaults were becoming a consistent diet for the COWBOYS. The 8th through the 10th at least one (1) lift per day was thrown in to keep the COWBOYS flexible and the Brigade maneuverable. Over 1000 "Sky Soldiers" were lifted during the period included. Rumors are starting to fly, that the COWBOYS will be getting their administration back with them from their Pleiku location.

i. The COWBOYS supported the Brigade with normal missions on the 11th of October in support of Operation Bolling.

At 1000 hours on the morning of the 11th many hard days of work and planning on the part of Major Lawson and 1Lt. Howell paid off as a convoy of 67 vehicles departed Camp Enari, Pleiku, for Phu Hiep. The night of the 11th, was spent at Quin Nhon and they arrived Phu Hiep the evening of the 12th.

j. On 13 October the COWBOYS supported the Brigade with a Combat Assault by lifting 361 "Sky Soldiers" in the assault. No enemy resistance was met.

k. Five (5) ships were put up on both resupply and General Support for the Brigade on the 14th. COWBOY 3 went on a recon late in the afternoon to plan for tomorrow's operation.

l. The lift went off as scheduled on the mooring of the 15th. Ten (10) COWBOY "Slicks" and a Falcon Light Fire Team made the lift. A total of 835 "Sky Soldiers" of the Brigade were placed into three (3) separate landing zones. The Falcons placed pre-strikes into the LZ's using 155 rockets, and 24,000 rounds of 7.62 ammunition. No enemy resistance was met.

m. On the 16th a small lift began the day with almost every conceivable mission performed during the days period.

n. On the 17th, 5 COWBOYS were called off their normally assigned missions at 1030 hours to participate in a Combat Assault of 70 "Sky Soldiers" into a suspected enemy infested area. All reports seemed incorrect as no resistance was met. Two (2) LRRP teams were placed in, to attempt to gather information and to capture a prisoner if possible.

o. At 1245 on the 18th, four (4) COWBOYS were called off their normal missions to place elements of E/17 Cav. in on a Search and Cordon of the village of Phu Sen. At 1640 the COWBOYS returned and extracted the recon team.

p. On 19 October the 335th Aslt Hel Co. continued their support of Operation Bolling. One (1) Combat Assault was conducted for the 4th Battalion and one for E Troop 17th Cav. Multiple LZ's were used for the E Troop mission that was a continued Cordon and Search of the village of Phu Sen. Over 400 troopers and 45 tons of cargo were carried in resupply and the General Support role of the 173rd Abn. Bde.

q. On 20 October the COWBOYS repositioned 412 "Sky Soldiers" of the Brigade. The 1st Battalion was repositioned from FSB Canoe to AO Gander and B Company, 4th Battalion was moved from LZ Sen to FSB Peak. All missions went as scheduled with the assistance of six (6) CH-47s in moving the larger equipment from Canoe.

r. At 1500 hours on the 21st the COWBOYS were called out of a TAC "E" by the 173rd. Troops were placed in an LZ near a unit of the 4th Battalion that was in contact.

s. 22 and 23 October found the COWBOYS in normal support of the 173rd Abn. Bde. in Operation Bolling.

t. On 24 October at 0800 hours a Falcon Light Fire Team departed to support the 48th Assault Helicopter Company and the ROK Division at Ninh Hoa who were in heavy contact. The Light Fire Team returned at 1900 hours, both ships were grounded with multiple hits received. No injuries were sustained, and the Falcons were credited with two (2) structures destroyed and several possible VC killed.

u. 25 and 26 October -- normal missions in support of the 173rd Abn. Bde. during Operation Bolling.

v. Routine missions were flown to provide continued support of the 173rd Abn. Bde. on Operation Bolling.

w. On the 28th the COWBOYS participated in an artillery raid with the 173rd. A B-52 strike was conducted on a suspected NVA headquarters, followed by artillery and then a reconnaissance of damage by fire of the Falcons. The mission appeared to be very successful.

x. On 29 October 135 troopers were lifted in an assault for the 4th Battalion of the 173rd Airborne Brigade. The Falcons placed in suppressive fire prior to the COWBOYS arrival. 280 passengers and 30 tons of cargo were carried on resupply and General Support.

y. Five (5) "Slicks" and a Light Fire Team supported the 4/503rd Infantry in their Combat Assaults. 187 troopers were assaulted. The Falcons placed in a pre-strike and suppressive fires on the landing zone as the COWBOYS assaulted.

z. Warrant Officer Machin closed the mission with a long day. It all began when he departed at 0630 to support the 281st out of Cam Ranh Bay. He ended up traveling over the entire III, Corps area and returning to Phu Hiep at 2030 hours.

III. MONTHLY STATISTICS:

	UH-1B	UH-1H	TOTAL
TOTAL SORTIES	470	5544	6014
COMBAT SORTIES	470	2328	2798
HOURS	466	1986	2452
PAX		11,262	11,262
CARGO (TONS)		776	776

IV. AWARDS RECEIVED DURING THE MONTH OF OCTOBER 1967

MAJ. LAWSON	DISTINGUISHED FLYING CROSS
PFC MARCHBANKS	BRONZE STAR W/ "V"
SP5 SELF	BRONZE STAR W/ "V"
SP5 BAKER	BRONZE STAR
1SG ORR	BRONZE STAR
CPT. TUCKER	BRONZE STAR
PFC PRATER	AIR MEDAL W/ "V"
PFC ERICKSON	AIR MEDAL W/ "V"
WO1 UNGERER	AIR MEDAL W/ "V"
SP4 FULLER	AIR MEDAL W/ "V"
PFC KITCHING	AIR MEDAL W/ "V"
WO1 BURKE	AIR MEDAL W/ "V"
WO1 ARCHER	ARMY COMMENDATION
SP4 RUTTERBUSH	ARMY COMMENDATION
SP5 CLARK	ARMY COMMENDATION

HISTORY OF THE
335TH ASSAULT HELICOPTER COMPANY
145th Combat Aviation Battalion
APO San Francisco 96227

1 November 1967 through 30 November 1967

Prepared by

1 Lt. PAUL C. HOWELL

Approved by

DONALD R. DRUMM
Major, Artillery
Commanding

335TH ASSAULT HELICOPTER COMPANY
145th Combat Aviation Battalion
APO San Francisco 96227

26 January 1968

Subject: Monthly History of the 335th Assault Helicopter Company for the period
1 November through 30 November 1967

To: Commanding Officer
335th Assault Helicopter Company
145th Combat Aviation Battalion
APO San Francisco 96227

I. ORGANIZATION AND DESIGNATION:

A.   Flight Platoons (2) -- COWBOYS

   (1)   First Airlift Platoon -- Ramrods
Platoon Commander: 1Lt. Thomas L. Anderson
Aircraft: 10 UH-1H "Slicks" -- Troop Carriers.

   (2)   Second Airlift Platoon -- Mustangs
Platoon Commander: Captain Albert R. Stewart
Aircraft: 10 UH-1H "Slicks" -- Troop Carriers.

   (3)   Armed Helicopter Platoon -- Falcons
Platoon Commander: Captain Phillip P. Osterli
Aircraft: 8 UH-1B "Guns" -- Armed Escort.

B.   166th Transportation Detachment.
(1) Commander: Major Robert A. Lawson
(2) 1 UH-1H recovery helicopter -- Horsethief.

C.   25th Medical Detachment.

D.   234th Signal Detachment.

159

II. OPERATIONS:

a. The month of November started with the 335th Assault Helicopter Company supporting the 173rd Airborne Brigade (Separate) in Operation Bolling in the Tuy Hoa area. 337 troopers were lifted in the morning when a change of mission was called in at 0600 hours. The lift commenced at 0700 hours and terminated at 1100 hours.

b. On the 2nd and the 5th of November the COWBOYS were in General Support of the 173rd Airborne Brigade in Operation Bolling. Falcon 612 was flying on a General Support mission for the Brigade when fire was received, and the ship took a hit. No injuries resulted from the incident.

c. On the 4th of November the extraction's scheduled for the morning were delayed for over an hour due to the weather. Once the lift was started, problems arose when previous unscheduled lifts were required. No fire was received, and no enemy movements were observed.

d. On the 5th of November after returning to Phu Hiep with half of the proposed extraction completed, five (5) UH-1Hs and a Light Fire Team were ordered to prepare for and close on Kontum today. Captain Stewart and the appropriate aircraft departed this area at 1400. At 2130 word was received that all aircraft arrived at Kontum and were setting up to stay.

e. No missions were scheduled at Phu Hiep today. One (1) small lift was performed at Kontum to support the Brigade's participation in Operation McArthur, A Light Fire Team was called out of Phu Hiep to attempt to assist the Special Forces Camp, 57 rockets and 1000 7.62 rounds were fired.

f. On the 7th of November the remainder of the flyable aircraft departed Phu Hiep for Kontum, and all arrived safely. Aircraft 648 crashed while flying resupply and had to be destroyed in place. All persons escaped without injury.

g. On the 8th of November ten (10) "Slicks" and three (3) Falcons departed Kontum for support of the Brigade at Dak To. 171 troops were carried on the assault and then the ships reverted to their normal missions. At 0630 aircraft 643 reported receiving fire, but no hits were received.

h. On November 9th, ten (10) UH-1Hs and three (3) Falcon gunships departed Kontum for Dak To to support the 173rd Abn. Bde. with a Combat Assault. At 0730 hour's aircraft 620 and 704 reported receiving fire, but no hits were taken. 640 passengers and 8 tons of cargo were carried during the assault.

i. On the 10th and the 11th of November Combat Assaults were performed for the 1st and 2nd Battalions of the 173rd. 470 "Sky Soldiers" and 12 tons of cargo were carried on the assaults. The remainder of the days' activities were in General Support of the Brigade.

j. A short lift on the morning of the 12th placed 257 troops and 20 tons of cargo for the LRRP and the 1st Battalion. General support of the Brigade in Operation McArthur comprised the remainder of the days' operations.

k. On November 13th, Warrant Officer Gary Bass while on an emergency resupply mission received fire and took three (3) hits. The ship was flown back to Kontum and Warrant Officer Bass took out another ship. No injuries resulted from the incident.

l. November 14th through the 17th the COWBOYS supported the 173rd Abn. Bde. with normal General Support missions in support of their participation in Operation McArthur.

On the 17th, WO Bryan flying a Falcon gunship was forced to autorotate when he had an engine failure. The heavily loaded gunship was landed on an unsecured road with no further damage and no injuries resulting.

m. On the 18th the COWBOYS flew General Support and resupply missions for the Brigade. 207 "Sky Soldiers" and 31 tons of cargo were carried.

n. On the 19th of November the 2nd Battalion, 503rd Infantry, 173rd Abn. Bde. (Separate) ran into heavy contact while assaulting Hill 875, to the Southwest of Dak To. No landing zone was available for ships to land with supplies and to pick up the wounded, so "sling loads" and "kick-outs" were required. Ship after ship attempted to get the loads into the area. All ships were covered with gunships, artillery and airstrikes. All ships received heavy automatic weapons and small arms fire. Five (5) ships were shot up and forced to set down at a fire support base. Warrant Officer Jerry B. Freeman received a scalp wound, completely destroying his helmet. Specialist Five Paul E. Rennie was wounded with a round through his shoulder.

On the 20th the COWBOYS continued to support the 2nd Battalion with all available flyable aircraft. Two (2) more aircraft were shot up and forced to land at a fire support base to await evacuation. One load that was dropped in was a landing zone kit so that the unit on the ground would be able to make an area large enough for our ships to land to resupply and carry out casualties.

Two (2) more aircraft were hit today while resupplying the 2nd Battalion on Hill 875. The battle is still raging. 11 tons of cargo was carried into the landing zone and 111 MEDIVACS were carried out.

On the 23rd Of November, Thanksgiving Day, the big assault for the Hill was made. The hilltop was taken in the afternoon by members of the 2nd and 4th Battalions, 173rd Abn. Bde.

The COWBOYS participation in the battle consisted of Combat Assaults and resupply missions under the most hazardous conditions of hostile fire. There were a total of nine (9) helicopters that received extensive combat damage during the period 19 November to 21 November and over ten (10) COWBOYS were wounded during the action.

o. On the 24th of November the COWBOYS performed an extraction for the 2nd and 4th Battalions, 173rd Airborne Brigade. Over 400 "Sky Soldiers" were extracted from the vicinity of Hill 875. In the General Support and resupply roles 240 passengers and 17 tons of cargo were carried. No significant enemy resistance was met during the day.

On the 25th and 26th of November the COWBOYS performed normal support missions for the 173rd Airborne Brigade in Operation McArthur.

p. 32 tons of cargo and 350 troopers were carried on the 27th and 28th of November in Operation McArthur Southwest of Dak To, Kontum Providence, RVN.

q. On the 29th of November the COWBOYS were delayed from their missions for almost an hour and a half due to the heavy layer of ground fog. Normal missions were performed during the day with no enemy resistance met.

r. On the 30th of November the COWBOYS supported the 1st Battalion with the extraction of 171 troopers. November has drawn to a close. What started as a quiet month for the COWBOYS ended up as one of the fastest moving and active months in some time.

III. MONTHLY STATISTICS:

	UH-1B	UH-1H	TOTAL
TOTAL SORTIES	807	4176	4983
COMBAT SORTIES	472	1487	1959
HOURS	596	1776	2372
PAX		7079	7079
CARGO (TONS)		422	422
AMMO - 2.75	1351		1351
7.62	200,000		200,000
40MM	490		490
MEDIVACS-VC/KBA			0
AIRCRAFT HITS	3	9	12
U.S./WIA/KIA			7 WIA
UH-1B MISSIONS	111		111

	UH-1B	UH-1H	TOTAL
AVG. ACFT HOURS	596	1776	2372
CA'S			13
EXTRACTION'S			8
REPOSITIONING			5
HIGH AVIATOR			143.8
LOW AVIATOR			0.0
AVG. AVIATOR HRS.			81.4

IV. AWARDS RECEIVED DURING THE MONTH OF NOVEMBER 1967

1Lt. LOWELL	BRONZE STAR
WO1 ANDERSON	BRONZE STAR
SP4 RHODES	BASIC AIR MEDAL
SP4 SCHIERS	BASIC AIR MEDAL
WO1 SWANSON	BASIC AIR MEDAL
SP4 BARTLETT	BASIC AIR MEDAL
SP4 DICKEY	BASIC AIR MEDAL
SP4 FERNANDEZ	BASIC AIR MEDAL
SP4 FUNK	BASIC AIR MEDAL
SP4 GRESHAM	BASIC AIR MEDAL
WO1 NORRIS	BASIC AIR MEDAL
PFC MUNOZ	BASIC AIR MEDAL
SP4 KOSCHMAN	BASIC AIR MEDAL
WO1 HOPKINS	BASIC AIR MEDAL
WO1 PICKLESIMER	BASIC AIR MEDAL
WO1 HILLIKER	BASIC AIR MEDAL
WO1 CZAPLICKI	BASIC AIR MEDAL
WO1 FERRARA	BASIC AIR MEDAL
WO1 REDDING	BASIC AIR MEDAL
PFC SCHMIDT	BASIC AIR MEDAL
WO1 SITZER	BASIC AIR MEDAL
SP4 ZARAGOZA	BASIC AIR MEDAL
PFC FREE	BASIC AIR MEDAL
SP4 HANSON	BASIC AIR MEDAL
SP4 TOLLEY	BASIC AIR MEDAL
MAJ. DICKERSON	ARMY COMMENDATION W/ "V"
SP4 THOMPSON	ARMY COMMENDATION W/ "V"
WO1 DANITZ	ARMY COMMENDATION
WO1 TEMEYER	ARMY COMMENDATION
SP4 WATSON	ARMY COMMENDATION

SSG BAKER	ARMY COMMENDATION
SP5 COSTILOU	ARMY COMMENDATION
SP5 DRIVER	ARMY COMMENDATION
SP5 HUFFMAN	ARMY COMMENDATION
CPT. OSTERLI	ARMY COMMENDATION
SP4 BREIT	ARMY COMMENDATION
SP5 CHEEK	ARMY COMMENDATION
WO1 IDELL	PURPLE HEART
SGT. RENNIE	PURPLE HEART
SP4 CHAMBERS	PURPLE HEART

HISTORY OF THE
335TH ASSAULT HELICOPTER COMPANY
145th Combat Aviation Battalion
APO San Francisco 96227

1 December 1967 through 31 December 1967

Prepared by

1 Lt. PAUL C. HOWELL

Approved by

DONALD R. DRUMM
Major, Artillery
Commanding

335TH ASSAULT HELICOPTER COMPANY
145th Combat Aviation Battalion
APO San Francisco 96227

30 January 1968

Subject: Monthly History of the 335th Assault Helicopter Company for the period
1 December through 31 December 1967

To: Commanding Officer
335th Assault Helicopter Company
145th Combat Aviation Battalion
APO San Francisco 96227

I. ORGANIZATION AND DESIGNATION:

A. Flight Platoons (2) -- COWBOYS

    (1) First Airlift Platoon -- Ramrods
        Platoon Commander: 1Lt. David C. Flett
        Aircraft: 10 UH-1H "Slicks" -- Troop Carriers.

    (2) Second Airlift Platoon -- Mustangs
        Platoon Commander: Captain Albert R. Stewart
        Aircraft: 10 UH-1H "Slicks" -- Troop Carriers.

    (3) Armed Helicopter Platoon -- Falcons
        Platoon Commander: Captain Ivol C. Kenner
        Aircraft: 8 UH-1B "Guns" -- Armed Escort.

B. 166th Transportation Detachment.
    (1) Commander: Major Robert A. Lawson
    (2) 1 UH-1H recovery helicopter -- Horsethief.

C. 25th Medical Detachment.

D. 234th Signal Detachment.

II. OPERATIONS:

a. December 1st, the beginning of a new month. The COWBOYS are anticipating being able to get the unit back together sometime in the month. Perhaps we will all make it back to Bien Hoa. If the first day is any indication it should be a quiet month, as far as enemy activity, with the COWBOYS still getting in a lot of flying.

b. The 2nd of December found the COWBOYS supporting E Company of 17th Cav. in an extraction. The remainder of the day was spent resupplying the forward elements of the Brigade with 250 passengers and 13 tons of cargo.

c. On the 3rd of December 300 "Sky Soldiers" were extracted for the 1st Battalion. No enemy contact was met.

d. On the 4th of December the COWBOYS began by assaulting 576 troopers of the 2nd Battalion into a suspected enemy infested area. No resistance was met on the assaults.

e. On the 5th of December the COWBOYS were in normal support of the Brigade in support of Operation McArthur with all available aircraft.

f. On the 6th, the 2nd Battalion, 173rd Abn. Bde. was supported by the COWBOYS in a Combat Assault moving 232 "Sky Soldiers."

g. General support missions in support of the 173rd Abn. Bde's. participation in Operation McArthur, Kontum Providence, RVN, composed the activities for the 7th, 8th and 9th of December.

h. On the 10th of December 210 "Sky Soldiers" were extracted for the 4th Battalion. On resupply and General Support 530 troopers and 17 tons of cargo were carried.

i. On the 11th through the 13th of December small lifts in support of the Brigade were supplemented by resupply and General Support. No significant troop activity was observed.

j. On the 14th and 15 the COWBOYS were given no missions as they made yet another move, this one was back to Phu Hiep to continue Operation Bolling. Two (2) ships remained at Kontum to help support the remainder of the Brigade at Dak To in Operation McArthur.

k. On the 17th and 18th, Combat Assaults of over 700 troops Northwest of Tuy Hoa were accomplished. The Brigade is setting up a forward base camp at Dong Tra.

l. On the 19th though the 22nd the COWBOYS supported the Brigade with mostly resupply and LRRP missions. An occasional Combat Assault was usually implemented into each day's activities to keep the COWBOYS flexible.

m. On the 23rd of December one LRRP team was placed in and later extracted. No hits were received and no injuries resulted.

n. During the Christmas Truce on the 24th and 25th of December, General Support of the Brigade was the only mission, hot Christmas dinner to the troops.

o. The 26th through the 28th found the COWBOYS being kept busy with Combat Assaults in moving the Brigade. Over 1200 "Sky Soldiers" were inserted and extracted from various landing zones and fire support bases throughout the operational area of Bolling.

p. On the 30th of December the COWBOYS performed strictly General Support missions in support of the Brigade. Marginal weather was prevalent throughout the operational area hindering many flights.

q. On the last day of the year 1967 the COWBOYS supported the 173rd Abn. Bde. with a Combat Assault of 220 "Sky Soldiers."

At 1200 hours on the 31st of December 1967 a change of command ceremony was conducted. Major Donald R. Drumm turned over the 335th Assault Helicopter Company to Major Frank M. Powell. At the ceremony rumors were verified by the 145th Combat Aviation Battalion Commander that the COWBOYS were being transferred to the 268th Combat Aviation Battalion at Phu Hiep but would still remain in direct support of the 173rd Airborne Brigade.

III. MONTHLY STATISTICS:

	UH-1B	UH-1H	TOTAL
TOTAL SORTIES	654	5082	5736
COMBAT SORTIES	583	4761	5344
HOURS	352	1779	2131
PAX		9293	9293
CARGO (TONS)		486	486
AMMO - 2.75	848		848
7.62	204,350		204,350
40MM	380		380
MEDIVACS-VC/KBA		2 MEDIV	9 VC/KBA
AIRCRAFT HITS			0
U.S./WIA/KIA			0
UH-1B MISSIONS	121		121
AVG. ACFT HOURS	352	1779	2131
CA'S			24
EXTRACTION'S			19
REPOSITIONING			17
HIGH AVIATOR			131.7
LOW AVIATOR			2.8
AVG. AVIATOR HRS.			74.5

IV. AWARDS RECEIVED DURING THE MONTH OF DECEMBER 1967

CWO LAWSON	DISTINGUISHED FLYING CROSS
WO1 MANKER	DISTINGUISHED FLYING CROSS

HEADQUARTERS
UNITED STATES MILITARY ASSISTANCE COMMAND, VIETNAM
OFFICE OF THE COMMANDER
APO San Francisco 96222

MACJ43-LM   12 December 1967

Subject: Letter of Commendation

To: Deputy Commanding General
     United States Army, Vietnam
     APO 96375

1. Our successes against enemy forces in the Dak To area during November can be attributed directly to the superb fighting team of combatant and logistical elements that we have developed here in the Republic of Vietnam.

2. While the success of combatant forces in South Vietnam is well known through the media of the press, what is not generally publicized is that the basis for their success is due, in a large measure, to an affective, responsive and flexible logistical system. A significant aspect of the Dak To operations was the tremendous logistics effort successfully carried out to reinforce the area with both troops and supplies. The requirement to rapidly increase logistical support for only 3 Battalions at the beginning of contact to 9 Battalions within a 15-day period presented a challenge that your logistics organizations very capably met in an effective and timely manner, during the peak period, resupply to Dak To of rations, petroleum, ammunition and other supplies, utilizing both airlift and motor transport means, exceeded 1,000 short tons per day. This is a significant achievement, especially since much of the motor transport movement was over a distance of 246 kilometers through a hostile environment. Such performance reflects not only effective, detailed planning and coordination, but evidences a "can do" attitude on the part of all individuals concerned. All units responsible for this fine performance can take pride in this outstanding accomplishment.

3. Our capability and flexibility to rapidly respond to similar enemy threats in any place he chooses has again been demonstrated. I wish you to pass to all the personnel involved in the logistics effort my professional and personal pride in their accomplishments and congratulations for a job well done.

        /s/W. C. Westmoreland
        /t/W. C. WESTMORELAND
          General, United States Army
          Commanding

AVHAG-PD (12 Dec. 67)   1st Ind.

Subject: Letter of Commendation   6 Feb. 68

TO: Commanding General, 1st Aviation Brigade, APO 96384

I take great pride in forwarding General Westmoreland's comments concerning the recent battle at Dak To. The success of this major engagement would not have been possible without the outstanding aviation support which was provided by your command to the heavily engaged infantry Battalions. The officers and men of the 1st Aviation Brigade who participated in the action accomplished their mission in an outstanding manner, bringing honor upon themselves and Army Aviation. Please extend my admiration and appreciation to those personnel who contributed to the defeat of the enemy at Dak To.

> /s/Bruce Palmer, Jr.
> /t/BRUCE PALMER, JR.
>   Lieutenant General, U.S. Army
>   Deputy Commanding General

AVHAV-PD (12 Dec. 67)   2nd Ind.

Subject: Letter of Appreciation

HEADQUARTERS, 1ST AVIATION BRIGADE, APO 96384, 6 Feb. 1968

TO: Commanding Officer, 17th Combat Aviation Group, APO 96240

    Forwarded to you with pride. Add my praise to that of General Westmoreland and Lieutenant General Palmer. The skill and courage displayed by the 17th Combat Aviation Group in support of ground operations contributed heavily to the allied victory at Dak To. Please convey my pride and admiration to the officers and men of your command for a job well done.

               /s/Robert R. Williams
               /t/ROBERT R. WILLIAMS
                  Major General, USA
                  Commanding

AVGD-CO (12 Dec. 67)　　　3rd Ind.

Subject: Letter of Commendation

HEADQUARTERS, 17TH COMBAT AVIATION GROUP, APO 96240　　　February 1968

TO: Commanding Officer, 268th Combat Aviation Battalion, APO 96316

 I wish to add my personal congratulations for those of you who participated in the battle of Dak To. The performance of all units was magnificent.

    /s/Bill G. Smith
    /t/BILL G. SMITH
     Colonel, Infantry
     Commanding

AVGD-E-CO (12 Dec. 67)   4th Ind.

Subject: Letter of Commendation

HEADQUARTERS, 268TH COMBAT AVIATION GROUP, APO 96316,   9 Feb. 1968

TO: Commanding Officer, 335TH Assault Helicopter Company, APO 96316

On a daily basis Army aviation in RVN demonstrates its tremendous and versatile capabilities. However, our true capacity for combat support of the ground forces was demonstrated at Dak To. The personnel of your unit are to be congratulated for their efforts.

/s/Donald E. Mulligan
/t/DONALD E. MULLIGAN
  LTC, Artillery
  Commanding

The following article was written by Major Jon R. Dickerson, Cowboy 3. Major Dickerson's first-hand account of the battle at hill 875 is further evidence of the fine job the COWBOYS did under extremely hostile conditions.

875 FROM THE AIR

A lot has been said about familiarity, some good, some bad. There was a time when two units being familiar with one another contributed immeasurably to the success of an operation.

Primarily, two units will be discussed; the 173rd Airborne Brigade and the 335th Assault Helicopter Company. The 335th is known as the COWBOYS.

The 335th habitually supported the 173rd. Prior to January 1967, the COWBOYS were assigned to the brigade. When the 335th changed parent units, the mission changed slightly. The COWBOYS supported the 173rd plus other units, American, ARVN and Australian.

On the 28th of May the 335th changed missions to that of direct support of the 173rd that was in the process of moving from Bien Hoa to Pleiku. The company, with attached units -- the 166th Transportation Detachment, the 234th Signal Detachment and the 25th Medical Detachment, headed for the Central Highlands and a date with destiny.

While at Pleiku, the units operated together for three weeks combing the local area for the elusive Viet Cong.

In June a Vietnamese force supported by American Special Forces sustained heavy casualties in an encounter with a unit of the North Vietnamese Army near the camp at Dak To. The 173rd was alerted and on the 18th of June, moved north and began sweeping the Dak To area for NVA.

There were a few significant encounters during the summer rainy season. Two of these were battalion sized and both sides suffered many casualties. These encounters will not be treated at this time, but rather one minor battalion operation will be discussed so that a later battle may be more easily understood.

Southwest of Dak To is a small unimportant river valley. The Dak Klong River begins in the hills at the southwest end of the valley and winds its way through the nine-by-one-kilometer valley on to join the Dak Pako. The valley floor is matted with bamboo, with only occasional trees and scrub brush filling in the gaps. The ground rises sharply on each side of the valley and becomes rolling jungle hills about two hundred meters higher than the valley floor. The growth on the hills is double to triple canopy jungle growth with thick undergrowth. One of these hills -- a very unimpressive one -- is Hill 875. During the summer monsoon the 2nd Battalion established a fire support base deep in the valley. From this fire support base, FSB 9, an ARVN battalion operated to the southwest for a while in the headwaters of the Dak Klong River. Later the 1st Battalion of the 503rd moved to FSB 9 and used it as a staging area. A B-52 strike had been directed at a suspected enemy force north of FSB 9 to the west of the valley. One crater was selected as the LZ. A close inspection revealed that the area was too small to land a UH-1. It was decided to use rappelling ropes and place a security force; then engineers with demolition be sent in to clear out the bamboo. It was a long, involved and slightly mixed up lift. Fortunately, "Charlie" wasn't home that day. It was known to the COWBOYS as "the LZ where we did the rope tricks." It was an area long remembered by all who participated. During the troop lift, the pilots on final approach to the pickup zone, could look at the hills to their front and see Hill 875. It was late summer now and all was quiet at Dak To.

In September the local population in the Tuy Hoa area was having difficulty with the rice harvest because of Viet Cong and NVA interference. The 173rd and the 335th moved from the mud at Dak To to the sandy beach south of Tuy Hoa.

It was during the stay at Tuy Hoa that the relationship between the two units reached new heights. Combat assaults and extractions were conducted daily. Many of these were made with little or no advance notice. The byword was "Kick the tire, light the fire, brief on guard, the first one off is lead." The members of the units were becoming quite familiar with each other's capabilities and limitations. Mutual respect was at new heights. It was autumn and the hills of Dak To were starting to dry out.

With the dry season in Dak To come the NVA Central Highland offensive. It was focused on the valley that runs from Dak To to Pleiku. The 4th Infantry Division met the NVA first while other units rushed in from all over the Corps area to thwart the efforts of the enemy.

Early in November the 173rd Airborne, minus the 3rd Battalion, 503rd Infantry, with the COWBOYS close behind, moved to the Dak To area. The brigade was quickly deployed west of Dak To to block further infiltration across the border and search out units that may be in the area.

Air mobile assaults were conducted frequently in an attempt to find the elusive NVA. On 10 November an LZ was selected for an assault on the 11th. It had been blasted out of the jungle by airstrikes and at first it was thought it would be necessary to rappel again. A low reconnaissance conducted by the COWBOYS Operation Officer and the brigade S3 indicated that it would be possible to bring the aircraft to a low hover and drop the troops off.

There was no difficulty encountered on the lift. The normal preparation was fired and the first of the 2nd Battalion, 503rd Infantry entered the landing zone. As soon as they could, the LZ was enlarged to accommodate CH-47s. When this was done, the remaining sorties of troops were lifted by Chinook. The LZ was on the top of a hill overlooking the Dak Klong River valley and old Fire Support Base Nine.

Within a short period of time the area was cleared to the southwest of the assault LZ for an artillery battery. This became FSB 16.

On the same day, in the afternoon, "C" Company, 1st Battalion, 503rd Infantry encountered an overwhelming force of NVA northeast of the new fire support base. The decision was made to commit "C" Company, 4th Battalion, 503rd Infantry to aid the beleaguered company. The COWBOYS were assembled from various missions. As each aircraft reported in, it was assigned a chalk number and sent to a nearby fire support base to pick up troops. The flight then formed and headed in the general direction of the landing zone. The Cowboy operations officer called the infantry battalion commander on the radio to obtain information on the landing zone. From the description it was obvious that the LZ had been used a few months ago. The flight leader reported into the area and was told that the landing zone was "the one where we did the rope tricks." The lead aircraft commander said, "Roger turning final at this time." This had been one of the fastest and best executed troop lifts conducted by the company while at Dak To. Familiarity with the area and the desires of the commander had cut the time involved to a minimum. The relieving troops arrived in time and a possible catastrophe averted.

Before the 2nd Battalion was firmly established at fire support base 16, it began moving out with three companies, A, C and D on search and destroy missions. They only had to search for a short time for on the 19th they ran into very heavy resistance on the way up Hill 875. By the time they reached a point three hundred meters from the top of the hill they were stopped. The paratroopers sustained heavy casualties on the way. Tactical air and artillery were called in on the top of the hill, while the infantry attempted to withdraw a short distance down the slope. The NVA employed very effective hugging tactics that made it impossible to break contact. Artillery and air were of little use because of the nearness of the lines.

The area where the battalion was located was thick jungle with no suitable landing zone. Two daring attempts were made to drop chain saws and demolitions to the paratroopers. Both times the helicopters received very heavy fire and had to make precautionary landings at a fire support base with oil, fuel and hydraulic leaks. Further attempts to get saws in were stopped for the time. The remainder of that day, close artillery and air strikes were used to the maximum to keep the Americans from being overrun.

On the 20th of November the 4th Battalion was moved to fire support base 16, where the three thousand meters walk to Hill 875 was begun. They ran into heavy resistance while enroute and sustained heavy casualties by the time they reached the north slope of Hill 875 and the 2nd Battalion.

The men of the two battalions were able to move the wounded down the slope about one hundred meters where a chain saw, and demolition were dropped to them. An LZ was cut and the prospects for a victory on Hill 875 looked a bit brighter.

The COWBOYS now began the long and tedious task of removing the casualties. The NVA was not finished though. Even though a constant barrage of air strikes and artillery had pulverized the top of the hill where the majority of the defenders were thought to be located, the enemy continued to fire at each helicopter. They could be seen standing outside their bunkers, between passes by the Airforce jets, firing at the aircraft who were on their mercy mission of medical evacuation. The armed helicopters circled the LZ lacing the outer edge of the friendly perimeter with machine gun fire and rockets each time a slick came in. Still the NVA kept shooting. Occasionally, enemy mortars were fired at the Americans, and one antiaircraft weapon was reported.

Day and night on the 21st and 22nd of November the intense fire on and around Hill 875 went on. B-52 strikes were directed at likely departure routes while fighters and artillery placed the close in fires.

It was obvious that the NVA was well dug in and intended to hang on as long as possible. They placed accurate small arms and mortar fire from Hill 875 on U.S. positions. They were well supplied with ammunition, at least for a while. Parts of their supplies were lost when a bomb missed the top of the hill by a short distance and landed on an NVA ammunition dump. Secondary explosions from that dump lasted approximately two hours.

At this point, it is necessary to interject a few lines about the COWBOYS that flew at Dak To. It would be unfair to other units to say that the COWBOYS were the best, but there are a few members of the 173rd who would not have any other unit support it.

There were so many deeds of a heroic nature that it is impossible to enumerate them. There were occasions when pilots had one aircraft damaged by hostile fire, returned to home base, picked up another and went back on their missions. There were several aircraft that although damaged continued to fly after a brief inspection. Never did a pilot hesitate to go into an area day or night to support the units with vital supplies. The aviators handled emergency situations like the professionals that they were. Several aircraft where landed on a stump covered slope of fire support base 16 with the hydraulics shot out. A loaded UH-1B was autorotated to a winding dirt road after a low-level engine failure. In each case there was no pilot caused damage.

For two days a buildup of supplies and troops went on. All of the causalities were removed from Hill 875. The COWBOYS evacuated in excess of two-hundred wounded. Elements of the 4th Infantry Division were lifted to a landing zone in the valley below Hill 875 on the 22nd of November. A continuous air and artillery barrage fell on the hostile positions while the lift was in progress. Some hostile fire was received by the lift helicopters and one sustained damage to the extent that it had to return to a secure area. The greatest hazard though, was friendly artillery and Tac Air. The command and control helicopter was nearly hit by a 175mm projectile as it flew by the left window in view of the pilot and passengers. One of the lift ships had the tail rotor damaged by twenty-millimeter brass that fell in the LZ from a jet strafing pass. It was later evacuated by Chinook.

The day ended with American units on the north and south of Hill 875, while artillery and air blocked escape routes to the west.

The attack was planned for 1100 on the 23rd of November, which was Thanksgiving Day. The 2nd and 4th Battalions of the 503rd would attack up the north slope while the 1/12th blocked the south.

Hanoi Hanna had announced earlier in the month that the NVA would have their Thanksgiving dinner at Dak To. She was just a little off. The COWBOYS were proud to deliver hot turkey to the top of Hill 875 to the "Sky Soldiers." The attack had been virtually unopposed, and the hill was won at 1120 hours.

After the battle for 875, things began to quiet down. The two units, the 173rd and the 335th had fought the good fight -- and won.

The war was not over though -- the team moved back to the Tuy Hoa area and began all over again.

Jon R. Dickerson
Major, Artillery
Cowboy --3

The following article was published in *Sky Soldier* magazine (volume 1, number 2, pages 18 and 19). *Sky Soldier* was an authorized publication of the 173d Airborne Brigade (Separate). It was published quarterly by the Brigade Information Office for the Sky Soldiers Association. *Sky Soldier* was printed by Dai Nippon Printing Co., Ltd., Tokyo.

FLYING COWBOYS

Versatile, aggressive, efficient and reliable--that's the COWBOYS of the 335th Assault Helicopter Company, who have supported the 173d Airborne Brigade ever since their arrival in Vietnam.

At that time the COWBOYS were the Brigade's Company A, 82d Aviation Battalion. In September 1966, the aviation unit was re-designated the 335th Assault Helicopter Company, 173d Airborne Brigade. Then during Operation Cedar Falls, in January, the COWBOYS were placed under their present parent unit, the 1st Aviation Brigade.

Although in separate units now, the association between the COWBOYS and the Sky Soldiers is greater than ever. According to company operations NCO, Staff Sergeant William Wade, Clarksville, Tenn., more than 50 percent of the company's gunners and crew engineers are former Sky Soldiers. Wade himself worked in the Brigade's Supply Office.

To fulfill the Brigade's aviation needs, the 335th consists of two platoons of "slicks" (UH-1H model) and one platoon of deadly gunships (UH-1B model).

Most paratroopers are more familiar with the "slick," the company's workhorse. These extra duty aircraft are used primarily for resupply missions, heliborne assaults, command and control, and medevac missions. A typical day for the helicopter crews often finds them flying all these assignments, averaging 10 hours a day in the air.

Flying long hours can become quite tedious at times, says Cowboy XO Major Frank Powell, Phoenix, Ariz. According to the major, "A good definition of aviation is hours and hours of pure boredom interspersed with moments of sheer terror."

During the bitter fighting around Dak To in November, the Cowboy helicopter crews have experienced more than their share of combat. At Hill 875, the company had 10 choppers shot down. Two choppers were completely destroyed while the others managed to limp back to nearby Fire Support Base 16 or other secure areas. Three pilots and five crew members were wounded or injured while attempting to resupply the fighting paratroopers and lift the wounded and dead from the battlefield.

For the week ending Thanksgiving Day, Cowboy helicopter crews dusted off 223 allied infantrymen from Hill 875 and other battle areas. The 335th lifted in 116 tons of supplies and spent 750 hours in the air supporting the Brigade.

Cowboy pilots described the one-ship landing zone carved out on the slope of Hill 875 as one of the most difficult they have ever had to land on. "The rough terrain eliminated all avenues of approach to the LZ," said Warrant Officer Jerry Freeman, cowboy pilot. "We were forced to hover the chopper 100 to 150 feet above the LZ before descending at 20 miles per hour," he said.

Pilots reported ground fire some of the fiercest they have ever flown through. "The NVA would stand out of their holes and fire at our ships as they circled the hill and attempted to land," said Major Jon R. Dickerson, Cowboy operations officer from Walla Walla, Wash. "The enemy stood their ground when our gunships laced the hill with rockets and machine-gun fire. They didn't run like the VC did down south," he said.

All the Cowboy pilots that landed on Hill 875, had high words of praise for the exceptional job turned in by their gunners and crew engineers. "They had to guide us in under extreme pressure," said one Cowboy pilot.

Recalled Specialist 4 Joe Prater, a door gunner from Temple, Okla., "Our chopper's rotor blade cleared the trees by just inches. It was hell landing, but we were too busy to be scared."

Another door gunner, Specialist 4 Dana Lockwood, Newfane, NY, spent nine months on line with the Brigade before transferring to the COWBOYS 16 months ago. "In case of a crash," he said, "it's a matter of teamwork. The crew engineer and the gunner would help the pilots out of the ship, retrieve our weapons and then set up a small perimeter. The aircraft commander and the pilot would become our ammo bearers. If necessary, we would destroy the ship to keep the enemy from getting the valuable radio."

In the air the gunner and crew chief are constantly watching for approaching aircraft and keeping an eye open for the pilots' safety. If the pilots were wounded, the crew engineer would take control of the ship, while the gunner administered first aid to the officers.

Keeping the COWBOYS flying takes long hours of work from dedicated people on the ground. Maintenance crews from the company's 166th Transportation Detachment work into the waning hours of the night and early morning to have the helicopters flying the next day. The delicate and highly expensive electrical systems are maintained by the 234th Avionics Detachment, and keeping the COWBOYS fit to fly is the responsibility of the 25th Medical Detachment. "It's one big team effort that keeps the helicopters flying," said Major Powell. "Morale is no problem here."

C◆WB◆Y

BULLSHEET

VOLUME 1   8 DECEMBER 1967   NUMBER 1

COWBOYS COME THROUGH WITH -- BULLSHEET

Welcome! to Volume 1 Number 1 of the COWBOY BULLSHEET, the NEW, (we just thought of it) UNOFFICIAL, (we aint got the 1st Sgt.'s permission) ORGAN, (eyes & ears only we hope) of FACT, (War is Hell) RUMOR, (have you heard a good one?) & FANTABULOUS FANCY (335th to be transferred to Los Angeles permanently). We want this to be your BULLSHEET so YOUR HELP is needed. Timely information, good (or bad) rumors, outrageous occurrences & convulsive coincidence are the stuff we shall thrive on. OUR SOURCES OF INFORMATION WILL BE CONFIDENTIAL!!! So, let's get the stuff IN COWBOYS, send info to BULLSHEET care of unit Mail Clerk.

A SPECIAL ALERT has been flashed to breweries & bartenders in Dreamland to brace themselves for the arrival of SP4 GROCE. Advanced warning is to allow them to stockpile enough Booze to handle his consumption. We know he will be back soon. Just can't support a thirst like that in the World. Lotsaluck Groce

RIDDLE OF THE WEEK: What can go up the chimney down, but can't go down the chimney up? Answer next week.

FLASH! Our insidious informer at high HQ has passed the word that a special Battle Star is being awarded to the COWBOYS at Kontum for having coexisted with the GLADIATORS without having suffered battle fatigue, shell shock or major casualties. GLADIATORS are the first unit in country to be attacked by a force of flashlight carrying Viet Cong! Thus far the GLADIATORS have a 3/4 tire confirmed kill!

Startling rumors concerning CHOW at the upper end of the range have been circulated in the old bunkhouse & COWBOYS were trying to get up there we decided to investigate. We reserved two seats & sent the S2 Sgt. up to check it out. His comment on return was "BUURRRP!!!"

Where did Boone tell that GLADIATOR to put His light bulb?

Which well-known COWBOY aviator recently refueled at BAN ME THUOT on a direct flight from Kontum to Tuy Hoa??

Our insidious informer tips us the word that a well-known COWBOY has had to resort to a Charles Atlas course down there at Bien Hoa to keep his manly figure? Well, there's the Bennies for ya COWBOYS...those sand bag details are for FREE!!

Word is out that business is brisk at the COWBOY PALACE at Kontum..., and all branding irons are RED HOT.

Insidious informer has dropped the word that Sgt. Johnson has been entrusted with new, highly important duties at BH...Do they really let you drive one of them vehicles now John?

Picked up the word Sgt. Pritchard has been sick. Sounds like a little too much of the COWBOY PALACE. Got to take it easy at first, till you get back in shape. Guess we will have to talk to the Mad Hungarian and have him hold you down. Sgt. Kinzinger has sent up a supply of drawers and trousers till things get back to normal.

Grapevine to the old Corral says Sgt. Givins is highly taken with the Airforce efficiency...Ya Man he literally RAVES about it!

Then there's the one about the gent that wanted to give a couple old minds a thrill one Halloween so he covered himself with a sheet and rang their doorbell. Said Hocus Pokus as they answered the door...and the old girls said, "to heck with the Hocus Big Boy."

A Bronze Star may not be awarded for heroism involving aerial flight.

Following COWBOYS are riding higher in their saddles due to acquiring an umbrella for their Eagles. Congrats to SPECIALIST FIVE Knox, Aschenback, Storesteen, Lawter, Chambers, Finch & Pritchett. We have checked it out & SP5 Karnes's orders are in the mail to him. S2 Sgt. smokes Dutch Masters. COWBOYS below have been awarded the Order of the Eagle and now answer to the title SPECIALIST 4: Bannister, Ellis, Sefert, Swanson, Montgomery, Wagner and Wannomae. Congrats COWBOYS.

As most of you COWBOYS know, Specialist Five Paul E. Rennie has been evac't to a hospital in Japan. Mailing address is: USAH Camp Zama, Japan.

Formerly Warrant Officer NOW 2LT. IDELL is still located at 71st Evac Hosp APO 96318...Congrats on the Demotion Sir and hope you are recovered soon!!

Got a whole bunch of COWBOYS who are leavin the range for a spread in the Land of the Brave and the Home of the Free: COWBOYS Hanson, Fischette, Prater, Lockwood, Barlow, Medlock, Carrol, Groce, and Mercado are all takin off for the States for Special Leave.

145th Aviation Battalion has a new CO LTC Deets assumed command on or about 1 December. SMAJ BASS is slated to leave the Battalion about 23 Dec. for Ft Rucker.

PLEASE SHARE THE BULLSHEET
PASS IT ON TO YOUR BUDDY

The Statue of Liberty weighs 450,000 pounds or 225 tons. From the heel to the top of the head the Statue is 111 feet & 1 inch.

CODE OF THE COW COUNTRY

It don't take such a lot of laws

To keep the rangeland straight,

Nor books to write 'em in, because

There's only six or eight.

The first one is the welcome sign

True brand of western hearts:

"My camp is yours and yours is mine"

In all cow country parts.

Treat with respect all womankind,

Same as you would your sister.

Take care of neighbors' strays you find,

And don't call COWBOYS "mister."

Shut pasture gates when passin thru,

And takin' all in all,

Be just as rough as pleases you,

But never mean nor small

Talk straight, shoot straight, & never break

Your word to man nor boss.

Plumb always kill a rattlesnake.

Don't ride a sore backed hoss.

It don't take law nor pedigree

To live the best you can.

These few is all it takes to be

A COWBOY--and a MAN!

NOTE: Certain papers COWBOYS are given are very important to you. A personal file should be established to include; Pay vouchers, General Orders pertaining to Decorations & awards, Special Orders for Flight Status or promotion, etc., etc. This will pay dividends for the man who takes the trouble to maintain it, & solve many problems for the Army and the individual!

BULLSHEET FACTS: FROM THE OLD SARGES NOTEBOOK

It is a fact that the Highest grade in the Armed Forces is General of the Armies, grade was established by the Congress for George Washington in 1799 but no record has been found to show that the appointment was ever made. As a result, John J (Blackjack) Pershing is the only officer to have ever held this rank. Only living Generals of the Army are Eisenhower and Bradley.

HOW DID THE HAND SALUTE ORIGINATE???

Hand raising as a formal greeting probably originated with the caveman, who used it to show they carried no weapons. Later armored knights raised the right hand to lift the helmet visor & show friendship by keeping the sword hand away from his weapon. Before the 19th century British Soldiers tipped their hats...or so says the National Geographic Society.

Have you ever heard of a compound helicopter?

A compound helicopter is one with both a rotor & wings for added lift in forward flight. The wings are usually short and stubby. The manufacture says it will go 302 mph, but the record is not official.

A camel is a horse designed by a committee! "Flying for a living consists of hours and hours of sheer boredom punctuated by seconds of stark terror." "There are lies, damned lies, and statistics" "Learn from the mistakes of others--You can't possibly live long enough to make them all yourself." George Washington, father of the country, was born in Westmoreland County, Virginia.

PROPHETIC PHRASES FROM THE PHANTOM

Who is the PHANTOM? He is your safety awareness. This is where YOU can express jewels of wisdom which can prevent accidents. And speaking of accidents, all accidents are included vehicle, fire, water, even, if you will, pregnancies, not just air craft. Why? Because any accident, regardless of how minor, can create the atmosphere for a major disaster! The watchword there is "Be Careful! The life you save may be your replacement." Did you know: Six US passengers or eight RVN passengers are max permitted in the Huey with a full fuel load? That's for the UH-1H, No passengers are permitted in Gunships UH-1B. A prime cause of recent accidents around the world is overweight for the conditions of flight. When was the last time YOU checked your aircraft and removed excess & extraneous junk such as extra "C" rations, tools, & ammo? You say YOU haven't HAD any accidents? FINE...Let your accident rate become ours. What rate is acceptable? ZERO ACCIDENTS! --The Phantom

Which well-known RLO was recently wounded in the battle of the LAMBRETTAS, at Bien Hoa??

REUP   --   REUP   --   REUP
ARMY

THE OLD SARGE SAYS:

This here bit of the BullSheet should prove of value to them thar young whipper snappers who are hankerin to have a sit-down at one a them thar promotion boards we been hearin about, Course most this stuff we all know, but it's kinda nice to kinda look it all over again. Fer instance we all know that the Medal of Honor is our highest military decoration, but how many had forgotten that there are two Medals of Honor; the Army & the Naval. AHA, I thought so. Now how many remember that the principal difference is the fact that the Army MH can be awarded only for COMBAT action, above and beyond the call of duty, and the Navy MH for his trip across the Atlantic. Course we all know that General of the Army McArthur is the only man to receive the MH twict. And speakin bout decorations, we all member that the Purple Heart is the Nation's oldest; established by General George Washington to reward Military Merit durin the Revolutionary War? Well troops that's it for this time, be glad to answer questions, and SETTLE spats for you young warriors anytime. Drop a line to the Old Sarge Care of the unit Mail clerk and We'll whip it on yuh. Till next time remember "OLD SOLDIERS NEVER DIE, THEY JUST SMELL THAT WAY." The Old Sarge

"Gee Mom, Why do I have to wear lipstick...none of the other fellows are? "Shutup Stupid we're almost to the Draft Board"

C◆WB◆Y

BULLSHEET

VOLUME 1	16 DECEMBER 1967	NUMBER 2

WELCOME BACK COWBOYS

Gals at the old COWBOY PALACE are in mourning as the COWBOYS return home. One of the first comments made by the returning heroes was: "When are our Cooks taking over the Mess Hall."

Sgt. Pritchard is rumored to be planning to manage the Mad Hungarian in a series of bouts with the local Nationals. After the exhibition he put on at Kontum, Pritchard figures he's a cinch for the Vietnamese:Fuzz: Weight Class!

Our insidious informer from higher headquarters finally came out of his bunker long enough to pass the word that the COWBOYS at Bien Hoa had been playing their own game of Combat, with a mortar attack near the compound. Hard Core John?

If you are looking for a definition of ### ask Sgt. Biddy. If you want to know what a Gentleman is good for...Ask SP5 Cook...if you want to know what happens to a two time looser, Cook can tell you that too.

BULLSHEET NEEDS HELP HELP HELP!

Into our second edition here and it looks as though the COWBOYS didn't get the WORD! This is your BULLSHEET and we need your help to fill each issue. After this issue, we are sure you will see for yourself it IS UNOFFICIAL and we hope all sources of information ### COWBOYS, you are the ones who are in the know as to what is happening and to whom. Cut the BULLSHEET in on the news and make it more enjoyable for all.

Our insidious informer at Maintenance tips us that everything is by the book now--even a main rotor track while at a hover...Old Sgt. Biddy is about to lose his fringe trying to figure out how to pull a tail rotor low track....And by the way Biddy....When you find the knob to adjust that ### the rest of the company in on the location.

ARE WE LOST: Certainly not, We are right here...The Trail is lost!

Belated congrats to SPECIALIST FIVE O'SULLIVAN who made the grade with the others mentioned in our last issue.

PHRASES FROM THE PHANTOM

HOLY MACKEREL! Whose head is harder than a tail rotor? If you really want first hand word on the danger of those whirling dervishes called rotor blades, ask the guy with the bandage around his head. His comment, after being soundly whacked on the noodle, went something like this: "They told us to watch those blades; don't walk around the tail boom and BE CAREFUL." He will vouch for the fact that one small, insignificant loss of memory or inattention to detail is extremely dangerous. It almost cost him his life. A fraction of an inch more and his skull would have resembled that box of egg shells seen next to the grill each morning. MORAL: Relax Safety standards for one instant and LOOKOUT, someone will get hurt. Usually in the Aviation Business you don't get a second chance to goof-up. Will you be the next one to forget? Will you become an accident statistic that "didn't think it could happen"? Remember, it's not always the "other guy," IT COULD BE YOU!

THE PHANTOM HAS SPOKEN

ANSWER TO LAST WEEKS RIDDLE: An umbrella can go up the chimney down but cannot go down the chimney up.

EXPERT--A drip under pressure

GO HARD CORE *****GO ARMY

Departed COWBOYS are in line to receive the following decorations: Major Davis-DFC, WO Temeyer-DFC & ARCOM, WO Manker-DFC & ARCOM, and the following persons are receiving ARCOMs WO Danitz, SP4 A. L. Watson, SP5 Huffman, SP5 Driver, SP5 Costilow, SP4 Hickey & SSG P. E. Baker. SP5 R. L. Baker received the BS. Following named Officers and EM have certificates in the Awards & Decoration Section to be picked up ASAP: WOs Bryan, Burke, Ungerer, SP4s Erickson, J. D. Brown, & PFC Allen. Work is progressing in the Awards & Decorations Section for the recommendation of all eligible persons for the Aircraft Crewman's Badge. There is a persistent rumor that the 335th has been or is being recommended for a unit citation or award. Personnel who are assigned to the company during the period for which the award is made, wear the award permanently. Personnel assigned after that period, wear the award while they are assigned to the unit. Unit awards and citations are affixed to the company Guide.

RIDDLE OF THE WEEK: What walks on four legs in the morning, two legs at noon and three legs in the evening??

WHAT TO GIVE THE GIRL WHO HAS EVERYTHING: A Bikini.

Definition of a PISTOL: A 105 Howitzer canister half buried at an angle.

FAMOUS QUOTES: WHO SAID, "THE DIE IS CAST" and what was the occasion?

DO YOU KNOW WHO THE COMPANY REUP SG IS?

THE NIGHT BEFORE CHRISTMAS

'T'was the night before Christmas, And all through the pad,

Not a creature was stirring, Thanks to Old Grand Dad.

The doors were left open, With uncanny care,

In hopes of some round eye Wandering in there.

The COWBOYS were sleeping, In fart sacks all bare,

While visions of Sweethearts, Danced through the air.

When out on the Flight Line, There rose such a clatter,

I sprang from my bed, to see what was the matter.

Away to the door, I flew like a flash,

Tripped on a beer can, And fell on my ash.

I picked myself up, My feet started beaten,

A trail to the Flight Line. Where I fell over Keaton.

The wind and the rain, Fell into our face,

The smell of old Nam, All over the place.

When what to my wondering Eyes should appear,

But all the mechanics, Just dead drunk on beer.

At last they had found a moment of peace,

Old Horsethief was rotatin And leavin the Far East.

With a jerk of my head, I heard some one exclaim,

Now Biddy and Murray, Don't call him that name.

Up Schweitzer, On Stocker, Now cut off their beer,

With all of this racket, You'll have Snuffy out here.

To the top of the roof, To the top of the wall,

It looked like the pilots Were out drinken them all.

When down through the middle, A small figure skittered,

He looked so darned funny, I just sat and twittered.

His eyes, how they twinkled, His dimples so merry.

A rarity amongst COWBOYS, Goin home with his Cherry.

With a twinkle in his eye, And a fifth in his hand,

He was so darned drunk, He could hardly stand.

His actions were shaky, Jerky and quick.

I knew in a flash, It had to be Old Six.

He turned with a jerk, And lowered his bag,

And called out to Woodard, Hey, don't be a drag.

Grabbing their Orders, Tight in their fists,

Six and Old Horsethief Finished their fifths.

Chief Falcon, Buzzard, Mustang and Dick,

Rushed up with refills, Unsteady, but quick.

And finally Snuffy, Stirred and awoke,

Looking for Bowser, Webb and some bloke.

Grabbing his whistle, Clipboard in hand,

The thunder of his feet, Could be heard on the sand.

With a crackle and static Avionics came through,

With a brand new rumor, To good to be true.

The COWBOYS is leavin This range around here,

Headin for home, And all they hold dear.

Old Howell gave a yell, Don't give me that stuff

I'm the S2 and I'll tell you sho nuff

The COWBOYS is stayin, Right where they am,

On the South China seacoast In the country of Nam.

The COWBOYS that were goin Were a miserable bunch,

Red eyed, hung-over, And loosin their lunch.

They'd done a good job During their year,

Bedecked with medals With grins ear to ear.

Mounting their Birds They got ready to fly,

With a wave of the hand, They took to the sky,

And they heard us exclaim, Ere they flew out of sight

Merry Christmas to ALL, And to all a good night.

The Old Sarge

C◆WB◆Y
BULLSHEET

VOLUME 1   24 DECEMBER 1967   NUMBER 3

MERRY CHRISTMAS COWBOYS

FLASH--When the cats away the meece do play is a well-known fact. But when the CAT recently arrived unexpectedly on CL St the play ground to a HALT! Sure, bet there were some cheesy excuses.???

WE KNEW IT COULDN'T LAST! Sgt. Murray finally fell off the wagon after establishing the phenomenal (for him) record of 16 DAYS without a drop of the liquid! We weren't sure his constitution could handle the prolonged drought, & his friends (?) were keeping a close watch. Sure was good to see him back to normal the other morning: redeyed & hungover!

Five will get you ten, that Sgt. Biddy will lose the rest of his hair along with his head if his Hooch Gal ever finds out that EXLAX is not an American candy. What a ****y thing to do Biddy!

The only gentlemen who prefer blondes are the ones who don't know how to defrost brunettes.

Girls who wear tight stretch pants usually have an elastic conscience to match.

Our insidious informer at higher HQ tipped us that the C Atlas Crs a well-known COWBOY studies, isn't so hot, as a matter of fact an old man was observed to out jump him the other night. We understand our Hero got his feet wet! Tisk Tisk. Course he wasn't too steady on his feet up at Pleiku either, wasn't on the Atlas kick then, and there weren't as many attractions as the big city!

FLASH - Sgt. Wade had the picture, & the application was all filled out. He was about to give the poor animal a rabies shot when he discovered under all that crud...he had WDA, a disreputable member of the 2d Plt. Sorry bout that Sarge!

Our insidious informer asks: Who was the VIP COWBOY who sank so deep in the cups at a 173d Bde Party that he couldn't find his parking spot? Tisk Tisk!

GOLDIGGER = A Sexpot looking for a Jackpot!

AGE = The difference between a stick up and a hold up.

BULLSHEET LETTER TO SANTA CLAUS

Dear Santy Claas,

This heres an altogether list a things the COWBOYS are a hankerin for fer Xmas: We all want to go home cept Givens and he's hard core. We all want hot showers that stay that way till your finished. We all want a permanent corral so long as it isn't at Bien Hoa. We all want shorter working hours and more medals fer to show our Gals. Now that list is fer all us. Got a few requests fer individuals: Fuzz needs singing lessons, Peterson wants a couple of sets of clean fatigues with all the buttons for WDA, Batton, Finch, Jackson and Granny are a hankerin for their front teeth, and Webb wants a Dog House for Troop so his late at nite visitors won't step on him again. Cormier wants flush toilets so's he can get offa that detail, Hill wants n interpreter so's he can unnerstan Boone when he'sa drinkin Snuffy's a lookin for a forty day drop and Biddy's givin up on Hair restorer and wants a toupee. Piggy is a hankerin for homemade Chili and Guaneri for a hunk a decent pizza, Knox needs civie shose and Bass a golden bar. 5 wants a sharper company and 6 is lookin to leave, 3 is gonna miss us, and 2 don't know if he should stay. Alphabet is buckin for Jayhawkers roost and Lester wants a pair of elevator shoes. Mustangs want to help set up the next set of classified plans like the last ones they had to burn in Kontum. Pritchard is wishin his name warn't mentioned so often in the paper, Graham is lookin for a lantern and a bucket to catch some cascading moonbeams, and Spring wants to know who in H--- Diogenes is. Blackwelder wants a cushioned seat in the latrine for the next time he passes out from overwork (?) (at the club (?)) He also would like all concertina wire removed from the company area since his radar doesn't operated effectively after 2 cases of Pabst. Schwietzer would like the entire war stopped and started over again the RIGHT way, Moore wants Santa to check and see if the "Shotguns" are still out back home in old West By God and says if Santa is bringing him a gift: "Please don't let it be a boy." Daniels wants at least ten new loves before New Year's and Ski would like a new rubber stamp to use on his rubber checks. Then last but not least Santa, we know he needs it but won't admit it, please bring Sgt. K a new girdle! He sprung his old one while he was at Kontum!

Thank you Santy Claas

The Cowboys.

POEM OF THE WEEK, Dedicated to WO Bass and Lt. Morse.

"TWINKLE TWINKLE GOLDEN BAR

HOW I WISH YOU WERE A SILVER STAR"

QUOTATION OF THE WEEK: Who said: "Return with your shield or on it"?

BULLSHEET FROM AROUND THE RANGE

A suggestion has been made to send a five man detail to the rear to service vehicles and drive for the Rear Detachment Commanders! Tough John!

What two Chief Warrant Officer Aviators recently left Bien Hoa for Vung Tau and landed in PHAN THIET!!

Does the sign on Turkey Road still say, "OFF LIMITS"?? Or does that just apply to enlisted types??

What Senior NCO learned that a jeep is out classed in an argument with a two and a half ton truck recently in Bien Hoa!!??

What RLO recently served notice on all NFGs (New Friendly Guys) that it doesn't pay to mess with the man that can make you look like a purple people eater?

Has anyone noticed how improved the mail situation is since the XO returned from Bien Hoa...Sure must have gotten the word to the APO people (?).

We understand that you have to walk a straight line BEFORE you go out at Bien Hoa these days?

BULLSHEET CLASSIFIED: DEAR PCH; Please come back home, all is forgiven. JCH & WLK

"She married a moron, moron than off"

ODDS & ENDS FROM THE OLD SARGE

A map is a pictorial representation of the earth's surface, drawn to scale on a plane. Clear, concise, and to the point. That's what your definitions before a Board should be. Too often the unprepared person "talks" himself into a corner, simply cause he hasn't considered the basics of his trade. All Soldiers reporting to a board, for promotion or for the selection of a Soldier of the Month should know there General Orders, the Chain of Command, and the basic definitions of the Soldiers trade. Failure to do so is asking the men on the Board to believe you don't really care for the promotion or selection that the Board can recommend for the individual. To wait till the day before the board and expect to learn everything at one slight session of review is to invite the board to recommend you be passed over for the promotion you may want. The time to get ready for the next promotion is the moment you got the rank you have. Any NCO will give as much assistance as he can to help a willing troop learn as much as he can about the Army. Study and application on the part of the individual is a must, in order to master the knowledge and philosophy required.

THE OLD SARGE

Radios and women are just alike--just try to get what you want, when you want it!

PHRASES FROM THE PHANTOM

At some time in the past an ancient philosopher defined a baby as "a large stomach connected with plumbing to a loud noise on one end, and no sense of responsibility on the other end." From the number of "silly" incidents & accidents that seem to be occurring, I wonder which end is which as we grow older. I read in the paper where a man was shot by an "unloaded" gun. At least he said, "I didn't know it was loaded." Where was his "responsibility to check before he pulled the trigger"? Still sitting on it? Fortunately, this did not occur to a COWBOY! But it COULD! Every day we handle weapons with live ammo. Remember, a rifle, pistol, or machine gun was designed to Kill!! Don't be caught sitting on your responsibility, making loud noises when care & caution should be used. Don't mar the holiday season or any other with an accident of any type! Every time you disengage your brain, responsibility slips to the wrong end and accidents result. Let's make our first New Year's resolution: Zero accidents in "68," and for this issue a Very Merry Christmas and a Happy Accident Free New Year!

THE PHANTOM HAS SPOKEN

ANSWER TO LAST WEEKS RIDDLE: Man.

ANSWER TO LAST WEEKS QUOTATION: Julius Caesar said: "The die is cast" as he crossed the Rubicon River in rebellion against the Roman Republic.

A WORD TO THE COWBOYS FROM THE DEPARTING COWBOY 3

"A departing Operations Officer a few months ago, made a statement to the effect that the COWBOYS were just another company, but on a Combat Assault no company, could hold a candle to the COWBOYS. That may have been true six months ago when it was stated, but I would argue NOW, to the point of mortal combat. At no time is the 335th "just another company!" On all missions we are COWBOYS, and no other company can hold a candle to us! We have been through some very harrowing operations. No other Avn company has undergone the austere living conditions and repeated moves that we have. No other aslt hel company supports sustained combat the way we do. Gentlemen no other Avn company is as good as the COWBOYS!! When you return to COWBOY HEAVEN and gather at the snack bar or billets, you don't have to listen to the teller of combat tales in wonder and awe. You were there! And you can tell him a thing or two. We have cussed the 173d and they have worked us hard, but the men and officers of the 173d have demonstrated their admiration and respect from the top down. There is no doubt in my military mind that the COWBOYS are the best in the world, your accomplishments may be equaled but can never be exceeded. I will be departing in a few weeks, and would like to express my feeling of pride in having been a COWBOY and a member of the finest Assault Helicopter Company"

COWBOY 3

BULLSHEET

VOLUME 1	31 DECEMBER 1967	NUMBER 4

HAPPY NEW YEAR COWBOYS

A MESSAGE FROM COWBOY 6

Upon my departure from the COWBOYS, I wish to express my sincere appreciation for a job "well done." There are other Assault Helicopter Companies in Vietnam, and all do their job, but none perform them as well as the COWBOYS. It's been a long time since the COWBOYS departed Bien Hoa on 28 May 1967. You have moved seven times, and never once failed to perform the mission in a typically outstanding "COWBOY" manner. It has been a pleasure to serve with the COWBOYS for the past eight months. The professional way in which you perform has made my job easy. I know you will give Major Powell the same support you have given me. A Happy New Year to all COWBOYS.

DONALD R. DRUMM
Major, Artillery
Commanding

A MESSAGE TO COWBOY 6

The COWBOYS would like to thank you for the outstanding job you have done during your stay with us. We all feel that a better commander could not have been found. We wish you the very best of luck in your new assignment and give you our best wishes for a Happy New Year.

THE COWBOYS

BULLSHEET RESOLUTIONS

In 1968, Brooks & Mc Cray resolve to play their "soul" records only 10 times a day, Winstead resolves to REUP for an Executive position like SFC K, & Sherman is resolved to think kind thoughts of SFC Batton, Baxter is going to make sure they are the right KIND of thoughts and Schweitzer is not going to be taken in even if they do stop the war and start it over again. Steve Morrell resolves to stop all technical BSing w/Stocker, & Sgt. Givens resolves not to mention 1st Cav. unless he's asked...he declines to comment on the significance of the black bar through the patch. Sprouse resolves to take no more early morning showers & Plattner resolves to teach D Smith to play the guitar, even if it does drive the billets' nuts. Lauch resolves to get rid of that "Sorrowful Jones" "Accident Cloud" that has been hanging over him for the past year and to expose the ID of the BULLSHEET's PHANTOM. Rook has resolved to smile & cheerfully pull the compressor housing on all compressor stalls in 68 just like he has in 67. Phillips is resolved to get his ship out of maint. sometime in "68" & Johannes & Mentzer say they are going to stop taking it easy and really work in the New Year. Hellickson will continue his fight to stay in the sheet metal shop & buck rivets, Miller is resolved to pull a PE in 10 hours instead of the usual 12. CPT Serrett resolves to continue reading his book (if he can find it) and COWBOY 45 resolves to find out the Phu Hiep Tower Freq. Neuman resolves not to sock any old fat men and Cook has resolved to stay out of the village except for Church & Sunday School. Biddy resolved not to give Hooch Maids any more chocolate candy and Murray is going back on the wagon to see if he can beat his record drought of 17 days. Keaton is going to teach 166 how to Twist & says it's what's happening. Batton is resolved to wear the two front teeth he got for Xmas.

PROPHECY FROM MAINTENANCE

In "68" Maintenance will do an even BETTER job in shorter hours. All work will be accomplished during the hr's of 0800-1630 Monday thru Friday. The uniform for maintenance will continue to be immaculate, starched, tailored, jungle fatigues or appropriate civilian attire. Shortly after the 1st of the year Major Lawson will suffer an acute case of nostalgia for the COWBOYS and the superior working condition & stable environment and will volunteer to return. Crew chiefs in the Flt Plts will be unable to make up their minds & consequently will vote both Sgt. Givens and Batton their "Favorite Sgt." in "68." Cook will be apprehended attending Sunday School and Murray will not break his record. Someone will "accidentally" sit on Brooks collection of "soul" music & CPT Serrett will find his book and finally learn how to track the main rotor while at a hover. During "68" BULLSHEET predicts that maintenance will not have to move even one time.

BULLSHEET RESOLUTION FROM RAMRODS.

Roybal resolves to seek a cure for his ailing back someplace other than nude on the Tuy Hoa beach, Carithers resolves to try a "Tonie" to keep his curl. Knox resolves to win a Hero medal like Carithers so he can wow the House Maids (he has a curl too) & hair cut...the one on his chest! Brown is resolved to insure his brain is engaged before putting his mouth into gear and Mills resolves to clear up the mystery of the identification of the OLD SARGE. Seabury resolves to find the Army Recruiter who gave him his "Romance Travel Adventure" tale to get him into all this.

BULLSHEET RESOLUTIONS & PREDICTIONS FROM THE FALCONS

Falcon 86 predicts a major medical breakthrough in hair transplant in 68. WO Enright resolves to revisit Ban Me Thuot and predicts Bien Hoa will be lost to a tidal wave. WO Bryan resolves not to suppress the COWBOYS, WO Quiberg resolves not to suppress the Falcons. Falcon 81 resolves not to mess with crossbows and all Falcons resolve to try to stop laughing at the Tiger Sharks!

LAST WEEKS QUOTATION: Spartan mothers reputedly told their sons "Return with your shield or on it" as they went off to battle.

BULLSHEET RESOLUTIONS FROM AROUND THE RANGE

WO Osterman resolves not to go wading without his rubbers. Welch and Erickson resolve to check out Rosie's Place in Kontum and see if they sell cancer too? Rear Detachment Commanders resolve to find the insidious informer who has been feeding the BULLSHEET. COWBOY 10 resolves to continue his selfless devotion to the COWBOY servant problem and will avoid Lambrettas in Bien Hoa. Webb resolves to build a dog house for Tramp, and Boone resolves to sleep ALONE. Upchurch resolves to sleep alone TOO. CWO Nelson resolves to find out who says he's an old man & predicts he can out jump any W2...Charles Atlas notwithstanding. Marley resolves not to tangle with any rear rotor blades and to read the PHANTOMS column every swinging issue! GALS at the COWBOY PALACE at

Kontum resolve to remain true. WO Peterson resolves to take a charm course & charm a well-known RLO out of enough paint to get rid of the dots on his helmet that make him look like a purple people eater. WO Bass resolves to be the same modest, brave, intelligent, handsome, lovable, astute, superior, shy, person as an RLO as he is as a WO. BULLSHEET resolves to continue reporting the facts as it overhears them ALL IN THE NEW YEAR OF 1968.

QUOTATION OF THE WEEK: "My wife must be above suspicion."

PHRASES FROM THE PHANTOM

The scientists and engineers have worked for centuries, trying to create life. Little did they know that a pair of bicycle repairmen and manufactures would accomplish this feat. Yes, The Wright Brothers did create life. The life of aero-machines. Since their first attempt, many engineers have refined and improved on the creation and the evolutionary process is still continuing.

But they created "Man" for flight. The "Women" came later, in the form of a whining, twisting, undulation helicopter. The engineers at Bell Helicopter took cold steel, aluminum, rivets, bolts and nuts, and made the body. She was sleek and graceful and a beauty to behold. From Lycoming they took an engine and gave her a throbbing heartbeat, but still she lacked life. They nicknamed her Huey. They petted her, caressed her and dreamed of all she could do. But still she lacked life. She sat on the ramp with the morning dew glistening like diamonds from the early sun. That morning she would receive her first transfusion of life.

The pilot assigned to fly her was not a superman nor a God. He was an Army Aviator, equipped with skill, imagination, and the mission to support the ground forces. The whine of her turbines made ripples of power and set them screaming across the landscape. She flexed her rotary arms and swept off on the morning breeze. The sun bather her lovely body with golden colors and she became an angel.

All day she swooped down in areas never before touched by a machine. She nourished the ground troops with the food she carried. She quenched their thirst and delivered their mail. She became nurse to wounded and injured soldiers. She became the first lap of the long ride home. She became life. The safe, sure hands that guided her, nudged her homeward and she was real. She savored her evening repast and snuggled contented and ready for sleep. She was caressed with loving care as she was wrapped up for the night. That was her debut! She was happy because she delivered happiness and help to many who needed it. She was ready for a long useful life. Little did anyone know, it was her first and last day of life. In less than 15 hr's she would lay twisted and broken and smoldering in the dense jungle over which she had hummed so gracefully today. She had confidence in those sure hands that had brought her to life. They caressed her and led her through many tight spots, and she had not let them down, But now, another pair of hands, rough & uncaring, cruel & erratic, would snuff out her life. These hands robbed her of her future. They stole the help she could have given to so many. With her dying breath she asked, "Why aren't all Army Pilots equipped with skill and finesse, gentle and sure hands, and fully aware of my capabilities & their limitations. There is so much more I could have done.

COWBOYS

UNIT HISTORY

1 JANUARY 1968 -- 31 DECEMBER 1968

NARRATIVE OF EVENTS

The 335th Assault Helicopter Company began the year of 1968 assigned to the 268th Combat Aviation Battalion, headquartered at Phu Hiep, RVN. During the period 1 January through 28 February the unit operated out of the Pleiku - Kontum - Dak To area in Direct Support of the 173rd Airborne Brigade. Throughout this period, the unit participated in Combat Assaults LRRP insertions and extraction's, resupply, medevac and numerous other missions in the area of An Khe, Pleiku, Kontum, and Bam Me Thout while maintaining maintenance base at Phu Hiep.

On 1 March, the unit was released from Direct Support of the 173rd Airborne Brigade and assumed the mission of General Support of the II Corps Tactical Zone. Four (4) "Slicks" and two (2) Gunships remained at An Khe in support of the Camp defense Battalion. The remainder of the unit returned to Phu Hiep to begin its new mission.

Beginning 1 March 1968, the unit provided aircraft for General Support missions throughout the II CTZ. The company was also involved in numerous CA missions for ARVN, ROK and U.S. Forces. At the same time, a major effort was underway to establish the containment area at Phu Hiep into a fairly livable condition. The basic structures were there, but an immense effort by unit personnel was required to make the area livable. A complete aircraft maintenance area also had to be built, to include hangar area, hardstand, Tech Supply, etc. Concurrently, required maintenance was performed on unit aircraft, and required availability of mission ready aircraft was maintained.

On 1 June 1968 the aircraft from An Khe returned to Phu Hiep, having been released from their mission. This was the first time in over a year the Unit had been together in its entirety.

On 20 June 1968, at Phu Hiep, Major Carl L. Cramer assumed command of the unit from Major Frank M. Powell, who had commanded the company since 31 December 1967. On 11 July 1968, the unit again provided aviation support to the An Khe area. Four (4) "Slicks," two (2) guns and a Forward Operation Center began work in that area. On 15 July, the unit was relieved of the An Khe mission and again returned to Phu Hiep, where they continued their mission of General Support for II CTZ. In accomplishing this mission, COWBOY aircraft operated from Phan Thiet to Dak To and from Tuy Hoa to Dalat. On 4 October the unit was awarded its first Meritorious Unit Citation and on 10 October received its second at ceremonies at Phu Hiep, RVN.

In November 1968, the unit was alerted once again for another major move, this time back to the III Corps area from where they had originally started. The move was to be a TDY one for a period of 90 to 180 days. It was scheduled to begin on 1 December with the unit becoming operational on 8 December. The General Support Mission for II CTZ was to continue through 30 November, Major Paul R. Riley, Jr. assumed command from Major Carl L. Cramer. On 25 November, a small advance party proceeded to Camp Martin Cox and began preparations to receive the main body. The main body began departing Phu Hiep (Tuy Hoa AFB) on 1 December with all elements closing the new location by 6 December 1968.

Upon arrival in the III Corps Area, the unit was attached for all purposes to the 214th Combat Aviation Battalion, headquartered at Dong Tam. On 8 December the unit began flying missions in support of ARVN Forces in IV CTZ under the OPCON of 164th Combat Aviation Group. Primary support was provided to the 7th Infantry Division (ARVN), 21st Infantry Division (ARVN), 44th STZ and IV Corps Headquarters. During the month of December, unit aircraft flew in all areas of the IV CTZ, providing aviation support where and when needed.

AWARDS AND DECORATIONS -- 1968

AWARD	RECOMMENDED	RECEIVED	PENDING
Distinguished Flying Cross	10	8	2
Bronze Star	19	6	13
Air Medal w/ "V"	15	14	1
Basic Air Medal	121	102	10
Army Commendation Medal	33	23	10

·

UNIT AWARDS

Meritorious Unit Citation

GO# 2309, HQ, USARV, dated -- 16 May 1968

For the Period 1 January 1967 -- 31 December 1967

Meritorious Unit Citation
(1st Oak Leaf Cluster)

GO# 2704, HQ, USARV, dated -- 5 June 1968

For the Period 5 May 1965 -- 4 May 1967

STATISTICS

January	Hours	UH-1B(A)	274
		UH-1H	2005
		TOTAL	2279
	Cargo (tons)	298	
	Passengers	7533	
	Sorties	UH-1B(A)	571
		UH-1H	3890
		TOTAL	4461
	Results (confirmed)	10 VC KBA	
	Aircraft Availability	UH-1B(A)	69%
		UH-1H	70%
		OVERALL	70%

February	Hours	UH-1B(A)	315
		UH-1H	1764
		TOTAL	2079
	Cargo (tons)	246	
	Passengers	7479	
	Sorties	UH-1B(A)	359
		UH-1H	4307
		TOTAL	4666
	Results (confirmed)	9 Structures	
	Aircraft Availability	UH-1B(A)	79%
		UH-1H	71%
		OVERALL	75%

March	Hours	UH-1B(A)	427
		UH-1H	1999
		TOTAL	2426
	Cargo (tons)	141	
	Passengers	7441	
	Sorties	UH-1B(A)	394
		UH-1H	4020
		TOTAL	4414
	Results (confirmed)	25 VC KBA	
		41 Structures	
	Aircraft Availability	UH-1B(A)	75%
		UH-1H	70%
		OVERALL	72%

April	Hours	UH-1B(A)	351
		UH-1H	1975
		TOTAL	2326
	Cargo (tons)	211	
	Passengers	5756	
	Sorties	UH-1B(A)	287
		UH-1H	3497
		TOTAL	3784
	Results (confirmed)	7 VC KBA	
		9 Structures	
		1 Sampan	
	Aircraft Availability	UH-1B(A)	80%
		UH-1H	73%
		OVERALL	76%

May	Hours	UH-1B(A)	291
		UH-1H	2201
		TOTAL	2492
	Cargo (tons)	319	
	Passengers	12661	
	Sorties	UH-1B(A)	309
		UH-1H	5153
		TOTAL	5462
	Results (confirmed)	3 VC KBA	
		6 Structures	
	Aircraft Availability	UH-1B(A)	69%
		UH-1H	66%
		OVERALL	67%

June	Hours	UH-1B(A)	310
		UH-1H	2037
		TOTAL	2347
	Cargo (tons)	208	
	Passengers	11184	
	Sorties	UH-1B(A)	466
		UH-1H	4516
		TOTAL	4982
	Results (confirmed)	4 Structures	
	Aircraft Availability	UH-1B(A)	67%
		UH-1H	60%
		OVERALL	63%

July	Hours	UH-1B(A)	343
		UH-1H	2191
		TOTAL	2534
	Cargo (tons)	373	
	Passengers	12729	
	Sorties	UH-1B(A)	426
		UH-1H	5742
		TOTAL	6168
	Results (confirmed)	4 VC KBA	
		12 Structures	
	Aircraft Availability	UH-1B(A)	71%
		UH-1H	80%
		OVERALL	75%

August	Hours	UH-1B(A)	368
		UH-1H	2184
		TOTAL	2552
	Cargo (tons)	370	
	Passengers	14735	
	Sorties	UH-1B(A)	900
		UH-1H	6181
		TOTAL	7081
	Results (confirmed)	3 VC KBA	
		4 Structures	
	Aircraft Availability	UH-1B(A)	78%
		UH-1H	76%
		OVERALL	77%

September	Hours	UH-1B(A)	474
		UH-1H	1858
		TOTAL	2332
	Cargo (tons)	225	
	Passengers	14100	
	Sorties	UH-1B(A)	691
		UH-1H	6043
		TOTAL	6734
	Results (confirmed)	3 VC KBA	
	Aircraft Availability	UH-1B(A)	87%
		UH-1H	76%
		OVERALL	82%

October	Hours	UH-1B(A)	324
		UH-1H	1836
		TOTAL	2160
	Cargo (tons)	306	
	Passengers	12287	
	Sorties	UH-1B(A)	575
		UH-1H	5545
		TOTAL	6120
	Results (confirmed)	2 Structures	
	Aircraft Availability	UH-1B(A)	72%
		UH-1H	79%
		OVERALL	76%

November	Hours	UH-1B(A)	249
		UII-1II	1930
		TOTAL	2179
	Cargo (tons)	291	
	Passengers	11177	
	Sorties	UH-1B(A)	477
		UH-1H	5297
		TOTAL	5774
	Results (confirmed)	None	
	Aircraft Availability	UH-1B(A)	80%
		UH-1H	79%
		OVERALL	79%

December	Hours	UH-1B(A)	600
		UH-1H	1828
		TOTAL	2428
	Cargo (tons)	52	
	Passengers	10407	
	Sorties	UH-1B(A)	650
		UH-1H	3961
		TOTAL	4611
	Results (confirmed)	36 VC KBA	
		51 Structures	
		39 Sampans	
	Aircraft Availability	UH-1B(A)	93%
		UH-1H	91%
		OVERALL	92%

NOTE: Statistics for December are for a 23-day period due to a stand down during unit move.

1968 Totals	Hours	UH-1B(A)	4296
		UH-1H	23808
		TOTAL	28104
	Cargo (tons)	3040	
	Passengers	126,907	
	Sorties	UH-1B(A)	6105
		UH-1H	58152
		TOTAL	64257
	Results (confirmed)	91 VC KBA	
		133 Structures	
		40 Sampans	

C◆WB◆Y
BULLSHEET

VOLUME 2   14 JANUARY 1968   NUMBER 2

FINALLY EXPENDITURES FROM UNIT FUND

FLASH- For the last six months two miserly men have dominated the Unit Fund Council Meetings, battling any hint of expenditures down with rare eloquence, requesting a strict accounting of every penny, insisting not a penny be spent until the COWBOYS get home. Finally, after six months of opening the meeting, counting the loot and hurriedly closing the meeting, 1st Sgt. Smith & SFC Kinzinger came to a meeting with a catalog in hand and that look in their eye. After a solid hour of "I make a motion to purchase," "I second that motion" "Not to exceed" etc., etc., the air cleared and out of the maze of notes scribbled by the Recorder, the following items appeared: An appropriation, not to exceed $15 for the purchase of a Plaque upon which the name of each COWBOY OF THE MONTH for the next twelve months will be engraved (at no cost to the fund). An appropriation, not to exceed $18.75 per month for the next twelve months to be used to purchase a bond for the COWBOY OF THE MONTH. An appropriation for the purchase of picture frames for the Chain of Command pictures & COWBOY Historical documents. And last but not least...an appropriation not to exceed $50 for the purchase of pre-cut HEADINGS for the COWBOY BULLSHEET. An appropriation for the purchase of mirrors for the showers was also passed. Even after these expenditures are made, the Unit Fund will still be worth over two thousand dollars. Of course, it would be a good idea to keep catalogs out of the 1st Sgt. & Kinzingers way...especially right before the next Unit Fund Meeting!

PONYTHIEF -- sure kicked up some dust climbing under Huey when he heard gunfire at Dong Tre the other day!

Any truth to the rumors on what you want that Forklift for Hill? We all thought you were short?

Insidious Informer wants to know if SFC Givens has any more shady deals he'd like to pull with PFC's?

We haven't forgotten you SFC Keaton, just couldn't get anything on you THIS ISSUE!

FROM THE HOSS's MOUTH

SABOTAGE is a word we all know. It is normally used in conjunction with some clandestine type operation where we work over the enemy lines of communications or he works over ours. But there is another type. When we sabotage ourselves! That's right, any action or job which you fail to complete properly is sabotage to our mission as surely as if Charlie hit us with a satchel charge. Any failure of an individual to perform his job, hampers our aviation support to the SKY SOLDIERS. There is also another form of "friendly sabotage": Stealing! That's what I said, friendly sabotage. Wrongful removal of parts from aircraft and other items of equipment is in violation of the Uniform Code of Military Justice, Article 121, and this act also borders on Aiding the Enemy. Removal of any parts or components from aircraft, vehicles, or other equipment, without proper authority will not be tolerated. Offenders will be dealt with accordingly. This includes unit property as well as sister organizations property. CASE IN POINT: The removal of the UHF and FM radios from 707 our C&C ship, during the night of 12-14 January. What better way does Charlie have to reduce COWBOY effectiveness than preventing COWBOY 3 from controlling CA missions?

COWBOY 6

One day two little old ladies went for a tramp in the woods, but he got away.

BULLSHEET FROM ROUND THE RANGE

Got a Trooper in the third Platoon who sure has been havin problems keeping up with his wall locker....damned thing wanders all over the barracks. Course it might be that the Charles Atlas enthusiasts are usin it to press. And speakin of the muscle bunch in the Falcons, we understand that the Platoon Sergeant has stopped kicking bunks to get the troops up in the morning since all that muscle has materialized!! Falcon Crew Chiefs and Gunners are a makin book that if the Red Baron goes any lower on his passes, they will be given additional MOSs for rice harvesting. Red Baron has already taken a bush from Viet Cong handson a looow pass the other day. Falcons figure the Baron thinks TRIM is something found only in the Barber shops. Speakin of the Falcons, wonder if any of them been sufferin from the bends...they were flying so high at Dak To and so low down here that there's a possibility that the bends could get the best of them. Some of the men have a heck of a time stayin in the ship on the real low passes. Rogers said he sticks a couple of bricks in his drawers to weight him down, but Bartlett clued us in that Rogers didn't have to put the bricks into his drawers just clean them out. Whole third Platoon wants Sehiers to know that there is only ONE THING short on him!! Now I wonder what that could be?

An Ass can never be a horse, but he can be a Sergeant!

FLASH FROM THE RAMRODS is that Smith made E4 again!, and Roybal made hard rank...sure is hard to take it off. Sgt. Pritchards still in the hospital and Carither's soundin more like the OLD SARGE every day. Ramrods say he's not really chicken- - - -, he's just got Hen House ways. Old Curley's not just hard-nosed and hard core! Insidious informer has a message for WO Mills "Next time you want to hit a grunt in the head...do it with somethin that doesn't cost $2,000." Insidious Informer tells us that WO Hopkins' givin lessons on how to cut an LZ with the main rotor blade, but heck, that aint so hot....WO De Curtis cuts his with his tail rotor. Got word that the second Platoon has the "Stretch" Champs of the battalion, at least the other night an Aircraft Commander from 2d Platoon was hauled up to Battalion HQ to get his reward for the game he played the other day. Insidious Informer said that SFC Givens has been a studyin the supply manuals for who laid the rail ever since he had a little chat with Old Hoss the other day. Still want to go to the Calvary Sarge?? Insidious Informer would like to know if WO Graham has found out who the Phantom is yet? Also need a report on the BJ's at Kontum from WO De Curtis. Understand Sgt. Upchurch might be goin to bed, but not for sleepin these days?? Old Hoss still considerin the possibility of putting that USARV Certificate of Achievement a certain section has in mourning until he found out that there just aint any fresh eggs to be had. Insidious Informer tips us that there is a Major at Bien Hoa in something of a tiff after learning that WO1 WONG is currently commanding the FALCON Gun Platoon, the Major commands a Fire Team down there.

ORTMAN MADE HARD RANK! All that rank in Operations things ought to be in ship shape now. Two Sergeants and if you count Kinzinger you could say four. We can remember when they didn't have any, took till eleven O'clock at night to get missions out then too. FLASH REPORT FROM MAINTENANCE: If you thought tracking a main rotor blade while at a hover was a good one, this one is calculated to kill. We understand that a VIP RLO in the 166th took off the other day without his crew. Cookie said he sure felt left out of things and Funk said he was so short that there was only ONE FLIGHT HE DIDN'T WANT TO MISS. Schwietzer, our oracle of the Tech Insp Div, has come up with a modification to the Huey....Duckbills in the swashplate....How's it work genius?

AIRCRAFT CREWMEN'S BADGES HAVE BEEN REQUESTED FOR ALL ELIGIBLE PERSONS WHEN ORDERS ARE CUT THEY WILL BE POSTED ON THE BULLETIN BOARD!!

A girl cocker spaniel used to meet the Postman and carry the letters to the house until one day she got a litter from her boyfriend.

PHRASES FROM THE PHANTOM

ALL RIGHT! Who was the clown who tried to amputate my toe? I'll tell you. ME! I was on my way to the shower with my mind on at least a dozen other things, I was probably thinking about R&R and Hawaii and my wife, etc., etc. Then all of a sudden something had hold of my big toe. My foot had become engaged with a strip of pierced steel planking, raised an inch or so off the ground. Fortunately, all I did was scrape the toe and stub it good. But when the catastrophe occurred, I was so busy cussing the PSP, hopping on one foot, holding my toe, that my brain became disengaged, and I fell flat on my dignity, skinning the ankle of my remaining "good" foot. If it hadn't been so funny I might have really gotten mad. Imagine a big pile of man wallowing on the ground, wrapped in a towel, trying to hold both feet simultaneously! Rather ludicrous isn't it. Fortunately, there was no one around to witness my foo-pah and injured pride. Yep! this was an accident! When did it occur? When I wasn't watching what I was doing. MORAL; Accidents can & do happen to everyone....even the Phantom, when strict attention is not paid to what you are doing.

THE PHANTOM***HAS SPOKEN

THIS WEEKS QUOTATION: Who said, "WAR IS HELL" (Before John Wayne if you please).

Write 100 using six 9's.

BULLSHEET FROM THE OLD SARGE

Troopers been asking bout the new Chain of Command fer the COWBOYS so thought I'd whip it on yuh!

PRESIDENT: L.B. JOHNSON

SEC DEF: HON MR. NCNAMARA

SEC ARMY: HON MR. RESOR

CHAIRMAN JCS: GEN WHEELER

C/S ARMY: GEN JOHNSON

USARPAC CMDR: ADMIRAL SHARP

USARV CMDR: GEN WESTMORELAND

1ST AVN BDE: MG WILLIAMS

17TH CMBT AVN GP: COL SMITH

268TH CMBT AVN BN: LTC MULLIGAN

335TH ASLT HEL CO: MAJOR POWELL

XO: MAJOR AKRE

1ST PLT LDR: LT FLETT

2D PLT LDR: CPT STEWART

3D PLT LDR: CPT KENNER

So thar she be!!!

Lotta talk round the old Corral bout them thar boards. Soldier of the month Board and promotion board. I already told you that thar wasn't goin to be no more cram classes, but thar will be a School of the Soldier every Wednesday night in the COWBOY Court House. General subjects will be gettin a goin over and I magin that a body might learn quite a bit about what might help him be a better soldier as well as pass a board or two.

THE OLD SARGE

Insidious Informer is wondering if PONYTHIEF is still holding his approach as directed by Phu Hiep Tower to whom he was talking on the wrong freq. AGAIN the other day?

Two cannonballs got married and had Beebies.

C◆WB◆Y
BULLSHEET

VOLUME 2   28 JANUARY 1968   NUMBER 4

MORIELLO RECOMMENDED FOR DFC

Specialist Five Anthony Moriello has been recommended for the award of a Distinguished Flying Cross for his valorous devotion to duty on the 7th of January 1968. Falcon enlisted personnel first brought Specialist Moriello's actions to the attention of COWBOY SIX, who concurred and made the recommendation.

First thing WOs Enright & Bryan did after the little action up on the north forty the other day, was to ask about damage to aircraft; last question was "Are there any casualties?" Hard Core? Falcons.

Understand that there's a movement started to rename the Falcons the Purple Heart Platoon?? Of course, that's not all they got that 's purple either!!

Insidious Informer is broken hearted to say that he couldn't dig-up one single boo boo on a well-known RLO in the 166th Transportation Detach. Is he clean or did he swear them all to secrecy??

A good masseur leaves no stern untoned.

NINETEEN, 19, XVIV, nineteen!!! Replacements arrived at the Old COWBOY Corral the other day, and Old Hoss had a grin on his puss as wide as the backside of Kinzingers drawers, just lookin at them. Sure are glad to WELCOME you all to the COWBOYS.

NORTH KOREA COMMITS ACT OF WAR!! Don't want to throw any wet water on that rotation gleam in Carither's eyes, but the seizure of the U.S. Intelligence Vessel in International waters sparked a call up of the reserves in CONUS. Sure would be a heck of a thing if all these "Short Timers" got extended for the duration plus six???

Insidious Informer tells us that PONYTHIEF finally grew up into a MUSTANG!!

Could that "Charm Course" WO Peterson got for Xmas be coming through? Understand that WO Besch climbed right into his lap the other night when the grenade rolled into the room??

FROM THE HOSS's MOUTH

In the past few short days, we have made great strides in our progress toward improvement of the basic school of the soldier. Our uniforms look better. Our haircuts are neater. Our billets are vastly improved, and our Company is beginning to resemble the "COWBOY CODE."

There is still a lot to be done. Much hard work required and I'm sure it will be done. Each of us, however, must begin a "self-analysis" program. Our work, our daily life, our habits and expressions, must begin to reflect only the highest standards. It won't be easy, but then there is little in life that is worthwhile that is "free." Hard work, dedication, and pride, can and does accomplish miracles!

In the ensuing days each of you will be required to put forth maximum effort. Don't wait to be told. If you see something that should be done, do it. In fact, do it now, not later.

COWBOY 6

Arrange the digits from 1 to 7 so that they will add up to 100...

A trader buys 100 head of animals and pays $100 for them. He buys cows at $10, hogs at $5, and chickens at 50 cents. How many of each does he buy?

What was the "Spartan Wall"?

BULLSHEET FROM ROUND THE RANGE

Fantabulous FALCONS have had another full week, Our Insidious Informer tells us that WO De Fide has developed a reputation for butterfingers because he drops the darndest things; it used to be Armorement didn't like him...now they hate him!! And by the way...those rumors bout Loesch & the new Barmaid at the club just aint so...he has a girl at home and wants everybody to know that his relationship with the Barmaid is strictly platonic...they are just comparing their collection of flowered drawers! Shore seems the shorter some FALCONS get...the higher they fly...crews are trying to scrounge oxygen masks & fur-lined flight suits...how bout that WO Wong? (Alias WB productions that is)...Educated Gunship WO Bryan got into the other day, broke its altimeter as soon as he announced the destination DAK TO...smart ship!! Insidious Informer says that palatial palace Fuzz moved into is lookin like a library with all the books he has policed up from the FALCONS...got word that he is now studying three lettered words, so he can mispronounce them... (What is this? Revenge for the five thirty wake up?) Message to the BLACK HAND from one who knows: Black Hand...be advised that a FALCON looks funny as hell, flying with a pot...better cut back and be satisfied with just thirds at the Mess Hall, or did SSGT Blackweller hire you to take over Mess Hall public relations?? What was that CPT Kenner?? "Hello CHALK FOUR!"

Insidious Informer says the rumor about the D 4/503d mascot being related to a Mustang Pilot just could be...strong resemblance....then to these's the same name...hummmm?? TWIGGY AWARD for the week went to...of course you have all guessed...Warrant Officer Ferrara....Understand that Mustang Bear has been nominated GRUNT OF THE MONTH for his inspiring dash and lonely vigil at the perimeter during the last alert. Insidious Informer tells us that Teeny Bobber Schmidt was up in the air during that alert too, but Mother P brought some P to bear and he got down pretty fast. And speaking of P, got the word that old Hoss brought some to bear on the Mustang Hero's that were playing with an unauthorized siren the other day...!!! Insidious Informer tipped us that WO Freeman has developed a totally NEW take off procedure...COWBOY Pilots better have him tell them about it...and how's that for real tact WO Freeman?? (BULLSHEET collects in cash.) Understand that "HOVER" Orders are being cut for SFC GIVENS for his exploits in Maintenance this past week...yeh we know, that's how they always do it in the Cav...but joking aside Insidious Informer tells us that SFC Givens has been awarded the SSC and BHC for the incident. For those not in the know...SSC is the well-known Scared S___less Citation and of course BHC is the very well-known BLEW HIS COOL award. BULLSHEET agrees...SFC Givens earned them both. A last minute tip from ONE WHO KNOWS that WO De Fide joined Jade in the hall of Fame as he too had trouble keeping his cookies in a wild ride with the notorious RED BARON...Insidious Informer says that RED BARON has written the 1st Aviation Brigade Publication "HAWK" demanding a retraction...RED BARON says that the picture was perfect, and of course he's very much alive...but at PHU HIEP NOT Long Binh...COWBOYS who want to examine the controversial photo and corrected caption will find it on the NOTAMS Board in Flight Opns.

FLASH FLASH As we go to press we are most happy to report all FALCONS are safe. The Editorial Staff of the BULLSHEET would like to commend the FALCONS and other victims/subjects of our pointed pens for the outstanding spirit and truly fine humor they accept the (ahem) literary tributes (?) reflected in these columns.

THIS SPACE IS FOR THE SECTIONS AND STORIES THAT WERE NOT GIVEN TO THE COWBOY BULLSHEET.

PHRASES FROM THE PHANTOM

Anyone remember the big pile-up of three duce and a half's a few weeks back? I sure do. Which brings up a point. SPEED! Do you know what the average speed law says? Usually a posted maximum speed is modified by law to also include "reasonable speed for road, traffic & weather conditions."

This means that just because the posted speed limit is 35 mph, you can still be stopped for reckless driving at 30 mph if traffic, road, and weather conditions won't support that speed.

Don't risk an accident by speeding! It only takes a few minutes at a safe speed to get anywhere. By speeding, you will not save time. In fact, it could take you forever to get there. Why? An Accident MORALE: SLOW DOWN AND LIVE!

THE PHANTOM***HAS SPOKEN

THERE WAS A YOUNG LADY NAMED ROOD WHO WAS SUCH AN ABSOLUTE PRUDE THAT SHE PULLED DOWN THE BLIND WHEN CHANGING HER MIND, LEST A CURIOUS EYE SHOULD INTRUDE.

THERE WAS A YOUNG MONK FORM SIBERIA WHO'S MORALS WERE RATHER INFERIOR, HE DID TO A NUN WHAT HE SHOULDN'T HAVE DONE, AND NOW SHE'S A MOTHER SUPERIOR.

ATTENTION COWBOYS WHO HAVE JUST BEEN PROMOTED OR WHO HAVE RECEIVED DECORATIONS IN THE MONTH OF JANUARY. If you want a hometown news release See SFC Kinzinger.

MAINTENANCE NOTES BY SPECIALIST SCHWIETZER

It has been said that, "Playing a piano by ear may sound nice after a fashion, but it's not very professional."

Some mechanics tend to play their maintenance by ear.

It is recognized that an individual's judgment plays a large part in trouble shooting, which components must be changed and what adjustments must be made. Aircraft require the installation of components, adjustments, inspections, and functional testing be accomplished with the greatest care and exactness.

Aircraft require the PROFESSIONAL approach by all concerned. Take time to look it up in the TM or other applicable directives. Be a Professional! DON'T PLAY IT BY EAR!

Soldiers YOU Should Know: The draftee who claimed exemption on the grounds of defective eyesight...& showed the draft board his wife to prove it...The COWBOY who reported, "I finally persuaded my girl to say yes." "Oh? When is the Wedding?" "Who said anything about a Wedding?" The old Sarge who caught a COWBOY with just one button unbuttoned and shouted, "Sunbathing Eh?" The very effeminate little clerk who gushed, "Isn't it just wonderful to be fighting for Aunt Sam?" ...and the poor 2d Lt. who received a cable from his best gal: "Couldn't wait for you a day longer, so have married your father, Love Mother!" And if you think these are sick....

Dominic Fino

C◆WB◆Y

BULLSHEET

| VOLUME 2 | 4 FEBRUARY 1968 | NUMBER 5 |

SP/4 CHRISTOPHER M. DANIELS MEMORIAL FUND GROWS

SADDENED COWBOYS GATHERED SUNDAY NIGHT TO HONOR THE MEMORY OF THE LATE SPECIALIST FOUR CHRISTOPHER M. DANIELS, KILLED IN ACTION ON 3 FEBRUARY 1968.

AS ARRANGEMENTS FOR FLOWERS ARE IMPRACTICAL, THE COWBOY COMMANDER IS CONTACTING CITY OFFICIALS IN THE DECEASED COWBOY'S HOME TOWN IN ORDER TO SELECT A BOY'S CLUB TO RECEIVE A CASH BEQUEST IN MEMORY OF SPECIALIST FOUR CHRISTOPHER M. DANIELS.

PERSONS DESIRING TO CONTRIBUTE TO THIS MEMORIAL FUND, MAY DO SO THROUGH THEIR PLATOON SERGEANTS, PLATOON LEADERS, OR THE COWBOY ORDERLY ROOM

THE EDITOR

FROM THE HOSS's MOUTH

The past few days have really been exciting. "Chuck" has elected to test the mettle of our efforts here in South Vietnam. Almost every major city and military installation has felt his wrath. This means that each of us will have to put forth additional effort.

Actually, the COWBOYS have not been badly harassed as yet. This is not true of our sister Assault Helicopter Companies in Vietnam. This means only one thing. We can and will increase our efforts to provide maximum aviation support.

The COWBOYS will continue to be called upon for additional effort. I know of no better way to display the COWBOY CODE than by adopting an old practice from the 13th Cavalry. There, any individual receiving an order saluted and replied, "It shall be done!"

COWBOY 6

The S in the dollar sign ($) is a corruption of the figure 8, from Spanish "piece of eight," which had a value of eight smaller coins. The parallel lines represent the pillar of Hercules, or passage between the Atlantic and the Mediterranean Sea. Dollar, derives from "thaler" a coin equivalent to a piece of eight but coming from Joachimsthaler, a silver-mining town in Bohemia.

The traditional three balls over the Pawn Shop are taken from the Medici Family of Florence.

BULLSHEET FROM ROUND THE RANGE

Warrant Officer Wong, of Falcon Fame departed this week with JayHawker, an honorary member of the BULLSHEET "Staff." WO Wong asked BULLSHEET Reporter, the Insidious Informer to pass on his fond farewells to all the COWBOYS, and his regret at the ending of the WB Productions. Word from "One Who Knows" is that the notorious BLACK HAND talks in his sleep (too). Soon as we can locate an Italian interpreter we will TELL ALL!! Big Question during the last alert was: Just what part of the perimeter is the Falcons supposed to man...or are they supposed to fake Charlie out with the fancy footwork? Red Baron's been a mutterin and cussin in his cups cause they won't let him shoot up no Charlie Critters...says he likes to be WHERE THE ACTION IS. Insidious Informer is nominating WO Wong & Bartlett for a SSC after the XO's neat little leg pull on an extension for everybody about to rotate. "One Who Knows" passed word down that when COWBOY Jones got wounded the other day...first thing he wanted was someone with a camera to take his picture. Usual COWBOY cry is for the

MEDAL first and then the camera...Also got word that Rogers quest for the quite life with the Ramrods has been almost as exciting as his exploits with the Falcons...Understand he set a new Worlds record for lightweight speed getting in to a bunker at Holloway the other day. Checked it out Rogers and don't worry Rogers, they won't really make you go down and look for that door. Insidious Informer says Sherman sure was sorry to see SFC Batton go...SFC Thompson's a lot bigger than he was...And from the Mustangs we are trying to find out who was in that Wall Locker with Vincent...maybe it was the California Kid?? All the COWBOYS are sufferin from them dish pan hands since the Hooch Maids aren't here to take care of the washing of clothing...Old Sarge really worked out the other night rinsing out his unmentionables...considering the size of them it was probably a full day's work,...he sure looked good in his passionate pink towel. Insidious Informer got his quota of chuckles the other day when old Hoss sank his teeth into the Vietnamese man who was foolin with the Hooch Maids...sorta sickish grin all over his face when the Old Man found out he had just had a piece of a PA&E Contractor. Might be WAR if the 1st Shirt really moves to put that there classy new report back in Operations. Here at the BULLSHEET we would like to stay impartial but in this case we have to root for Operations...sorta fraid if it does go to Ops...we will be stuck on it...!! Understand that Russo has a thing bout spiders...dropped a case of ammo the other day and was out of the area before the box hit the ground when he came eye to eye with a big one. How bout that BLACK HAND!!

NOTES FORM THE OLD SARGE

Troops are startin ter git them fancy education coursed we sent fer here a few weeks back. I reckin we'll see now jest which ones has got the gumption to finish all them lessons. Anybody can start one a them USAFI courses, n anybody can find all sorts excuses why he can't finish...I sort a wonder what could have happened if old Abe Lincoln hada used any of the several good excuses he had and said to heck with education...I'm pretty sure he wouldn't have been President! Education is its own reward! Sounds ter me like a heap a truth in that. N while we're a talkin about rewards I wonder how many of us have larn't ter reward hisself...How many have been a studyin life enough to see that the only important reward is that one we all feel when we know we have done a damned good job, or the right thing. A body has got to feel sorry for the man who knows he doesn't deserve a reward he got. There'll be a good many times when you bust your gut to do a job n get a clop in the snout fer it, but if you HAVE DONE A GOOD JOB, and you know that you have, you can still look back with a feeling of pride for your part in the endeavor. Learn now to reward yourself, and you can learn later to laugh at "the slings and arrows of outrageous fortune." One of the world's greatest Fairy Tales is the story of The Emperor's New Clothes which, if you will read it, isn't so much of a "Fairy Tale" after all!!!

THE OLD SARGE

PHRASES FROM THE PHANTOM

In the study of aircraft and missile design, one important aspect is FATIGUE. Here fatigue is defined as follows: "When a part is subjected to repeated loads, stresses are created within the part which continually very with time." Let me add to that; the unknown quantity of changing loads, and look at fatigue under a new light.

What I am leading up to, is a statement that fatigue in man is much the same as fatigues in metals. The basic difference is that man does not have a mandatory time change for his components. (Even an occasional "oil change" won't count) The microscopic cracks that occur to each of us under the changing loads of our duties are not as easily detected and measured as those in metal.

Fatigue in a rotor head is a killer, no doubt. But do you really realize that fatigue in us is also a killer? It can cause us to forget a safety wire, miss a low rotor RPM, overlook an item on preflight or "go to seep at the switch."

These are trying times, demanding maximum output from each individual. During these times be especially watchful for those insidious "cracks of fatigue" in yourself and your friends. Let you safety conscious be your shield against personal fatigue.

THE PHATOM***HAS SPOKEN

ODDS & ENDS ROUND THE CORRAL

Arrange the digits 1 to 7 so that they will add up to 100 in the following way: 15+36+47+2=100!

A trader buys 100 head of animals and pays $100 for them. He buys cows at $10, hogs at $5, and chickens at 50 cents....He buys the following: One cow, nine hogs, and ninety chickens.

What was the Spartan Wall? The Spartan Wall was the men of Sparta, each one considered a brick in the wall defending the city...!!

TRY THESE FOR NEXT WEEK......Farmer A said to Farmer B, "If you will sell me 7 acres of your farm, I will have twice as much land as you." But Farmer B said to Farmer A "If you will sell me 7 acres of your farm, I will have just as much land as you." How much land did each Farmer have?....Answer next issue.

What is the difference between six dozen dozen and a half dozen dozen? Answer next week....

If three cats can catch three rats in three minutes, how many cats could catch one hundred rats in one hundred minutes?

George Washington was inaugurated first President of the country on the balcony of the Old Federal Building located at Broad & Wall Streets in New Your City. His inauguration took place 30 April 1789.

BULLSHEET

VOLUME 2   13 OCTOBER 1968   NUMBER 26

SECOND MERITORIOUS UNIT COMMENDATION

AWARDED TO COWBOYS BY LIGHTNING 6

CWO WEIDNER AWARDED DFC

EXECUTIVE OFFICER PROMOTED TO MAJOR

BATTLE STAR FOR TET COUNTER OFFENSIVE

LTC ORLANDO E. GONZALES presented a second award of the Meritorious Unit Commendation to the COWBOYS at an awards and decorations ceremony in the COWBOY Corral on the 10th of October 1968. Many COWBOYS presently in the unit will take this award as a permanent part of their uniform. The period of service covered is 1 Jan 67 to 31 December 1967 and all personnel who were assigned to the 335th or 166th/234th Detachments during that period are permitted to wear the Meritorious Unit Commendation as a permanent part of their uniform. ALL COWBOYS while assigned to the COWBOYS now wear the Meritorious Unit Commendation with 1st Oak Leaf Cluster and the Cross of Gallantry with Palm. COWBOYS rotating to the States wear these decorations until they sign in at their next unit or until they are discharged.

CWO Weidner was presented with the Distinguished Flying Cross & some twenty other COWBOYS were decorated by LTC Gonzales during the awards & decoration ceremony on 10 Oct. 68. CWO Weidner's DFC was awarded for action with the 61st AHC. CONGRATS COWBOYS!

A Battle Star for the Vietnamese Service Medal has been awarded for the period 30 Jan - 1 Apr 68. All personnel assigned during this period now have TWO Battle Stars and persons arriving AFTER 1 Apr 68 wear only one Battle Star. The Seventh Campaign, commencing 2 April 1968 has not yet been named and a cutoff date for it has not yet been established. The TET Counter Offensive is the sixth campaign of the Vietnamese Conflict.

FROM THE HORSES' MOUTH

It would appear that the wet weather is here to stay. Low clouds and reduced visibility are associated with this weather in the form of precipitation. The test is upon each of us who are required to determine if we have enough weather to safely make the flight. The long days of flying causes one to become very tired & leads to dulling of your reflects. Attempting a flight through rain after darkness requires one to be fully alert to cope with problems. Weigh these factors and make a decision based on them. If you determine that an RON is the best decision, insure that Operations is notified. It is better to sit out the weather than not be around to make the next decision.

Motor Maintenance is improving. Each of us must do our part, today, to insure we have something to accomplish the mission with tomorrow.

Aircraft Maintenance continues to meet the challenge. Projects which will receive emphasis this week are: Washing and continued improvement of the appearance of aircraft. Police of the Maintenance area to include the shops. Crew Chief & Gunner working on their aircraft while in PE.

I was very proud to invite the Battalion Commander down to decorate so many COWBOYS. The 2d Meritorious Unit Commendation and the individual awards reflect what the COWBOYS have done in the past and what they are capable of doing now! Keep up the good work and keep them flying COWBOYS!

COWBOY 6

SAFETY SPOOK

To the United States Army, who trusts that I am technically qualified for the tasks expected of me. To the aircrews & pax, who trust their lives & safety to my mechanical skills. To my unit, which expects me to be a professional mechanic as well as a good soldier. To my fellow mechanics, who as team members must depend upon me for a task completed. To myself, for the personal satisfaction of a professional job well done. To all whom I have named I recognize my obligation . . . TO DISCHARGE THIS OBLIGATION . . .

I WILL perform maintenance of the highest quality to assure the safety of every flight. I WILL always be sure of my work, or consult a superior when in doubt. I WILL strive to improve my professional skill by attention to duty & self-education. I WILL NOT allow my personal desires or considerations to affect my job. I WILL NEVER attempt to perform duty when my mental or physical condition might lead to maintenance mistakes. I WILL keep my tools and equipment in first class condition to insure a job worthy of the professional mechanic that I am. I PLEDGE ADHERENCE TO THESE PRINCIPALS TO REFLECT CREDIT UPON MYSELF, MY FELLOW WORKERS MY UNIT, AND ARMY AVIATION. And if YOU DO this unit will not be haunted by the SAFETY SPOOK.

INSIDIOUS INFORMER

BULLSHEET FROM 'ROUND THE RANGE

CONGRATS MAJOR LOGAN on your promotion. The troops are all waiting for you to set the date for free beer in honor of the occasion. A little tradition we are trying to get started.

Words out that CONGRATS are also in order for VANCE . . .he almost got a Huey to his credit, . . . as a matter of fact the Huey he was riding in . . . and got the RLO peter-p a little shook.

The company party last Sunday was a great success, 1st Sgt. Mess, Sgt. Grundy, Tipton, and Kinzinger. . . sounds like a roll call of company NCOs when we name the people who hit the drink.

We could sure tell that SGTs Hair, Ellert, and Smithson were gone. . . we had 17 cases of beer left over.

All of the COWBOYS were happy to see WO Woolsey before he left and wish him a speedy recovery.

Insidious Informers says Mustangs are overdue for a class on the installation of the short shaft. . . seems that they have to do it twice or three times to get it right. (HOW BOUT THAT SUPER SHAFT).

A report from Indian Country says Big Chief Indian vetoed the Braves plans for a lounge and Bar in the new annex. Word is out the Newman of the FALCONS is steady fighting a hairy problem, & intrepid FALCONEERS CHICKEN HAWK AND FANTASTIC FAL were really pretty shook up the other days at Bong Son when the quest for LAW & ORDER took them to an enemy emplacement equipped with 50 Cal machine guns. GEE WHIZ CHICKEN HAWK! DID YOU REALLY KISS THE GROUND WHEN YOU LANDED? TURKEY . . you got to look out better for CHICKEN HAWK during your fearless flight against crime!

OUR reporter in Da Nang says, "WHO TUCKED SFC Hair in bed the other nite?"

Tipton says that Dong Ba Thin is really where the action is, but that story he is passin out about old buddies is just a line because SOME have seen the pics and believe us: we should have such a BUDDY!

No CHICKEN LITTLE. . .the sky is not really falling, you probably got into the helicopter up-side-down.

We were trying hard to get something good on Old Wrangler this week. . .but we found out that he didn't do anything! Of course, there are those who are holding their breaths for fear some of his sketches may fall into the wrong hands.

Got the word that SSGT Smithson was heard to say that he would give a $100 to have SFC K with him in Taiwan. . . course we kinda figured that the Babes there would be too much for him, but we didn't think that he would call for help when it could be heard!

Words out that Foltz is lookin forward to keepin his hands clean now that he is Engine TI. FEARLESS FALCONS respectfully request FALCON SIX be more careful with the pussy mounts. . . SSGT COLES can be BAD about stuff like that and the Plt. was hurtin till they were found.

SOMEONE QUICK! Show WO Besch how to do INSPECTION ARMS WITH A 38!!!

THE OLD SARGE

On 12 May 1962, General of the Army DOUGLAS MacARTHUR, speaking to future officers of the United States Army, had this to say about us:

" . . .And what sort of soldiers are those you are to lead? Are they reliable, are they brave, are they capable of victory? Their story is known to all of you; it is the story of the American man-at-arms. My estimate of him was formed on the battlefield many, many years ago, and has never changed. I regarded him then as I regard him now--as one of the world's noblest figures, not only as one of the finest military characters but also as one of the most stainless. His name and fame are the birthright of every American citizen. In his youth and strength, his love and loyalty he gave--all that mortality can give. He needs no eulogy from me or from any other man. He has written his own history and written it in red on his enemy's breast. But when I think of his patience under adversity, of his courage under fire, and of his modesty in victory, I am filled with an emotion I cannot put into words. He belongs to history as furnishing one of the greatest examples of successful patriotism; he belongs to posterity as the instructor of future generations in the principals of liberty and freedom; he belongs to the present, to us, by his virtues and by his achievements. In twenty campaigns, on a hundred battlefields, around a thousand campfires, I have witnessed that enduring fortitude, that patriotic self-abnegation, and that invincible determination which have carved his stature in the hearts of his people. From one end of the world to the other he has drained deep the chalice of courage."

THE OLD SARGE

C◆WB◆Y

BULLSHEET

VOLUME 2	27 OCTOBER 1968	NUMBER 28

SPECIALIST FIVE UNTALAN
BATTALION SOLDIER OF THE MONTH

SPECIALIST FIVE UNTALAN earned the distinction of being the first COWBOY selected to be Lightning Soldier of the Month. LTC Gonzales made the announcement during a surprise visit to COWBOY RANCH HOUSE (Orderly Room). Specialist Five stripes were won with the coveted title. CONGRATS & WELL-DONE SP5 UNTALAN!

Specialist Four Reboletti was awarded a commendation for safe driving by Major Cramer. Driving over ten thousand miles without accident or DR is quite an achievement in this country. Best of luck to SP4 Reboletti on his return to Paradise!

Over twenty happy COWBOYS are departing from the Old Corral this month! Quite a Posse of COWBOYS to be going all at one time. Best of luck to you COWBOYS and save some of the world for us!

COWBOY CARRIAGE HOUSE (Motor Pool) was the subject of an extensive news article this week. The hard work and initiative that went into many fine innovations are truly outstanding. COWBOY 6 also appointed a new CARRIAGE HOUSE MASTER, WO Snow. COWBOY CARRIAGES are really in for a good "Snow Job" from now on! CONGRATS to all CARRIAGE HOUSE PERSONNEL on a FINE JOB!

LADIES DAY AT COWBOY FLIGHT OPERATIONS! FLASH! COWBOY 3's fabricated fantasy concerning his relationship with the young lovely who visited COWBOY Flt Operations this week has not hoodwinked the Insidious Informer who is trying hard to learn just how the seemingly shy CPT. managed to swing a line that was so good it brought a genuine ROUND EYE to visit him. In a country where the male to "that-kind-of-female" ratio is something better than twenty thousand to one, Insidious Informer says he's got to get whatever the CPT'S. got! BULLSHEET Editor says he figures the CPT. is telling the truth . . . cousins would explain the phenomena. If not, if what the CPT. has can be boxed and sold it'll make a fortune!!

FROM THE HORSES' MOUTH

Well, this week has seen some more wet weather, but COWBOYS keep getting off on time and getting their daily missions accomplished. Maintenance had 15/5 flying for the best record in sometime. Keep up the good job Maintenance! I see more people working on their aircraft than ever before. The Guns have gotten their last tail rotor blade, Lt. Smith informs me. He better be right!

We sure have had money trouble lately with the change of MPC. It brought to light that many people were keeping too much money on hand. Many people have needlessly lost money out of foot lockers or wallets. Send your money home or put it in Soldier's Savings where it is safe and will work for you! Insure that you don't make it easy for someone to have a good time on your hard-earned money!

Rations Cards are a Controlled Form since they are a valued item with which people can secure more items from the PX then they are supposed to. Is your ration card buying beer and radios for the VC?

COWBOY 6

SAFETY SPOOK

Brigade Safety Officer's visit to the Old Corral found COWBOYS in fairly good shape. SAFETY SPOOK is really happy to see the presentation of a Safety Award to SP4 Roboletti and says others are in the mill!

Keep flying SAFELY COWBOYS

Safety Spook

PRAYER OF THE LIEUTENANT

Twinkle
Little Bar

How I wish
You were a Star!

INSIDIOUS INFORMER

BULLSHEET FROM 'ROUND THE RANGE

Insidious Informer says he always figured that some RLOs found those bars in cracker jacks boxes but when a SP4 in Flight Operations had to give a Jr. RLO a class in Map Reading the other day, it was a case of suspicion confirmed!

When BULLSHEET Editor asked Insidious Informers in Maintenance for the word this week, all he got was "What about the critical shortage of Butter?"

So much, and so many different colors of paint going on COWBOY Aircraft that we won't have to worry about getting a Christmas Tree this year . . . is the "word" from COWBOY CREW CHIEFS.

So far, we have heard all the lies and listened to all the speculation on the patch over Smithson's eye . . . and we really don't believe the favored rumor that the big Babe in the Mess Hall gave it to him . . . and we don't think that Webster whipped it on him . . . but he may have been wearing sunglasses when he went to visit his girlfriend!

Insidious Informer got a "scoop" on the dapper Dan of 2nd Plt however which is too good to keep. Seems Smitty has a "thing" about complexion care and is using a really great formula of Calamine Lotion that makes his face "Lovely to Live with" . . . He calls that LIVING? We suggest amputation of everything above the shoulders!

COWBOY Brice has really figured out a smooth way to handle the "Guard" problem . . . stop writing home, and you can get taken off guard to write a letter in the Old Man's Office! Neat Huh?

Got word that the enthusiasm for the "Training Films" shown in the EM Club last Sunday almost knew no bounds. Word is up that the men are all eager to have a practical exercise . . . wonder if the Old Man would go for that . . . we got the 1st Shirt sold!

Words out that the COWBOYS got the INDIANS about four times this week . . . COWBOY SIX got CHIEF INDIAN that is! Speaking of the Indians . . . they almost split a Wigwam when a Sr. CWO in Maint spent thirty minutes telling them how important it is to make sure the battery in the Birds is off, and showing them how to check it . . . then started to walk off with the battery switch still ON!

COWBOY T. J. Smith lowered the boom on a Vietnamese who clobbered his Bird with a rock Saturday. Major Logan & the pugnacious Crew Chief had pulled him off the Aircraft three or four times and when he got tossed off the last time he wound up the pitch and crashed a rock through the window . . . T. J. put him OUT!

FALCON close support of Ramrods almost got WO Krutul the well-known SSC (Scared S_____less Citation) & Sheet Metal says the FALCONS can knock that off any old time now.

Speaking of Sheet Metal, word is out that old 579 was just too much for them and the old Hoss is heading to Qui Nhon and the glue factory.

A report came in that COWBOY McCollough found and bought a "Burning Ring of Fire" in Bangkok recently! Understand they sell Cancer there too!

Miracle Maintenance want's Sgt. Preston to measure the pitch fit between his ears . . . How bout that! Got the word that Old Wrangler was stranded with CHIEF PACK RAT in Qui Non for three days this week . . . bet that was about as tough as "Strangers in Paradise" . . . understand that Old Wrangler tried to brain himself on the rotor when they finally had to start back . . . ah well into each life some rain must fall!

Who reported Elrod as the winner of 75 points out of a possible 15 for Dud of the Week? Are they trying to tell us something Elrod?

SERGEANT Foltz has been elevated to NCOIC of the Allied shops we understand. Course he's pretty dejected to find that he still has dirty hands . . . we figure that is a dirty shame.

We were asked to give Tech Supply a plug in this issue . . . course we couldn't find a plug but we got a clue that there are two men in the Tech Supply . . . the Hider and the Hunter . . . wonder if they are trying to tell us something.

What Mustang Crew Chief pulled a daily by the book and filled three pages with write-ups?

What FALCON Plt Sgt. blindfolds his driver when they go to Tuy Hoa??

THE OLD SARGE

SCHOOL OF THE SOLDIER CLASSES will commence at 1830 hours 28 Oct. 1968 in the COWBOY BULLSHEET OFFICE. Classes are strictly voluntary & will be conducted each Monday, Wednesday and Friday night that COWBOYS show up for them. COWBOYS who want a crack at the Soldier of the Month Board and the promotion boards might find it to their advantage to be in attendance.

USAFI . . . USAFI . . . UNITED STATES ARMED FORCES INSTITUTE!

ARE YOU OVERLOOKING A BET?

Now more than ever before COWBOYS have an opportunity to cash in on "In-Service" education! If you are planning to return to school when you get out, a refresher course NOW will assist you in reacquiring the study habits you will need to make the grade. Courses taken from USAFI can be used for credit toward your degree.

For COWBOYS who already have a profession or a job to return to, a USAFI course can materially assist you in advancing in your chosen field. To be considered also is another fact of education; to make our lives more enjoyable, fuller, richer, and more meaningful through exploration of our surroundings.

Education is not only the means to a well-paying job and affluence. As a matter of fact, not many years ago most people considered college more a preparation for life, than a preparation for a career or job.

Education can be the key to unlock the doors of art, literature, music, and the fascinating world around us . . . genetics, law, biology, anthropology. We live in a wonderful era in which the great mysteries are being unfolded. Without education we miss so much!

Your interest is mechanics? Courses are available. Agriculture? Come see me. Aerodynamics? I'll fix you up. Specialist Five? We'll give it a good try!

HAVE YOU A MILITARY QUESTION YOU NEED AN ANSWER FOR?

Possibly the answer lies in the Field Manual & Technical Manuals in the OLD SARGES Library. It's in the BULLSHEET Office!

THE OLD SARGE

C◆WB◆Y

BULLSHEET

VOLUME 2	3 NOVEMBER 1968	NUMBER 29

CHIEF WARRANT OFFICER QUIBERG
PREPARES TO DEPART
WELLS FARGO OFFICE NEARS COMPLETION

CHIEF WARRANT OFFICER LEON R. QUIBERG, senior COWBOY in the company will be hanging up his spurs and riding over the clouds to COWBOY HEAVEN before another issue of the BULLSHEET is off the press. Arriving in the Company in March 1967, just five months after the unit was activated, FALCON 81 is one of the few remaining COWBOYS who can boast of the battles of Bien Hoa and remember the days before the wandering in the wilderness. One of the most revered officers in the company, CWO QUIBERG was presented a plaque from the FALCON Enlisted Men in the COWBOY PALACE Sunday afternoon. All COWBOYS JOIN THE BULLSHEET IN WISHING CHIEF QUIBERG THE BEST OF LUCK IN HIS NEW ASSIGNMENT.

WELLS FARGO OFFICE NEARS COMPLETION . . . First Shirt is waxing pretty frisky as the finishing touches are being applied to the new COWBOY MAIL ROOM. Under the skilled supervision of SFC. Thompson a major improvement to the COWBOY CORRAL is about to become a reality . . . GOOD WORK Commish.

COWBOY T. J. Smith will represent the COWBOYS at Lightning for the CREW CHIEF of the Month competition. SP4 Norwood goes for SOLDIER of the Month. CONGRATS COWBOYS!

Plans for the UNIT DAY Party, to be held on the 10th of November are firming up. Permanent plaques for Tug-o-War, Volley Ball, Horse Shoe, and Ping-Pong are being prepared. PLATOONS are urged to GET THEIR TEAMS READY!! Each Platoon is also expected to come up with an entertainment feature for the Company. This can be an instrumental group, singing or a skit . . . but EACH PLT WILL HAVE SOMETHING.

FROM THE HORSES' MOUTH

This week saw the COWBOYS compete another successful month of operations. While the weather reduced our flying hours, we still managed to fly 2265 hours. This is considerable more time than any other company within our Battalion.

It is the fruit of you hard labor that makes these figures outstanding. The high time slick for the month was 653 with 127 hours, SP5 Dennis Smith, Crew Chief. The high time Gun was 664 with 93 hour's SP5 Chambers, Crew Chief.

Chaplain Doggett tells me he found a COWBOY up at the chapel the other night borrowing nails. He would not tell me his name, however. I would say we have one lucky trooper.

Accidents continue to be a problem. It's not the big things but the little ones. Personal injury accidents account for many wasted man hours and much suffering on the part of the parties involved. Play it safely and don't take a chance. Mr. Greenwell will tell you it is hell having to stay in the hospital. Let's keep the COWBOYS record on accidents low so each of us can enjoy the years to come. Keep them flying safely, COWBOYS!

COWBOY 6

SAFETY SPOOK

Reinforcement and repair of Crew Chief Stands in Maintenance are the sort of positive Safety Awareness that will prevent accidents BEFORE they happen. Most anybody can figure out what to do AFTER an accident has already occurred, we need to be the kind of people who can see what can cause the accident before it happens. Look over YOUR area and try to come up with AT LEAST one POSITIVE SAFETY IMPROVEMENT TODAY!

Safety Spook

INSIDIOUS INFORMER

BULLSHEET FROM 'ROUND THE RANGE

"A Blond in hand is worth $20 in the bush" or at least says the Old Sarge when the 1st Sgt. offered $20 to the chubby little SFC. at the TUSAC NCO Club the other night . . . Insidious Informer said it was the first time in memory that anyone can recall Kinzinger doing deep breathing exercises. When the lovely lassie hinted at a crack at the slot machines Old Kinzinger was in a real hurt . . . you can't play the one-armed bandit with your hands in your pockets!

Word is out that COWBOY 6 can be VERY SIX at 0230 in the morning.

What COWBOY OPERATIONS OFFICER got a real hint that all was not well with the gal of his dreams called for the Duty Driver to come and pick him up??

What FALCON AC took off from a Vietnamese out post without his Gunner and couldn't figure out why he couldn't get an "ALL Clear to the Right" . . . What FALCON Crew Chief laid in a supply of Silvertex for his forthcoming trip to Siam . . . Not buying any cancer this trip FALCON?? FANATIC FALCON T. J. Smith, the COWBOY OF THE MONTH this month really got POd when Fonteno stopped a fight between a Vietnamese man & wife the other day . . . Smitty hasn't liked the Vietnamese much at all since one threw a rock through the window of his Bird last week.

Words out that Personality Petes circle approaches have the Mustangs in a tizzy they are so dizzy . . . but maybe when you are dizzy to begin with . . .!

Insidious Informer wonders if a senior CWO in Maintenance will be a little more careful about whom he sends for a vehicle late at night!

FLASH Lateral in 354 was finally determined to be an unbalanced eight-day clock . . . source of this info is hush hush but his initials are POPA.

Got word that a magazine in Kirkbride's desk has been making things hard for him . . . tisk.

Got word also that Chief Quiberg is going to give classes on how to sleep comfortably across the front seat of a jeep . . . Take one quart of Old Crow . . .!

Insidious Informer says COWBOY Sheehan dropped his load at about 15000 the other day.

XO is really after WO Harrell to get some BALLS . . . can't have a Ping-Pong tournament without them!

FALCON Chambers was reportedly mixing with the Brass during his recent trip to Guam . . . A COLONEL's Daughter no less!

Have you heard about the Crew Chief who asked the TI to come over to the shack to check his short shaft because he was afraid if he tried to carry it to the TI he might drop it??

What Crew Chief made the mistake of telling the Old Man that he was pulling an Intermediate by memory!

What FALCON PLATOON SGT. was found to be sleeping at attention by COWBOY SIX at 1400 hours Wednesday. AHHH for the HARD LIFE of a Flight Platoon SGT.!

COWBOY FEEDBAG says all these FNGs should have no trouble finding the place with the new sign they just put up . . . considering all, maybe we ought to draw a couple of pictures too.

Three-time loser JALBERT couldn't get the right kind of lights in three trips to the Air Base the other day . . . good-looking Donut Dollies over there or did you stop in the village Jalbert?

THE OLD SARGE

This weeks "The Old Sarge Says" column features a guest writer. Chaplain Doggett, or Lightning Top Sacred, has been kind enough to pen the following:

I had an opportunity to visit the COWBOY CORRAL this past week and had a good chat with The Old Sarge. He whipped a request on me to write a little something for the COWBOY BULLSHEET, and so I said I would try. I would like to commend the BULLSHEET Editor for putting out one of the most interesting and readable papers I have come across in a long time. It is really "Up Tight."

I came across this little statement and thought I would pass it along to you this week in the BULLSHEET. "THE REASON THE 10 COMMANDMENTS ARE SO CLEARLY WRITTEN AND SO EASILY UNDERSTOOD IS THAT THEY WERE HANDED DOWN DIRECTLY AND DID NOT REQUIRE THE CONCURRENCE OF MANY STAFF SECTIONS."

The "NEW" chapel is coming along nicely. What is that the NCO's call it? I want to say a big "THANKS" to the COWBOY Sheet Metal Shop for making our chapel lights. They really look great! Also, a big THANKS to all the COWBOYS who have worked on the chapel since we began way back in July!

Thanks again for letting me have this little bit in the BULLSHEET. Hope to see you in chapel Sunday!

"CHAPPY"

Thank you LIGHTNING TOP SACRED, err Chaplain Doggett that is . . . Interested COWBOYS should take note that the Chapel is nearing completion. Assistance is still required on some indoor projects and COWBOYS who would like to help would be most welcome. Work continues each evening . . . take a walk over and lend a hand!

THE OLD SARGE

C◆WB◆Y
BULLSHEET

VOLUME 2   23 NOVEMBER 1968   NUMBER 31

A FAREWELL TO THE COWBOYS

Well, today I write my last lines for the BullSheet. It doesn't seem that it has been five months since I first wrote. The time really flies.

I would like to say, that it has been a very rewarding experience. I will not mislead you into thinking that all my decisions were easy or popular, but those are the breaks of the game. I have watched each of you over the past months, doing the job that had to be done. You operated like true COWBOYS upholding our end of the mission. I am very proud to have had the opportunity to be your commander.

I regret that I cannot accompany you in future operations, however, I have binding commitments elsewhere, just as have each of you.

I am scheduled to assume command of the 29th Transportation Company (DS) in Germany. If you are in the area or need an assignment please stop in.

I know that as COWBOYS you will be tops regardless of the mission

Goodbye COWBOYS and keep them flying safely!

> CARL L. CRAMER
> Major, T. C.
> COWBOY 6

INSIDIOUS INFORMER

BULLSHEET FROM 'ROUND THE RANGE

It might have been expected, in spite of 01' Mame and right in front of the Group Commander and all the dignitaries assembled for the COWBOY change of Command, the call came out "Scramble the FALCONS" . . . and out of the formation they went! In a way, far more than any of the speakers could say the FALCON SCRAMBLE demonstrated what it is to be a COWBOY. THIRTEEN MINUTES from the time that the call came into Flight Operations COWBOYS were in the sky!

Insidious Informer in the Miracle Maintenance Department tells us about a VERY INTERESTING flight the other day . . . SFC. Grundy was so shaken he closed the aircraft door on his hand and hasn't been able to talk about much else since. Popa almost brained himself getting out of the ship, (and for Popa to brain himself would be pretty much of a feat in itself), and WO Webb, the Hawaiian Hero was caught holding up half the Air Force!!! ENEMY ACTION? ENGINE FAILURE? NO! DONUT DOLLIES! Yep! Old Grundy, Webb and Popa had a labor of LOVE carrying two sweet young things on a small hop to the Air Force Base. Great care was evidenced in keeping the trip a dark SECRET from Lt. Grabowski . . . sorta looks like the trio was afraid he might beat their time. Insidious Informer says that in flight a chicken plate fell to the floor of the aircraft and Grundy almost collapsed. Upon landing at the AFB Monty took his helmet off in order to say sweet nothings to the Babes and when he recovered his equilibrium four F100's were backed up behind him on the ramp and the Control Tower Operator discovered a whole new vocabulary of profanity he never realized he knew. All told the mission was really a flight to remember.

We got word that Chicken Little has been taking Lt. Blake with him lately on flights. Logging Pilot time seems to indicate that maybe Big Chief Indian has been keeping Chicken Little right side up. We figured something happened because he doesn't look half as dizzy as he used to.

One Who Thinks He Knows is about to finger Lt. Johnson for the dastardly deed of hoisting all the wire out of COWBOY 1's room. The disappearance of Lt. Allue's wire coincides too neatly with the installation of that new wall plug in Lt. Johnsons' pad.

Got the word that WO Zawiski is banned from watching COMBAT any more until he gets over having nightmares from all the action.

With all the nasty old men in maintenance we find the story about Hague rather difficult to believe. Ranney made a whole barracks happy with the packing and sending of his speakers home!

A FAREWELL TO MAJOR CRAMER

Dear Major Cramer,

Over the period of the past five months, COWBOYS have not been called upon to engage in spectacular operations, make major moves, or impress the world with our exterior abilities and virtues. Possibly some might feel that it has been an uneventful period in COWBOY History.

For the COWBOYS who write that history as well as the COWBOYS who have been here working through the period, a somewhat different perspective will prevail.

Behind each successful operation, contributing to the ability to make major moves, and supporting the surface accomplishments of any Army Unit; a solid base of training, discipline, experience, and esprit, must exist. Mission accomplishment must become habitual, and individual effort must become commonplace.

Over the period of the past five months, each element of the COWBOYS has reformed from the inside out. Motor Pool and Mess Hall, Supply and Avionics, Operations and the Orderly Room, have all made significant strides that insure accomplishment of their parts of the company's tasks and missions. In the COWBOY Maintenance Establishment, a new era has arrived! Never has our Maintenance accomplished so much, so willingly, so well!

Anything the COWBOYS are tasked for will be done only as a result of this internal reworking of the unit effort and pride. This can hardly be considered "insignificant" in the history of any organization.

Each step of the way, your support, guidance, and effort, has guided this development of the COWBOYS. You have truly "Talked straight, shot straight, and never broke your word to man nor boss!"

Major Cramer, you have been a straight-shooting commander and the COWBOYS are proud to salute you!

FAREWELL!

THE COWBOYS

Dominic Fino

C◆WB◆Y
BULLSHEET

VOLUME 2   8 DECEMBER 1968   NUMBER 33

MAJOR RILEY NEW COWBOY COMMANDER

COWBOYS MOVE SOUTH AGAIN

COWBOYS TEACH DEMONS TO FLY

NOW IT CAN BE TOLD: COWBOYS moved south once again in a lightning move which was completed in less than 96 hours and employed Air Force asst. all the way from Japan and the Philippines to move oversized equipment of the COWBOYS. Previously not reported for security reasons, COWBOYS exhibited truly magnificent effort and heart in preparing for and executing the rapid move of the unit.

COWBOY PILOTS are reputedly a bit apprehensive about the impeding visit of LIGHTNING SIX to the new COWBOY CORRAL . . .to say COWBOY exuberance on departing the Phu Hiep area got slightly carried away is an understatement.

HEY! Those ships have the COWBOY Diamond! Was the reaction of Third generation COWBOYS as they returned to 12th Combat Avn Group ranges this week!

A WELL DONE to the COWBOY CHUCK WAGON and staff who have really come through in establishing a fine mess in short order in the new area. Well done to the Advance Party who accomplished minor miracles in making the new area habitable (In spite of the obvious attractions of the local Steam Bath Bien Hoa, etc., etc.) and Well Done to the entire COWBOY COMPANY for the hard work they accomplished.

MAJOR PAUL R. RILEY, JR. assumed command of the COWBOYS in ceremonies conducted on the COWBOY Maint. Ramp at Phu Hiep Army Airfield just prior to COWBOY departure for the south on 23 November 68. COWBOY 6 makes his debut in the BULLSHEETS' "FROM THE HORSES MOUTH" Column.

SUSPICIONS CONFIRMED DEPARTMENT:

As COWBOYS prepared to move out in the closing days of Nov. they were given the final task of training Demon Pilots in the art of providing COWBOY support to the many units previously supported by the COWBOYS! In the relatively short training period that time permitted a significant improvement could be detected in Demon technique. WO Story is reputed to have given added instruction above and beyond the call!

FROM THE HORSES' MOUTH

On this, my first effort at producing a column for the BULLSHEET, I would like to express my distinct pleasure in receiving the title "COWBOY SIX." My predecessor Major Carl Cramer has done an outstanding job and leaves me a mighty big pair of shoes to fill.

In the coming months COWBOYS will be facing another challenge. The mission is an important one and I am sure that COWBOY pride and sense of mission accomplishment will insure a continued outstanding record for the unit.

I only ask that each man do his job to the best of his ability, keeping safety in mind. With teamwork and professionalism, we will be able to keep the name "COWBOY" at the top of the list where it belongs!

COWBOY 6

SAFETY SPOOK

A hauntingly familiar thought occurred to me today as I was on my way to the COWBOYS for this edition of the BULLSHEET! SEAT BELTS! Been a while since we rattled that chain! Seat belts and restraining devices are installed to protect YOU! In this country, being thrown from the ship in a crash can put you under the aircraft in several feet of water, or unconscious face down in a rice paddy. . . in either event you wind up very dead . . . permanently.

Speaking of winding up dead. . . riding down Highway One to Long Bien and Bein Hoa can be a lasting experience . . .your very lasting one. The other day I saw two accidents within three miles of each other. If you are a driver, or think you are a driver, remember to drive defensively and watch out for the other guy. Vehicles are altogether too difficult to come by, to have one wrecked by negligent driving . . .and by the way. . . the outer lane on the four lane highways are for bicycles and lambrettas . . . I know they are not marked that way . . .but I believe the big burley MP who stopped me & told me so . . . You believe him too!

Last but certainly not least, we want to remember our Malaria Pills. The change of climate and many mosquitoes in this part of the country make it imperative for extra precautions against Malaria . . .don't let them reduce your effectiveness. HAPPY HAUNTING COWBOYS ** THE SPOOK

INSIDIOUS INFORMER

BULLSHEET FROM 'ROUND THE RANGE

Speakin of the new area. . . from the satisfied look all over Hookers face and the STEADY stream of COWBOY Pilots a headin for the local Steam Bath (and the equally Unsteady COWBOYS departing form it) Insidious Informer deduces that underaged Warrant Officers should be permitted to visit the establishment only in the company of their Platoon Sergeants.

ONE WHO KNOWS tells us that CB6 is being very careful bout asking where the materials for all the current construction is coming from, and has already identified the culprits who got the Artillery on the warpath. As a matter of fact, 1st Sgt. Bourland had a couple three cigarettes all lit up & a smoking right after an Arty representative told him he would have to move the Old Man out of the hooch he was living in . . .we wouldn't want to come right out and say he was shook . . .But!

Lightning Six seemed satisfied with all he saw on his visit . . .and he thought the COWBOY overflight was very impressive . . he didn't approve of the "smoke" on La Bah, however!

We wouldn't want anyone to get the impression that BEAR CAT is hot but Insidious Informer tells us that SP5 Matos got rid of 3 cases of soda the first day he was here.

Speaking of drinking, quite a few COWBOYS came all the way down in a daze what with all the farewell shin digs at Phu Heip for departing COWBOYS.

The NCOs had their "thing" and were in really great shape for the long wait on the ramp at Tuy Hoa, and the 180th Officers really threw a Whig ding for COWBOY Pilots and Officers. More than one COWBOY woke up at BEAR CAT trying to remember how he got there.

SFC K was sure that the Company was down with the GIs out on the ramp at Tuy Hoa then at 1630 hrs it stopped short, and after the second day the rotund NCO figured out that the GI's, the Rest Room in the Passenger Terminal, and the Snack Bar just outside were all sorta connected.

Latest rumor from the Home Range is that the Battalion Comdr. dropped in on the Rear Detachment at bout 1000 hrs the other day and caught them all in the sack . . .same rumor has it that they are all assigned to 268th now!

CRIME DOES NOT PAY! Insidious Informer tells us that when you see WOs Bliss & Baetzel looking their most youthfully innocent it's time to get a good grip on your trousers. . .Under that outward display of wide eyed innocence lurks the nature and propensities of thieving packrats!

First Shirt & Chuck Wagon Chief found out that it just don't pay to try to out drink these Aussies last night . . .and the biggest gas in the Company is to hear old Rebel Warlick try to put on an English Accent to tell you how the Aussies called him "Old Chap"!

Insidious Informer relates that WO Speanburg has been host to a bunch of visitors (Gobble Gobble) . . .Warrants are all hoping he left them all in Phu Heip.

We have all heard bout the guy that was so tough he ran the Devil out of Hell . . .Well the word is out that WO Story managed to knock a few Demons out of Phu Heip!

And so went another week in the COWBOYS!

THE OLD SARGE

THE JOB: What is the JOB! "Well he isn't the best Soldier in the world but he does a good job" . . . "He isn't a Soldier but he works as hard as any man on the job"

How often have we heard or said something very similar to these statements? They are becoming increasingly familiar clichés in the vocabulary of the military.

How often have we really considered what the job REALLY is . . .? What we are paid to accomplish, what is expected of us. As a matter of fact, our job is to be the very best Soldier that we can possibly be! That is the Job! It goes without saying that a GOOD SOLDIER must also know his MOS. MOS=Military Occupational Specialty and nothing more. It is presumed that the individual already possesses the basic qualities of SOLDIER! If a man accomplishes the duties of his MOS in an outstanding manner he cannot be credited with having done a GOOD JOB unless his performance as a SOLDIER is also considered.

Proper uniform, proper haircut, military bearing, military courtesy, discipline, shined shoes, good attitude; are all parts of the total job of being a Helicopter Mechanic, Company Clerk, Crew Chief, or POL Specialist, just as truly as pulling a PE, typing a Morning Report, packing a short shaft, or establishing a field refueling station.

Because of the importance of the MOS functions of each COWBOY to the successful accomplishment of the unit missions, the equally important military aspects of individual performance are frequently overlooked.

"EQUALLY IMPORTANT" in that the military aspects of individual performance indicate the status of discipline, training, and professionalism in the unit. Not too long ago a Commander could gauge the degree of discipline in his unit by observing the quality of the hand salutes that were rendered to him. A proud outfit salutes proudly!

Located so close to the Brigade Headquarters, and under a close scrutiny of a new Battalion & Group Commanders and their staff, COWBOYS have a unique opportunity to demonstrate the inherent superiority of the COWBOYS to all other Assault Helicopter Companies.

Let's remember to do THE ENTIRE JOB while we are here in the south!

THE OLD SARGE

COWBOYS

UNIT HISTORY

1 JANUARY 1969 -- 31 DECEMBER 1969

History of

335th Assault Helicopter Company
214th Combat Aviation Battalion
1ST AVIATION BRIGADE

Prepared by
WO1 JOHN T. JONES
UNIT HISTORICAL OFFICER

Approved by
VANCE S. GAMMONS
MAJ. INFANTRY
Commanding

BEAR CAT, REPUBLIC OF VIETNAM
APO 96530

CHAPTER 1 HERALDRY

The unit of the 335th Aviation Company (Assault Helicopter) shows the "COWBOY'S" extremely aggressive attitude towards getting the job done. The crest also indicates the efficiency and reliability of the "COWBOY'S" operations against the enemy.

This unit is one of the few select units to fully support the 7th Infantry Division (ARVN). The "Mustangs" and "Ramrods" provide the lift capability while the "Falcons" provide aerial fire support for this daily mission in the Delta. Basically assigned a particular area within the Delta, the COWBOYS have participated in combat throughout the Delta area. Logging an average of 2700 hours monthly the COWBOYS fought the enemy while suffering very little combat damage. The 335th Aviation Company is known for its combat ability to get the job done regardless the obstacles. Employing only the finest of men and machines the COWBOYS have been victorious both day and night against the hostile forces within Southern Vietnam.

VANCE S. GAMMONS
MAJ, IN.
Commanding

CHAPTER 2

From the South Eastern shores of the United States to the South Eastern shores of Vietnam the 335th Aviation Company can easily lay claim as the most experienced Aviation Company in Vietnam. Initially the 335th Assault Helicopter Company was stationed at Ft. Bragg North Carolina and was Company "A" 82nd Avn Bn. As the Vietnam conflict progressed the need for helicopter aviation was apparent and the 335th was selected for deployment to Vietnam. Early in 1965 the 335th was made ready for the big move and by April were settled at Bein Hoa, Vietnam. The 335th remained at Bien Hoa until May of 1967 when another move was dictated because the unit being supported, the 173rd Airborne Brigade, was relocated to Kontum, Vietnam. Two more moves were in store for the COWBOYS. One in August of 1967 that made Phu Hiep their new home and area of operation in support of the 173rd Airborne Brigade. Again, in December of 1968 the 335th relocated to a new area of Vietnam, to work under the operational control of 164th Combat Aviation Group.

CHAPTER 3

1969 saw the COWBOYS commanded by three of the best commanders in its history:

MAJ. RILEY, PAUL R. JR.	AT	053-xx-xxxx	23 NOV. 68 -- 25 MAY 69
MAJ. STILES, HOWARD J.	IN	081-xx-xxxx	25 MAY 69 -- 08 NOV. 69
MAJ. GAMMONS, VANCE S.	IN	411-xx-xxxx	08 NOV. 69 -- PRESENT

CHAPTER 4

January had the COWBOYS, under operational control of 164th CAG, back in the III Corps area at its new location, Bear Cat, just South of the unit's first home, Ben Hoa.

During the early months of 1969 the unit was in continuous direct support of the 9th ARVN Division in the provinces of Vinh Long-Ken Hoa, providing needed ships for Combat Assaults, troop movement and many types of resupply and administrative work. The unit also helped support the 9th U.S. Division until 31 May when the operation was completed successfully.

The COWBOYS first change of command, in 1969 came on 25 May when Major Howard J. Stiles took command from Major Paul R. Riley, Jr.

The middle months of 1969 saw the COWBOYS major support gradually change from the 9th ARVN Division to the 7th ARVN Division. The unit, by early August, was providing the 7th ARVN Division with the same support given the 9th ARVN Division and the operational area shifted slightly North and East into Dinh Toung-Kien Hoa and Go Cong provinces.

On July 1st, the 335th Aviation Company was officially released from the 17th Combat Aviation Group and reassigned to the 214th Combat Aviation Battalion, 164th CAG. This reassignment did not affect the COWBOYS mission, giving aviation support to the 7th and 9th ARVN Divisions.

The final months of 1969 also saw Major Howard J. Stiles, on 8 Nov., turn our command of the COWBOYS to Major Vance S. Gammons.

In early December the COWBOYS made their annual move. No one complained too loudly as this move was just across the street to the much better quarters left by the 6/15 Artillery Battalion Headquarters. During this time the 335th Avn Co. continued its normal support activities in the Delta.

The year's most memorable occasion came in late September when Major General Allen M. Burdett, Jr., Commanding Officer of the 1st Aviation Brigade, came to Bear Cat and presented the Presidential Unit Citation, for heroism during Operation "McArthur" in Kontum Province between 6 Nov. 1967 through 27 Nov. 1967, to the COWBOYS who received it with the greatest of pride.

CHAPTER 5

Equipment and Installations

I. A. 6 -- UH-1B Gunships

        1. 4 heavies: 38 rockets

        2. 2 lights: 14 rockets -- 2 mini guns

    B. 22 -- UH-1H "Slicks" -- Utility helicopters

        1. 1 -- Command and Control ship

        2. 1 -- Night Hawk ship -- xeon light -- mini gun

        3. 19 -- Troop Carrying ships

        4. 1 -- Maintenance ship

II.

First Platoon	Ramrods
Second Platoon	Mustangs
Third Platoon	Falcons

AWARDS RECEIVED DURING THE YEAR

SILVER STAR	KRUG, ROBERT	SP4
	LUKE, ROBERT	SP4
DISTINGUISHED FLYING CROSS	STEIN, JAMES	CPT.
	GOULD, THOMAS	CPT.
	RYAN, JON	CW2
	KNEIP, NEIL	WO1
	DUPUIS, DENNIS	WO1
	NICHOLAOU, MICHAEL	WO1
	BLAIR, ROBERT	WO1
	FERNANDEZ, VINCE	CPT.
	STILES, HOWARD	MAJ.
BRONZE STAR	STEIN, JAMES	CPT.
	DAMERS, ANDRE	CPT.
	BROWN, DANIEL	CPT.
	KNEIP, NEIL	WO1
	KINNAN, MORRIS	WO1
	BLAIR, ROBERT	WO1
	WOOD, WILLIAM	WO1
	BISSON, DONALD	CW2
	WILLIAMS, AUSTIN	CW2
	FENDEL, JACK	CPT.
	EADS, LARRY	CPT.
	GOULD, THOMAS	CPT.
	NICHOLAOU, MICHAEL	WO1
	WILLIAMS, JAMES	WO1
	FREEMAN, WILLIAM	WO1
	SCHRAY, WILLIAM	WO1
	THOMSEN, PAUL	CPT.
	POSEY, RAYMOND	1Lt.

Presidential Unit Citation
GO# 42, HQ, DA, dated -- 16 June 1969
For the Period 6 Nov. -- 23 Nov. 1967

	JAN	FEB	MAR	APR	MAY	JUN	JUL	AUG	SEP	OCT	NOV	DEC	TOTAL
HOURS UH-1H	2004	1613	1874	1971	2037	2011	1922	2291	2262	2509	2129	2216	15,694
UH-1B	596	563	727	569	538	616	474	543	465	595	544	471	6,601
TOTAL	2600	2176	2601	6980	2575	2627	2396	2834	2718	3107	2673	2687	27,537

	JAN	FEB	MAR	APR	MAY	JUN	JUL	AUG	SEP	OCT	NOV	DEC	TOTAL
CARGO (TONS)	23	29	127	32	9	7	10	81	138	135	176	90	757
PASSENGERS	19,115	18,810	19,438	16,981	18,832	17,390	19,466	28,254	27,016	28,500	23,513	23,324	130,023
SORTIES UH-1H	6444	6160	6294	5832	6010	5829	6403	8450	9470	9341	8469	6709	85,411
UH-1B	1108	1255	1627	1148	995	1186	1210	1696	1412	1515	1703	1556	16,411
TOTAL	7552	7415	7821	6980	7005	7015	7615	10146	10882	10856	10172	8265	61,549
RESULTS KBA	47	20	78	160	88	89	81	15	34	58	24	7	701
STRUC DEST	93	19	222	200	258	233	149	124	134				1,432
STRUC DAM	0	23	3	18	87	19	5	76	35				266
SAMPAN DEST	7	5	5	38	64	51	28	6	25				229
SAMPAN DAM	0	5	18	0	10	3	0	6	24				66

The following article was published in **_HAWK_** magazine in September 1969, the author is not listed. The article describes a typical day in the 335th.

335th Assault Helicopter Company. . . RIDES HERD ON CHARLIE

The shrill whine of the jet-powered turbine grew from a muted murmur to a high-pitched scream and slowly dissolved to the familiar steady clatter of the rotor blades as the UH-1B shivered awake in the predawn darkness.

The sound of the lone Huey readying itself for flight was joined by the sound of another further down the line. Soon the entire flight line came alive with the noise as the rest of the crews finished logging in at operations and began making preparation for lift off.

As helicopter crews from other companies were still fighting their way out of sleep, the men of the 335th Assault Helicopter Company, COWBOYS," were moving their machines out of the revetments for the standard 0600 take off.

High in the air over the airfield it was cool, even cold, as the ten slicks formed up in two five-ship formations, the same formations in which they would operate all day. Far below the twinkling lights of Bear Cat faded behind as the ships turned south. Off to the right the huge military base at Long Binh was briefly visible and soon the brightly lit skyline of Saigon slid by.

Slowly the darkness gave way as the sun rose on the left and slightly behind the choppers as they continued the flight. Later, after almost two hours of flight time, they touched down at Vinh Long, deep in the Delta, for fuel. Then after liftoff they flew southwest, settling forty-five minutes later at a small airstrip at Chi Lang as the base of Mt. Nui Coto. There the helicopters shut down awaiting word from the C&C ship to begin the first lift of 9th ARVN Division troops which the 335th supports on a daily basis.

The word came, and the choppers began cranking. Moments later the first five slicks, Alpha Team, went down in the Pickup Zone (PZ), gathered in a load of ARVN's, lifted out and headed for the Landing Zone (LZ) as Bravo Team followed.

Meanwhile the C&C ship, piloted by CPT Vincent Fernandes II, 335th Executive Officer, was over the LZ with two of the B-model Hueys. The other two gunships were at Chi Lang on standby.

The 335th, unlike many other helicopter companies, fly their Command and Control ship close in rather than orbiting it high above the action. They call it a "LOHing Charlie-Charlie."

"It gives us a better feel for what is actually happening on the ground," explained CPT Fernandes. "We can scout the area before the slicks get here, indicate targets for the gunships and give directions for suppressive fire to the lift ship door gunner. It also gives the ARVN commander and his American advisor a chance to see exactly how the troops are doing down there."

"Alpha Team leader, this is Charlie-Charlie."

"Roger, Charlie-Charlie, this is Alpha Team leader."

"This is Charlie-Charlie, we're dropping smoke."

High above the LZ, pilots could see the red smoke billowing up around a small clearing

"This is Charlie-Charlie. The smoke is good. Full suppression on the left into the tree line. There should be friendlies on the right. Execute left turn on lift off."

"Roger Charlie-Charlie. We see the smoke. Full suppression on the left."

"Bravo Team leader, this is Charlie-Charlie. Do you see the smoke?"

"This is Bravo Team leader, Charlie-Charlie. We see the smoke. Execute left turn on lift off."

"Roger that."

Alpha Team dropped down, swiftly, with a stomach clenching suddenness, as the door gunners on the left cut loose. The ships touched down, the troops scrambled out and Alpha team pulled pitch, banked left and directed more fire into the tree line. Bravo Team followed swiftly.

When both inserting elements were safely out of the LZ, the C&C ship, along with the two primary gunships, left to recon the next LZ. Skimming along at treetop level over an area that included the LZ, CPT Fernandes scouted a wide area so that any enemy below would not be tipped to the drop point. High overhead the guns circled like vultures waiting for the word. The word came.

"Falcon One-Five, this is Charlie-Charlie. We have just dropped smoke."

"Roger that, Charlie-Charlie, we see the smoke. What about those wooden structures to the left?"

"Bust 'em."

The two big B-model Huey's went down, flaking off like fixed-wing fighters, leveling off at lower than treetop level, miniguns roaring, rockets and M-60 rounds striking all around the area of the smoke. As the first ship passed over the area the door gunners lobbed out hand grenades and more smoke. Moments later the second gun came by inundating the area with deadly firepower. Back up they went, orbiting, hungrily waiting for the word on a second run.

Off in the distance the troop-laden slicks could be seen bringing the second load of ARVN's to the LZ. Smoke was popped, and the slicks came in again.

And again. And again. All morning long. Stopping only long enough to refuel and form up again. Finally, in the early afternoon a break came and the crew broke open C-rations, rearmed, checked the ships or tried to catch some sleep in the dusty, hot afternoon.

The C&C ship, meanwhile, was "LOHing around" over the next set of LZ's. After refueling they sent back word and the slicks and gunships cranked, pulled pitch and were off again.

Deep into the afternoon the action continued until all operational assignments for the day were completed. Then the long trip home in the deepening dusk of the Vietnamese evening.

But the day was not over yet. Late into the night the crew chiefs and door gunners worked along with maintenance crews getting the ships in shape for the next day.

This is the way the war is for the men of the 335th Assault Helicopter Company. This is the way it has always been.

The 335th, commanded by MAJ Howard J. Stiles, originally came to Vietnam in April 1965 as Company A, 82nd Aviation Battalion (AML), organic to the 82nd Airborne Division. Their designation was changed on September 1, 1966, to the 335th Aviation Company (Ambl Lt) when the unit became a part of the 173rd Airborne Brigade.

January 1, 1967 was the date the 335th was redesignated the 335th Assault Helicopter Company and added to the growing number of 1st Aviation Brigade units.

The 335th has had a long history of geographic moves throughout the history of their Vietnam tour. They have been based at Bien Hoa, Tay Ninh, Pleiku, Dak To, An Khe, Vung Tau and now Bear Cat to name a few. Their present location marks the first time that all three platoons of the unit, the "Ramrods," "Mustangs" and "Falcons," have been stationed together in the same place at the same time.

The 335th is a part of the 164th Aviation Group (CBT), but is based in III rather than IV Crops. This makes for the early wakeup call--3:30 a.m.--and the long flying time to the AO--1 1/2 to 2 1/2 hours. This makes it more difficult on the crews and makes for more maintenance on the ships, but the men of the 335th do not seem to mind it.

"The Cowboy Spirit," says MAJ Stiles, "binds these men together. I've seen crews working well past midnight, so their ship can fly in the next day's mission. It's a point of pride with them. Often a crew will work all night and fly all the next day. But I hear no complaints."

The 335th has recently been awarded the Presidential Unit Citation for extraordinary heroism in connection with military operations against an armed enemy during Operation MacArthur in Kontum Province from November 6 to November 23, 1967. Also known as the Battle of Dak To, Operation MacArthur reduced the 174th North Vietnamese Infantry Regiment to combat ineffectiveness and drove back and scattered the 24th, 32nd, and 66th North Vietnamese Regiments with their supporting artillery.

The enemy in IV Corps can well imagine how Indians of the Old West must have felt as these modern COWBOYS come swooping down out of the sky to lay waste to Charlies plans in the Delta.

This is an actual News Release. The Originating Office was the Information Office, 214th Combat Aviation Battalion. The Releasing Office was the Information Office, 1st Aviation Brigade, Long Binh.

Release No. 7-69-015

Title: 335th "COWBOYS" RIDE OVER ENEMY, KILL 7 VC.

Bear Cat, Vietnam, July 21-- COWBOYS of the 335th Assault Helicopter Company, 214th Combat Aviation Battalion yesterday rode roughshod over the Viet Cong (VC), killing seven Reds in the Mekong Delta while airlifting Army of the Republic of Vietnam (ARVN) troops and aiding Navy patrol boats.

Several 335th Huey helicopters were making an approach to insert 9th Division ARVN soldiers outside Tray On when the VC opened up with 30 caliber fire from a nearby wood line.

"I could see the tracers coming from both sides," said Warrant Officer Tom Story, Risco, Mo., commander of one of the choppers. "My crew opened fire with machine guns and I began punching off rockets."

The return fire killed one VC and drove the other Communists off. An hour later, a Navy patrol boat called for chopper aid after spotting a platoon of VC in an open field just outside of Vinh Long. Story and Warrant Officer Ronald Wallace, Neosho, Mo., raced over and as Story dipped in on a pass at the rice-paddy site, three VC opened up with automatic weapons from camouflaged bunkers.

Story circled back and fired three rockets into the bunkers. Two scored direct hits, killing three Communist troops.

"Everything broke loose then. There were VC running everywhere," said Specialist Four Clyde R. Justice, Hillsboro, Ore., a gunner on Story's copter.

"One of the soldiers had web gear and an AK-47 rifle. He was running north to a wood line when all of a sudden, he stopped, turned around and opened fire on the aircraft."

Justice dispensed of the Red regular with a burst of M-60 machine gun fire. A later sweep of the blood-stained rice-paddy revealed six VC bodies.

This article is from the Stars and Stripes

Falcons fly support for ARVN, kill 33

VINH LONG -- Falcon gunships of the 335th Assault Helicopter Co. accounted for 33 NVA in one day's action as they provided suppressive fire in support of the 7th ARVN Division in Kien Hoa Province.

During the morning, slicks (troop-carrying helicopters) of the 335th's COWBOYS of the 214th Combat Avn. Bn. were making troop insertions in Kien Hoa Province four miles southeast of Ben Tre (50 miles south-southeast of Saigon), when the heliborne assault force received intense enemy fire from nipa palm groves along a canal close to the intended landing zone.

On the initial insertion, the Falcon gunships were credited with three enemy killed. As they continued operations in the area, they were advised by the ARVN assault force that the three enemy soldiers were NVA dressed in blue uniforms and had been armed with automatic weapons.

Throughout the day, the COWBOYS lifted additional elements of the 7th ARVN Division into the area. Later in the afternoon, enemy contact was again heavy-and very close to the LZ.

That time the gunships killed eight more enemy troops and destroyed 30 hooches, while the ARVN assault force captured some enemy documents as well as their weapons. The contact was made at midafternoon and continued throughout the afternoon.

A sweep through the area later in the day revealed that the gunships had accounted for 28 NVA.

1969 335th COWBOY

During the early months of 1969, the unit was in continuous direct support of the 9th ARVN Division in the provinces of Vinh Long - Kien Hoa providing needed ships for combat assaults, troop movement and many types of resupply and administrative work. The unit also helped support the 9th U S Division until 31 MAY 68 when the operation was completed successfully.

25 MAY 69 - Maj. Howard J Stiles took command from Maj. Paul R. Riley Jr.

14 JUN 69 - The COWBOYS commend the actions of WO Rick Dorer, Lt Tom Gould, SP4 Ted Crafton & PFC Edward Martinez and compliment them on a job well done when their aircraft sustained heavy damage and the gunner was lightly wounded, the 2 pilots working together were able to land the aircraft safely in what could have been a dangerous situation.

20 JUN 69 - The COWBOYS commend WO Dave Bowsher and WO Steve Lyons for the outstanding job done when they went back into an extremely hostile area with their 2 aircraft to evacuate wounded ARVN soldiers.

1 JUL 69 - The 335th AHC was officially released from the 17th CAG and reassigned to the 214th CAG. This reassignment did not affect the COWBOYS mission, giving aviation support to the 7th and 9th ARVN Divisions.

21 JUL 69 - TRAY ON COWBOYS kill 7 VC during 9th ARVN insertion, Story, Wallace, Justice.

8 NOV 69 - Maj. Vance S. Gammons took command from Maj. Howard J. Stiles.

This article is from the Stars and Stripes

October 17, 1969

'Cowboys' Get PUC

LONG BINH (Special) -- Maj. Gen. Allen M. Burdett Jr., commanding general of the 1st Aviation Brigade, presented a Presidential Unit Citation to the 335th Helicopter Co. COWBOYS during ceremonies at Bearcat recently. The award was for heroism demonstrated by the 335th during operation MacArthur two years ago in Kontum Province.

History of the 335th A.H.C. – 1969

The Vietnam conflict has ushered in the era of the helicopter. Each day history is made. You, the officers and men of the 335th Aviation Company (Aslt Hel) are part of that history. The COWBOYS have traveled the length and breadth of Vietnam. You the soldiers of today inherit a proud tradition.

The COWBOYS were originally Company A, 82nd Aviation Bn, and were stationed at Fort Bragg, North Carolina. With the increase in troop strength in early 1965, Company A, 82nd Aviation Battalion was selected for deployment to Vietnam. In April 1965, the COWBOYS settled in Bien Hoa and were the direct support of the 173rd Airborne Brigade. The Ramrods, Mustangs, and Falcons became synonymous with truly outstanding airmobile support as the COWBOYS rode herd on "Charlie" throughout the III Corps Tactical Zone. Bien Hoa was home until May 1967 when the 173rd Airborne Brigade moved to the Pleiku, Kontum, Dak To area. In August, the unit again moved. This time to Phu Hiep just south of Tuy Hoa on the south China Seacoast. These were rough days as the COWBOYS lived out of duffel bags and Bien Hoa was still considered home. In November, the 335th Avn Co (Aslt Hel) once again flew to battle in the Dak To area. While supporting the 173rd Airborne Brigade on Operation MacArthur, the COWBOYS were awarded The Presidential Unit Citation. On 31 December 1967, the 335th Avn Co (Aslt Hel) was reassigned to the 17th Combat Aviation Group and to the 268th Combat Aviation Battalion located at Phu Hiep.

The unit's mission was still to support the 173rd Airborne Brigade. The mission finally changed in March of 1968, and the unit was in general support of the II Corps Tactical Zone.

In December, the COWBOYS were once again on the move. This trail lead to Bear Cat. The unit was attached for all purposes to the 214th Combat Aviation Battalion. The COWBOYS began flying missions in support of ARVN Forces in the IV Corps Tactical Zone supporting the 7th and 9th ARVN Divisions.

In July of 1969, the COWBOYS were assigned to the 214th Combat Aviation Battalion, 164th Combat Aviation Group. Today, home is still beautiful downtown Bear Cat.

This book is dedicated to COWBOYS past, present and future.

Dominic Fino

C◆WB◆Y

BULLSHEET

VOLUME 3   23 JANUARY 1969   NUMBER 1

BULLSHEET ENTERS THIRD YEAR

OF PUBLICATION

COWBOYS GET NEW RANCH FORMAN

FIRST SERGEANT THOMPSON

CAPTAIN FERNANDES NEW COWBOY FIVE

With this issue COWBOYS BULLSHEET has entered its third year of publication in the Republic of Vietnam. Referred to lovingly by the COWBOYS as the rag that "HEARS ALL, SEES ALL, TELLS EVERYTHING" the COWBOY BULLSHEET has succeeded in its self-appointed task of chronicling the glories and gaffs of COWBOYS from Dak To, LZ English, and Ahn Khe, to Bam Me Thuot and the Mekong Delta. Policy has continued as originally stated to print the news, good rumors, and well-stated speculations without regard to persons, places, or the fact that you want to send each copy of the BULLSHEET home to mother! As always this, is YOUR BULLSHEET! WE DEPEND UPON YOU FOR THE NEWS TO KEEP IT GOING! Three COWBOY COMMANDERS have not been able to penetrate the secrecy surrounding the ID of the INSIDIOUS INFORMER who has again and again scooped the Company!

Among the many NFG's arriving at the COWBOY CORRAL since the first of the year two new COWBOYS are already on the way to being OLD TIME COWBOYS. First Sergeant Thompson has assumed his duties of RANCH FORMAN and SFC. K would like to hasten to report that he really isn't Chicken S___, he just has "Hen House" ways. CAPT. Fernandes, new COWBOY Executive Officer, has his new duties well in hand and is about to assume command of the COWBOYS while COWBOY SIX has a well-earned rest on R&R. At his age you go on R&R for rest! Most COWBOYS are convinced that DA has a wire crossed as the number of NCO's newly assigned continues to mount . . . one COWBOY was heard to comment "It looks more like a zebra farm than the old COWBOY CORRAL." To all new comers (NFG's that is) WELCOME!!!

FROM THE HORSES' MOUTH

Well, our first weeks here in the Delta have shown that the COWBOYS have continued their normal routine of providing outstanding support to the ground units. It has meant a lot of long, hard hours for everyone, but you can all take a great deal of pride in the unit's accomplishments.

We are all aware of the importance of aircraft maintenance. I hope that in the past few weeks we have become more aware of the importance of vehicle maintenance. Our mission is dependent upon vehicles as well as the effort of each man.

Speaking of the efforts of the men, I would like to interject a thought about maintaining that outstanding effort through something called preventive medicine . . . it is making sure our shots are up to date and avoiding the adverse effects of sudden temperature changes or sleeping under a fan. A cold can deprive us of the effort of a man just as well as a bullet from Charlie. In this country the danger of infection greatly increase. Treat your cuts and watch closely for the first sign of infection. An extra tetanus shot is only common sense when you consider the horrors of lockjaw.

Next week Captain Fernandes will write this column as I am going for a few days' rest. I am confident COWBOY performance will continue outstanding.

COWBOY 6

SAFETY SPOOK

HI COWBOYS! Remember me? I'm your safety awareness. I am the pricking that you feel when you do the right thing and double check a "cleared" weapon, or the prompting that makes you slow down as you notice a potentially dangerous situation on the road. You don't know me? You have never heard my frantic calls for more care, greater attention? The rattling of chains that directs your attention to the safety aspects of a job, an action, or a plan?

Frequently I can't get through to people. They get angry, or they are in a hurry, or maybe they don't believe in me. They consider seat belts a bore, and driving safety for sissies, weapons' safety to them is for the squares. I know them very well . . . you see after their carelessness has killed themselves they become the remorse that is felt when someone is injured through a lack of SAFETY AWARENESS. This remorse is not nice and gentle like I am; it forces its way upon you and makes you sad. Please Please listen to me, and practice what I teach you so remorse won't get you!

Hauntingly
Safety Spook

INSIDIOUS INFORMER

BULLSHEET FROM 'ROUND THE RANGE

FLASH report that Indian 6 had been attacked by a monkey was scotched the other day as it couldn't be determined who was chasing whom . . . but we would like to advise Lt. Blake that "penetration, howsoever slight . . . etc. etc.!"

Insidious Informer at Operations reports that with two new Operations Officers we are only two days behind in CA's.

Inside report just arrived that 623 is alive and well and working with the DEMONS at Phu Hiep.

What Flight Operations Sgt. got a confirmed skid on 019 the other day?

Is it really true that Lt. Burlinson has a bind in every cyclic he uses? Or is that just what happens when you fly them up-side-down Chicken Little?

What chubby Intelligence Sgt. has nominated SSG Smithson for the Florence Nightingale of the year Award.

What FALCON Platoon Leader couldn't hack that cushy life in Operations and returned to his Plt. to come up with a 52-rocket answer to the Cobra. By the way Cpt. Smith is it really true that it is the only aircraft in the country that takes off at a 5-foot hover?

Senior Sergeants are eyeballing the new Property Book Officer with some envy as he managed to get one of his troops (?) a haircut for the first time since his arrival. SFC. K reputedly stated that he even got Cammallere into something resembling a uniform.

FALCONS report that OLD-TIME FALCON RANDY CHAMBERS was the only one to remember them at XMAS with a box of cookies. FALCONS have been working hard at the renovation of a new Ammo bunker. SSG Coles had them recovering sand bags for it for some time now. FALCONS all like the bright effect of new bags.

Words out that CPT. "Crash" J is getting to be Ole Twiggy (Bones). Thomas' favorite AC!

Insidious Informer reports that the FEARLESS FOURSOME (Smithson, Ellert, Coles & Webster) are not employed as doormen in the local Thai Social Clubs, but they may be taking head count in an effort to have such a facility installed for the COWBOYS!!

Who said that Hobbs was trying to get a corner on the Market for Saigon Tea? By the way Hobbs, that Babe wants you to come back.

Tip that Lt. Wisell & CPT. McLaughlin really scarf up the C's. Before the egg dries on their chin from breakfast they are checking out what to hit for dinner.

Old eagle eye Layton gave all the chickens in the Delta a break the other day when he called the FALCONS in on a REAL ENEMY TARGET!

Got the word that Jalbert really gets along well with the Thai's . . . has he started kissing them back yet??

Troops at Maintenance have got to learn that when Fontenot says, "the Major says" he means "THE MAJOR SAYS!" DOGGONEIT!

Latest craze to capture COWBOY Pilots has been the rash of hammocks that sprout up during standby at Ben Duck . . . EM say the hammocks can stay but taking boots off has to go!

Insidious Informer says Lt. Allue has a thriving business selling coke bottles back to the little Old Mama-san who sells them there at Ben Duck. A penny saved is a penny earned?

FALCON ACE WIEDNER got a confirmed pig the other day, and Nichols got a confirmed drip! How about that Pussycat!

OK Hunzinga we agree halitosis is better than no breath at all and the other guys are envious!

Insidious Informer says CPT. Grabowski has gone through three transmissions in three weeks . . . the other day he offered to fly Sgt. La Brie to Saigon before he would let him use the jeep! Status or something??

THE OLD SARGE

"HE'S BUCKING FOR A PROMOTION!"

WOW! What a gross injustice. The individual who can say that about a fellow is showing more than just tail feathers!

Someone you may think of as "Bucking for a promotion" is probably an individual you can't get along with, someone who is doing his best to be a soldier . . . and doing his best to get his job done properly.

If willingly working long hours is "Bucking" for promotion . . . then someone should tell the President of the United States to quit bucking! If polished boots and a clean uniform are "Bucking" for promotion where does pride in ourselves and self-respect for our personal appearance come in at. Is it "Bucking for promotion" to be proud of our uniform; is it "Bucking for promotion" to accept and believe the fact that personal appearance and conduct reflect upon our country, our leaders, our families, our upbringing, as well as ourselves? If this is "Bucking for promotion" HURRAH FOR IT!

Is it "Bucking for promotion" to do our best on the maintenance line, or is it regard for the safety and well-being of our friends who fly these aircraft, that prompts us to do our best? Does the Crew Chief who really keeps his ship up, parts on order, and PM pulled, really put in the extra effort for the promotion . . . or is it because he knows how important his ship can be to a LRRP Team that needs extraction?

Is it bucking for promotion to recognize that you are following in the footsteps of fathers, brothers, uncles, and grandfathers, who have worn the uniform of the United States Army before us? Does promotion have to do with Nathan Hale, the men at Valley Forge, Sergeant York and Roger Young, in whose tradition we are following?

The next time you hear the expression "He is bucking for promotion" think a second more. Are you sure it shouldn't be: "He is trying to do things right," or "He is more ambitious than I."

If we can't admire and respect ambition, then what is left? Indifference? Does anyone really admire a "Don't give a damned" attitude?

Are each of the men in Maintenance and all the Crew Chiefs who have worked so hard to maintain the COWBOY COMMITMENT "Bucking for promotion?" Or are these the men who have consistently distinguished this unit! Are you REALLY good enough to count in their number? Have you EARNED the respect that we show them?

Try thinking this over, you may find some answers.

THE OLD SARGE

C◆WB◆Y

BULLSHEET

| VOLUME 3 | 30 MAY 1969 | NUMBER 4 |

COWBOYS WELCOME NEW SIX DURING BIG WEEKEND

The weekend at the home of the COWBOYS in Bear Cat, began Friday with the presentation of Air Medals to the following officers: First Lieutenant Vance E. Fisher, Gerald W. Hendley, Robert M. McIntosh and Warrant Officers David B. Bowsher and Larry L. Ross. CW2 Duane H. Johnson received the ARCOM for his outstanding record while flying in RVN.

Sunday morning the change of command ceremony at Bear Cat commenced with the award of the DFC for achievement and the Bronze Star for meritorious service to Major Paul R. Riley, commanding. After the citation was read and awards presented, Major Riley relinquished the command of the 335th A.H.C. to Major Howard J. Stiles. Among the dignitaries present, LTC Stevens expressed his appreciation to Major Riley for a job well done and expressed confidence in continued success under the leadership of Major Stiles.

The COWBOYS welcome Major Stiles from his Assistant G-1 position at 1st Avn. Bde. HQ. The new Cowboy "6" graduated from the U.S. Military Academy in 1959. He is dual qualified and has attended the Aviation Safety Course at U.S.C. as well as the Aviation Maintenance Officers course.

With the outstanding credentials, Major Stiles saddled up to lead the COWBOYS and also govern the Ranch House back at Bear Cat.

Sunday drew to a close as 1st LT. Richard L. Mellen was promoted to Captain and the COWBOYS partook in the closing celebration of the big weekend with a "Bought Bar" by our new Captain.

FROM THE HORSES' MOUTH

I am very pleased and proud to be the new Cowboy six. It is with humility that I assume command and dedicate my entire effort to your well-being. We are an air mobile company and mission accomplishment means placing the ground troops in battle at the right place and time. However, total mission orientation means much more. It means having a mess hall that provides outstanding chow. It includes, but is not limited to, an administrative organization that keeps the paper flowing, a maintenance effort that practices "Zero Defects," a motor pool that is an example to all, and people that are dedicated to achieve better and higher standards. Total mission orientation is what I am asking you to strive for with maximum effort from all concerned. I feel confident the COWBOYS can and will attain the highest of goals in the future.

COWBOY 6

SAFETY SPOOK

Last week if you'll remember, Randy Spastic caught his toe on a stake in the ground. True to our promise we've managed to get an interview this week. Of course, we had to work our way to the 3rd Surgical Hospital at Dong Tam to locate him. Seems he had neglected his injury and infection had set in.

He's in good spirits though and claims he's learned his lesson about being safety conscious at all times.

"I just can't get over some of the ways these soldiers overlook such an important thing as safety," he commented. "I mean every day you see some jerk playing around with his weapon or horsing around with his airplane. The best way to screw yourself is to use something for what it isn't designed to be used for or isn't even designed to do."

"A good point Randy--we hope you're out and back with us soon."

Just as we walked off we heard a blood curdling scream and an earth jarring crash. Seems old Randy had braced himself up with the little portable night table by his bed and since it didn't have square wheels.......

INSIDIOUS INFORMER

Lt., Nicholson, those fire extinguishers sure are hard to stop once you check them to see if they work, aren't they???

It's rumored that the crew of 592 is going to requisition field glasses and fur coats for when they cover C&C with a certain Falcon AC.

Sgt. Critchlow, do you really think your tape recorder works better if you feed it a whole can of beer?

CWO Weidner had a pleasant surprise Thursday. During the mission he received word of a 15 day drop and he is to leave country in two days. He completed the mission and also got credit for one last kill, even if it did take six sets of rockets!!

We would like to congratulate 86 for "doing his thing" last week at Tan An. Talk about smiling the skids, this ship was really roaring!!

BROTHERS...The 335th now has two brothers in the company. PFC Michael and SP/4 Robert Luke. Mike is a clerk in the Orderly Room and Robert is a crew chief.

None of the AC's in first platoon want to fly with LT. Gould. Could it be because he has been shot up three times and twice the AC took shrapnel in the face? Just stay away from Me Magnet A__!

The COWBOYS are getting a new sign signifying the Cowboy Corral. It should be up in a few days. The sign was painted by Sgt. Bull.

It looks as if we will have to get an extra gunship to fly C&C. Those gunnies sure get in your way during gun runs don't they, FALCON 25!

Nobody lets an old major run off and leave them now, do they COWBOYS? We can run 50 or 60 yards a day with him, he surely can't last too much longer!

It seems as if the personnel in the Orderly Room are taking turns. This week another one turned up "ill." Isn't that right Bork?

FLYING FICKLE FINGER OF FATE

It has been suggested to us to start the 4-F program, so after consideration we think it could be a lot of fun IF we can get EVERYONE'S' participation. The award will be given to ANYONE in the company who is deserving of such an inferior award. Everyone is eligible for the award and ANYONE can nominate. So, let's get into the act COWBOYS and show our disappreciation for an unjust act or decision. The award consists of the "Finger" which the winner (?) gets to keep till the following week. We encourage your participation COWBOYS so let's get with it.

Did 89 really expend again on ONE VC that was in a canal? THE SECOND TIME IN TWO WEEKS, NO LESS!

NOBODY BUT NOBODY gets written up for the same thing in the BullSheet TWICE, But...Second platoon in case you didn't notice, the sand bags around the gas tanks have fallen down again!

BULLSHEET

VOLUME 3   4 JUNE 1969   NUMBER 5

FANS QUITE A HAZARD TO THE

COMPANY

WHAT!! SGT. GRUNDON WORRY??!!

The BULLSHEET is constantly looking for new material to print and this week we think we have come up with some very good material with sincere messages. We hope you find these as interesting and heart stirring as did we.

The following was written by Jackie Wojnicki, whose brother, PFC Jim Wojnicki, is stationed here with the COWBOYS.

NOW THAT HE'S GONE!!

You live with him for all of your child life and a good portion of your teen life, not appreciating him, but putting him aside as a piece of furniture. All of a sudden that piece of furniture seems to be one of the most important parts of your life. The rooms in the house are filled but filled with loneliness and memories of him. It didn't seem like much then but now when you look back at the past when little things he said or did meant nothing, are now the BEST memories of your life! That's right -- look back! "You never know till he's gone."

FROM THE HORSES' MOUTH

May was a big month for the COWBOYS as we flew 2500 hours. As you know, the majority of that time was combat assault. For those who have never been to the AO (Area of Operation), we support the 9th ARVN Division on pacification operations in the Delta region of Vietnam.

I mentioned last week the need for total mission orientation. Each of you contributes to the success of our flying mission, and each of you should be proud of the record the COWBOYS are establishing. Whether you are a clerk, mechanic, cook, pilot, or what have you, each of you contributes to our total mission accomplishment, and each one of you are to be congratulated.

The IG inspection will be on 11 June. Continue to improve your area of responsibility. Strive for excellence, and on the 11th of June, look sharp and be sharp.

COWBOY 6

SAFETY SPOOK

Next week Randy will be taking his R&R, Sidney, he says. One reminder he has is to be sure your shot record is current or it might mean a sore arm or two the first few days from late shots.

"Wednesdays' shower was a real good blast for some people," he recalled. "Something like that could cause a few bad accidents on the roads. Remember the ditches that were nearly washed over, and that driving wind coupled with wet roads is definitely a hazard."

The increasing rain means damp cloths and boots. It's important to keep as dry as possible. I had a bad rash because I didn't change wet clothes and believe me, it is not exactly comfortable.

INSIDIOUS INFORMER

The Insidious Informer would like for Machado to read the Safety Spook twice this week. It seems he knows all too well what wet roads can do as Wednesday night the jeep he was driving suddenly became submerged in about five feet of water. This happened, not because of his driving, but because of the rain covered roads. Let us all learn from this injury free accident while we can, not as we are laying in the ditch ourselves.

Mr. Knoblauch and Mr. Lowell did an outstanding job on the lettering of the 2nd platoon hooches. Now if they would only learn to spell, the signs would look much better. It's plaToon fellows, not plaNoon!

Who was it that forgot about the drainage ditch between the hooches during the last big rain and nearly drowned in it on his way to the shower, but walked away from the scene as though it was something he did every day? Know anything about that, Polacke?

Fans are quite a hazard to a few people in the Company. Topito has quite a cut on his arm due to a "booby trap"? Sp/4 Dill caught his WHAT in the fan while blowing off talcum powder! That's worse than catching it in a zipper, isn't it Rodriguez?

It seems as if Bittinger turned his head just long enough to run about 150 feet of film onto the floor of the EM club this week. He also did a double take at the Officers' club that night. Smooth move, Xlax!

SGT. Grundon, do you really have IT? With only 22 days left in country too. "Well, honey it's like this.......

Lt. Nicholson, how did you end up standing "in ranks" at Vung Tau last week? You were supposed to have followed Major Stiles all the way to the bleachers. OH! SOME LIEUTENANTS!

A few maintenance write-ups for the week:

458 was turned into the 6/11 for a short in the wiring. Was written up as, "STRUCK BY LIGHTNING!"

FM Homing inop. -- No FM Homing stations in South Vietnam. Come on, Avionics!

The Falcons were skunked this week by C&C. Score: C&C 4, Falcons 0!

Perez, no one uses 1500 rounds to kill one VC. Did you finally kill him or did he just die of fright after the first 1000 rounds?

First platoon's water tower is still standing after one week of completion. Of course, they haven't put the tank on top of it yet!

'PROUD I AM'! PROUD WE STAND'!

How many have walked here before me? How many will walk here after I'm gone?

The men I have worked with were good men! They were sincere in their beliefs, proud in their laughter, understanding in their sorrow! They had a damn good reason for their actions, They were proud, they were Americans.

"I'm getting old now, too old to fight but I'm not worried, these new fellows have shown me that they can be just as much "American" as were those that I fought with."

You will see me every now and then, I'm not hard to find. Oh, you can call me "Troop," all my friends do!

AWARDS

On 30 May, the following personnel were presented the Air Medal for sustained achievement in flight: Sp/4 Andrew E. Hooker, Michael A. Lee, Frank G. Machado, Paul K. Perry, David R. Ranney, John F. Topito, also, PFC Thomas L. Setino.

C◆WB◆Y

BULLSHEET

VOLUME 3	14 JUNE 1969	NUMBER 6

The rangeland is now changing its tone from the normal BullSheet brown to the bright colors of the COWBOYS. Their red and white diamonds are now decorating every door in the company. In addition, the platoons hope to paint the platoon insignia on each appropriate door. The big diamonds sure have made a difference in company appearance.

The company is also being gifted with new urinals. Of course, we all have our own names for them. They should be used for one purpose and that isn't "dunking" your friends in head first, or for losing your dinner, although they come in quite useful for that. Let us also remember that after a quite night at the club, we must not lose our footing and step in one. That trick is reserved for the jet set.

The IG is now over and both clubs were busy with celebration. Everything was going well until we were awakened early Thursday morning for a "Flyby" for an NBC filming. We came through in the normal Cowboy fashion and ###.

FROM THE HORSES' MOUTH

Gentlemen, the AGI is behind us now and I wish to thank each and every one of you for your outstanding performance and hard work. Such team effort, from the Maintenance Line to the Motor Pool, makes the COWBOYS the cohesive unit they are.

The swimming pool is now open and I encourage each of you to take time for a dip. While in the general area, visit the library. They have a wide selection of books, newspapers, and magazines. Also, the library is air-conditioned.

A word of appreciation is also in order for those individuals who have been responsible for sprucing up the company area. May the red and white diamonds live forever.

I'll mention a word about safety in closing. During the Monsoons, it is imperative that each of us be aware of the hazards present. We have wet roads, wet and slippery aircraft decks, lightning, and hazards to flight. Stay alert and stay alive.

Again, I appreciate the effort on everyone's behalf for the AGI. Thank you.

COWBOY 6

SAFETY SPOOK

This edition of the BullSheet will find the Safety Spook haunting the 1st Aviation Bdg. Safety conference at Vung Tau.

With the entire company giving a good showing for the AGI team, we had a good reason to let off some steam built up from the pressures of the IG. However, this is a time to be overly conscious of each individuals' responsibility to THINK SAFETY.

A quick look at the record shows that the 214th Battalion accident rate is the lowest since July and is on a downward trend. Let's not reverse this trend by complacency.

April was an accident free month for us and we nearly made it through the month of May. We are doing really well this far into June.

INSIDIOUS INFORMER

The NBC "Flyby" went off in the usual Cowboy fashion and with no major problems. The Bear Cat tower is to be congratulated. They not only coordinated Cowboy aircraft in formation, but also kept traffic moving smoothly in the opposite direction.

The 1st SGT says, "If you mess up, you make the BullSheet." Well Top, what were you and Sandy doing in that bunker together? Daily inspections?

SGT. Bull, I hear you switched to Thursdays again. Are those finger marks on your wall the reason you went back? Been climbing the walls?

Perico, what happened to your Walrus? (I don't get it!)

SGT. Peacock, you don't check the fire extinguishers by squeezing the handle. If you don't believe me, ask Lt. Nicholson. He's tried it too!

Hey Lundberg! Do you really have a black eye because you went to sleep in the latrine and fell off the pot?

Someone was blowing a whistle the other night at 2300 (11:00 PM) and two EM hooches fell out for formation.

Mr. Jongejan, you have it backwards, you don't give the girls a shower at the steam bath, they give you one! (Did you give her a massage too?)

With only a few days left, Topito is starting to drip like the rest of the orderly room. Taking lots of pills hey?!

It has turned out that SGT. Grundon really had nothing to worry about after all. Maybe he was never really exposed to the illness!

Who was the pilot that started up with the exhaust cover on? A thorough preflight, huh?

Major Stiles, in case you can't figure out why your jeep wouldn't start, someone filled it up with diesel fuel. Better watch those clerks!

Maintenance write ups: -- Pilots attitude inop. Removed nut from behind cyclic!

WHAT IS A SOLDIER?

Between the security of childhood and the second childhood we find a fascinating group of humanity called Soldiers. They come in assorted sizes, colors, and states of sobriety. They can be found anywhere, on leave, in the PX, in bars, in love, and always in debt. Girls love them, towns tolerate them, and the government supports them.

A Soldier is laziness with a deck of cards, bravery with a tattooed arm, and the protection of the world with a playboy. He has the energy of a turtle, the slyness of a three-star general, the sincerity of a liar, the aspirations of a Casanova, and when he wants something, it's usually connected with a GI pass. Some of his likes are; girls, women, females, broads, dames, and the opposite sex, (just to name a few). His dislikes are, answering letters, shaving, his uniform, his superior officers, the chow, and getting up in the mornings. No one can cram into a uniform pocket, a little black book, a package of gum, a picture of Tuesday Weld, a comb, a candy bar, and what's left of last month's pay. He likes to spend some of his money on poker and girls and the rest he spends foolishly. A Soldier is a magic creature. You can block him out of your house, but not out of your heart.

He's your long away from home, good for nothing, bleary eyed, bundle of worry. But of all your shattered dreams become insignificant when your Soldier comes home and looks at you with those bleary bloodshot eyes of his and says, "Hi, gee it's god to see you again."

C◆WB◆Y
BULLSHEET

VOLUME 3   21 JUNE 1969   NUMBER 7

COWBOYS AWARDED AT SA DEC

On the 19th of June in an award's ceremony at Sa Dec the 9th ARVN Division awarded CW2 William Weidner, who at this time has DEROSed, CW2 Tom Story, WO William E. Newman, WO Jerry Wells, SP/4 Charles O'Neal, SP/4 Julian Perez, SP/4 Ronald Trouard and SP/4 Paul Larson, who is on R&R the Vietnamese Cross of Gallantry with Bronze Star for valorous gunship action on 20 May 1969.

CONGRATULATIONS

Congratulations to the following COWBOYS on their respective promotions, Capt. Martin LeGault, CW2 Mike Hallock, CW2 Pete Knoblauch, SSG Earl Blackwell, SP/5 Jack Hunnicutt, SP/5 Milan Gruber, SP/4 Dominic Fino, Jr., and SP/4 Louis Byrne.

STAY ALERT, STAY ALIVE

FROM THE HORSES' MOUTH

Gentlemen, I can see a fantastic amount of teamwork and cooperation throughout the company. With each individual carrying his load, success in all our ventures is assured.

Rumors about a move are prevalent. There is nothing definite, and it may never be definite.

The attitude we must all have is to disregard the rumors, continue to build and improve our present area, or we will be hurting ourselves in the long run.

On 14 July, we will have a Battalion CMMI, keep your respective areas "UP TIGHT." Our attitude must be one of -- Be Ready, Not Get Ready.

COWBOY 6

SAFETY SPOOK

Randy is back from R&R already. To brush up on his reading he reviews the Weekly Summary put out by USABAAR. He says it's really unbelievable the number of accidents and amount of incident damage caused by pilot error or judgment. He has pointed out numerous incidents involving maintenance or material defects that were compounded by hasty or unnecessary maneuvers by pilots. It's difficult to understand how some pilots make a decision to move their aircraft after making a precautionary landing. Randy related one accident where a pilot made a successful landing following an engine stoppage. He restarted on the ground and took off--the engine stopped at 150 feet due to fuel starvation and it cost four lives.

This same reason applies to vehicles. If you become involved in an accident wait for the appropriate person to make the decision to move the vehicle.

We're cracking down on safety--and that means you.

INSIDIOUS INFORMER

SFC Meers it is rumored that your platoon is giving you range estimation exercises, did that ditch ever find out what hit it.

"16" remember to "Carry on if that's your bag." WO James Williams why do all the guys on the maintenance line call you Tom Terrific.

Maintenance personnel take note, it's First Aid not take pictures.

WO Rick Dorer why do the first platoon pilots draw straws to fly with you, also have heard that the AC's are doing the same with 1LT. Tom Gould.

SP/4 Coyaso, our latest reports tell us your nerves are shot, that was pretty close wasn't it.

WO McClellan and WO Mayl, will we ever hear the true story about your overnight stay in Saigon, did you really get stranded or was that planned.

SP/4 Bowlin we hope those girls didn't embarrass you, girls have to go too.

LT. Gould this is the Army not the circus, really now, walking the log with a starscope, who would believe your diversified talents.

SSG Webster and SSG Gower was that snake really watching TV.

SP/4 O'Garra did you get your pants back from the laundry at Vinh Long yet.

LT. Cyclic has been having his troubles with maintenance, those star clusters with play and those scissors bearing that go clank, clank, oops, change that to boom, boom are really rough.

Let's give a big hand to the "Sunshine Boys" LT. Allue and PFC Elliott.

SP/4 Krug we've heard that the guys in the third platoon appreciated the trench you dug from the hooch to the bunker in the last mortar attack.

SP/4 Hesselberg when will you learn you can't run through large boulders.

FINK WINS THREE DAY R&R

Our own SP/6 Richard Fink won a three-day R&R to Vung Tau for his safety slogan sent to battalion and printed in the Cougar News.

TRAFFIC HASTE MAKES HUMAN WASTE

WELL DONE COWBOYS

The COWBOYS commend the actions of WO Rick Dorer, 1LT. Tom Gould, SP/4 Ted Crafton and PFC Edward Martinez and compliment them on a job well done. On the 14th of June their aircraft sustained heavy damage and the gunner was lightly wounded, the two pilots working together were able to land the aircraft safely in what could have been a dangerous situation.

A well done also to WO Dave Bowsher and WO Steve Lyons for the outstanding job done on the 20th of June when they went back into an extremely hostile area with their two aircraft to evacuate wounded ARVN soldiers.

C◆WB◆Y

BULLSHEET

VOLUME 3   28 JUNE 1969   NUMBER 8

COWBOYS AWARDED

COWBOYS LOOSE THREE TO SAD FAREWELL

On 23 June 69, the Bronze Star was awarded to Captain Hanning for meritorious service while with the COWBOYS. The Air Medal was awarded to CW2 Steven Tichnor, WO's Walter Payne, James Johnson, Donald Lowell, Sp/4's Wallace Coyaso, Louis Lapan, James O'Garra, Norman Polacke and David Ranney. The Purple Heart was awarded to Sp/4's Louis Lapan and Charles O'Neal. We say congratulations to everyone except Lapan and O'Neal. We hope you fellas don't get any OLC's for your award.

The COWBOYS have temporarily lost three of our favorite members. They are CW2 Ed Eget, WO1 Leo Scott, and Sp/5 Larry Gerbitz, who were wounded in action last week. We will miss their good humor and quick wit and wish them the best of luck and a speedy recovery. Here's the address of CW2 Ed Eget; I'm sure he would appreciate a few get well cards. US Army Hospital, Camp Zama, APO San Francisco 96343.

IT'S BETTER TO BE OVERSAFE THAN UNSAFE!

FROM THE HORSES' MOUTH

Gentlemen, this month we are asked to contribute to the Army Emergency Relief Fund campaign. The Army Emergency Relief serves the Army family during times of financial emergency.

All members of the Army, both active and retired and members of their families are eligible for AER assistance. Aid may be given under varying types of emergencies, conditions, or situations that may be caused by the demands of military service which cause financial hardship that is beyond the ability of the soldier or his family to meet.

Financial assistance is extended either as a non-interest-bearing loan, or as an outright grant, or a combination of both, whichever is considered the most appropriate.

The Army Emergency Relief, through the organization of the American Red Cross, offers many varied services to members of the Army and their families through Red Cross chapters located in the United States and in overseas areas wherever troops are located.

Help the Army help its own. Make a contribution.

COWBOY 6

SAFETY SPOOK

The COWBOYS have surpassed the 30-day mark in accident free flying. 23 May was the last accident we had. The past week we've also been lucky by keeping the whole flight flying...well, except for combat damage which has been taking its toll.

We haven't had a vehicle accident in ages. Except for one near incident a couple of days ago. Somehow six (6) live rounds found their way into a trash burner. They were spotted before a fire was started. These near misses should be carefully studied for contributing factors and corrective actions the same as an incident.

Anyway COWBOYS, congratulations for the fine record this month. Let's not spoil it!

INSIDIOUS INFORMER

SGT Rivera, how did you end up with Top's teeth in your desk? On the other hand; Top, how did he end up with your teeth in his desk?

WALK THE STRAIGHT AND NARROW....We can't....Who ever built the side walk between the orderly room and the mess hall didn't follow the line and it ended up the "crooked and narrow." With a few words of "encouragement" from Top, the builders immediately remodeled it and we now have our straight and narrow walk way. By the way gentlemen, it looks very nice!

It seems as if a certain club manger flew as a gunner the other day and everything was hunky-dory except for a couple of self-made holes in the skids! You've got to admit it is just a little different than opening cans or taking inventory.

After the last rain, Cpt. Le Gault got into his truck just in time to have a lot of water dumped in his lap from a hole in the canvas top. We thought he would turn into a mud puddle, oh, what, "dirt bag."

SGT Gower don't look now but who ever gave you your last haircut didn't make the sides very even. What a coincidence that you should cut your head. It covers up your bad haircut!

Jonesy is starting a new class, "How to Defule an Aircraft."

Wayne says, "Only dumb gunners lose their weapons on their first day of flying." All I can say is, "Welcome to the Dummy club, Toad."

It seems that two truck drivers "misplaced" a truck and spent all night in Saigon looking for it. C'Mon Fellas! That's as bad as a couple of Helicopter drivers getting stranded at Hotel "3" overnight. Do you fellas know something we don't!?

Looks can give the wrong impression, as a certain gunner knows. He thought the engine for a chopper was started by the button on the clock. He said, "Every time the pilot pushed that button, the engine would start!"

SGT La Brie, says, "What's a bull among cows," of course he shouldn't be talking since he is really "in trouble."

Some people have all the luck, a certain Cowboy thought everything was going smoothly until he dropped from that window right into the arms of the Provost Marshall.

Certain Cowboy C&C's still need lessons in dropping smoke from altitude. Instead of the LZ he almost put the smoke right in lead's cockpit! "Bombs Away."

In case no one has noticed, the first platoon water tower has tanks on it again. We're taking bets, on when the tanks are full this time.

SGT Peacock & SGT Meuser we appreciate the excellent maintenance on aircraft but two days to do a thirty-minute job on a forklift, you guys better stick to your PMOS.

BE A PROFESSIONAL: STAY ALERT -- STAY ALIVE

Again, we wish a fond farewell for our departed or departing COWBOYS. Captain Donald Hanning, CW2 Steven Tichnor, Sp/4 Glenn Higashi, Sp/4 Roger Lopez, and Pvt. Henry Cadieux; Sp/4 Michael Nix has been reassigned to the 3/17th.

VOLUME 3   5 JULY 1969   NUMBER 9

Not long ago Red Skelton presented on his show an interpretation of the Pledge of Allegiance. With Flag Day and the 4th of July recently passed, we feel it will be appropriate to reminisce on this meaning of patriotism.

THE PLEDGE OF ALLEGIANCE
by Red Skelton

I remember this one teacher. To me, he was the greatest teacher, a real sage of my time. He had such wisdom. We were all reciting the Pledge of Allegiance, and he walked over. Mr. Lasswell was his name. He said:

"I've been listening to you boys and girls recite the Pledge of Allegiance all semester, and it seem as though it is becoming monotonous to you. If I may, may I recite it and try to explain to you the meaning of each word."

"I--me, an individual, a committee of one.
"PLEDGE -- dedicate all of my worldly goods to give without self-pity.
"ALLEGIANCE -- my love and my devotion.
"TO THE FLAG -- our standard, Old Glory, a symbol of freedom; wherever she waves, there is respect because your loyalty has given her a dignity that shouts freedom is everybody's job.
"OF THE UNITED -- that means that we have all come together.
"STATES -- individual communities that have united into 48 great states; 48 individual communities with pride and dignity and purpose, all divided with imaginary boundaries, yet united to a common purpose, and that's love for country.
"AND TO THE REPUBLIC -- republic, a state in which sovereign power is invested in representatives chosen by the people to govern; and government is the people and it's from the people to the leaders, not from the leaders to the people.
"FOR WHICH IT STANDS --
"ONE NATION -- the nation, meaning, so blessed by God.
"INDIVISIBLE -- incapable of being divided.
"WITH LIBERTY -- which is freedom and the right or power to live one's own life without threats, or fear, or some sort of retaliation.
"AND JUSTICE -- the principle or quality of dealing fairly with others.
"FOR ALL -- which means, boys and girls, it's as much your country as it is mine.
"And now, boys and girls, let me hear you recite together the Pledge of Allegiance:

"I pledge allegiance to the flag of the United States of America and to the republic for which it stands, one nation, indivisible, with liberty and justice for all."

"Since I was a small boy, two states have been added to our country and two words have been added to the Pledge of Allegiance; "Under God.""

"Wouldn't it be a pity if someone were now to say, "That's a prayer" and that would be eliminated from our schools too?"

FROM THE HORSES' MOUTH

And the rains came -- and they continued to come. From the Flight line, motor pool, and our sidewalk builders too, everyone is getting wet. I appreciate your dedicated efforts to continue to get the job done in spite of such adverse conditions. Keep smiling, in a couple of months, everyone can complain of the dust.

The COWBOYS will stay at Bear Cat as you should know by now. The Dong Tam units will move. In the near future, we should begin to support the 7th ARVN Div. It appears both we and the EMUS will provide aviation support to them.

Lastly, a word about safety. The roads are slick so if you're a driver, reduce your speed. The skies are full of thunderstorms so if you're a pilot don't extend yourself. Make a 180 while you have the ability too. On the maintenance line, don't lose your step on slippery decks or maintenance stands. Safety must be a way of life.

COWBOY 6

SAFETY SPOOK

The results of careless or negligent handling of weapons is scarcely given a thought until someone is MEDIVACED.

If possible, a jammed weapon should be cleared away from a populated area. If the weapon has to be cleared on the ground, a moments prior planning with attention given to BODY POSITION will at least protect the individual should the weapon discharge.

Everyone should consider himself a supervisor if an unsafe act is noticed. One might think a person is being BOSSY if he mentions a safety hazard -- but at least listen to what he says, he might save your life!

INSIDIOUS INFORMER

Mr. Jongejan why does everyone call you the "Dean Martin of the Thai's?"

The cowboys have been having a pretty sever epidemic of diarrhea going around as one T.I. knows. While climbing up to check the head, he completely ruined one set of undershorts!

"Safety pays" says "6". Right after our last safety meeting he got a little too close to a truck bumper and broke the antenna off his jeep!

Did Mr. Morrison really get cleared through artillery above 10,000 or was he up on company uniform when he called for clearance?

Say, where are our maintenance personnel when we need them? Could it be they could be found in the "Panther" club?

It seems the word about staying in Saigon is spreading. Friday night Sgt. LaBrie, Sgt. Bull, and Mr. Williams were in there "picking up parts for maintenance."

Talk about patriotism, Hagashi has it. He was scheduled for ETS on the first of July but he doesn't leave Vietnam till the 7th. Knowing he's loving spending another week with us!

It seems as if a couple of Falcon Pilots couldn't agree on a certain mission. It's a good thing those Lt.'s had a CWO to take over and set them straight, huh, Mr. Story?

I know PFC's are pretty good at everything they attempt, Keeling, but try not to do any more acrobatics off the back of a deuce and a half, OK?

The last time I wrote about falling in a urinal, Sp/5 Childress couldn't wait to try it. He went out the very next night and fell in one up to his waist! Way to go, "Dummy!!"

The platoon that sinks together stays together is very appropriate to the first platoon. All five of their ships had to restart and move because they were sinking up over the skids while on stand-by this week.

C◆WB◆Y
BULLSHEET

VOLUME 3	12 JULY 1969	NUMBER 10

COWBOYS AWARDED PRESIDENTIAL UNIT CITATION

Recently the 335th received notification that they had been awarded The Presidential Unit Citation. The citation was awarded to the COWBOYS for their "extraordinary heroism" against an armed enemy during Operation MacAuthor in Kontum Province, RVN from 6 Nov. to 23 Nov. 1967. The 335th was instrumental in the 173 Airborne Brigade's defeat of a "heavily armed, well-trained, well-disciplined and numerically superior enemy operation largely from well-prepared and heavily fortified positions." From the combat assault on Hill 823 on 6 Nov. to the final victory on Hill 875 on Thanksgiving day, the battle of Dak To was characterized by countless displays of gallantry, relentless aggressiveness and quick reaction, resulted in a hard-fought and unprecedented victory, rendering the 174 North Vietnamese Infantry Regiment combat ineffective. This defeat of the 1st North Vietnamese Division frustrated a major enemy attempt to control the Dak To area and the surrounding highlands.

Several old COWBOYS remember well that the 335th conducted combat assaults and resupply missions under the most hazardous conditions of hostile fire. There were, a total of nine helicopters bearing the white and red diamond that received extensive combat damage and over ten COWBOYS wounded during this action. The COWBOYS flew over 4,000 sorties, and 2,000 hours. They lifted over 7,000 troops and 420 tons of cargo. They expended over 1300 2.75mm rockets (FFA) and 200,000 rounds of 7.62mm machine gun ammunition. This is truly "In keeping with the highest tradition of the military service and reflects great credit upon the unit and the United States Army."

This makes the fifth unit award received by the COWBOYS. Others include two meritorious unit commendations and two Vietnamese Cross of Gallantries with Palm -- Unit awards.

New entries to the Cowboy bunkhouse include: 1LT Cseak, WO1 Bramblett, WO1 Freeman, Sp/5 Smith, PFC Goerlitz and Pvt.'s Henwood and Lutes. Our recent list of promotions includes two new CPT's; CPT Bower and CPT Nicholson. COWBOYS who have or will depart our midst shortly are: CW2 Hallock, CW2 Knoblock, Sp/5 Ashenback, Sp/5 Reavers, Sp/5 Gruber, Sp/4 Hicks, Sp/4 Norred and Sp/4 Lopez R. Our accomplishments as a unit were attained with their help and continued success is wished for them in their next assignment.

FROM THE HORSES' MOUTH

Congratulations to maintenance as we had the best availability in the Battalion the last week of June. Our goal is to sustain the high level of perfection we are gaining.

Once again, the Battalion CMMI is 14 July. Let's BE READY -- NOT GET READY.

Also on the 14th, we'll have a company party and a floor show. Thanks to LaPan and crew, we'll have a nice stage. Hopefully, if everyone behaves and no incidents mar the occasion, we can have more shows in the future.

The COWBOYS once again have been rewarded for outstanding support and extraordinary heroism. The Presidential Unit Citation was recently awarded for action 6 November, to 23 November 1967. Members of the company during that period are authorized to wear the award. Ours is a proud heritage. Keep up the good work.

Lastly a word about our morning take-off. One of the many items the Battalion Commander measures our professionalism by is our take-off. This along with reports, inspections, mission accomplishment, etc. -- causes the man to form an impression. Last month, we were the worst in the Battalion with 23 late take-offs. People are late arriving on the flight line. Also cranking 15 minutes prior to takeoff does not give miracle maintenance time to make a fix. The COWBOYS deserve better than being last. We're selling ourselves short. Thus the present procedure. Two and a half hours prior to take-off is get-up. Two hours prior AC and CE preflight and run up the aircraft. During this period, pilot and gunner eat and get organized. Approximately one hour prior to take-off, they go to the flight line while AC and CE return to eat. This gives maintenance a minimum of an hour to fix aircraft, solve avionics problems, etc. This system will help put the COWBOYS back on top where they belong. Let's all support the program.

COWBOY 6

SAFETY SPOOK

"Sleep, who needs it?" Sometimes we kid ourselves with that worn out phrase, "Hell, I can get by with 3 or 4 hours sleep with no sweat."

Only now with the new wake up policy, it's hard to get sufficient rest unless we break away from the club or TV. Crew Chiefs, you're going to have the roughest time, but get as much rest as you can. If you're dragging that bad, let the old platoon Sgt. know you're too tired. Don't just make idle talk about it.

Now that we have the doors back, we'll all keep decently dry during the "light drizzles." AC's make sure these doors are back and securely locked into position during flight. (CA's, etc.) If they aren't locked into position they will gradually wear around the rollers and jump the track. Don't take the chance of a door going through a rotor blade.

Cowboy 6 helped dedicate the new NCO club Saturday night. It looks like a very nice club fellas, and I'm sure you won't be selling anything but sodas. RIGHT? Especially with someone like Mr. Adams (CIV.) attending it. It seems he goes out of his way to keep from corrupting the minds of our young officers. He doesn't even let the NCO's read a nice, clean, sex novel! (Smile)

INSIDIOUS INFORMER

Lt. Hendley, why did they make the fearless Falcon killer the Civil Affairs Officer?

It seems like the NCO's had quite a time trying to build their new club. It took Sgt. Peacock almost THIRTY minutes to drive just one nail in the ceiling!

It seems like some of the people in the company just watch certain NCO's to see that they make the BullSheet but this week we're not going to mention Top and Sandy.

We're sorry to hear that SGT. LaBrie has been ill. Since when did they start giving penicillin for TONSILLITIS? Come to think of it, you were one of the guys that went into Saigon for "supplies," weren't you?

We would like to congratulate Mr. Biggs, who ruined his whole R&R by getting married. He must have been nervous, he fell through a greenhouse just before he left!

I wouldn't even laugh at the fact that Lt. Allue fell off the top of his chopper last week.

C◆WB◆Y

BULLSHEET

VOLUME 3	19 JULY 1969	NUMBER 10

KINGS CROSS REVIEW AND COMPANY PARTY A BIG SUCCESS

On the 14th of July, the COWBOYS christened their new stage with an Australian floor show, "The Kings Cross Review." The COWBOYS were very grateful for the show which climaxed a hectic week of hard work on preparation for the CMMI inspection which was completed that very afternoon. That the next day was a stand-down was all the more reason for the cowboys to celebrate.

The evening was started with a free Bar-B-Q of chicken and ribs and the free drinks were provided by each appropriate club.

The evening continued with a ribbon cutting ceremony on the new stage and a special thanks went to Louis LaPan and associates for the outstanding job of construction.

The floor show commenced amidst a tremendous applause and the constant flashing of flashbulbs.

The COWBOYS have again shown their great spirit and morale by the big Cowboy welcome as well as a loud Cowboy good-bye. We think the show was a great success and are hopefully looking for more shows in the future.

FROM THE HORSES' MOUTH

The COWBOYS left the beautiful beach of Phu Heip last November to Participate in Operation Speedy Express. The TDY, as you all know, has been extended and down town Bear Cat is now home.

For the units' participation in Speedy Express, we have received a letter of commendation signed by General Cao Van Vien, Commanding General, Joint General Staff, RVNAF. The COWBOYS can be proud of their contribution. Thank you all.

Yes, the diamonds must go. Our efforts to retain them were turned down. As a member of the 214th CAB, we must adopt their tactical marking. We didn't in the past because we were attached. The decision has been made, let's accept it and live with it. As beauty is only skin deep, the loss of the diamonds does not alter the composition of the COWBOYS. The unit and the people have not changed -- so let's continue to charge in our usual manner. The COWBOYS are and will continue to be versatile, aggressive, efficient, and reliable. Keep up the good work.

COWBOY 6

SAFETY SPOOK

Would anyone mind spending a three-day passion....uh pass, in Vung Tau? If you have a good slogan that might help prevent the rash of accidental weapons discharges that is plaguing Vietnam, you might spend three days stroking... ah, strolling in Vung Tau. Turn your slogan in to Sp/5 Childress or Sp/4 Luke in the Orderly Room not later than 08:30 (for you US's, that's 8:30 AM!) Wednesday, 23 July. GOOD SHOOTING!

All you rotary wing aviators remember what you were taught to do when you untie the blades at night? Several people have mentioned that they've encountered some ships running up with no lights FLASHING BRIGHT til you pick it up! Crew Chiefs, do all your lights work?

INSIDIOUS INFORMER

Mr. Williams nearly brought a little embarrassment to the Major last week when he furnished him with some scissors that wouldn't even cut the tape during the dedication ceremony. Wouldn't you say that's about par for a Warrant Officer?

I hear someone is taking up a collection to buy Lt. Thompsen a "Lady Norelco." He keeps cutting his head with his razor.

Everyone had on nice, clean fatigues and shined boots for the inspection last week; that is until Sgt. Meeve marched a platoon right through a BIIIGGG mud hole. You should have heard the comments!!

There are lots of brave men here in Nam that face death every day. Mr. Nicholaou had rather take his chances with Charlie than compete against false teeth! At first sight of those "Falsies" he starts climbing the walls.

No Polacke, a pedestrian doesn't have the right-of-way over a hovering Huey!

Rumor has it that a certain Cowboy 6 has bought a WALLABY costume and is looking for the herd to come back!

The EM sent their thanks to Sgt. Meers. It seems as if he has lost the list of personnel who were caught with dirty rifles.

Who is the prominent figure in the company that "walks softly and carries a big stick"? Could it be the same person that has been nick-named "Major Moses"?

It seems as if Sp/4 Phillips of the Falcons was complaining about a foot injury, then got so enthused with killing Charles that he forgot to limp when he got back on the ground. Hurts, huh?

Top, do you still deny that Sandy has anything to do with your eye injury?

Sgt. Bull was following the advice of an officer the other night, but not to the step. It seems as if Mr. Morrison made it all the way across the ditch and Sgt. Bull fell off the walk into the mud. It was a 4-foot drop into one foot of mud, which included hitting his face!

Sgt. LaBrie be careful! Alcohol and penicillin just aren't compatible.!

Let's hear it for Sgt. Rodman! Last week while climbing around on the ships, he ruined TWO more pairs of undershorts! Will some of you married men please write home for some diapers, the PX is out of underclothes!!

Could anyone tell me why Sgts. Meers and Peacock have become known as the "Bobsey Twins"? Is it because they are always together?

Maintenance Officers are OK but even they aren't qualified to start the engine with the rotor tied to the revetment. Right, Cpt. LaGault?

Mr. Story is looking for the man that stole Ben Tre last week. He said it just wasn't where it used to be and he couldn't find it!!

Lt. Czeak, just because you are new doesn't mean you have to wait on those NCO's when one of them yells for a KP!

Specialist Bailey, your buddies want you to start sleeping in your own bed from now on. (This was passed on to you as a hint.)

BE PROFESSIONAL * DO IT RIGHT THE FIRST TIME

C◆WB◆Y
BULLSHEET

VOLUME 3	26 JULY 1969	NUMBER 11

FINAL RESULTS OF 9TH ARVN SUPPORT

IN MEMORIAL

Our deepest sympathies are sent to the families of four members of the 135th, AHC, our sister company, who lost their loved ones in a helicopter accident earlier this week.

Our prayers and consolations go to the families of WO1 Bernadino F. Genchi, WO1 Allen E. Starr, SP/4 Larry G. Pool, and SP/4 Gail L. Whitlatch.

We assure you, their loss is felt as deeply in the 335th as in their own company. May God lead and comfort each of their loved ones and friends in this time of need.

The members of the 335th AHC
COWBOYS

On June 21st, the COWBOYS started to support the 7th ARVN DIV. The COWBOYS were supporting this unit when we first moved to the Delta from the mountains of Phu Heip in December 1968.

After four months of supporting the 7th ARVN in which the COWBOYS established an outstanding record, the 335th transferred their support to the 9th ARVN DIV. Now, after only 21 weeks with the 9th, the COWBOYS are supporting the 7th ARVN once more.

In a comparison of results, the time spent with the 9th ARVN was even more satisfactory than the first few months in the Delta.

Our support of the 9th ARVN began on 21 March and ended 21 July. The following results are applicable to that time period: We flew over 8,700 combat hours and 25,500 sorties, carrying over 70,000 passengers and 68 tons of cargo. The vast majority of this was in combat assaults, as is shown in our hit and kill record.

The COWBOYS have had 73 aircraft take hits by at least 193 enemy rounds. This is very minimal though, considering our ships have recorded 428 confirmed kills while destroying over 900 structures and 167 sampans and damaging over 150 others. In accomplishing this feat, the COWBOYS have had 17 flying personnel wounded and no fatalities.

This is an outstanding record COWBOYS. Let's keep up the good work and again show the 7th ARVN why we are the Best in the Delta.

FROM THE HORSES' MOUTH

Hopefully--the days of 0610 report times to Tra On are over. As mentioned earlier, the COWBOYS are now supporting the 7th ARVN. The EMU's are also supporting the 7th, and this combination looks like it will work to our advantage. The plan is that when operationally feasible, one company will be released after the morning mission. Thus, on alternate days, we could get released early, while on the next day, we'd standby until late afternoon release. Crew chiefs and gunners should benefit, and as a result, the entire company. Let's all show a lot of professionalism as we start back with the 7th.

This month everyone gets a raise. That extra money can go to work for you by the purchase of U.S. Savings Bonds or Freedom Shares. The Savings Deposit Program can get you a Whopping 10% interest.

On 4 August, the Bn. inspection team will be back to reinspect unsatisfactory areas. The main problem areas are billets and weapons. Let's pull together and get the job done.

Incidentally, the diamonds on the vertical fin look pretty good!!

COWBOY 6

SAFETY SPOOK

A good point was made in the Haunted House the other day. Do some of you pilots still wear the old leather gloves? There's a chance they may get caught on the window catch (this is primarily for ACs) There are two courses of action -- NOMEX gloves or tuck them up your sleeves!!

Everyone is cooperating fully in preventing aircraft accidents. We're accident free from 23 May, but we still have those incidents.

It's been said that an incident is just an accident that couldn't find the right place to happen. REMEMBER . . . IT'S EASIER TO PREVENT AN ACCIDENT THAN TO EXPLAIN WHY!!!!!

INSIDIOUS INFORMER

Sgt. Marin, why do you take reducing pills if you are still going to eat SIX pieces of chicken??!!!

Who is the officer that couldn't start his chopper the other morning because the ignition circuit breaker was out? It's probably the same one that washed down the console of his ship and ruined all the radios, huh, Lt. Allue?

Mr. Adams, how do you expect to tow anything with that Honda when you can't even ride it? Incidentally, you owe us one compressor!!

SP/6 Fink said he never made the BullSheet because he was straight. Well, he better put that plywood back before I tell where he "borrowed" it!!

Mr. Wood said he could receive but not transmit on Uniform. He must have good ears because the whole UHF radio was missing!!

SP/4 Sousa, how in the world did you end up with your shorts on backwards and in someone else's bed??!!

Our congratulations to Lt. Shaver and Lt. Stein who got a tail stinger THREE times on ONE approach last Wednesday.

Need tips on couth while eating in a Chinese restaurant?? Just ask Lt. Wissell. He tells all, including how to smell the hot, steaming wash cloth!!

I heard Condry flew gunner in a gunship this week just to show everybody that a Bravo model could take off with a load and a half!!!

SP/4 Garcia and SP/5 Condry have challenged anyone to a wrestling bout -- for the welterweight championship!! Come on fellas!!

For the second time in one week, Mr. Gilles has made two trips to operations to turn in a forgotten flight plan. DUHH, I'M A PILOT, DUH!

C◆WB◆Y
BULLSHEET

VOLUME 3   1 AUGUST 1969   NUMBER 13

COWBOYS RECEIVE SURPRISE FLOOR-SHOW!

The COWBOYS had a bit of a surprise last week, thanks to a "short-timer" in the company. Sp/4 Goodnough, alias -- "the scrounge," just happened to be "in-the-know" with the right people in Saigon and as a personal favor, received the floor show as a going away gift for the company.

To show our appreciation for the show, the COWBOYS "passed the hat" to help pay for the expenses incurred by the group.

The show, "Rick Arellano and the Juniors," proved to be an outstanding group. They kept the audience laughing and clapping, even without the help of our company's "professional photographers" who were getting a few "close-ups" of members of the band.

An interesting note: Rick, the comedian who received many favorable comments from the COWBOYS, has previously won an award from his native country (equal to our Emmy) for his outstanding performances on television.

BOREDOM CAN BURY YOU * STAY ALIVE!

FROM THE HORSES' MOUTH

The COWBOYS are soon to be awarded the Presidential Unit Citation in a ceremony at Bear Cat. Details will be announced as they become available. The heritage of the COWBOYS is a proud one. This unit has helped write the history of the 1st Aviation Brigade. The COWBOYS have roamed the length and breadth of Vietnam providing airmobile support. To attest to our professionalism are two Meritorious Unit Commendations, two Vietnamese Cross of Gallantry's with Palm, and the Presidential Unit Citation. As we approach each day, our challenge is to continue the tradition. Be proud and be professional.

Over the weekend, let's have max effort on weapons and billets. Keep the Old Man out of Jail!

Let's also keep up our accident prevention program. Think safety whether you are flying, driving, or just working I the area.

KEEP CHARGING!

COWBOY 6

SAFETY SPOOK

GOOD -- "as it should be," "better than average," "effective," "providing favorable results," "beneficial."

There is not one pilot in this company who cannot be a good pilot, however, there have been some indications that a few are starting to think they are better than their own ability or can surpass the stresses imposed on the aircraft to perform safely. A man who pulls 45 pounds of torque in an empty ship, proceeded by a cyclic climb is not a good pilot.

A good pilot is not one that can hold his proper angle and move into 1/2 rotor disc and fly from here to Dong Tam without losing his position. A good pilot is one who can fly the aircraft the way it is built to perform, while following the regulations and SOP's on Safety.

Gentlemen, good formation flying cannot be stressed too much. Our own SOP calls for 2-3 rotor discs distance in V's and staggered formation, and 3-5 while in trail or at night. Let's keep these distances in mind and give the other guy room to maneuver in case of an in-flight emergency or in case he runs out of pedal in an LZ. Two rotor discs will give him room to turn without hitting another aircraft. This is especially true in trail. Allow yourself enough room in case the man in front of you flares. This too, might cut down on our number of stinger and tail rotor strikes.

Remember AC's -- today's Peter-P, is tomorrow's AC. Let's make him a good one!

INSIDIOUS INFORMER

Who is the AC that pulled a good lower preflight then found that his head was missing when he climbed up on top? Do you know, Lt. Gould?

Hey Shepherd, I hear you were really smooth when you drove that water truck right straight into the ditch, right next to a driveway!

It seems Fink had to return the plywood. I guess the Major found out where he "borrowed" it!

I hear Mr. Gilles had another extra trip to operations this week. This time to return an SOI he had forgotten!

Maintenance, you don't have to worry. I won't tell anyone what went on (?) in your hooch payday night. (For a piece, uh, er, price, that is!)

When I asked what the 1st Sgt. had done this week, they said, "That's just the trouble, he ain't done nothing!"

Sgt. Rodman, diapers are going to become a mandatory supply item for you if you ruin one more set of undershorts. I think THREE sets are enough for ANY Sgt. to ruin!

Mr. Adams, were you really looking for a HONDA SHOP in Saigon? At 05:00!!

Sgt. Yelle, Blackwell said, "Stay in your own bed, I'm not young and tender!"

Sgt. Rivera said those doors were so drunk he didn't know which one to go through. It seems he picked the wrong one and sprained his hand!

Sgt. Webster and Sp/5 Childress must be given credit. After two years each in Nam, they went to Saigon together and were taken for $50.00 each. CONGRATULATION, FISH!

For the second time, Sp/5 Childress went into one of our urinals. I guess we ought to congratulate him but I still don't think it compares to Army chow!

Who is the officer that manages to eat at the Chinese restaurant ONLY when "6" is flying? Know anything about that Cpt. Fernandes?

Our outside-insidious informer tells us that the 135th is now starting a newspaper. It will be called "EMU BIRDSHEET"!

I've been asked why the EDITOR of this paper never gets written up. Well, it's because I NEVER do anything wrong! (Ed.)

Sgt. Meers really busted his _____ when he fell down the stairs of the maintenance trailer yesterday!

C◆WB◆Y

BULLSHEET

| VOLUME 3 | 10 AUGUST 1969 | NUMBER 14 |

There seems to be some controversy throughout the company as to the validity of the BullSheet. That even one person thinks the BullSheet doesn't print the truth--the whole truth--and nothing but the truth, is the most preposterous, impetuous, insolent, outlandish piece of rumor I've ever heard.

Now why would the solid-reported paper like the BullSheet want to print lies? Our informers are of nothing but topnotch quality. Heaven only knows that our NCO's don't lie, or even stretch the truth, -- I mean, who knows the real truth about Top and Sandy, -- except Top and Sandy. Is Sgt. La Brie really in trouble? Only his hooch-maid knows for sure!!!!

So you see COWBOYS, although we can't print the real truth, we can let a little of it invade some of our lines and still get it printed.

Now keep that information coming in. I'm sure they can't censor all of it!!!!

BE PROFESSIONAL
STAY ALERT * * * STAY ALIVE

FROM THE HORSES' MOUTH

You guys are OUTSTANDING. The barracks really looked good. Our challenge is to maintain the high standards we have attained.

Would you believe we have another battalion inspection 15 Sept.? This will be another CMMI type inspection. I also have a very strong suspicion we will receive a 1st. Aviation Brigade CMMI during September. That's the granddaddy of 'em all.

Sgt. La Brie has taken over as Re-enlistment NCO. I know a lot of you have questions on the VRB and/or your re-enlistment options. Please feel free to contact Sgt. La Brie, Lt. Gould, or myself anytime you have a question. Remember--$8,000 bucks can be yours--RE-UP!

The battalion Commander recently reiterated his policy on flight uniforms. Everyone will wear NOMEX flight suit, NOMEX gloves, leather boots, a chicken plate, helmet, and ID tags. Let's get behind this policy. It's for our safety.

COWBOY 6

SAFETY SPOOK

071002 -- UH-1H--Major*-AC misjudged height of hut during LOW LEVEL flight. Tail stinger hit ground causing major structural damage to tail boom. (USABAAR Weekly Summary 14-20 July)

No height was listed for the hut in question, but how many HUTS have you seen that are more than 10 feet high? Even 15 feet is still too low for helicopter pilots. The circumstances of the LOW-LEVEL flying are not given, but still wouldn't justify being that low.

A speculated guess would be: "demonstrating low level technique and proficiency to a new pilot, with emphasis on cyclic manipulation to avoid obstacles in flight path." Or maybe: "high speed contour flying, demonstrating evasive maneuvers."

Anyway, it's looked at, flying at hut level is a blatant display of mental slowness, a lack of sound reasoning, and deliberate misuse of Government property!!

INSIDIOUS INFORMER

Sgt. Bull has a good thing going in the company with his "strip tease" act. I hear it is really outstanding and the pictures Sgt. Marin got of it are NUMBAH ONE!!!

With an outstanding display of military boarding, Cpt. LaGault diligently marched to the front of the platoon, did a left face and in a military voice gave "close ranks, march" -- while Lt. Czeak was in the third rank inspecting rifles!

Who were the men that were caught in Long Thanh last week by the Mousekateers? Their excuse sounded legitimate, they were buying a duck for the company party! The Mousekateers let them go!

Someone in the orderly room went to the Dr. this week "just to be sure." It's a good thing he did, he had it!!!

Hey Wannamae, that peanut butter taste in your mouth was exactly that. The hooch maids fed you peanut butter in your sleep and you didn't even know it. Light sleeper, huh?

Sgt. Longo, you had better watch who you tell to come see you if he wants to talk to you. Especially if it's a Major and he's standing right behind you!

I asked Locke if he had anything for the paper this week and he said no and walked off. I found out later that he had driven a truck into the ditch this week. Just didn't want to talk about it, I guess!!

Cpt. Johnson found out the hard way that courier missions are not for snivs. With only a few days left, he was shot down while "sniving."

Is it true that things are so dull for the Falcons now that they are making rocket runs on cemetery stones?

Sgt. Marin was seen running frantically toward the latrine this week. Could he be another Sgt. Rodman?!

When the cat's away, the mouse will play. It seems as if Sgt. Critchlow has been making eyes at Sandy while Top has his back turned!

I heard that Ready had a pretty good fall this week--from the top of a chopper. Never fear though, he had a good cushion. Old lightweight himself, SP/5 Condry was there to cushion his fall.

Did you hear about Gorup backing over an APU? With a three-quarter, no less. He put that truck right on top of that little ole startin' machine.

Sgt. Peacock, FIVE TIMES! (HA, HA!) IMPOSSIBLE! You were only in Saigon one day, NOT two weeks!

It seems as if he isn't the only one who goes to Saigon for supplies and got it . . . the supplies too!

Since we're on the subject, we had a few EM's get caught by the Mousekateers the other night. They were just sitting behind this table in the dark when the Mousekateer found them with his flashlight!

MIRACLE MAINTENANCE: 572 was written up for a rod end bearing so Hurley went out and changed it, -- on 527!

Sgt. Peacock and Sgt. Meers have been keeping a dog in their hooch. It turns out now that she is pregnant. BUT I'M NOT INSINUATION ANYTHING, SARGE!

C◆WB◆Y

BULLSHEET

VOLUME 3   16 AUGUST 1969   NUMBER 15

OPERATION RE*UP AND TIGHTEN-UP IN EFFECT

The rangeland is starting to look pretty strak now since the beginning of "Operation tighten-up and RE-UP."

The company has started tightening up with the procurement of enough paint to change the color of the exteriors of all the hooches in the company. Coinciding with the new "spring" look is the planting of palm trees in appropriate places to help bring a "livable" look to our company area.

The RE-UP portion of the operation is being supervised by SSgt. La Brie, who just recently took over the job as re-enlistment NCO. The cry, which not too long ago was banned from being said in the COWBOYS when morale dropped to an all-time low, is now being spoken again. "RE-UP" can now be heard from early morning till late at night. Moral is climbing toward a height long unknown by the COWBOYS and many of our "first termers" are now seriously considering the re-enlistment benefits.

Let's keep up the outstanding work COWBOYS, and not only say but also prove to our competitors why we are the Best in the Delta.

FROM THE HORSES' MOUTH

A lot of you have heard me talk about khaki corpuscles. What am I referring too? Basically, I'm directing my comments toward a "state of mind"--an attitude--a philosophy.

Now wait you say--You didn't ask to join the Army nor did you ask to come to NAM. True; however, the fact remains here you are in beautiful downtown Bear Cat.

Whether you're a lifer or one of Uncle Sam's' chosen few, your attitude can make your stay more enjoyable. Your attitude also contributes to the team effort. The team effort contributes to the morale and sprite that makes the company go.

I enjoin each of you to check your attitude. Are you contributing? It takes each and every one of you to make the COWBOYS the Best in the Delta. Do your part.

COWBOY 6

SAFETY SPOOK

A lot has been written about Aviation safety but no matter how many accident free months a company has on its Aviation record, the accent and/or glory seems to be pointed toward the rated aviator or pilot. No one seems to give a second thought to the other two members of the crew that gives that familiar sound, "Clear Right, Sir," or "Clear Left, Sir." The only time the crew is mentioned is when a weapon accidentally discharges or when suppression is needed.

It is about time all Aviators say thanks to each crew chief and each gunner, for without their familiar: "Clear down right, Sir," "Aircraft at Three O'clock, Sir," "Don't swing your tail, Sir," or any other of the numerous phrases spoken by them, Aviation would definitely have a great many more accidents.

So thanks crew. You are our eyes to the left, right, and rear, and you're doing one helluva job!!

EVERYONE SHOULD BE WEARING NOMEX FLIGHT SUITS AND HAVE GLOVES. LET'S "TIGHTEN-UP!"

INSIDIOUS INFORMER

Another one of the competitors of Top asked Sandy to sit on his lap. Everything was going fine till the chair collapsed. Isn't that right, Sgt. Meers??!!

Rodriquez was holding a famed position of the hand the other day and Major Stiles walked out the door. It's surprising how fast he can straighten out those fingers!

SP/5 Berryman went to Saigon to visit "his" girl the other day. This time he walked in and found Sgt. Peacocks' name scribbled on the wall. Not bad for an old man, Sarge!

Childress is well again. He's hitting the bottle once more. In fact, he has become a member of the "Blue Blazer" club.

Sgt. Yelle has started a "Blue Blazer" club. Anyone wanting to join may contact him. He said the initiations rough.

I hear the Falcons are changing their name to the 335th Penicillin platoon. I'd never guess why unless it's that moldy bread (sic) they're keeping!

Mr. Ross and Mr. Store hit a "little" bird and cracked the windshield. Fellas, "little" birds don't fly at 2500 feet!!!

Our motor pool Sgt. had a flat tire on his truck. That's OK, except he had to "beat" the lock off to get to his jack. Keys do wonders, Sgt. Critchlow!!

One of our EM's was on all fours making "oinks" like a pig then singing "You are my Sunshine" to his hooch-maid. No resemblance, I hope!!

Hollaman, there's a regulation about impersonating a Major. Just because you put on an old hat you found. Did it really help you get the parts you wanted??

Maintenance write-up on 545: Pilots attitude inop. (No offense, Lt. Shafer!)

Say Mr. Mayl, did Bear Cat tower really move runway 05 or were you just practicing hovering over the berm with your landing light on??

We have a new couple in the company (boy and girl, that is). It looks like Popa and Linda, from the EM club.

No Machado, we weren't given life preservers because they are planning a CA on Borneo! Mr. Speanberg, you better quit Bull_____ our younger EM too!

Mr. Story is definitely having his troubles. Last time he couldn't find Ben Tre, this time he couldn't find Schroeder, No Mr. Story, they don't keep moving those places to confuse Charlie!

Sgt. Webster is now walking on crutches and missed out on three days in Saigon. That's OK Sarge, If you blew $50.00 in five minutes one morning, you couldn't afford three days in Saigon anyway!

Who are the guys that were stopped by the Mousekateers just for driving by Rosie's and looking suspicious? Maybe Rodriquez or Glover could tell us!

It is now time for us to reiterate weapons' safety. No weapons or ammo in the billet's area. Let's not accidentally zap a buddy!

THIRTY SECONDS FOR SAFETY

C◆WB◆Y

BULLSHEET

VOLUME 3   23 AUGUST 1969   NUMBER 16

COWBOYS BRAVE STORM TO SEE FLOOR SHOW

The COWBOYS proved this week that they are not only versatile but also completely DIEN CAI DAU when it comes to watching a floor show.

A rain storm was situated over Bear Cat that had caused an electrical power failure. The COWBOYS defeated that little obstruction by bringing a generator from the flight line to the company area. So now we had the electricity and the rain had even stopped so everything was "go" with the show.

The show commenced amid applause and cheers. Just as everyone started to relax and shun the chills brought on by the previous storm, another rain started. A few were sent running for rain jackets but the majority braved the storm and ended up getting soaked. Nevertheless, the show continued and so did our photographers.

Once again, the COWBOYS prove the old Chinese cliché, "Neither lack of electricity nor rain can stop the show." Remember that one?

SAFETY IS EVERYONE'S BUSINESS

FROM THE HORSES' MOUTH

F.O.D. -- FOREIGN OBJECT DAMAGE.

What is a foreign object? When we are talking about a turbine engine, we're referring to screwdrivers, dzus fasteners, safety wire, and the like. Foreign object damage is when something other than air is ingested into the engine. The turbine blades get chewed-up, power is lost, and an engine is ruined. Let's all be aware of FOD. For safety reasons, and economical reasons, let's fight FOD.

Another show is planned for 31 August and on 1 September, we'll have a company party. Then we'll have to put our noses to the grindstone for the CMMI. I want the COWBOYS to be the best in the battalion. Don't let the COWBOYS down. Do a little extra.

COWBOY 6

SAFETY SPOOK

"Margin of Safety" is a split-second decision at a critical time of emergency. It is a hair trigger reflex action. It is an observant crew chief or gunner who are our eyes in the backs of our heads. It is an AC who insists on running a "tight ship."

PFC Clark, 2nd, Plt. CE, observed an AC's door had become unlatched and was vibrating enroute to the LZ. Plenty of time to make the necessary adjustments before it became a dangerous condition during the approach or landing. WELL DONE--you prevented a possibly serious incident.

Full suppression doesn't mean the pilots have to suppress with an M-16 or his 38. Our job is to fly them-- SAFELY! The pilot who is not on the controls should monitor the instruments, be ready to take the controls IMMEDIATELY if necessary. Suppressing out his door will not allow immediate reaction and distracts from more important duties.

INSIDIOUS INFORMER

Say Mr. Troxell, don't you know you can't fire rockets by pressing the force trim button? Even your gunner knew that!!!

What's this about Jones digging in the garbage can for chicken? You really don't have to do that; the mess hall would have given you seconds.

What's this about one of our maintenance officers running up 385 without any engine oil? Maybe you know, Lt. Czeak!! I'm not even going to mention what happened to it this week!!!

Hurley, are you really going to RE-UP for a haircut?? Dig those bennies, man!!!

Which one of our cooks can't go to sleep at night unless he's sucking his thumb?? What's wrong Orr, don't you get enough to eat??!!!

I think everyone in the company ought to get a pink shirt like Hibbards. He said it really helped him get the girls while on R&R. The pink shirt plus some long green, that is!!!

If someone doesn't do something about the rain we're having around here, the COWBOYS will have to name their stage "The Mud-A-Go-Go."

KIDS WILL BE KIDS . . . Lt. Goulds' girl sent him a Frisbee for his birthday.

Two NCO's were walking to the shower the other night when they heard a beautiful wolf whistle. When they turned around, who was standing there but our sexless "6." Looked good, huh?

Would you believe Jones is trying to get to Saigon for three days? His excuse is his mother is there and he wants to see her!

It is rumored that Cpt. Fernandes is going to move his office closer to the Officers' club. Could it be because of the new girl they have working there?

Mr. Speanberg actually had a lesson on sanitation from a mama-san this week on defecating in a rice paddy. Embarrassing, huh?

Sgt. Critchlow was showing one of his young troopers how to fill out a requisition form this week with a sample copy. I don't know what he ordered but somehow it got forwarded to the 590th with the other forms. It was returned marked, UNAVAILABLE HERE, CHECK SAIGON!

Mr. Morrison became an official "Blue Blazer" this week. Not bad for a guy that doesn't even drink....

Mr. Bisson, how in world did you ever earn the nickname "Sam Sincere"?

Mr. Bramblett, I'm supposed to write you up but I don't know how to word it. All I can say is, ALL you maintenance Officers are really coming through!

What's this about a Cowboy Free Press starting just so they can get this editor's name printed once in a while.

The COWBOYS have many personnel with many varied talents. The following is an article submitted by one of our EM's who likes to write.

'SHE'

I had just laid down and made myself comfortable when I felt something was wrong. Then I knew. Wave after wave of evil mysticism cascaded through my mind and body. I was fighting a losing battle and felt the end was near. Then she was there with me. I felt her pulling the covers tighter and tighter around my neck. All my doubts were absolved when I reached up to the head of my bed to feel her long fingers pull yet tighter on the blanket constricting my throat. Terror clutched my mind and I said, "Why?" Her only answer was, "For the one you sent in your place!"

THIRTY SECONDS ISN'T LONG COMPARED TO A
LIFETIME. TAKE TIME FOR SAFETY!

C◆WB◆Y
BULLSHEET

| VOLUME 3 | 8 SEPTEMBER 1969 | NUMBER 17 |

COWBOYS RAGE BECAUSE BULLSHEET EDITION IS LATE!!!

Why is it when I ask someone what they have for the BullSheet the reply is, "I'm getting short!" Even the ones that have more time left over here than myself tell me they are short.

What is this short-timers' attitude that starts to develop within two months after arriving over here?

Is it a way of kidding other more recent arrivals? Maybe it's a way we have of kidding ourselves that "a year isn't really too long."

Well, let me tell you--a year really isn't too long--if you're with your girl, or maybe in your favorite bar, or just "back in the world." BUT . . . (and that's a big BUT) let me say that a year over here is 365 LLOONNGG days--8,710 grudgingly long hours, or one hell of a long time when you're just waiting for it to pass!!

I'm only a double-digit midget but I'm still "short" compared to 3/4 of the company. So, eat your hearts out fellows and I'll see you "BACK IN THE WORLD!"

ACCIDENTS ARE PLENTIFUL, BUT DON'T
SHARE ONE WITH YOUR BUDDY!

FROM THE HORSES' MOUTH

ZAP! -- There went the Brigade CMMI team. It's over. We were satisfactory (by the skin of our teeth). The lesson learned I believe is that we lack quality control in all areas relating to our equipment. Operator maintenance is the key to success. Let's all jump in with both feet and benefit from the inspection. I want to thank all of you for the hard work and cooperation. We're going to try again for our show this Sunday night.

I feel I must say a word about driving. Too many people speed. The maximum speed limit on this post is 20 MPH. A lot of streets are posted 15 MPH. The roads are full of holes and ruts. Going slow and hitting these ruts is bad enough but hitting them while speeding is causing the vehicles to be damaged. Conserve our equipment. Drive Carefully. Speeding tickets are given and a few people have paid the fine recently.

Let's all enjoy the show Sunday. Also, we'll have a BAR-B-Q on Monday.

COWBOY 6

SAFETY SPOOK

The following is a strange but true story: A helicopter landed at a certain airfield with the pilot as the only person on board. After landing, the pilot left the ship while it was still running. An instant later the helicopter was observed to be approximately two feet off the ground and rapidly spinning counterclockwise. The pilot avoided the tail rotor then began to run in the same direction as the helicopter was rotating. He caught up with it, climbed in the right side and brought the aircraft down to the ground. In a few minutes he called the tower, said he knew what happened and requested takeoff clearance. This was given and he departed the area.

Even though this pilot kept his cool after things started happening, it was a mental lapse on his part that caused the incident. It is a lot easier to think before acting than trying to recover gracefully.

INSIDIOUS INFORMER

I say congratulations to Howard in the mess hall for brushing his teeth with Brylecream. Did a little dab really do you??!!

Several officers became Blue Blazers this week. Among those are Major Stiles who burned his lip and Lt. Czeak who scorched his mustache.

Reese really pulled a boner this week. He installed a cyclic backwards then wondered why the buttons were on the wrong side. Way to go, dumb-dumb!!

Mr. Williams earned his flight pay this week for the next 2 1/2 months. He finally flew and ended up logging 11 hours.

Mr. Proulxs' R&R was not only expensive but he is still paying for it. OUCH!! Those shots sure do smart!!

Who was it that was eating breakfast the other morning and just flat fell out of his chair?? Just what did you have in your coffee, Finney??!!

Wojnicki has now joined Sgt. Rodman as a full-fledged member of the "Diaper Club." How are we going to explain this to your wife? Incidentally, to become a member, one must___his pants!!

Someone told me that "big, fat, Ernest" didn't have a thing to do except lay down and roll through the green house!!

Sgt. Peacock said that he wasn't going to Saigon anymore because it broke him -- physically and financially. I guess he has something better here in the company Incidentally, those little white pups sure are cute!!!

I hear the suggestion box in maintenance is being changed to request for promotion box.

Just wanted to let everyone know that Jones didn't get his three-day pass to Saigon to see his mother. Good try, Jonesie!

Sgt. Critchlow isn't talking to Sandy much since Top has returned to the company. Don't worry Sgt. Critchlow, right after an R&R an old sergeant like that is too weak to be dangerous!

SP/4 Thompson was given $10.00 to get quarters for the jute box for the EM club. He came back with $10.00 worth of MPC divided up neatly into twenty-five cent stacks!!!

Mr. Speanburg is really a dirty old man, but I don't dare print why, for the sake of my own health!

Well, maybe it isn't all as bad as the headline's state--in fact, no one has even missed the BullSheet. One EM missed it, I heard him tell a cook he wished the BullSheet would come out, the latrine was out of paper. That doesn't make me feel bad though, look at Mr. Sears, or Mr. Roebuck. They spent 40 years doing nothing but printing pretty toilet paper--in booklet form, no less!! So, one of these days fellas, you might be able to say, "I knew BullSheet 6 when he first started out, printing one sheet of toilet paper at a time!"

C◆WB◆Y
BULLSHEET

VOLUME 3   13 SEPTEMBER 1969   NUMBER 18

YEAH!! YEAH!! COWBOYS REACH 100% AVAILABLOOP!!!

The word heard around the company for our three-day standby was "100% availability for the slicks and gunships." That slogan was put to a rough test Thursday morning when 385 went down just prior to takeoff. Fifty minutes later, 527 was down at Dong Tam for an Engine chip detector light. Only a short time after that, C&C went down with what was thought to be FOD. It was FOD all right--a round through the engine!! When the secondary fire team was called out, they were unable to get off the ground because of a dead battery and an inoperative fuel control. While all this was taking place, 775 had just taken a round in the transmission from a VN (?) that had just gotten off his ship.

The word quickly reached our maintenance and the word was passed, "Send one slick to the AO" --which was immediately changed to "send one slick and one gunship," "No, send two slicks and one gun!" The final word became law, "Send ALL the slicks and guns to the AO!"

Finally, after little hesitation, a "Bravo" team was enroute to relieve the "A" team that had just made its first insertion with a grand total of three slicks!

The join-up between the teams was made in the AO but now one more problem arises. What to do with the maintenance personnel who brought the ships in relief? The answer: stay at Dong Tam until a ship becomes available for a one-way flight home. AAHH . . . SIGH!! A full commitment at last . . . OH NO!! WHAT'S THIS??!!! One of the relief ships is now breaking out of the flight because of negative radio communications. Now what? The hooks are weathered in and won't be able to get to the downed aircraft till the ceiling rises.

Finally, everything seemed to get straightened out--after much contemplated suicide on the part of Charlie-Charlie.

It seemed as if our 100% availability turned into a slapstick of comedy for the COWBOYS. Oh well, we'll try again tomorrow--MAYBE!

FROM THE HORSES' MOUTH

Yes, I think you could say Thursday was "The Week That Was" all in one day! Guess it's all in a day's work. Congratulations go to the maintenance team headed by WO Ross and WO Williams, Jr. Also, BOC (If they can read) we appreciated the rapid hook response.

The three days down last week gave everyone a nice rest, and maintenance a chance to catch up. Let's keep up the high availability. KEEP CHARGING!

COWBOY 6

SAFETY SPOOK
(Aviator Code of Conduct)

1.   I am an American flying man. I am entrusted with the technical maintenance and mechanical operation of 335th Avn. Co. (Aslt Hel) aircraft. I will fulfill these responsibilities to the best of my ability and training.

2.   I am responsible for the life and welfare of the air crews and passengers who ride my aircraft. I will perform the highest quality preflight inspection and follow all regulations to assure the safety of each flight.

3.   I will allow no personal considerations of desire to affect performance of duty. I will remember that a crew as a team is no stronger than its weakest member. I will endeavor to be a crewman of sound technical training and good moral character.

4.   I will keep my tools and equipment in top condition. I will remember that a clean aircraft is a well-maintained aircraft, and a clean crew a good crew.

5.   I will keep both myself and my flying machine within the flight envelope. I will never push my aircraft beyond its capabilities, nor will I perform duty when my own mental or physical condition ....pilot error.

6.   I pledge perpetual loyalty and faithfulness to my God, my country, my fellow-airmen, and myself. I will do everything possible to ensure the success of each mission and the safe return of the aircraft.

INSIDIOUS INFORMER

Let us welcome Mr. Schray and Mr. Bother to the COWBOYS. Mr. Schray reported in wearing crew-members' wings and Mr. Bother bought a new lock and locked both sets of keys in his locker!! AND YOU'RE REALLY EXPECTING TO FLY?

Are you smoking more and enjoying it less? Mr. Blair doesn't think so. Why just the other night, he came into the EM club with two cigarettes hanging out of his nose. Must be drinking with those Blue Blazers again!

SP/6 Fink almost blew his mind the night of the party. He came into the EM club and found Major Stiles circle red X'd. Status: Checked and found within limits!

I've heard of good clubs, but Mike Medalis must run the best one in Vietnam. Eleven people were carried out the other night. Just what are you putting in those cokes anyway, Mike?

I've seen Sgt. Popa walking around with an FM on Mines and Booby traps. Maybe he can tell us what happened the other night down at the old supply room!

I guess Golden and Ranney are getting ready for next summers' Olympics. Fellas, the pool opens at 10:00 A.M. and is much larger than the ditches in the company!

Hey Moore, did you really fill up your 3/4 with diesel fuel?

I hear SP/4 Bailey is opening up his own education office. It's located right across the street from the panther club and only costs $5.00 per course. Just what are you teaching anyway?

Maybe Hooker should take a little math course. While taking a field phone out to bunker 21, he was challenged with a pass number. We all know that 9 and 6 don't add up to 14. Isn't that right, Hook?

Did you know that our ships won't start without the ignition circuit breaker in? One of our maintenance pilots didn't. Right, Mr. Bisson?

Sgt. Meuser was showing a new gunner how to jettison the rocket pods and did it right in the revetment. Next time sarge, unload the rockets!

Did I see Lt. Czeak swimming in the ditch by the maintenance hooch the other night?

Say McKay, you didn't really drive a deuce-and-a-half into the PC trailer, did you?

Hurley is really a Sad Sack. In fact, just outside camp Swampy there is a town named Hurleyburg, right, Sack.

So, you really thought the VC were shooting at you, huh Golden? Next time try securing the chains on your truck, stupid!

(WHEN YOU'RE OUT OF HAMMS--YOU'RE OUT OF BEAR!)

C◆WB◆Y
BULLSHEET

VOLUME 3	10 OCTOBER 1969	NUMBER 20

TO THE HOMEWARD BOUND RANCH HANDS

With a number of illustrious COWBOYS about to depart on DEROS, it seems only appropriate to warn you that you aren't leaving "Marvin the Arvin" behind you. Indeed, your observations regarding the superior knowledge, intelligence, and coordination of Marvin may continue to flourish long after your return to the world.

At Fort Bragg recently; the activation of the fire alarm system at John F. Kennedy Hall emptied the building and brought fire trucks with sirens screaming and red lights flashing. A thorough search revealed no fire. An investigation uncovered the culprit--a Vietnamese Jr. Officer student whose understanding of English was quite literal. With a cigarette poised between his lips, needing a light, he did what the sign on the was said: "PULL FOR FIRE."

At Fort Wolters a few months ago the tower operator made the following radio transmission; "Aircraft hovering on 'Charlie Panel' say ID." A response with a distinct Vietnamese accent came back saying nonetheless exactly what was asked of him: "ID."

So, to you destined COWBOYS soon to depart from the confines of our temporal city of Bear Cat for the world we say: Marvin is already there--TDY.

FROM THE HORSES' MOUTH

A special welcome to the new "Cougar 6," LTC Baughman. In 1966, he was Cowboy "6" as the COWBOYS supported the 173rd Airborne Brigade. Let's show him the COWBOYS are still tops in aviation support.

A special thanks to the "Proud Crowd." The aircraft availability has been outstanding.

Everything is sailing along smoothly now. Let's keep up the good work especially in vehicle and aircraft maintenance.

COWBOY 6

SAFETY SPOOK

UNABLE TO READ

INSIDIOUS INFORMER

Rumor has it that the 335th is getting one of the biggest groups in the world to come play here. We don't know much about it, so any more questions should be directed to ### "6." I wonder how many orphans they have.

Mr. Dilts is a real killer. Why, the other day he got a Dink with his Tail Rotor Blade. I think the "Falcons" might be scoping him out.

Speaking of the Falcons, I hear the VC started throwing mud at your ship "83" you know you must be doing something right.

We hear the NCO Club has done it again. The victims this time were Critchlow, Lundberg, and Mr. Smith. Those bottles of wine sure were strong weren't they, MEN?

1st Sgt. tells us that Hibbard is the only trooper he knows that gets four day's bed rest for getting the Thai Club Infection. Sure must have been hard to take, right Hibbard?

Lutes, I hear you aren't getting your money's worth. Your section leader told us all about your stay in Saigon, King. There aren't many people who get lost in Saigon, are there?

SPORTS FLASH ******

Volleyball--Sin City OFFS 22, 2nd Plt EM 20 despite the efforts of Jumping Bean Copeland and Bouncing Bailey the all-stars defeated them by the close score of 22 vs. 20. Things looked good for the All-Bear Cat and All-Vietnam EM Champs, but then a resounding comeback by the Sinners led by Leaping Bleekert and Speedy Fisher, the Officers squeaked by to win.

How does it taste, Bailey? Also, about that mike cord. Avionics will forgive you someday but those Dinks, NEVER!

Are you shaving more and getting more and more cut up? Souza has the easiest answer. He does it every day. He shaves without a blade in his razor. Try it sometime won't you?

There is a rumor going in the 2nd Plt Officers Hooch that Mr. Schray and Mr. Galloway might become permanent duty officers. Now you know what I was talking about. All the Newbees get all the details.

There is only one man in the 335th who sits down when shaking a Colonel's hand. What did they teach you in Basic, Brown? How You Gonna Act?

EDITORIAL

WO1 Larry Morrison left for Japan early Friday morning the 10th of October. His work around the Cowboy Corral for the past few months is still really appreciated. We only wish our thanks could be expressed in a bigger way. Mr. Morrison held down the job of full time AC in the 1st Platoon and additional duties of the 1st Platoon IP (flying on his days off), Officer Club custodian (making detailed reports to HQ each month) and editor of our Delta Famous "BULLSHEET," plus anything that was asked of him during one of his busy days. Mr. Morrison's symbolic of the phrase; "Give a busy man something extra to do and he'll find the time to do it."

Larry, the COWBOYS of the 335th wish you a speedy recovery from your operation in Japan and a safe return flight back to the world.

THOUGHT FOR THE WEEK

"Some people's idea of free speech is that they are free to say what they like, but if anyone says anything back, that is an outrage." WINSTON CHURCHILL

C◆WB◆Y

BULLSHEET

| VOLUME 3 | 18 OCTOBER 1969 | NUMBER 21 |

THE COWBOY

The rooster crows. The mist rises in the subdued valley. Moisture drapes from the trees. A few lights flicker on into the early morning darkness. A man wipes sleep from his eyes. Putting on his boots takes a little time, for our hero is still a little weary from a long night. After a quick shave and a strong cup of coffee, he feels it's time for him to move out for a full day's work. He checks his weapon and looks over his fine young horse. He must make sure they are in good condition for it's his bread and butter. Without one or the other his job would be no more. The sun is starting to rise over the mountains in the distance and our friend saddles up and gets ready to ride out. A long ride is ahead of him. He finally reaches his destination and is now prepared to carry out his long days work. He knows his area of work very very well, for he has been over it time and time again. He must ride hard today to cover the vast swamps, deep rivers and the land of many trees. He glances up into the clouds to see if it is going to rain. There have been many many days, he remembers that he has ridden through the cold uneasy rains, that chill his bones and wet his clothes. But still he rides on. He senses danger in the air as he nears a river. All is still except for the pounding of his horse. Suddenly, a flash, then smoke and it's all over. Our hero wins again. It goes on like this day after day never stopping to rest, always on the trail. Daring to do what others are afraid to do. The darkness sets in and he heads for home waiting for another day, thinking of what it will bring.

FROM THE HORSES' MOUTH

As the time comes to relinquish the reins as Trail Boss, I cannot help but reflect back over the past 5 months. The COWBOYS have come a long way. The reason we have come a long way is PEOPLE. You, the officers and men of the unit, who go out and do the job. The pleasure of seeing a unit function efficiently, of knowing each man knows his job and wants to perform to the utmost, is most rewarding. That's what puts the COWBOYS on top. As the Senior Advisor to the 9th ARVN said last week, "It's good to work with professionals again." You -- each and every one of you are professionals. Each man contributes to the overall mission accomplishment. We are on the top. The challenge now is to stay on top. Everyone must strive for maximum output. Do not get complacent. KEEP CHARGING

COWBOY 6

SAFETY SPOOK

Landing in Water

For years there has been a debate among helicopter pilots about what to do when you ditch a helicopter. Roll it left, roll it right, don't roll it. What you do depends on the type of helicopter you fly, but two things always hold true for all cases. One, have all the doors open when you contact the water. Two, don't prematurely evacuate the helicopter; wait until the main rotor stops. A lot of injuries and fatalities are caused by rotor blades striking the crew members who have departed early.

INSIDIOUS INFORMER

I hear Steve Floyd, the night spoon, and his coffee machine don't get along too well. I know we have strong coffee but not enough to knock you on the floor. Better check the gas next time, Old Buddy.

The words out. We found out what Mr. Lyons real job is. If you haven't relieved yourself more than three times a day, don't tell anyone. I still don't see how you can keep records up on a thing like that.

Is it true that the COWBOYS have a phantom ship? I don't know, but when Mr. Williams the test pilot avoids flying 649 you know there's something spooky about that. Tell Mr. Williams the crew chief is a ghost too.

It seems to me that Sp/5 Dorris has a new enemy to fight during the day. With the help of a few brave proud crowders the damning NCO led an assault on the powerful enemy. They dropped in smoke and fire bombs and when this failed to drive the force from their positions Sp/5 Dorris attacked single-handily. We all know the outcome of this fierce battle. 1000 Yellow Jackets were driven from their home on the maintenance fork lift and old Dorris managed to escape with one-each-sore head from a hostile Wasp Sting.

I hear the Falcons are giving Avionics personnel OJT flight training. We all know that you can't fly a Ship from the outside, or can you?

Who the HELL is Cowboy One?

Things are really getting up tight with water around here at night. The other night the 1st Sgt. came into the orderly room wearing his shower shoes, and a towel wrapped around his waist with a bar of soap in his hand. I know we keep a fair amount of water in our cooler, Top, but there's not enough to take a proper shower and in the orderly room!

Sp/4 Root has been reading those Sgt. Rock comic books again. The other day while guarding 028 which had gone down in a rice paddy, he was getting kind of shaky when the Grunts got into some contact nearby. He started looking for the crew chief's gun and soon found out that he had taken it with him. Well, the EM did what any good Cowboy EM would do. He grabbed an M-60 barrel and set up his position trying to outfox the VC with his good looks. I know now why they didn't attack.

Capt. Allue is getting pretty short. The other day he called the MP's when his duty truck was missing. As it turned out the truck had run out of gas and was stuck out on the road. Really now, sir, we know you can do a lot with your MACV credit card but road service? You had just better wait till you get back to the world then you can really put a tiger in your tank.

Falcon 90 is really Chicken Man........

1st Lt. Gould lived up to his name as the Midnight Cowboy. The other night while leaving the EMU Officer Club, the upstanding 1st Lt. fell into a ditch of an unbearable smelling substance without spilling a drop of his Scotch and Water. Outstanding job, Lt. Gould, an outstanding job!!!

The Class 6 Store has a new item in stock, wine in steel bottles which are guaranteed unbreakable. This should be a real advantage to the Cowboy Motor Pool, right Tom.

THE MISADVENTURES OF JOHNNY SMACK

We begin our story at the Ft. Benning Induction Station where we find our friend Johnny Smack taking his physical exam for the US Army. "Well you seem fit enough" the doctor said to Johnny. "I feel really great and I can't wait to start Basic Training" (little does he know). After waiting in line for hours and signing his name to piles of papers Johnny is rushed off to the Reception Center at Ft. Benning. Still wearing his best sport coat, his good silk pants and his wing-tipped shoes Johnny steps out of the bus only to be met by a fierce and loudmouthed PFC. Of course, Johnny wants to do his best in the Army and he has read all the Sgt. Rock comic books he could get his hands on so he whips a fine salute on the higher-ranking soldier. "What do you think you're doing Trooper?" the PFC asks: "I work for my money and that's what you guys are going to do." After being rushed through all kinds of paper work, Johnny finally makes it to bed. Sleep at last, (that's what you think Johnny) (pick up the next issue of the BullSheet and find out if Johnny gets some sleep or goes AWOL his first night in the Army) A. HOOKER

COWBOYS

UNIT HISTORY

1 JANUARY 1970 -- 31 DECEMBER 1970

NARRATIVE OF EVENTS

The 335th Assault Helicopter Company began the year of 1970 assigned to the 214th Combat Aviation Battalion, Headquarters, at Vinh Long, RVN. Until August 31 the unit was stationed at Bear Cat, eight miles Northeast of Saigon. Flying in support of the 7th and 9th ARVN Divisions the period of January 1 through May 2nd proved uneventful with Combat Assaults and resupply missions becoming a matter of daily routine.

The month of May ushered in unprecedented action for the COWBOYS. With President Nixon's announcement of the Cambodian invasion the COWBOYS were called upon to fly ground elements and needed supplies into this relatively unknown area of Indochina. Enemy contact was light but with long turn-around flights between home base and the area of operations twelve to fourteen-hour days became commonplace. This held true not only for the flight crews but for everyone in the company. Maintenance teams working around the clock made fourteen ship commitments possible. Following the Cambodian Campaign, the unit received a Presidential Citation for their untiring effort to complete the mission. May 30th found the 335th AHC with a new Company Commander, CPT. Thomas A. Teasdale. Upon completion of their involvement in Cambodia, the COWBOYS returned to support work for the 7th and 9th ARVN Divisions.

Rumors to the effect that the COWBOYS were in for another move started around the company area, however the summer months passed by and no move materialized.

Tragedy struck the unit in July with the death of WO1 Donald A. Krumrei. Mr. Krumrei was killed when his aircraft experienced a tail rotor failure while on short final to a LZ West of Ben Tre. A fine officer and true gentleman, his life was a great loss to the unit, his family, and all his country.

August brought new fire to the transfer rumors and the 31st proved to be the day of truth with the first of many convoys carrying men and equipment South to Dong Tam, the COWBOYS new home. The move was monumental in that aircraft were still flying missions during the four day move.

A new commander, Major Henry J. Raymond was installed and initiated into the COWBOYS on September 1970. October 15 saw history made again with arrival of five (5) Vietnamese Airforce pilots. They were to fly on actual combat missions with COWBOY ACs which, since the move to Dong Tam, carried them to all corners of IV Corps.

Winter arrived and with it the sun and dust. Dong Tam became a virtual "Dust Bowl." PZs and LZs with IFR dust conditions were met without any incidents or accidents whatsoever. Christmas came with a cease-fire and a day of rest.

December 29 was to become a day the COWBOYS would not soon forget. While making a third and final extraction from a PZ in the U'Minh Forest a flight of five (5) "Slicks" was caught in an ambush staged by NVA Regulars as the aircraft were lifting off. WO1 Peter L. Smith in the lead aircraft was critically injured with five (5) rounds which resulted in five (5) wounds. Seconds later the engine failed and his copilot, WO1 Alex Garcia autorotated the aircraft to a safe and upright position. Without any gunship coverage Chalk 2 dropped down to rescue the stranded and injured crew members while the remaining three "Slicks" suppressed the enemy held tree line. Mr. Smith was taken to Binh Tui and later medivaced to Ft. Lenard Wood, MO. 1970 closed with another cease fire, celebrating and hopes for a better 1971.

AWARDS AND DECORATION 1970

AWARD	RECOMMENDED	RECEIVED	PENDING
Army Commendation Medal	391	347	44
Basic Air Medal	78	66	12
Distinguished Flying Cross	37	19	18
Bronze Star	97	76	21
Purple Heart	14	12	2
Air Medal "V"	83	75	8

	TOTAL HOURS	CARGO	PAX	SORT	HITS H/B	VC KILLS	VC STRUC	SAMPANS
JAN	2119	10429	46	6421	14/64	20	106	43
FEB	2879	26028	142	7991	7/7	21	65	7
MAR	2928	15007	127	1940	11/41	57	212	165
APR	3229	20868	98	1643	10/30	55	366	12
MAY	3102	14643	77	6478	4/16	28	174	113
JUN	3044	16523	189	8570	8/22	87	347	383
JUL	2488	18464	122	7886	7/10	80	474	172
AUG	2572	15496	81	7449	20/50	120	478	263
SEP	1805	14771	147	5996	7/40	56	86	77
OCT	2083	11274	99	6150	24/38	62	98	63
NOV	1899	11274	95	5904	7/16	38	69	54
DEC	2472	11421	78	6419	3/23	21	235	227
TOTAL	30,610	184,898	1,396	84,856	122/357	645	2,610	1,669

History of the 335th A.H.C. – 1970

The Vietnam conflict has ushered in the era of the helicopter. Each day history is made. You, the officers and men of the 335th Aviation Company (Aslt Hel) are part of that history. The COWBOYS have traveled the length and breadth of Vietnam. You the soldiers of today inherit a proud tradition.

The COWBOYS were originally Company A, 82nd Aviation Bn, and were stationed at Fort Bragg, North Carolina. With the increase in troop strength in early 1965, Company A, 82nd Aviation Battalion was selected for deployment to Vietnam. In April 1965, the COWBOYS settled in Bien Hoa and were the direct support of the 173rd Airborne Brigade. The Ramrods, Mustangs, and Falcons became synonymous with truly outstanding airmobile support as the COWBOYS rode herd on "Charlie" throughout the III Corps Tactical Zone. Bien Hoa was home until May 1967 when the 173rd Airborne Brigade moved to the Pleiku, Kontum, Dak To area. In August, the unit again moved. This time to Phu Hiep just south of Tuy Hoa on the south China Seacoast. These were rough days as the COWBOYS lived out of duffel bags and Bien Hoa was still considered home. In November, the 335th Avn Co (Aslt Hel) once again flew to battle in the Dak To area. While supporting the 173rd Airborne Brigade on Operation MacArthur, the COWBOYS were awarded The Presidential Unit Citation. On 31 December 1967, the 335th Avn Co (Aslt Hel) was reassigned to the 17th Combat Aviation Group and to the 268th Combat Aviation Battalion located at Phu Hiep.

The unit's mission was still to support the 173rd Airborne Brigade. The mission finally changed in March of 1968, and the unit was in general support of the II Corps Tactical Zone.

In December, the COWBOYS were once again on the move. This trail lead to Bear Cat. The unit was attached for all purposes to the 214th Combat Aviation Battalion. The COWBOYS began flying missions in support of ARVN Forces in the IV Corps Tactical Zone supporting the 7th and 9th ARVN Divisions.

In July of 1969, the COWBOYS were assigned to the 214th Combat Aviation Battalion, 164th Combat Aviation Group.

The year 1970 brought sweeping changes to the COWBOYS," the most important of which was the move to Dong Tam. On August 31 the transfer commenced, lasting 4 days, while still flying the missions provided by battalion.

A new commander, Major Henry J. Raymond, succeeding Cpt Thomas Teasdale, was installed and initiated into the COWBOYS on Sept. 19.

October 15th saw history made again with the arrival of five (5) Vietnamese Air Force pilots. Vietnamezation of the war had become a reality to the 335th AHC and for the COWBOYS it meant a big step had been taken on the long road home.

This book is dedicated to WO1 Donald A Krumrei, a fellow Cowboy who gave his life for his country.

COWBOYS

UNIT HISTORY

1 JANUARY 1971 -- 31 DECEMBER 1971

History of the 335th A.H.C. – 1971

The Vietnam conflict has ushered in the era of the helicopter. Each day history is made. You, the officers and men of the 335th Aviation Company (Aslt Hel) are part of that history. The COWBOYS have traveled the length and breadth of Vietnam. You, the soldiers of today inherit a proud tradition.

The COWBOYS were originally Company A, 82nd Aviation Bn, and were stationed at Fort Bragg, North Carolina. With the increase in troop strength in early 1965, Company A, 82nd Aviation Battalion was selected for deployment to Vietnam. In April 1965, the COWBOYS settled in Bien Hoa and were the direct support of the 173rd Airborne Brigade. The Ramrods, Mustangs, and Falcons became synonymous with truly outstanding airmobile support as the COWBOYS rode herd on "Charlie" throughout the III Corps Tactical Zone. Bien Hoa was home until May 1967 when the 173rd Airborne Brigade moved to the Pleiku, Kontum, Dak To area. In August, the unit again moved. This time to Phu Hiep just south of Tuy Hoa on the south China Seacoast. These were rough days as the COWBOYS lived out of duffel bags and Bien Hoa was still considered home. In November, the 335th Avn Co (Aslt Hel) once again flew to battle in the Dak To area. While supporting the 173rd Airborne Brigade on Operation MacArthur, the COWBOYS were awarded The Presidential Unit Citation. On 31 December 1967, the 335th Avn Co (Aslt Hel) was reassigned to the 17th Combat Aviation Group and to the 268th Combat Aviation Battalion located at Phu Hiep.

The unit's mission was still to support the 173rd Airborne Brigade. The mission finally changed in March of 1968, and the unit was in general support of the II Corps Tactical Zone.

In December, the COWBOYS were once again on the move. This trail lead to Bear Cat. The unit was attached for all purposes to the 214th Combat Aviation Battalion. The COWBOYS began flying missions in support of ARVN Forces in the IV Corps Tactical Zone supporting the 7th and 9th ARVN Divisions.

In July of 1969, the COWBOYS were assigned to the 214th Combat Aviation Battalion, 164th Combat Aviation Group.

The year 1970 brought sweeping changes to the COWBOYS," the most important of which was the move to Dong Tam. On August 31 the transfer commenced, lasting 4 days, while still flying the missions provided by battalion.

October 15th, 1970 saw history being made again with the arrival of five (5) Vietnamese Air Force pilots. This trend has continued and the 335th has trained approximately twenty-five VNAF pilots to date.

A new commander, Major Marvin W. Schwem, succeeding Major Harold L. Bowen, was installed and initiated into the COWBOYS on 11 July 1971.

The number of combat assault missions has been decreasing at a steady rate as the Vietnamese Air Force has started to take over the load in the Delta. Vietnamization appears to have become a reality for the 335th A.H.C. and for the COWBOYS it may mean a big step has been taken on the long road home.

COWBOYS

UNIT HISTORY

1 JANUARY 1971 – 5 NOVEMBER 1971

DEPARTMENT OF THE ARMY

335TH ASSAULT HELICOPTER COMPANY

APO San Francisco 96359

AVBAWW-K   John E. Morrissey, III – Admin Officer

SUBJECT: Unit History 1 JAN 71 – 5 NOV 71

New Year's' Day-1971 found the COWBOYS still in Dong Tam under the able command of MAJ Henry J. Raymond. It was during the month of January that the "Night Hawk" concept of the two-ship Hunter-Killer team was reinstituted in anticipation of the Tet Offensive on "Chuck's" part. In its early days, the "Night Hawk" was to fly the sole mission of defending Dong Tam from attack ground or mortar. As the 7th ARVN Division became aware of the obvious advantages of this system, the scope of its employment was expanded to include the entire area within a 15-click radius of Dong Tam. It was a rare night when the "Night Hawk" came home without being able to claim a kill. During its first week of operation it came to the aid of three ARVN company's in heavy contact with a VC force of unknown size. It descended upon the scene in the midst of heavy enemy small arms fire. Within 40 minutes, the minigun and xeon light of the Low Ship, combined with the 50 cal. Fire of the High Ship, wrought lethal judgment upon the VC force. The following morning the ARVN forces moved into the area and counted 21 VC bodies. On several occasions when crisis arose, the "Night Hawk" team was dispatched far from the AO to come to the aid of a besieged ARVN outpost or a friendly unit that had been ambushed. The team has been credited with saving innumerable Allied and U.S. lives.

The TET Holiday proved to be fairly quiet as did most of the months of January, February, and March. In addition to the "Night Hawk," the COWBOYS continued to fly their standard missions of combat assaults, "wings," and inspection and survey.

In the beginning of March one of the Cowboy swing ships successfully "kidnapped" its cargo of 8 NFL-AFL football players from VIHN BIHN Province and treated them to a steak dinner at the Officers Club. Before the night was over, they had been "initiated" into the COWBOYS at each of the clubs. The "Night Hawk" team was again called upon to tie them in and fly them back to Tra Vinh.

The end of March brought an increase in enemy activity, especially in Vinh Binh Province, a long-time VC stronghold. On 23 March 1L/T Marvin B. Coon and CPT William T. Carter, flying chalk 4 in aircraft #361, took a direct hit in the engine with a B-40 round on take-off from the LZ, five clicks west of Tra Vinh. Due to the outstanding flying proficiency of the pilots, the aircraft was brought to the ground with no injury to the crew. Both pilots were awarded the Distinguished Flying Cross for their actions.

At approximately the same period CW2 Bill Belsher, 335th Unit Test Pilot, took AK47 hits while test flying an aircraft shortly before sunset in the Dong Tam traffic pattern. Within days of this incident, CPT John Barnowsky took an AK47 hit while on short final at Dong Tam in the "Night Hawk" high ship shortly after sundown. It became obvious that Chuck wasn't playing games.

On 20 March, the COWBOYS said farewell to MAJ Raymond as he returned to the States. On 29 March MAJ Harold L. Bowen assumed command of the 335th Assault Helicopter Company. Major Bowen came to the COWBOYS with the primary mission of improving the company's safety record. While the COWBOYS had compiled an outstanding combat record in regard to the number of hours flown, KBA's sampans and structures destroyed, passengers carried, and aircraft availability, the company had been plagued by a rash of aircraft accidents resulting in the aircraft involved being partially or totally destroyed. The unit had the worst Safety Record in the 164th Combat Aviation Group and was nearly the worst in the First Aviation Brigade. However, through Major Bowen's constant tutelage, his goal of a perfect Safety Record was finally realized. From 3 March to 4 October, the Unit's last mission in the Republic of Vietnam, the Cowboy's achieved a perfect accident-free safety record, the best in Battalion, the best in Group and near the top of the list in Brigade. This accomplishment can be considered to be even more remarkable as it was achieved during the months of the Delta's worst flying weather – the end of the dry season accompanied by the constant haze of the burning rice paddies and ever-present IFR conditions of the Rainy Season.

On 20 June the COWBOYS were called upon to increase their already heavy load with the move of their sister company, the 135th Assault Helicopter Company to Di An. In addition to flying combat assaults more frequently, the 335th increased their number of daily swing and I&S missions and picked up the one-time 135th daily mission of supplying the personal ship for the 7th ARVN Division Senior Advisor. The COWBOYS met the challenge and continued to provide their much-needed support in an outstanding manner.

With the loss of the EMU's the COWBOYS were the only major American aviation unit remaining at Dong Tam. During the first few weeks of this period there was some apprehension that the VC might step up activity against the base camp, however this did not occur. There was no significant change in the local tactical situation.

On 11 July MAJ Bowen returned to the States for a compassionate reassignment. MAJ Marvin W. Schwem assumed command of the 335th AHC on this date. The months of July and August were relatively slow for the COWBOYS in regard to the number of combat assault missions that they were required to fly. Instead of having CA's every other day as they had been averaging in the past, swing ship missions and I&S began to take up the time as it became apparent that the VNAF were beginning to assume a more aggressive combat role in the Delta.

The month of August proved to be a true test of the Cowboy's flexibility and professionalism as they developed a critical shortage of Aircraft Commanders and experienced crewmembers due to a "rash" of August DEROSes. Although the majority of the pilots and crewmembers were "Newbees," their willingness to learn and their ability to react efficiently when the pressure was on, proved that they were professionals in every sense of the word. The requirements of every mission were met with utmost efficiency and the 335th's perfect safety record was maintained.

Near the end of August, there were pretty strong rumors in the wind that the 335th was soon to receive orders to standown. Although most of the pilots were new, the officer strength was now at a point where the company could meet the mission requirements put forth by Battalion, with relative ease. It was at this point that the COWBOYS ceased to receive any new unit personnel. It had become apparent that the initial phase of the standown had begun although the unit had not as yet received official orders.

With the beginning of the Vietnamese political campaigns, the COWBOYS picked up a new mission. Every night the 335th was to have a "Mini-Pac" which was to consist of two gunships, two slicks, and one C&C. The initial concept of this mission was to provide a reactionary standby which would be able to drop troops at any location within the 7th ARVN Division AO within a 15 – 30-minute period after any significant contact with the enemy had been established. After employing the package in this manner on several occasions, it became apparent that it could be effectively employed to prevent the enemy from establishing these contacts. Since the VC maneuver primarily at night, ARVN forces could react to their intelligence information by inserting troops between the enemy and their objectives at any hour of the night through employment of the "Mini-Pac." This method of employment proved to be extremely successful in reducing, and in several cases entirely eliminating, the number of enemy attacks on the ARVN outpost.

As the Vietnamese elections drew nearer the NVA began to take a more active role in the Delta. At approximately 0300 Hours 19 September in a region known as the "Hump," south of Rac Soi, a Falcon gunship was shot down. The COWBOYS lost three of their best men in what would prove to be the opening blow of a new offensive in the long-time VC-NVA stronghold known as the U Minh Forrest. Aircraft Commander WO1 Gerald F. Vilas, Crewchief SP5 Fred A. Thacker, and Gunner SP5 Lynn G. Jones lost their lives in the crash while Pilot WO1 Robert Robinson was seriously injured. This incident proved to be a serious blow to the COWBOYS as there had been no fatalities in the unit for 14 months. The unit reacted to the incident with a vengeance. The Falcons began a nightly mission into the U Minh in search of the NVA strongholds. Although in the first few nights of this mission the gunships, flareship, and C&C took heavy 50 and .51 caliber fire, along with AK47, the area soon quieted down and the Falcon gun team would find itself on reactionary stand-by at either Rac Soi or Ca Mau.

During the same period, the COWBOYS were still operating their "Mini-Pac." The low ship of the "Night Hawk" team with its xeon light was being utilized to locate and illuminate the LZ's for the "Mini-Pac's" slicks. During the daylight hours, the company was still providing a ship for the 7th ARVN Division Senior Advisor as well as support ships for provinces throughout the Mekong Delta. The scope of these mission requirements demanded the full cooperation of every individual in the unit. From aircraft maintenance to the mess hall the men of the 335th worked together to provide the necessary support in maintaining aircraft and equipment availability to perform the required missions.

In the month of September, the COWBOYS received official notification that the unit would standown beginning 5 October with a completion date of 5 Nov. The Unit Colors, a Company Cadre, and aviation-associated equipment along with some aircraft would be redeployed to Ft. Riley, Kansas. The unit was to cease flying missions as of 2400 hrs on 4 Oct. In spite of the extra work required of the unit in preparation for the eminent standown, the COWBOYS continued to fly full mission schedule of daily I&S, swings, "Mini-Pacs," and "Night Hawk."

On the day of 4 Oct 1971, the COWBOYS of the 335th Assault Helicopter flew their last tactical mission in the Republic of Vietnam. In answer to a call to provide fire support for an ARVN tactical element under attack, near Vi Than, the Falcons expended four times on a location concealing a possible battalion strength NVA unit. When the ARVN's swept the area after contact had been broken, they found 29 bodies that the enemy had been unable to carry away. At approximately 2345 hrs, the "Night Hawk" claimed one KBA, one sampan, and numerous supplies destroyed. In all, the COWBOYS and the Falcons claimed a total of 30 confirmed enemy kills on their last day of flying.

The morning of 5 October found the men of the 335th in a new role. Everybody from pilot to cook found himself in a temporary MOS of "packer and mover." In only one month, everything and everyone from the COWBOYS would be gone from Dong Tam. There would be a daily drain of personnel from the unit as these EM with more than 90 days and officers with more than 60 days left to serve in the Republic of Vietnam, were returned to USARV control for reassignment. The majority of the COWBOYS were retained by their own 214th Combat Aviation Battalion and were assigned to either the 175th or 114th Assault Helicopter Company. Of the personnel eligible for the "drop," only one officer (CPT William T. Carter – Cadre CO) and approximately 20 enlisted men were to remain with the 335th as cadre when it was to reach Ft. Riley. The remainder of those without drops went to their new PCS stations with adjusted DEROSES. The standown proceeded like clockwork and on the morning of 5 NOV 1971, the Cowboy cadre departed the Republic of Vietnam with a history and tradition that it was determined to maintain at home in the nation that it had fought for.

COWBOYS

UNIT HISTORY

1 JANUARY 1972 -- 31 DECEMBER 1972

DEPARTMENT OF THE ARMY

335TH AVIATION COMPANY (ASSAULT HELICOPTER)

Fort Riley, Kansas 66442

WGPQAA A   30 MAR 73

SUBJECT: Annual Historical Supplement

Commander

1st Infantry Division (Mech) & Fort Riley

ATTN ALBFDO-PP

Fort Riley, Kansas 66442

The 335th Avn. Co. (Aslt. Hel.) COWBOYS was originally Company A, 82nd Avn. Bn., assigned to Fort Bragg, North Carolina. In April 1965, the COWBOYS deployed to Bien Hoa, South Vietnam to support the 173rd Airborne Bde. The COWBOYS were in the Republic of Vietnam until 5 Nov. 1971. During this time the unit flew a total of 136,500 hours. The unit carried out every type of mission imaginable in a professional manner as is reflected in the list of decorations received. A brief description of these decorations follows. 2 Legions of Merit, 3 Silver Stars, 103 Distinguished Flying Crosses, 187 Bronze Stars, 358 Air Medals with Vs, plus other air medals. The past performance of the COWBOYS is commendable; however, this supplement will primarily be concerned with the COWBOYS during the calendar year of 1972.

In Nov. 1971, the 335th stood down to be assigned to Fort Riley, Kansas. When the unit stood down, Cpt. William Carter helped bring it back and became the COWBOYS Operations Officer in its new stateside assignment. Major Jerry Black became the Commander of the COWBOYS. On 27 Nov. 1971 the first morning report was turned in consisting of 3 Commissioned officers, 1 Warrant officer, and 17 Enlisted men. 1972 would see the COWBOYS reaching new peaks in performance.

1972 saw the COWBOYS receiving its full complement of aircraft thus enabling the unit to add a third dimension to the 1st. Inf. Div. training in the form of airmobility. The 335th provided a wide range of support for both the 1st Inf. Div. and 5th Army. The COWBOYS provided support for numerous VIP flights, range safety, disaster relief, civil disturbance operations, and displays. Almost immediately after becoming operational at Fort Riley, the Unit of Choice recruiting office began requesting aircraft and crews for support in their activities. The 335th has flown hundreds of hours in support of the Unit of Choice recruiting for skydiving and aircraft display. Let us not forget the primary mission of the 335th to provide support for the Big Red One. From 1 Jan until 31 Dec. 1972, the COWBOYS flew many hours of simulated combat assaults to help in the training of the Infantry units on the hill. The advent of Summer also meant the arrival of over 2,000 ROTC Cadets from all over the 5th Army area for summer camp. This meant a lot of flying, as the COWBOYS flew several simulated combat assaults and numerous resupply missions. During 1972, two arimobile briefing teams were organized consisting of four men each. These teams travel to the National Guard units over the 5th Army area to help the units better understand and acquire a working knowledge of airmobile operations.

In June of 1972 the 335th began providing aircraft to Flight Standards on a daily basis to train non-instrument rated pilots to receive their standard instrument ticket. At one time, as many as eight aircraft per day were provided. Also in June, Major Black rode 22 miles on a bicycle for the Saint Judes Hospital for Crippled Children. This effort was backed by the men of the 335th by pledging donations per each mile ridden by Major Black. The end result was over $740 donated to the foundation. The floods of South Dakota brought the COWBOYS into action as they flew much needed food and supplies to the victims of Rapid City. November 10th was designated Unit Day and the festivities included free steaks for everyone and helicopter rides for the non-aviators of the unit. The COWBOYS celebrated Christmas by sending five fully loaded helicopters to Oklahoma to a needy Indian reservation. The toys and clothes were received with great appreciation. The 335th ended the year in support of OPLAN MISSOURI.

As before mentioned, personnel of the 335th received a large, well-deserved complement of medals. The unit itself also received its share of citations. In May 1968 the unit received its first Meritorious Unit Citation for action in the Republic of Vietnam for the period covering 1 Jan to 31 Dec. 1967. This was followed by the first Oak Leaf Cluster awarded on 5 June 1968 for the period covering 5 May 1965 to 4 May 1967. On 16 June 1969 the 335th was awarded the Presidential Unit Citation (ARMY) for the period covering 6 Nov. 1967 to 23 Nov. 1967. The company's first annual IG was held in May of 1972 only 6 months after the unit became operational. After the IG Team had completed their inspections, the company was given a "Very Satisfactory" rating. Later in the year, the 5th Army safety inspection team came and it was determined that the 335th had one of the best safety programs on Fort Riley. Although busy with missions the 335th has never neglected its training obligations. Early in April 1972, two aircraft and four crews flew to Colorado for cold weather mountain training. All through the summer different types of training were performed. Most recently, however, is the initiation of low level and nap-of-the-earth routes. Even though the 335th has flown over 6,000 accident-free flying hours since its first mission stateside, the personnel involved realize that it is important for the unit to train to maintain its professionalism in the years to come.

JERRY L. BLACK
MAJ, IN
Commanding

COWBOYS

UNIT HISTORY

1 JANUARY 1973 -- 31 DECEMBER 1973

DEPARTMENT OF THE ARMY

335TH AVIATION COMPANY (ASSAULT HELICOPTER)

Fort Riley, Kansas 66442

24 Jan 74

SUBJECT: Annual Historical Supplement

Commander

1st Infantry Division (Mech) & Fort Riley

ATTN ALBFDO-PP

Fort Riley, Kansas 66442

    The 335th Aviation Company (Assault Helicopter) COWBOYS was originally Company A, 82nd Avn. Bn., assigned to Fort Bragg, North Carolina. In April 1965, the COWBOYS were deployed to Bien Hoa, South Vietnam to support the 173rd Airborne Bde. The COWBOYS were in the Republic of Vietnam until Nov. 1971. The past performance of the 335th is commendable, however, this supplement will primarily be concerned with the COWBOYS during the 1973 calendar year.

    The 335th departed the Republic of Vietnam on 5 Nov. 1971 for reassignment to Fort Riley, Kansas. On 10 Jan 1972 the unit joined the 1st Avn. Bn. (Prov.) at Marshall Army Airfield. It wasn't until 27 Feb. 73 that the unit attained full operating strength of 23 UH-1 (Huey) and 6 (AH-1 (Cobra) helicopters. The 335th consists of the company Headquarters with flight safety, flight operations, 1st Airlift Platoon, 2nd Airlift Platoon, 3rd Aerial Weapons Platoon, and the service platoon. When the unit returned from the Republic of Vietnam, MAJ. Jerry L. Black became the units new Commanding Officer. He held the reins of the COWBOYS until 11 April 73. At that time, MAJ. Black went to Omaha, Nebraska to school and MAJ. David A Measels took command. Maj. Measels is Airborne qualified, a Senior Aviator with over 2400 hours of flight time, he wears the expert Infantry Badge and the Vietnamese pilots wings. His awards include the Good Conduct Medal, Air medal with 31 OLC, Air Force Commendation Medal, Purple Heart, and the Bronze Star. Maj. Measels was commissioned in Sept. of 1963. His various assignments include 1 tour in Korea and 2 tours in Vietnam. He has attended flight school, Infantry Officers Advance Course, Degree Completion Program at University of Tampa and the Military Assistance Training Advisor Course.

    During the first part of the year, the unit started out by keeping a crew on 24-hour alert as a range medical evacuation aircraft. Early in the year the unit began very active support of the unit of Choice program. Aircraft were sent to all parts of the central states for static displays and for dropping skydiving teams as part of the central states recruiting effort for Fort Riley. Missions for this cause were sent as far away as North Dakota, Minnesota, Indiana and Mississippi. The unit flew a total of 835 hours in support of this mission. Many local missions were flown for the same effort. During the summer months many weekends were devoted to flying the skydiving team for their practices at Marshall Airfield. The unit also had a briefing team which traveled extensively to ROTC and National Guard units in Kansas and other States. The team briefed many soldiers and soldiers to be about helicopters and how they are used in combat. Following the discussion the men were taken on helicopter rides, usually information, to reinforce and to clarify the classroom training. For many of these men it was their first ride in a helicopter. The summer months were extremely busy as the company logged over 700 hours in support of ROTC summer camp and National Guard and Reserve unit training. Practice combat assaults were accomplished both day and night. This important phase of training is vital to the development of a well-rounded soldier. The 335th has two VIP aircraft, which have logged 400 hours, for use by visiting dignitaries during their tours of the post. These aircraft have modified seating to afford maximum comfort to the passengers. The mobility of the helicopter affords commanders a maximum amount of time for personal checks of field training exercises on various parts of the post. During early September the Aerial Weapons Platoon flew to Camp McCoy, Wisconsin to requalify the pilots in aerial gunnery. During Combat Assaults the Gun Platoon fly's protective cover for the UH-1's as they fly in formation. The 335th has one UH-1 aircraft with a xenon search light installed for use on fire fly missions. These usually occur on payday week ends in conjunction with the military police to reduce the possibility of crimes on Fort Riley. Other missions for the Night Hawk ship included search and evacuation of injured civilians during the tornadoes and floods that hit October of 1973, and search and rescue for downed aircraft. The COWBOYS have logged over 50 hours on these search missions.

In August of 1973 the 335th went to the field in support of the 1st Inf. Div. (Mech) Field Training Exercise. During the exercise, the COWBOYS flew 160 hours of simulated combat assaults, and courier missions. The unit used all slack time available to improve overall proficiency of the flight crews. The company also played a small part in Reforger V this year. Two aircraft were kept on 24-hour standby during the time of loading for the exercise. These aircraft were used for control and command and for such duties as air liaison officers. The unit celebrated its Unit Day on Nov. 23 as was designated in the enclosed letter. In Dec. of 1973 the 335th once again went to the field, this time, on their own. Emphasis was placed on Cold Weather Training and mainly on low level flying techniques to avoid enemy radar. The unit flew 150 hours in the form of single ship missions, day and night airmobile assaults, and search and rescue. Valuable experience was gained in these field exercises which helped to maintain the proficiency of the company.

While the unit was in Vietnam, it received its share of awards. In May 1968 the unit received its first Meritorious Unit Citation for action in the Republic of Vietnam for the period covering 1 Jan. to 31 Dec. 1967. This was followed by the first Oak Leaf Cluster awarded on 5 Jun. 1968 for the period covering 5 May 1965 to 4 May 1967. On 16 Jun. 1969 the 335th was awarded the Presidential Unit Citation (ARMY) for the period covering 6 Nov. to 23 Nov. 1967. On 6 Jul. 1973, the 335th achieved 10,000 hours of accident free flying hours since returning from Vietnam. On 24 Jul. 1973, Brig. Gen. Jack R. Sadler personally congratulated the 335th for this accomplishment. By the end of the year, the unit had passed the 12,000-hour mark for accident free flying. Although busy with missions the 335th never neglected its training obligations. Through the year the COWBOYS flew as many training flights as possible to maintain their proficiency in the form of Field Training exercises or just individual tactical training.

DAMH-HSO (11 Jun. 73) 1st Ind.

SUBJECT: Request for Change of Unit Day

DA, CMH, TEMPO C BLDG, WASH DC 20315

TO: Commander, 335th Aviation Company, Fort Riley, KS 66442

In accordance with recent telephone conversations between Mr. Stark of this office and personnel of your company, a Unit Day Certificate attesting to the selection of 23 November as your Unit Day is enclosed.

FOR THE COMMANDER:

WALTER L. MCMAHON
Colonel, Infantry
Chief, Historical
Services Division

COWBOYS

UNIT HISTORY

1 JANUARY 1974 -- 31 DECEMBER 1974

DEPARTMENT OF THE ARMY

335TH AVIATION COMPANY (ASSAULT HELICOPTER)

Fort Riley, Kansas 66442

COWBOYS

30 Jan 75

SUBJECT: Annual Historical Supplement

Commander

1st Infantry Division (Provisional)

ATTN AFZN-AV

Fort Riley, Kansas 66442

Commander

1st Infantry Division & Fort Riley

ATTN AFZNDO-PH

Fort Riley, Kansas 66442

Headquarters

Department of the Army

ATTN: (DAMH-HSO) TEMPO ABC

Washington, D.C. 20315

1. The 335th Aviation Company (Assault Helicopter) was originally Company A, 82nd Avn. Bn., assigned to Fort Bragg, North Carolina. In April 1965, the Company was deployed to the Republic of Vietnam, where it was redesignated the 335th Aviation Company (Assault Helicopter) on 10 November 1966. The company was deployed to Fort Riley, Kansas from Vietnam in November 1971. The period covered in this supplement will be calendar year 1974.

2. The organization, mission, key personnel, and brief biological sketch of the commander are as follows:

   a. Organization: See Enclosure 1
   b. Mission: The mission of the company is to provide tactical air movement of troops, supplies, and equipment within the combat zone.
   c. Key Personnel

   (1) Commander

      (a) Major David A. Measels   01 Jan 74   22 Feb 74
      (b) Major Myron D. Davis   22 Feb 74   31 Dec 74

   (2) Executive Officer

(a) Captain Roger A. Groth	01 Jan 74	30 May 74
(b) Captain James Hilton	30 May 74	28 Jun 74
(c) Captain Barry H. Adams	28 Jun 7 4	31 Dec 74

(3) Operations Officer

(a) Captain Alan Duguette	01 Jan 74	07 May 74
(b) Captain Merrill B. Richardson	07 May 74	31 Dec 74

(4) 1st Airlift Platoon Commander

(a) 1Lt William Hathaway	01 Jan 74	07 Aug 74
(b) Captain Arthur R. Labelle	07 Aug 74	31 Dec 74

(5) 2nd Airlift Platoon Commander

(a) 1Lt John G. Senor	01 Jan 74	04 Apr 74
(b) 1Lt James R. Kolstad	04 Apr 74	31 Dec 74

(6) Armed Platoon Commander

(a) Captain William Lyons	01 Jan 74	02 Jun 74
(b) CW3 Robert P. Lynn	02 Jun 74	31 Dec 74

(7) Service Platoon Commander

1Lt Lawrence B. Morra	01 Jan 74	31 Dec 74

(8) First Sergeant

(a) 1SG Franklin D. Wyant	01 Jan 74	19 Dec 74
(b) SFC Philip D. Souve	19 Dec 74	31 Dec 74

3. Biographical Sketch of Commander: Major Myron D. Davis assumed command of the company on 22 February 1974 from Major David A. Measels. Major Davis is a Senior Army Aviator with over 4,000 flight hours. His awards include Combat Infantry Badge, Expert Infantry Badge, Distinguished Flying Cross, Bronze Star, Meritorious Service Medal, Air Medal, and the Army Commendation Medal. He was commissioned in July of 1961 from North Georgia College, and he entered active duty in March of 1962. His various assignments include one tour in Korea and two tours in Vietnam. Prior to his present assignment, he served as S-3 and Executive Officer, 1st Battalion (Mechanized), 58th Infantry, 197th Infantry Brigade, Fort Benning, Georgia. He is a graduate of the Infantry Officer Advanced Course.

4. Personnel Management: As evidenced by the list of key personnel, there was turbulence in that area. Often, personnel were assigned to leadership positions who were junior to the authorized grade structure. Each of these personnel proved to be competent in their assignments; however, because of lack of experience and expertise, a considerable amount of time was spent in their training as well as their platoons. There was little turbulence in the non-commissioned officer corps. Most were extremely competent and contributed greatly to the training fundamentals required of the company.

5. Training and Operations: In February the Airlift Platoons qualified personnel in the M-23 weapons systems, and the Armed Platoon maintained proficiency through line fire exercises. In March, the company successfully completed its first Army Training Test. In April, personnel armed with M-16 rifles were qualified. Field training exercises were conducted in July and August. In September, the company successfully completed a "No-NOTICE" exercise that saw the entire company move to Salina for a simulated move to Puerto Rico. Throughout the year, the 335th supported the 1st Infantry Division in airmobile operations, as well as the 3rd ROTC Region Advanced ROTC Summer Camp. The company supports the Provost Marshall with a "Nighthawk" aircraft during those periods when crimes are more probable to occur. In November, one airlift platoon flew to Fort Carson, Colorado in support of Operation Brave Shield. All training goals were reached during the year.

6. Logistics Management: The company underwent 2 MTOE changes during the year. All equipment changes were requisitioned in a timely manner, and because of that, the equipment on hand, together with dedicated maintenance management, remained at a high level of readiness.

7. Inspections:

(a) The company successfully completed a Department of the Army Inspector General Inspection in January.

(b) A FORSCOM Aviation Safety Inspection was successfully completed in April.

8. Awards:

(a) Unit: In November the company received a FORSCOM Certificate of Achievement for excellence in Aviation Safety for Fiscal Year 1974. On 6 November, the company reached a level of 3 years and over 16,000 hours of accident free flight and was submitted for a Department of the Army Award of Honor for this achievement.

(b) Individual:

(1) WO1 Tommy T. Penrose was awarded the Army Commendation Medal in August by BG Kingston for saving a man from drowning in an automobile accident in June.

(2) 1SG Franklin D. Wyant was awarded the Army Commendation Medal in December for his service as First Sergeant.

(3) CW3 George B. Davis and SFC Arnold Jurgens ware awarded the Army Commendation Medal upon their retirement from the Army.

MYRON D. DAVIS
MAJ., Infantry
Commanding

COWBOYS

UNIT HISTORY

1 JANUARY 1975 -- 31 DECEMBER 1975

DEPARTMENT OF THE ARMY

335TH AVIATION COMPANY (ASSAULT HELICOPTER)

Fort Riley, Kansas 66442

SUBJECT: Annual Historical Supplement

Commander

1st Aviation Battalion (P)

Fort Riley, Kansas 66442

G3/DPT

1st Infantry Division and Fort Riley

ATTN AFZN-DPT-PH

Fort Riley, Kansas 66442

1. UNIT ORIGIN AND ORGANIZATION:

a. The COWBOYS of the 335th Aviation Company (Assault Helicopter), were attached to the 1st Avn. Bn. (P) on 10 Jan. 72 for administrative and operational control. Commanded by Major Myron D. Davis, the 335th Avn. Co. began supporting the "Green Mittens" mission in Grand Forks, North Dakota, on 7 Jan. 75. Five UH-1 aircraft, crews and maintenance personnel supported the combined SAFCOM-ARMCOM mission on a continuous basis through 1 September 1975. Grand Forks, North Dakota, provided an excellent opportunity for the COWBOYS to experience and train in severe cold weather operations. While supporting "Green Mittens" the 335th Aviation Company (AH) continued its annual training and support of the First Infantry Division, ROTC and UOC at Fort Riley, Kansas.

b. On 27 May 1975 Major Stephen D. Ballard assumed command of the 335th Aviation Company. A physical fitness program was immediately implemented which has greatly increased the unit's esprit de corps and combat readiness. Brigadier General Johns, Assistant Division Commander, has participated with the 335th soldiers during physical training and has complimented the unit on its physical training program.

2.   TRAINING AND OPERATIONS:

a. On 6 & 7 February 1975 flight personnel of the 335th Avn. Co. conducted .38 caliber pistol training and qualifications.

b. An unexpected April snowstorm provided a challenging environment for the unit's Annual ORTT that was satisfactorily completed on 3 April 1975.

c. The first week in May involved moving the Armed Helicopter Platoon to Fort Knox, Kentucky, where annual aerial gunnery qualification was conducted.

d. On 13 and 14 May the company conducted M-16 firing and qualifications. Those not required to qualify took part in range operations to insure safe and successful training.

e. From 1 July to 11 July the COWBOYS supported cadets of the Reserve Officer Training Corps attending summer camp at Fort Riley, Kansas. Over two thousand cadets were transported on tactical airlifts employing contour level flight techniques.

f. The unit provided support for the First Infantry Division on pre-REFORGER '76 FTX's from 22-24 July and 25-28 August.

g. In keeping with the Nation's Bicentennial, the 335th COWBOYS provided a "Vietnam Era" color guard. Clothed in camouflage jungle fatigues the unit has honored the Nation at a Kansas City Chiefs Football game on 18 August, the Sedgwick Fall Festival Parade at Sedgwick, Kansas on 13 September, the Arkalalaa-Festival at Arkansas City, Kansas on 25 October and the Will Rogers Parade in Claremore, Oklahoma on 1 November.

h. On 22 September the unit again qualified personnel with the .38 caliber pistol. From 23-28 September, M-16 qualification was conducted with emphasis on known distance and night firing.

i. On 3 October the unit participated in its annual advanced PCPT. Conditioned by a vigorous physical training program, the unit scored an average of 409 on the proficiency test.

j. From 4 October to 11 November the COWBOYS supported REFORGER '75 providing 11 officers and 6 enlisted men for the First Infantry Division.

k. Those at home were involved with UH-1H door gunnery from 15-17 October, qualifying crew chiefs with the door mounted M-60 machine gun.

l. Escape and evasion took place on 24 November. Temperatures dipped in the low teens as 60 participating air crew members completed the 12-kilometer course.

m. Unit athletic highlights involved winning the tug-of-war event during the Battalion Organizational Day. The motorcycle race was also won by a member of the 335th Avn. Co. Post Flag Football competition found the COWBOYS in second place, losing 6-0 in the Post Championship Finals. The COWBOYS were honored with the Main Post Championship.

3. UNIT AWARDS:

a. The 335th Avn. Co. was awarded the FORSCOM Aviation Award for Accident Free Flying for the period July 1972 to July 1975.

b. The 335th Avn. Co. also received the Aviation Accident Prevention Award for 1 year and 3-year periods during 1975.

STEPHEN D. BALLARD
MAJ., Infantry
Commanding

COWBOYS

UNIT HISTORY

1 JANUARY 1976 -- 31 DECEMBER 1976

DEPARTMENT OF THE ARMY

335TH AVIATION COMPANY (ASSAULT HELICOPTER)

Fort Riley, Kansas 66442

31 January 1977

SUBJECT: Annual Historical Supplement

Commander

1st Avn. Bn. (Prov)

Fort Riley, Kansas 66442

1.   335th Avn. Co. was organized on 10 November 1966 in Vietnam. It was formed out of Company A, 82nd Avn. Bn. While in Vietnam, it was awarded one Presidential Unit Citation, 2 Meritorious Unit Commendations and 3 Vietnam Cross of Gallantry with Palms. On 10 December 1971 it was reassigned to Fort Riley, KS and attached to the 1st Avn. Bn. It is a FORSCOM unit.

2.   In CY 1976 the 335th COWBOYS flew 3656 hours. Some of the highlights include loss of the gun platoon (6 AH-1G Cobras) due to a TOE change; aircraft support for Operation Rocking Force at Grand Forks ND from Jan-Apr 76; successful completion of the ORTT in Apr 76; support for training of National Guard units at Ft. McCoy, WI Jul-Aug 76; furnished instructors and support personnel to ROTC Summer Camp Jul-Aug 76; conducted aerial gunnery training in Sep 76; began a tactical instrument training program in Oct 76; and moved from the old World War II wooden billets to permanent barracks in Nov 76. The unit was awarded a FORSCOM Safety Award for flying for the 75-76 period. The AGI was completed Jun 76. The unit football team took 3rd place in the Post Flag Football Tournament.

3.   Organization Changes:

    CO MAJ Barry H. Adams took command from MAJ Stephen D. Ballard Jun 76
    XO CPT Judd Clemens Jan-Mar 76
        CPT William Garrison Mar-Oct 76
        CPT Arthur Labelle Oct-Dec 76
   1SG Charles Hadley Jan-Jun 76
      SFC Benedict A. Pieri Jun-Sep 76
      1SG William Belcher Sep-Dec 76

1st Flight Platoon 11 UH-1H Helicopters	CPT Arthur LaBelle Jan-Oct 76
	CPT Joseph Kulik Oct-Dec 76
2nd Flight Platoon 11 UH-1H Helicopters	CPT Timothy Lenzmeier Jan-Dec 76
Service Platoon 1 UH-1H Helicopter	CPT William Garrison Jan-Mar 76
	1LT William Biggar Mar-Apr 76
	CPT James Armstrong Apr-Sep 76
	CPT Robert W. McElwain Sep-Dec 76
Operations Officer	CPT Daniel McClung Jan-Mar 76
	CPT John Hayne May-Dec 76

                                 BARRY H. ADAMS
                                 MAJ, FA
                                 Commanding

Note: The following list only includes helicopters that were in the 335th AHC after September 1966. The primary source of this information is the U.S. Army Goldbook. Accuracy is estimated to be about 80% to 95%.

Model	Tail Number	Built Date MMYY	Begin In Unit YYMM	Begin In Unit Hours	Finish In Unit YYMM	Total Hours	Hours In Unit
AH-1G	67-15621	568	7303	2185	7512	2344	159
AH-1G	67-15764	968	7303	2005	7501	2069	64
AH-1G	67-15822	1168	7402	1838	7406	1901	63
UH-1B	63-08560	264	6905	2757	6907	2957	200
UH-1B	62-01967	363	6903	1965	6904	2077	112
UH-1B	64-13976	365	6805	1932	6810	2280	348
UH-1B	64-13978	365	6610	809	6708	1086	277
UH-1B	63-08606	464	6807	2177	7005	3578	1401
UH-1B	63-08610	464	6612	1413	6709	1585	172
UH-1B	63-08612	464	6710	1602	6805	2031	429
UH-1B	64-14004	465	6806	1682	6912	3024	1342
UH-1B	62-02019	563	6812	2662	6908	3382	720
UH-1B	64-14023	565	6811	2130	6909	3069	939
UH-1B	62-02025	663	7003	2929	7101	3439	510
UH-1B	62-02028	663	6906	1999	7001	2680	681
UH-1B	63-08648	664	6610	597	6801	1140	543
UH-1B	64-14049	665	7003	2754	7012	3468	714
UH-1B	62-02056	763	6709	1690	6803	1970	280
UH-1B	63-08664	764	6709	3	6902	1066	1063
UH-1B	63-08676	764	7007	3959	7011	4151	192
UH-1B	62-02094	863	6805	3160	7002	4269	1109
UH-1B	63-08685	864	6710	1546	7001	3007	1461
UH-1B	63-08703	864	6709	2070	6802	2340	270

Model	Tail Number	Built Date MMYY	Begin In Unit YYMM	Begin In Unit Hours	Finish In Unit YYMM	Total Hours	Hours In Unit
UH-1B	62-04579	963	6711	2138	6810	2714	576
UH-1B	62-04592	963	6808	2496	7006	3781	1285
UH-1B	62-04594	963	7002	1909	7101	2716	807
UH-1B	63-12916	1064	7005	2988	7007	3240	252
UH-1B	63-12928	1064	6610	1333	6702	1445	112
UH-1B	63-12930	1064	6610	1398	6710	1659	261
UH-1B	63-12932	1064	6610	1053	6611	1073	20
UH-1B	63-12934	1064	6610	1454	6705	1783	329
UH-1B	63-12935	1064	6610	1493	6702	1683	190
UH-1B	63-12945	1164	6610	839	6807	1736	897
UH-1B	62-01901	1262	6610	1952	6702	2133	181
UH-1B	64-13919	1264	6610	1682	6709	2010	328
UH-1B	64-13924	1264	6807	2214	6903	2422	208
UH-1B	64-13925	1264	6803	1964	6807	2122	158
UH-1B	64-13926	1264	6908	2291	7003	2956	665
UH-1C	66-15071	367	7010	1439	7102	1775	336
UH-1C	66-15141	567	7102	1862	7104	1980	118
UH-1C	64-14112	865	7101	1057	7102	1129	72
UH-1C	66-00591	966	7012	1250	7012	1279	29
UH-1C	66-00629	1066	7010	1675	7012	1868	193
UH-1C	64-14167	1165	7010	1865	7101	2033	168
UH-1D	64-13557	265	6610	1238	6706	1627	389
UH-1D	64-13561	265	6610	981	6707	1438	457
UH-1D	64-13567	265	6610	1157	6703	1603	446
UH-1D	65-09671	266	6805	1532	6805	1589	57
UH-1D	65-09674	266	6610	376	6612	618	242

Model	Tail Number	Built Date MMYY	Begin In Unit YYMM	Begin In Unit Hours	Finish In Unit YYMM	Total Hours	Hours In Unit
UH-1D	65-09679	266	6610	367	6707	863	496
UH-1D	64-13570	365	6610	1165	6612	1410	245
UH-1D	64-13609	465	6610	1268	6702	1699	431
UH-1D	64-13610	465	6610	1206	6704	1640	434
UH-1D	64-13611	465	6701	1024	6707	1235	211
UH-1D	64-13614	465	6610	1027	6611	1143	116
UH-1D	65-09902	566	6610	43	6702	195	152
UH-1D	65-09910	566	6610	75	6707	527	452
UH-1D	64-13701	765	6610	726	6703	1201	475
UH-1D	64-13735	765	6610	735	6610	735	0
UH-1D	64-13736	765	6610	906	6707	1311	405
UH-1D	64-13738	765	6610	789	6704	1054	265
UH-1D	64-13747	865	6805	1739	6808	1870	131
UH-1D	65-12849	866	6611	0	6707	255	255
UH-1D	64-13773	965	6805	1634	6806	1690	56
UH-1D	65-12858	966	6611	0	6707	374	374
UH-1D	65-12868	966	6611	0	6707	385	385
UH-1D	66-00799	1066	6611	0	6703	144	144
UH-1D	66-00879	1066	6701	0	6707	268	268
UH-1D	64-13884	1165	6610	635	6706	1034	399
UH-1D	66-00900	1166	6701	0	6706	57	57
UH-1D	65-09569	1265	6610	472	6707	863	391
UH-1H	66-01091	167	7208	1935	7509	2670	735
UH-1H	67-17173	168	7008	1956	7112	3335	1379
UH-1H	67-17192	168	6912	2185	7112	4067	1882
UH-1H	67-17197	168	7010	2408	7112	3637	1229
UH-1H	67-17224	168	7510	3271	7512	3302	31

Model	Tail Number	Built Date MMYY	Begin In Unit YYMM	Begin In Unit Hours	Finish In Unit YYMM	Total Hours	Hours In Unit
UH-1H	67-17225	168	7012	1861	7102	2064	203
UH-1H	69-15036	170	7007	260	7011	621	361
UH-1H	69-15046	170	7008	732	7010	1041	309
UH-1H	66-01208	267	7105	2226	7112	2872	646
UH-1H	66-16090	267	7012	2301	7112	3306	1005
UH-1H	66-16094	267	7105	1960	7109	2145	185
UH-1H	67-17292	268	7007	1678	7012	2067	389
UH-1H	69-15118	270	7011	373	7101	575	202
UH-1H	69-15127	270	7010	715	7112	1548	833
UH-1H	70-15725	271	7105	86	7112	785	699
UH-1H	66-16118	367	7010	1992	7010	2041	49
UH-1H	66-16184	367	7012	2875	7112	3728	853
UH-1H	67-17354	368	6806	235	6902	1179	944
UH-1H	67-17361	368	6806	223	7102	3485	3262
UH-1H	67-17380	368	6805	0	6905	1377	1377
UH-1H	70-15711	371	7208	401	7512	1321	920
UH-1H	66-16258	467	6903	1029	7004	2336	1307
UH-1H	66-16308	467	6911	1069	7007	2055	986
UH-1H	66-16319	467	7208	2489	7405	2651	162
UH-1H	66-16321	467	6807	759	6907	2067	1308
UH-1H	67-17426	468	6805	0	6808	555	555
UH-1H	67-17427	468	7002	1387	7112	3704	2317
UH-1H	67-17452	468	7208	1570	7509	2105	535
UH-1H	69-15271	470	7208	1248	7405	1780	532
UH-1H	66-16363	567	6812	630	6901	820	190
UH-1H	66-16385	567	6807	616	6909	2016	1400
UH-1H	66-16408	567	7004	1563	7011	2500	937
UH-1H	66-16437	567	7208	2874	7512	3367	493

Model	Tail Number	Built Date MMYY	Begin In Unit YYMM	Begin In Unit Hours	Finish In Unit YYMM	Total Hours	Hours In Unit
UH-1H	66-16458	567	6903	436	6905	678	242
UH-1H	69-15378	570	7007	0	7110	1688	1688
UH-1H	65-09986	666	7409	3797	7512	4007	210
UH-1H	66-16498	667	6709	0	6806	1000	1000
UH-1H	66-16522	667	7208	2116	7412	2636	520
UH-1H	66-16545	667	6904	513	6912	1434	921
UH-1H	66-16557	667	6910	552	6911	735	183
UH-1H	66-16572	667	6907	568	7009	1990	1422
UH-1H	66-16581	667	7010	1905	7112	3121	1216
UH-1H	69-15441	670	7105	449	7112	951	502
UH-1H	69-15474	670	7208	680	7512	1527	847
UH-1H	69-15481	670	7511	1143	7512	1162	19
UH-1H	66-16620	767	6709	0	6902	1625	1625
UH-1H	66-16621	767	6709	0	6906	2054	2054
UH-1H	66-16623	767	6709	0	6812	1551	1551
UH-1H	66-16633	767	6709	0	7004	2738	2738
UH-1H	66-16635	767	6801	187	6801	291	104
UH-1H	66-16637	767	6709	0	6805	833	833
UH-1H	66-16638	767	6709	0	6805	728	728
UH-1H	66-16639	767	6709	0	6907	2082	2082
UH-1H	66-16643	767	6709	0	6805	825	825
UH-1H	66-16647	767	6709	0	6711	147	147
UH-1H	66-16648	767	6709	0	6710	162	162
UH-1H	66-16649	767	6709	0	7001	2514	2514
UH-1H	66-16651	767	6709	0	6805	910	910
UH-1H	66-16653	767	6709	0	6905	1802	1802
UH-1H	66-16654	767	6709	0	6907	2025	2025
UH-1H	66-16656	767	6709	0	6808	1340	1340

Model	Tail Number	Built Date MMYY	Begin In Unit YYMM	Begin In Unit Hours	Finish In Unit YYMM	Total Hours	Hours In Unit
UH-1H	68-16053	769	6908	0	6909	295	295
UH-1H	68-16070	769	7011	1652	7112	2714	1062
UH-1H	68-16073	769	7208	1838	7512	2629	791
UH-1H	68-16076	769	6908	0	7003	1025	1025
UH-1H	68-16090	769	6908	0	7010	1737	1737
UH-1H	64-13740	865	7512	4577	7512	4577	0
UH-1H	66-16701	867	6709	8	6806	1032	1024
UH-1H	66-16702	867	6709	17	6803	705	688
UH-1H	66-16704	867	6709	0	6906	2060	2060
UH-1H	66-16706	867	6709	10	6907	2137	2127
UH-1H	66-16707	867	6709	0	6906	2072	2072
UH-1H	66-16708	867	6709	0	6907	2079	2079
UH-1H	66-16717	867	6709	0	6907	2019	2019
UH-1H	67-17744	868	7005	2357	7006	2537	180
UH-1H	68-15775	869	6908	0	7102	1880	1880
UH-1H	68-16118	869	6908	0	7102	2004	2004
UH-1H	68-16160	869	6909	0	6910	259	259
UH-1H	68-16194	869	7009	926	7010	999	73
UH-1H	69-15627	870	7208	374	7512	981	607
UH-1H	66-16797	967	7511	2709	7512	2749	40
UH-1H	67-17806	968	7105	2417	7111	2783	366
UH-1H	68-16224	969	7105	1395	7112	1965	570
UH-1H	68-16254	969	7012	1588	7112	2552	964
UH-1H	68-16272	969	7012	595	7112	1617	1022
UH-1H	68-16278	969	6910	0	7008	757	757
UH-1H	66-16925	1067	6908	1218	7009	2518	1300
UH-1H	66-16928	1067	6902	435	6902	486	51
UH-1H	66-16948	1067	7005	2238	7010	3024	786

Model	Tail Number	Built Date MMYY	Begin In Unit YYMM	Begin In Unit Hours	Finish In Unit YYMM	Total Hours	Hours In Unit
UH-1H	67-17828	1068	6910	1049	7011	2588	1539
UH-1H	67-17832	1068	7010	1663	7112	2958	1295
UH-1H	68-16373	1069	7005	353	7109	1977	1624
UH-1H	68-16384	1069	6912	36	7005	807	771
UH-1H	69-15757	1070	7012	0	7112	1320	1320
UH-1H	64-13861	1165	6911	2112	7110	3469	1357
UH-1H	66-17051	1167	6903	1060	6909	1737	677
UH-1H	66-17058	1167	6903	1006	7009	2899	1893
UH-1H	67-19522	1168	6909	828	7008	2101	1273
UH-1H	67-19527	1168	6901	0	7004	1544	1544
UH-1H	68-16481	1169	6912	0	7009	1258	1258
UH-1H	69-15817	1170	7012	0	7012	100	100
UH-1H	69-15836	1170	7208	932	7512	1714	782
UH-1H	66-17090	1267	7409	2456	7512	2691	235
UH-1H	68-15242	1268	6901	0	7004	2087	2087
UH-1H	68-16592	1269	7002	0	7006	821	821
UH-1H	69-15884	1270	7102	0	7112	982	982
UH-1M	66-15005	167	7011	1553	7110	1976	423
UH-1M	66-15016	267	7012	1831	7110	2415	584
UH-1M	66-15017	267	7107	2387	7112	2569	182
UH-1M	65-09493	366	7105	2188	7108	2333	145
UH-1M	65-09528	466	7012	1834	7107	2125	291
UH-1M	66-00492	666	7105	2580	7110	2738	158
UH-1M	66-00635	1066	7012	1666	7110	2125	459

GLOSSARY OF ABBREVIATIONS

A/C	Aircraft
Abn. Bde.	Airborne Brigade
ACM	Army Commendation Medal
AFB	Air Force Base
AHC	Assault Helicopter Company
ALA	Airlanded Assaults
ALR	Airlanded Resupply
ALSC	AUSTRALIAN LOGISTICAL SUPPORT COMPANY
AM	Air Medal
AML	Airmobile Light
APC	ARMOR PERSONNEL CARRIER
ARA	Aerial Rocket Artillery
ARVN	Army of the Republic of Vietnam
AVN	Aviation
B.S.	Bronze Star
BAM	Basic Air Medal
BN	Battalion
BOQ	Bachelors Officers Quarters
C&C	Command And Control
CA	Combat Assault
CAL	Caliber
CAPT.	Captain
CAV	Cavalry
CL	Command and Liaison
COL.	Colonel
CONUS	Continental United States
CP	Command Post
CTZ	Corps Tactical Zone
CWO	Chief Warrant Officer
DEROS	Date Estimated Return Overseas Service
DFC	Distinguished Flying Cross
DIV	Division
EH	Escort Helicopter

EM	Enlisted Men
FSB	Fire Support Base
GO#	General Orders Number
INF.	Infantry
KBA	Killed By Action
KIA	Killed In Action
LFT	Light Fire Team
LOLEX	LOW LEVEL EXTRACTION
LRP	Long Range Patrol
LRRP	Long Range Reconnaissance Patrol
LT	Light
Lt.	Lieutenant
LTC	Lieutenant Colonel
LZ	Landing Zone
MACV	Military Assistance Command Vietnam
MAD	Mortar Aerial Delivery
MAJ.	Major
MED.	Medical
MEDIVAC	Medical Evacuation
NCO	Non Commissioned Officer
NVA	North Vietnamese Army
P.H.	Purple Heart
PAX	Passengers
PFC	Private First Class
POL	Petroleum Oils and Lubricants
PSP	Perforated Steel Plate
PZ	Pickup Zone
R&R	Rest and Recuperation
RAA	ROYAL AUSTRALIAN ARTILLERY
RAR	Royal Australian Regiment
RPM	Revolutions Per Minute
RNZA	ROYAL NEW ZEALAND ARMY
RVN	Republic Of Vietnam
SGT.	Sergeant
SSGT	Staff Sergeant
TAOR	Tactical Area of Operational Responsibility

TDY	Temporary Duty
TF	TASK FORCE
V	Valor
VC	Viet Cong
VR	Visual Recon
WIA	Wounded In Action
WO	Warrant Officer

Cowboy Monument Memorial Dedicated 10/26/2017
Fort Rucker Alabama Veterans Park

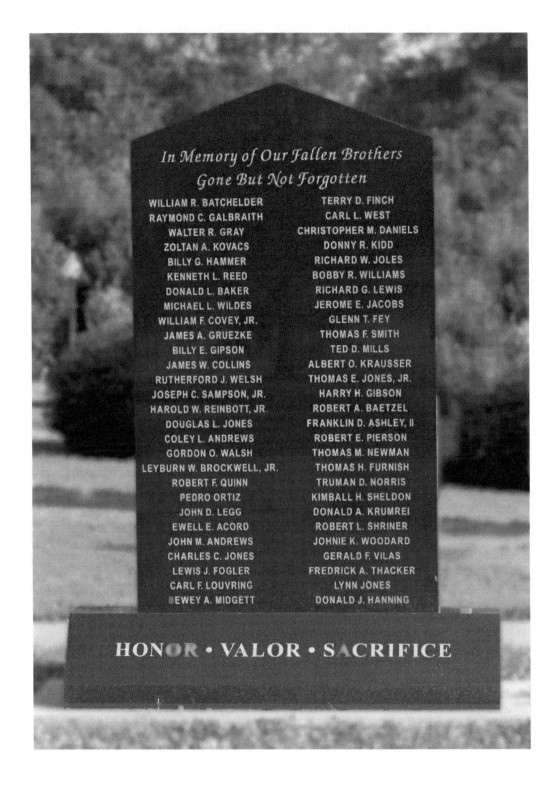

Pathway to the Air Museum at Fort Rucker Alabama

Order of Events

October 22, 2016

One year and two days ago, Jack Hunnicutt laid out a plan to have a Monument Memorial dedicated to the 335th Assault Helicopter Company. He solicited feedback from the troops and found that there was a great deal of interest in pursuing his idea.

Jack posted a draft of what the structure might look like, and many COWBOYS contributed ideas as to what should and should not be included. Jack put together a committee to review all the suggestions and a consensus was reached.

The Cowboy mission was now set. Jack was flying lead with Jim Stein flying wing on this project. We also had boots on the ground in the names of Tom Gould and Jerry Hendley.

Fund raising began

We were a bit concerned as to the timing of this solicitation for funds because the holidays were coming and there were many folks that had suffered with hurricanes in the East, tornadoes in the Central part of the country and wild fires out West.

November 2016

Jack and Tom Gould visited some local stone companies and obtained estimates. At the same time, Jack and Jim Stein met with the folks at Fort Rucker to obtain approval for locating the structure at Veterans Park.

Fund Raising efforts continued and we reached our Goal 5 days before Christmas. December 20, 2016. That's **57** days to raise the **$15069**

A notice was sent out telling everyone the goal had been reached and that there was no need to send more donations. Well, the COWBOYS never a group to always follow orders, continued to send money creating a surplus to be used for the Dedication. We raised **$17920**. **$2851** over the cost of the monument memorial.

March 2017

Stone slab was ordered

April 2017

Final approve to place the monument was granted on April 21, 2016 by Commanding General, Installation Management Command.

July 2017

The stone slab of Black Granite was received in Georgia and fabrication began. That is the etching, sandblasting and polishing necessary to complete the project.

Planning efforts for the unveiling ceremony also began.

August 2017

Stone fabrication completed.

Stone delivered and placed at Fort Rucker August 22.

September 2017

Dedication Ceremony occurred October 26, 2017.

The terms Monument and Memorial.

• Monument is a structure, statue, or a building that is built to honor someone notable or a special event.

• Memorial is a structure or a statue that is built to remember a dead person or a group of people who died in an important past event.

The Cowboy structure is like a coin. It does not have a front and back. It simply has two sides.

On one side is the Memorial dedicated to the 56 men who gave all in the service to their country.

On the other side is a Monument dedicated to all who served with or were attached to the 335th.

The monument memorial represents the blood sweat and the lives of all those that served in or were attached to the 335th Assault Helicopter Company and they shall never be forgotten.

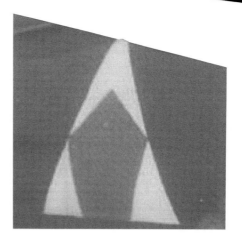

Diamond was on the Tail Boom of all Cowboy Aircraft. The center diamond was bright red and outer larger diamond was white.

Cowboy Tail Boom Diamond was replaced with the white Triangle with dayglow orange Pentagon Design 19 JULY 1969.

A-Company, 82nd Aviation attached to the 173rd Airborne Brigade, Bien Hoa. Made in Bien Hoa. 1965 or 1966.

Cowboy Business Card

The only patch used by the 1st Platoon.

The only patch used by the 2nd Platoon.

1st Aviation Brigade Patch

234 Signal Detachment

Pocket and hat patches. 1965 82nd Aviation Btn.
Used in Vung Tau before moving to the 173rd ABN
in Bien Hoa.

An original 335th AHC door emblem

335th AHC COWBOYS Detachment Patch

Old or first Cowboy Patch

Newer or later Cowboy Patch

43975454R00179

Made in the USA
Lexington, KY
04 July 2019